The *Other* Orlando

What To Do When You've Done
Disney & Universal

Kelly Monaghan

The Other Orlando

What To Do When You've Done Disney & Universal

Published by The Intrepid Traveler
P.O. Box 531, Branford, CT 06405

Copyright © 2002 by Kelly Monaghan
Second Edition
Printed in Canada
Book Jacket: George Foster, Foster & Foster, Inc.
Maps designed by Evora Taylor
Library of Congress Control Number: 2001099728
ISBN: 1-887140-41-7

Publisher's Cataloguing in Publication Data. Prepared by Sanford Berman.

Monaghan, Kelly

The other Orlando: what to do when you've done Disney & Universal. Branford, CT: Intrepid Traveler, copyright 2002.

"Revised update of. . . Orlando's other theme parks: what to do when you've done Disney" (1999).

PARTIAL CONTENTS: SeaWorld Florida. -Discovery Cove. -Cypress Gardens. -Gatorland. -Splendid China. -Holy Land Experience. -Kennedy Space Center. -Busch Gardens Tampa. -Water parks. -Dinner attractions. -Who's who of zoos. -Moving Experiences. Balloon rides. Boat rides. -Sports scores. -Spectator sports. Arena football. Auto racing. Jai-alai. Rodeo. -Shop 'til you drop.

1. Orlando region, Florida--Description and travel--Guidebooks. 2. Theme parks--Orlando region, Florida--Guidebooks. 3. Recreation--Orlando region, Florida. 4. Sports--Orlando region, Florida. 5. SeaWorld, Florida--Description and travel--Guidebooks. 6. John F. Kennedy Space Center, Cocoa Beach, Florida--Description and travel--Guidebooks. 7. Busch Gardens, Tampa, Florida--Description and travel--Guidebooks. 8. Shopping--Orlando region, Florida--Guidebooks. 9. Discovery Cove, Florida--Description and travel--Guidebooks. 10. Cypress Gardens, Florida--Description and travel--Guidebooks. 11. Gatorland, Florida--Description and travel--Guidebooks.

I. Title. II. Title: What to do when you've done Disney & Universal. III. Title: Orlando IV. Intrepid Traveler.

917.5924

Trademarks, Etc.

This book mentions many attractions, fictional characters, product names, entities, and works that are trademarks, registered trademarks, or service marks of their various creators and owners. They are used in this book solely for editorial purposes. Neither the author nor the publisher makes any commercial claim to their use.

Cover Photo Credits

Other Books by Kelly Monaghan

Universal Orlando:
The Ultimate Guide To The
Ultimate Theme Park Adventure

Home-Based Travel Agent:
How To Succeed In Your Own
Travel Marketing Business

The Travel Agent's Complete Desk Reference
(co-author)

Air Courier Bargains:
How To Travel World-Wide For Next To Nothing

Fly Cheap!

Air Travel's Bargain Basement

Table of Contents

List of Maps

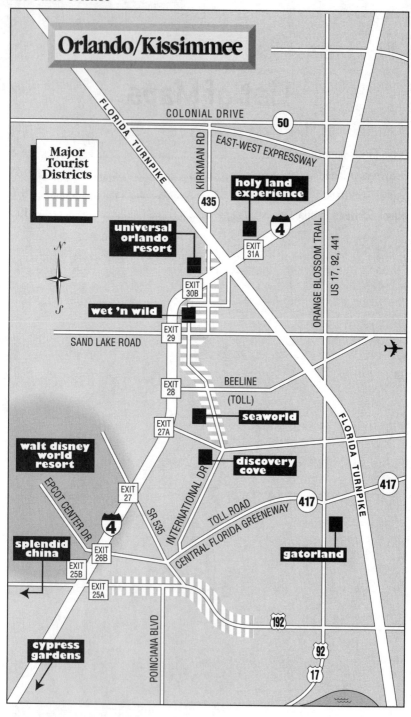

CHAPTER ONE:

Introduction & Orientation

Don't get me wrong. I love Disney World and Universal Orlando. I visit these splendid theme parks every chance I get. However, as a travel writer, I must cast a canny eye on the marketplace. In doing so, I determined two things. First, my publishing company already has a book on Disney World. I refer, of course, to *The Hassle-Free Walt Disney World® Vacation* by Steven M. Barrett (Intrepid Traveler, $14.95). Second, a terrific guide to Universal Orlando has also been written, this time (fortunately) by me. It's called *Universal Orlando: The Ultimate Guide To The Ultimate Theme Park Adventure* (Intrepid Traveler, $14.95).

Because Disney World and Universal are the 900-pound gorillas of Central Florida tourism, any general guidebook to Central Florida must, of necessity, devote so much space to their multitude of attractions that the area's other attractions receive short shrift, if they are covered at all. This book, then, turns away from Disney World and Universal, not out of disdain, but to lavish on Orlando's other attractions the in-depth treatment that Disney has long enjoyed and that Universal is now beginning to attract. I suspect that readers of this book have already visited Disney World and Universal, perhaps many times, and are ready to explore the other possibilities of a Central Florida vacation. As you will see, they are myriad. In fact, there are so many things to see and do in the Orlando area that at the end of this Introduction I have included a list of "hidden" treasures you might overlook.

When to Come

There are three major questions you must ask yourself when planning a trip to Orlando: How crowded will it be? What will the weather be like?

9

When will my schedule allow me go? For most people, the third question will determine when they go, regardless of the answers to the other two. The dictates of business or the carved-in-stone school calendar will tend to determine when you come to Orlando. For those who can be flexible, however, carefully picking the time of your visit will offer a number of benefits.

During slow periods, the crowds at Orlando's major theme parks are noticeably thinner than they are at the height of the summer or during the madness of Christmas week. On top of that, hotel rates are substantially lower and airfare deals abound. Likewise, Orlando in winter can seem positively balmy to those from the North, although it's unlikely you will find the temperature conducive to swimming (except in heated pools). Spring and fall temperatures are close to ideal.

Let's take a look at these two variables: the tourist traffic and the weather.

Orlando's Tourist Traffic

Most major tourist destinations seem to have two seasons — high and low. For most of Florida, the high season stretches from late fall to early spring, the cooler months up North. Low season is the blisteringly hot summer, when Floridians who can afford it head North. Orlando, thanks to its multitude of family-oriented attractions has five or six distinct "seasons," alternating between high and low, reflecting the vacation patterns of its prime customers — kids and their parents.

Orlando hosts over 40 million visitors a year. The heaviest tourist "season" is Christmas vacation, roughly from Christmas eve through January first. Next comes Easter week and Thanksgiving weekend. The entire summer, from Memorial Day in late May to Labor Day in early September, is on a par with Easter and Thanksgiving. There are two other "spikes" in attendance: President's Week in February and College Spring Break. Various colleges have different dates for their Spring Break, which may or may not coincide with Easter; the result is that the period from mid-March through mid-April shows a larger than usual volume of tourist traffic. The slowest period is the lull between Thanksgiving and Christmas. Next slowest (excluding the holidays mentioned earlier) are the months of September, October, November, January, and February. Tourism starts to build again in March, spiking sharply upward for Easter/Spring Break, then dropping off somewhat until Memorial Day.

Another thing to bear in mind is that, when we speak of crowds, we are speaking of the major theme parks: Disney World, Universal Orlando, SeaWorld, and Busch Gardens. Here are annual attendance figures for Orlando area parks for 2001, the latest year for which figures are available, as estimated by the trade paper *Amusement Business*:

Rank*	Park	Attendance
1	The Magic Kingdom	14,700,000
3	EPCOT	9,000,000
4	Disney-MGM Studios	8,300,000
5	Disney's Animal Kingdom	7,700,000
6	Universal Studios Florida	7,200,000
7	Islands of Adventure	5,500,000
8	SeaWorld Orlando	5,100,000
11	Busch Gardens Tampa	4,600,000

Numbers represent the parks' national rankings. Disneyland, California, was number two, Universal Studios California was tied with SeaWorld Orlando for number eight.

In other words, on any given day, the largest crowds will tend to be at the Disney parks and Universal. If you've been a Disney regular, SeaWorld will seem quite manageable by comparison. And regardless of when you visit, any attraction other than the big ones will seem almost deserted compared to Disney.

The best advice is to avoid the absolutely busiest times of the year if possible. If you do come during the summer, as many families must, plan to deal with crowds at the major parks when you arrive and console yourself with the thought that, if you're concentrating on the attractions covered in this book, you've automatically avoided the worst crowds.

Orlando's Weather

Orlando's average annual temperature is a lovely 72.4 degrees. But as we've already noted, averages are deceptive. Here are the National Weather Service's generally cited "average" figures for temperature and rainfall throughout the year:

	High (°F)	Low (°F)	Rain (in.)
January	71	49	2.3
February	73	50	2.8
March	78	55	3.2
April	83	59	1.8
May	88	66	3.6
June	91	72	7.3
July	92	73	7.3
August	92	73	6.8
September	90	73	6.0
October	85	66	2.4
November	79	58	2.3
December	73	51	2.2

Use these figures as general guidelines rather than guarantees. While the average monthly rainfall in January might be 2.3 over the course of many years, in 1994 there were 4.9 inches of rain that month and in 1996 almost 4 inches fell in the first two days alone. January of '96 also saw lows dip into the twenties.

I find Orlando's weather most predictable in the summer when "hot, humid, in the low nineties, with a chance of afternoon thunderstorms" becomes something of a mantra for the TV weather report. Winter weather tends to be more unpredictable with "killer" freezes a possibility. As to those summer thunderstorms, they tend to be localized and mercifully brief (although occasionally quite intense) and needn't disrupt your touring schedule. I was once in Orlando for a summer week when it rained somewhere every day but never on me. Another thing to bear in mind is that June through September is hurricane season, with July and August the most likely months for severe weather.

Getting Oriented in Orlando

Orlando can be confusing. The Orlando metropolitan area comprises three counties and, since you will often hear location indicated by naming the county, it is worth knowing their names and relation to one another. From north to south they are Seminole, Orange, and Osceola. Orlando is in Orange County, Kissimmee is in Osceola. Most of the attractions covered in this book are in Orange and Osceola; only a few are in Seminole or more distant counties.

The area is dotted with lakes, both large and small; so streets stop, start, and take circuitous detours. In European fashion, streets change names as they cross municipal boundaries. On top of that, the area's major highway, Interstate 4, which runs east-west across the state, runs roughly from northeast to southwest through the Orlando metropolitan area and almost directly north-south in the heart of Orlando's tourist district. As a result, streets that are "east" or "south" of I-4 at one point are "west" or "north" of it at another. (See map, page 8.) All of this complicates the process of giving, receiving, and following directions.

Fortunately, most of the Orlando area's attractions are located in two fairly compact tourist districts: International Drive in Orlando and US 192 in Kissimmee, with I-4 forming a direct and easy-to-follow link between them. Attractions that are not located in these two areas are seldom more than a short drive away from an I-4 exit.

International Drive (sometimes abbreviated I Drive and pronounced "Eye Drive," just as I-4 is pronounced "Eye Four") is in Orlando. It is a meandering boulevard that roughly parallels I-4 from Exit 30 on the north to

Exit 26 on the south. Many of the major attractions profiled in this book are on it or near it. At the northern end, you will find Universal Orlando (just across I-4) and Wet 'n Wild. At the southern end lies SeaWorld. In between, there are some dinner attractions and a number of smaller attractions, along with dozens of hotels, scores of eateries, several discount outlet malls, and the mammoth Orlando Convention Center. International Drive is glitzy, garish, hyperactive, and a traffic nightmare in the evening and at rush hours.

The second major tourist axis is US 192 (also called Highway 192, and Irlo Bronson Highway), which runs east to west through Kissimmee crossing I-4 at Exit 25. West of I-4 you will find Splendid China and the entrance to the Disney properties; to the east of I-4 is a gaudy strip of hotels, restaurants, dinner attractions, smaller attractions, miniature golf courses, and discount shopping outlets. This strip is thoughtfully marked with numbered "Mile Markers," which I have used in the text to give directions.

Tip: Chances are you will be staying in or very close to one of the two major tourist areas. When you are traveling from Point A to Point B in the Orlando area, my advice is to travel via US 192 and I-4. This may not always be the most direct or shortest route but it will be the surest route and very often the quickest. When I give directions in this book I try, wherever possible, to route you via these major arteries.

Keeping Posted

For the very latest information about what's going on in Orlando, your indispensable source of information is the *Orlando Sentinel*, the local daily newspaper. It costs 50 cents, except Sunday when it is $1.50. If you purchase the paper from a vending machine (as opposed to a store), you avoid paying the sales tax. Cheapskates take note.

Every Friday, the *Sentinel*'s "Calendar" section offers an entire week's worth of information about films, plays, concerts, nightclubs, art exhibits, and the like, along with capsule reviews of many of the area's restaurants and a guide to area radio stations. Music buffs will appreciate the exhaustive listings of who's playing what where and film fans will find show times for every multiplex from Orlando to the Atlantic coast. There is even a listing of area attractions and a section of personal ads just in case you start feeling lonely. On other days of the week, a one-page "Calendar" section gives details on events for that day, including lesser happenings that don't rate mention in the weekly section. Those who want to get an advance peek at what's going on in Orlando, can visit the *Sentinel*'s "Calendar" section on the Internet at http://calendar. orlandosentinel.com.

Orlando has a free weekly newspaper, the *Orlando Weekly*, that is especially strong on the pop music scene. You will be able to find it in racks near the entrance to book stores, coffee shops, supermarkets, and drugstores.

The Intrepid Traveler, the publisher of this book, maintains a web site containing updated information about all of Orlando's non-Disney attractions along with other valuable information. Log on at:

http://www.TheOtherOrlando.com

The Orlando FlexTicket

Borrowing a page from the Disney marketing manual, several of Mickey's competitors banded together to offer what has long been a Disney staple — multi-day, multi-park passes at an attractive price. The participating parks are Universal Studios Florida, Islands of Adventure (IOA), SeaWorld, Wet 'n Wild, and Busch Gardens Tampa. It's called the Orlando FlexTicket and it works like this:

4–Park, 14–Day Orlando Flex Ticket — Universal Studios Florida, IOA, SeaWorld, Wet 'n Wild

Adults	$180.15
Children (3 to 9)	$143.05

5–Park, 14–Day FlexTicket — adds Busch Gardens Tampa

Adults	$215.46
Children (3 to 9)	$175.12

Prices include tax. These passes offer unlimited visits to all four or five parks for two weeks and represent an excellent value. On top of that, they offer the come and go as you please convenience of annual passes, albeit for a much shorter time.

FlexTickets may be purchased at any of the participating parks' ticket booths or through your travel agent before coming. They are valid for fourteen consecutive days beginning on the day you first use them. As for parking, you pay at the first park you visit on any given day. Then show your parking ticket and Orlando FlexTicket at the other parks on the same day for complimentary parking.

A number of attractive vacation packages include the Orlando Flex-Ticket. Global Travel International, an Orlando-based travel agency, offers a number of these packages. For their best prices, call (800) 715-4440 and use PIN number 42468001.

All About Discounts

Throughout this book, I have listed the standard admission price for every attraction. However, thanks to the cutthroat competition for the attention of tourists in tourist-saturated Orlando, an entire industry of dollars-off coupons and discount ticket outlets has grown up. With a little effort, you will seldom have to pay the posted price.

Coupons

The most ubiquitous money-saving vehicle is the coupon. Coupons are distributed via attractions' sites on the Internet and through a variety of free visitors' guides — magazine-sized publications filled with ads for area attractions and restaurants. The coupons you want are either downloadable or found in the freebie publications' ads or separate coupon sections (some booklets are nothing but coupons). There's a good chance you will find several of these throwaway publications in your hotel room or be handed them with your room key or when you pick up your rental car. If not, look around for displays at the airport, car rental agencies, hotel lobbies, and restaurants in the tourist areas. You won't have to look far.

Another source of dollars-off coupons is the brochures for individual attractions. Many of them contain a coupon. You will find them in the same places you find the larger, magazine-format coupon books. Many lobby and restaurant display racks contain dozens of these brochures.

The discounts available from dollars-off coupons are relatively modest, usually a few dollars. Some attractions make their coupons valid for up to four or six people, hence the headlines that shout "up to $16 off!" You are unlikely to find coupons for museums, botanical gardens (except Cypress Gardens), and state parks (although anything is possible in this overheated competitive environment).

My suggestion is that you collect as many free visitors' guides as you can get your hands on. Browse the brochure racks and pull out those that appeal. Then, in the comfort of your hotel room, select and cut out offers that appeal to you and keep them in your rental car for ready use.

Yet another option for getting a wide range of modest discounts is the Orlando Magicard. Sponsored by the Orlando Convention and Visitors Bureau, the Magicard looks like a credit card. Flashing it will get you discounts at most area attractions and dinner shows, as well as at some restaurants and area hotels. You can obtain a card prior to your arrival by writing to the Orlando Visitors Center, 8723 International Drive, Orlando, FL 32819. Or call (407) 363-5872. Or order on the Web at www.orlandoinfo.com/magicard. They will send you the card free of charge. You can also pick up the card at the Center once you are in Orlando. Along with the card, you will receive a brochure with the current list of discount offers. The card is good forever; the list of attractions, restaurants, and hotels offering discounts changes periodically.

Tip: If you find yourself near an attraction you'd like to visit but don't have a coupon, stop into nearby restaurants, or even the entrance to a nearby attraction, and look for brochure racks. Chances are you'll find a brochure and coupon for the attraction that caught your eye.

Ticket Brokers

The second major source of discounts is ticket brokers. There are dozens of them scattered around the tourist areas, many of them located in hotel lobbies. Ticket brokers concentrate on the major attractions and the dinner shows. Discounts can be substantial — except for Disney. A 4% discount on Disney tickets is pretty standard. On the other hand, some brokers offer Universal at nearly 15% off and some dinner attractions at 34% off.

Using ticket brokers requires careful comparison shopping since discounts can vary widely from outlet to outlet. As a general rule, the discount ticket booths you find in your hotel lobby or in local restaurants seldom have the best prices. You'll do better at the free-standing ticket outlets. Nonetheless, it's a good idea to shop around. Sometimes even the lowest of the low-price dealers will be undercut by someone else for a particular attraction. Virtually every reputable ticket broker will have a printed price list; collect a goodly supply of these and examine them later in your hotel room to smoke out the best deals.

Protecting Yourself

While fraud is rare, it does occur. So take some simple precautions:

- Ticket brokers are regulated by both the state of Florida and local authorities. They are required to prominently post the appropriate licenses. If you don't see these certificates displayed, ask to see them.
- Ask about "restocking fees." If you find a lower price elsewhere, you may be able to return your tickets, but many outlets charge a 15% fee when you do so.
- Does the printed price list contain the name, address, and phone number of the broker? The absence of these elements does not, in and of itself, signal fraud, but there is no reason for a reputable broker to omit them.
- Look for brokers that advertise that they will meet or beat any advertised price. That way, if you find a better deal, you will be protected.

"Free" Tickets

It is actually possible to get "free" (or very cheap) tickets to some major attractions. The catch is that, in return, you must agree to sit through a presentation for a local timeshare resort. You will be assured that there is no obligation, no high-pressure sales pitches. If you insist that you will never, ever buy a timeshare, they will tell you that's no problem, that you'll be able to tell your friends back home about their resort and that's good enough for them.

All this may be true. But for me, sitting through a timeshare presentation is about as appealing as a visit to the dentist for root canal work. If you feel different, you can find this kind of offer through ticket brokers or little booths along the tourist strips emblazoned with the words "FREE TICKETS."

How This Book Is Organized

Chapters 2 through 7 cover the major Orlando area attractions, ones which will occupy anywhere from a half a day to several days of your time. I have attempted to cover them in some depth, offering guidance on dining and shopping. Chapters 8 and 9 cover Kennedy Space Center to the east and Busch Gardens Tampa to the west. These, too, are major attractions.

The remaining chapters are omnibus chapters; that is, they cover three or more attractions that all have a common theme. The attractions described in these chapters are scattered throughout the Orlando area.

There is an index of rides and attractions, which will be most useful in locating the smaller attractions covered in chapters 11 through 19. It can also be used to locate descriptions of specific attractions at the major parks.

As a general rule, I have tried to restrict the geographic scope of this book to Orlando and its immediate environs. That means that the farther you drive from Orlando, the more likely you will be to encounter attractions not covered in this book. For example, with the exception of Kennedy Space Center and the nearby Astronaut Hall of Fame, I have not included any attractions on the Atlantic coast. Nor have I mentioned the many things to see and do in the Tampa Bay area aside from Busch Gardens and Adventure Island, its next-door water park.

Price ranges for restaurants (cost of an average meal without tax and tip) and hotels (cost of one night's stay in a double room without tax) are indicated as follows:

	Restaurants	Hotels
$	Under $5	Under $50
$$	$5 – $10	$50 – $100
$$$	Over $10	Over $100
$$$$	Over $20	Over $150

Finally, a note on highway and route abbreviations. I stands for Interstate; US for United States (i.e. federal) Highway; SR for State Route; CR for County Road.

Hidden Highlights of the Other Orlando

Since there is so much information in this book and since I worry that you might overlook something wonderful, here is a brief and highly opinionated list of lesser-known attractions I think are worth considering:

Dinner shows. Of those listed in Chapter 11, my favorite is *Arabian Knights*, but don't overlook the spectacular *Mysterious Kingdom of the Orient* show at Splendid China (Chapter 6).You can see the show at a bargain price without touring the park.

Animal encounters. Discovery Cove (Chapter 3) gets all the press, but at Amazing Exotics (Chapter 14) you can play with monkeys and apes and pet a tiger. Also worth singling out is the *Serengeti Safari Tour* at Busch Gardens Tampa (Chapter 9) that lets you hand feed giraffes and other denizens of the Serengeti. During spring, bird watchers will want to flock to the *Alligator Breeding Marsh* at Gatorland (Chapter 5), where hundreds of cranes and egrets come to build their nests and rear their young, protected from their natural predators by the gators below.

Natural wonders. Bok Tower Gardens (Chapter 15) is actually a cunning man-made creation but those who appreciate the art of landscape architecture will find it ravishingly beautiful. For a more down-home experience in the great outdoors, plunge into the natural spring swimming hole at Wekiva Springs State Park (also in Chapter 15).

And all the rest. The Kissimmee Rodeo (Chapter 18) is a touch of the Old West in Florida and offers a lot of entertainment value at a modest price. Fantasy of Flight (Chapter 12), with its evocative dioramas depicting the history of flight and its extensive antique plane collection, is worth a side trip for aviation buffs. Fans of Frank Lloyd Wright won't want to miss the largest collection of his buildings to be found in one place (Chapter 16). And the ritzy town of Winter Park, with its fabulous art museums and theater (Chapter 16) and the boat tour past the homes of the rich but not so famous (Chapter 17), is worth a day or two all by itself.

In addition to those mentioned above, chapters 2 through 9 contain my personal choices of the must-see or -do attractions at each of the major parks.

Accuracy and Other Impossible Dreams

While I have tried to be as accurate, comprehensive, and up-to-date as possible, these are all unattainable goals. What's most likely to change, alas, are prices. I have quoted 2002 prices. However, some attractions may decide to raise their prices later in the year. Perhaps more disconcerting will be the disappearance of entire attractions, usually smaller and/or newer ones. I sincerely hope that none of the wonderful attractions listed here close down before you get to experience them. Before driving any great distance, however, you may want to call ahead to make sure the attraction that caught your eye is still open and double check the hours and pricing.

Once again I refer you to my web site for updated information:
http://www.TheOtherOrlando.com

CHAPTER TWO:

SeaWorld Orlando

I've been to Disney," people will tell you, "But y'know what I think is the best thing they've got down there in Orlando? SeaWorld!" I heard it over and over again. In a way this reaction was somewhat surprising. After all, compared to the Magic Kingdom or Universal, SeaWorld is downright modest, with only a smattering of thrill rides.

Of course, we could simply ascribe this "I-liked-SeaWorld-best" attitude to one-upmanship — that quirk of human nature that makes us all want to look superior. After all, SeaWorld is educational and how much more flattering it is to depict yourself as someone who prefers educational nature shows to mindless carnival rides that merely provide "fun." I'm just enough of a cynic about human nature to give some credence to this theory.

However, I think the real reason lies elsewhere. No matter how well imagined and perfectly realized the attractions at Universal or Disney might be, the wonders on display at SeaWorld were produced by a creative intelligence of an altogether higher order. The animated robotics guys can tinker all they want and the bean-counters in Hollywood can give them ever higher budgets and they still will never produce anything that can match the awe generated by a killer whale soaring 30 feet in the air with his human trainer perched on his snout. No matter how much we are entertained by Universal and Disney, at SeaWorld we cannot help but be reminded, however subliminally, that there are wonders in our world that humankind simply cannot duplicate, let alone surpass.

It's a feeling of which many visitors probably aren't consciously aware. Even if they are, they'd probably feel a little awkward trying to express it. But I am convinced it is there for everyone — believer, agnostic, or atheist. It's the core experience that makes SeaWorld so popular; it's the reason people will tell you they liked SeaWorld best of all. To paraphrase Joyce Kilmer's magnificent cliché about human inadequacy,

> *I think that Walt will never do*
> *A wonder greater than Shamu.*

Before You Come

Gathering Information

You can get up-to-date information on hours and prices by calling (407) 351-3600 and pressing "2." Between 8:00 a.m. and 8:00 p.m. you can speak to a SeaWorld representative at this number.

For the latest on SeaWorld's animals, you can check out the Anheuser-Busch Adventure Parks animal information site on the World Wide Web. The address is www.seaworld.org. For Shamu fans the site to check out is www.shamu.com. Yet another web site provides information for both Sea-World Orlando and its sister park, Busch Gardens Tampa. The address is www.4adventure.com.

Doing Your Homework

There's no real necessity to "bone up" on marine mammals before coming to SeaWorld. The park itself will give you a good introduction to the subject if you half pay attention. However, it is possible that parents might want to generate some interest in their younger children who, perhaps, might not be able to fully appreciate why they should go to SeaWorld instead of spending another day with Mickey and his friends.

There have been a number of excellent videos about SeaWorld that you may be able to find in your local library or video store. Probably easier to come by will be the video of *Free Willy*, the hit movie about a boy's struggle to liberate a killer whale from an amusement park. When your children get the idea that they can meet the star of this movie (one of his cousins actually) at SeaWorld, they should become enthusiastic boosters of the visit.

When's the Best Time to Come?

Even at the height of summer the crowds at SeaWorld are quite manageable compared to those you'll encounter at, say, Disney. Still, it is a good idea to plan on arriving during the off-season, if at all possible. Crowds in January are negligible and the weather cool to moderate, perfect viewing conditions for the outdoor shows. Regardless of the time of year you visit, I would recommend arriving early and planning to stay until the park closes. There are two reasons for this. Early arrivals breeze right in; as the morning wears on, the lines at the ticket booths lengthen. As for staying 'til the bitter end, some of the best shows (including what is arguably the best show) are only performed in the hour before closing. Compensate for the long day with a leisurely lunch.

Getting There

SeaWorld is located just off I-4 on Central Florida Parkway. If you're coming from the south (i.e. traveling east on I-4) you will use Exit 27A and find yourself pointed directly towards the SeaWorld entrance, about half a mile along on your left. Because there is no exit directly to Central Florida Parkway from Westbound I-4, those coming from the north (i.e. traveling west on I-4) must get off at Exit 28, onto the Bee Line Expressway (Route 528). Don't worry about the sign that says it's a toll road; you won't have to pay one. Take the first exit and loop around to International Drive. Turn left and proceed to Central Florida Parkway and turn right. It's all very clearly marked. This route, by the way, offers a nice backstage peek at *Kraken*, SeaWorld's roller coaster. As you get close to SeaWorld, tune your AM radio to 1540 for a steady stream of information about the park. This will help while away the time spent waiting in line at the parking lot.

Arriving at SeaWorld

Parking fees are $7 for cars and $8 for RVs and trailers and are collected at toll booths a short drive from the entrance. If you'd like to park close to the front entrance, you can opt for Shamu's Preferred Parking, available for cars only, for $10. Annual passholders pay nothing for regular parking and get a 50% discount on preferred parking.

Handicapped Parking. Several rows of extra large spaces near the main entrance are provided for the convenience of handicapped visitors. Alert the attendant to your need for handicapped parking and you will be directed accordingly.

The SeaWorld parking lot is divided into numbered sections, and you will be ushered to your space in a very efficiently controlled manner. While the lot is not huge, it's still a very good idea to make a note of which section and row you're parked in. If you are parked any distance from the entrance, you will be directed to a tram that will whisk you to the main entrance. If you arrive after noon, however, you may find yourself on your own. Fortunately, the farthest row is never too far from the park perimeter. You can orient yourself by looking for the centrally located *Sky Tower*; it's the blue spire with the large American flag at the summit.

Once you reach the beautifully designed main entrance, you will find a group of thoughtfully shaded ticket booths where you will purchase your admission. To the left of the ticket windows are the Guest Relations window and the annual pass center. Once inside the park, walk straight ahead to the Information Desk. There you can pick up a large map of the park. On the back you will find a schedule of the day's shows as well as information on any special events happening that day.

Opening and Closing Times

SeaWorld operates seven days a week, 365 days a year. The park opens at 9:00 a.m. and remains open until 6:00, 7:00, 8:00, 9:00, 10:00, or 11:00 p.m. — or even until 1:00 a.m. — depending on the time of year. Unlike Universal and Disney, SeaWorld does not practice soft openings (admitting guests early). During very busy periods, they will start admitting people at 8:30, but these early arrivals are held in the Entrance Plaza (or "mall") just inside the gates, until the park proper opens at 9:00. By the time the last scheduled shows are starting (about 45 minutes to an hour prior to the posted closing time), most of the park's other attractions have either shut down or are in the process of doing so.

The Price of Admission

SeaWorld has several ticket options, including some that offer admission to its sister park, Busch Gardens, in nearby Tampa. Most visitors will be looking at either a one-day admission or the Orlando FlexTicket. At press time, prices (including sales tax) were as follows:

One-Day Admission:
Adults:	$52.95
Seniors (55+):	$49.77
Children (3 to 9):	$43.41

Children under age 3 are admitted **free**.

Value Ticket:
(One day each at SeaWorld and Busch Gardens.)
Adults:	$88.34
Children & Seniors:	$72.37

SeaWorld participates in the **Orlando FlexTicket** program described in *Chapter 1: Introduction & Orientation*. Prices for the FlexTicket (including tax) are as follows:

4-Park, 14-Day Pass — Universal, IOA, SeaWorld, Wet 'n Wild
Adults	$180.15
Children (3 to 9)	$143.05

5-Park, 14-Day Pass — adds Busch Gardens Tampa
Adults	$215.46
Children (3 to 9)	$175.12

The Discovery Cove Option

If you are also planning to visit Discovery Cove (described in Chapter 3), be aware that your admission fee there includes a seven-day pass to Sea-World. The pass is valid for seven consecutive days, starting the day of your first visit, and can be activated either before or after your Discovery Cove visit. To get the pass, stop into Guest Relations and show your Discovery Cove confirmation letter You will be issued a non-transferrable credit-card-sized pass. You may be required to a produce photo ID each time you enter the park using this pass.

If you would like to make SeaWorld the centerpiece of your Orlando vacation, you might consider using this "Discovery Cove option." Although the full Discovery Cove experience, the one that includes the dolphin swim (and costs $210.94, including tax), books up months in advance, you may be able to purchase the cheaper non-swim ticket ($126.14, including tax) on shorter notice. It's pricey, but amortized over eight days it comes out to under $16 a day. Running the same calculation on the all-inclusive Discovery Cove admission, yields a per-day cost of just under $26.50 a day. Read *Chapter 3: Discovery Cove* to decide if this option might make sense for you.

Adventure Express

For those short on time and long on cash, SeaWorld offers a guided six-hour VIP touring option that guarantees you will hit the highlights and be treated like a celebrity along the way. You start the tour at 11:00 a.m. and get to feed stingrays, dolphins, and sea lions and pet a Magellanic penguin. You will also be given reserved seats at the Shamu show, which means Shamu will practically be in your lap. Similar preferred seating is offered at either the sea lion or dolphin show, depending on scheduling on the day of your visit. Guests on the Adventure Express who meet the minimum height requirements (see ride reviews, below) also get front of the line privileges at the big thrill rides, *Kraken, Journey to Atlantis*, and *Wild Arctic*.

None of this comes cheap. The cost is $65 for adults and $60 for children 3 to 9 (younger children tour free) — and that's in addition to the regular price of admission! At least tax and a box lunch with a choice of sandwich and soft drink are included in these prices. There are only 16 spaces available for the Adventure Express, so you may want to reserve a spot by calling (407) 363-2380 or (800) 406-2244.

If that's not exclusive enough, you can opt for a private version of Adventure Express, dubbed Elite Adventure Express. This private tour offers the same privileges, but is limited exclusively to your party. The tab is $424 including tax for 1 to 6 guests and $742 for 7 to 16 guests, plus the regular one-day admission. You pay extra for lunch on Elite Express tours, $10 per person, but kids under three tour free. So if your party included 6 people age three or older and 2 kids under 3, you'd pay the $424 price, but you'd have to pay for all eight lunches if you wanted sandwiches for everyone. Book at least one week ahead, and preferably two, for the Elite Express.

Which Price Is Right?

For most people, a one-day pass will suffice, assuming that you arrive early and stay until closing. Of course, if you've taken my advice and come during one of Orlando's slow periods, there's an excellent chance SeaWorld will offer you a second day free.

The major advantage of taking two days to see SeaWorld is that you can adopt a much more leisurely pace than otherwise, lingering to commune with the sharks or hanging around until something interesting happens at the killer whale observation area. Second day tickets, when available, must be used within seven days. If you'll be visiting Tampa and you are not using the Orlando FlexTicket, the Value Ticket, offering one day each at SeaWorld and Busch Gardens, is a good buy.

Annual Passes & EZ Pay

SeaWorld has several annual pass options that are so reasonable you may want to consider them as an alternative to a one-day admission. For example, the adult annual pass costs less than twice as much as a one-day admission. Some people might consider that worth it for the convenience of coming and going as they please during their Orlando stay. If you plan another Orlando vacation within the next 12 months, the annual pass options become almost irresistible, especially now that SeaWorld offers an EZ Pay option.

Opt for **EZ Pay** and you pay for your annual pass on a monthly basis, interest-free, over the life of the pass. Payments are charged to your credit card; no fees are added.

The passes, called "Passports," take the form of a credit card sized photo ID. Silver Passports are valid for one year and Gold for two. In the following list of prices, which include tax, the Silver Passport price is given first, followed by the Gold Passport price. Children's prices apply for those 3 to 9, Seniors to those 55 or older.

SeaWorld Passports
Adults:	$84.75 / $132.46
Children & Seniors:	$74.15 / $121.85

SeaWorld - Busch Gardens Passports
(Annual Passes to both SeaWorld and Busch Gardens)
Adults:	$138.40 / $186.32
Children & Seniors:	$127.75 / $175.67

You can add Adventure Island, Busch's water park in Tampa (see *Chapter 10: Water Parks*) to either of the SeaWorld/Busch Gardens passports for an additional fee of about $32, including tax.

Annual passes offer unlimited admission, free parking in the regular lot, and an array of discounts, including a 10% discount at SeaWorld restaurants, 10% or 20% discounts at the shops, plus a 50% discount on preferred parking and all guided tours. The pass itself is a photo ID card which is checked carefully at the gate, to make sure it's really you visiting the park, and you may need to show a second ID.

I have noticed that annual passes are especially popular with local residents, so much so that during periods when SeaWorld offers its discounts to Florida residents, it can take a good 30 to 45 minutes to have your annual pass processed.

Discounts

You can get a 10% discount on one-day admission tickets by buying online at the SeaWorld/Busch Gardens' web site, www.4adventure.com. Failing that, look for dollars-off coupons in the usual tourist throwaway publications and at the guest services desk at your hotel. A typical discount is $2.50 off per person for up to six people. Steeper discounts are available from discount ticket brokers (see *Chapter 1: Introduction and Orientation*). Members of AAA receive a 10% discount off regular prices. The deaf, the blind, and those with mental handicaps receive a generous 50% discount. Active military personnel can get a discount by purchasing tickets at their military base.

Buying Tickets

You can purchase your tickets online (see above) or when you arrive at the park. To save a bit of touring time, you can come by a day or two earlier, in the afternoon when the lines are nonexistent, and buy tickets for use another day. The best way to do this is to park in the lot of the Renaissance Orlando Resort across the street and walk the short distance to the SeaWorld ticket booths.

Staying Near the Park

If SeaWorld is your primary Orlando destination, you may want to consider staying at one of the handful of hotels that are within walking distance of the front gate. Because of their proximity, none provides shuttle service. They are listed here in order of their distance from the park.

Renaissance Orlando Resort
6677 Sea Harbor Drive

Orlando, FL 32819

(800) 468-3571; (407) 351-5555; fax (407) 351-9991

A luxury resort hotel with a huge central atrium, first-rate restaurants, and many amenities.

Price Range: $$$ - $$$$

Amenities: Olympic-size pool, tennis, volleyball, health club, three restaurants, two lounges, 24-hour room service

Walk to Park: 5 minutes

Hilton Garden Inn

6850 Westwood Boulevard

Orlando, FL 32821

(800) 445-8667; (407) 354-1500; fax (407) 354-1528

Mid-scale hotel with many amenities.

Price Range: $$ - $$$

Amenities: Heated pool, jacuzzi, kids' play area, restaurant, lounge, evening room service, onsite convenience store, complimentary 24-hour business center

Walk to Park: 5 minutes

Sheraton World Resort

10100 International Drive

Orlando, FL 32821-8095

(800) 327-0363; (407) 352-1100; fax (407) 354-5068

An upscale motel that caters to conventioneers.

Price Range: $$ - $$$$

Amenities: Three heated pools, two kiddie pools, mini-golf, fitness center, restaurant, lounge, poolside bar

Walk to Park: 5 to 10 minutes

Travelodge Orlando South & Villager Premier

6263 Westwood Boulevard

Orlando, FL 32821

(800) 346-1551; (407) 345-8000; fax (407) 345-1508

Standard mid-range motel and its extended-stay facility, which offers both weekly and daily rates.

Price Range: $$-$$$$ Travelodge; $-$$ Villager

Amenities: Pool and poolside bar at Travelodge

Walk to Park: 5 to 10 minutes

Hawthorn Suites Orlando SeaWorld

6435 Westwood Boulevard
Orlando, FL 32821
(800) 527-1133; (407) 351-6600; fax (407) 351-1977
All-suite format with kitchenettes in every room.

Price Range: $$ – $$$$

Amenities: Free buffet breakfast, large heated pool, kiddie pool, poolside BBQ grills, children's play area, game room, convenience store, Nintendo and video cassette players in rooms

Walk to Park: 10 to 15 minutes

StudioPlus & Extended Stay America

6443 Westwood Boulevard
Orlando, FL 32821
(888) 788-3467 for both; (407) 351-1982, fax (407) 351-1719 for StudioPlus; (407) 352-3454, fax (407) 352-1708 for Extended Stay
Basic all-suite format with kitchenettes; daily and weekly rates.

Price Range: $$–$$$ StudioPlus; $ Extended Stay

Amenities: Seasonal pool and exercise room at StudioPlus

Walk to Park: 15 to 20 minutes

Dining at SeaWorld

Dining at SeaWorld is almost entirely of the fast-food variety. There is only one full-service restaurant open as we go to press, the Bimini Bay Cafe. A new sit-down venue located in *Terrors of the Deep* may be open by the time you visit. The good news is that the food in all the eateries is well above average theme-park fare. On top of that, the prices at all of SeaWorld's eateries are less than those you'll encounter at other area theme parks. Their lower prices on soft drinks ($1.49, $2.09, $2.39) will be especially appreciated by hard-pressed parents who felt ripped off at Universal and Disney World.

There is beer to be had, as you might expect at a park owned by Anheuser-Busch, but it seems less omnipresent than it does at some other parks. Indeed, many of the fast-food establishments are alcohol-free. On the other hand, you can get a mixed drink here, at the outdoor Sunset Beach Tiki Bar.

You can also get great desserts here. They're made right on the premises and most of the eateries offer them. I especially recommend the chocolate cherry and carrot cakes (about $3), but those whose taste runs to fruit for dessert won't be disappointed. Fresh strawberries are readily available.

SeaWorld lets you eat while waiting for or watching the big outdoor stadium shows; there are even snack bars (offering ice cream bars and nachos) conveniently located near the entrances to the stands. Not all eating establishments are open throughout the park's operating hours. A "Dining Guide," listing the various restaurants and their operating hours, is available at the Information Desk in the Entrance Plaza.

Shopping at SeaWorld

Of course, SeaWorld is dotted with strategically located gift and souvenir shops ready to help you lessen the heavy load in your wallet. Inveterate shoppers can soothe their conscience with the thought that a percentage of the money they drop at SeaWorld goes towards helping rescue and care for stranded sea mammals.

Most of the wares on display are of the standard tourist variety but some items deserve special mention. Many of SeaWorld's shops offer some very attractive figurines and small sculptures. They range from quite small objects suitable for a bric-a-brac shelf to fairly large pieces (with fairly large price tags) that are surely displayed with pride by those who buy them. Prices range from under $20 to well over $2,000. If you're in the market for a special gift for a friend or relative who collects this sort of *objet d'art*, or are a collector yourself, you will want to give these items more than a cursory look.

Good Things to Know About . . .

Access for the Disabled

All parts of SeaWorld are accessible to disabled guests and all the stadium shows have sections set aside for those in wheelchairs. These are some of the best seats in the house. Wheelchairs are available for rent at $8 per day. Electric carts are $32 per day.

Babies

Little ones under three are admitted free and strollers are available for rent if you don't have your own. Single strollers are $8 for the day plus a $2 deposit, double strollers are $14 plus the deposit. There are also diaper changing stations in all the major restrooms (men's and women's). In addition, there are "non-gender changing areas" at *Wild Arctic*, the Friends of the Wild shop, and the *Anheuser-Busch Hospitality Center* where you will find diaper vending machines. There is a nursing area near the Friends of the Wild shop.

Drinking

As a reminder, the legal drinking age in Florida is 21 and photo IDs will be requested if there is the slightest doubt. Try to feel flattered rather than annoyed. Taking alcoholic beverages through the turnstiles as you leave the park is not allowed.

Education Staff

It's hard to say too much in praise of the education staff at SeaWorld. There are some 100 employees whose job it is to hang around and answer your questions. They are invariably friendly, enthusiastic, and more than happy to share their considerable knowledge with you. Don't be shy. Taking advantage of this wonderful human resource will immeasurably increase the enjoyment and value of your visit to SeaWorld. Just look for the word "Education" on the employee's name tag. In fact, even employees who are not with the Education Department will likely have the answer to your question.

Emergencies

As a general rule, the moment something goes amiss speak with the nearest SeaWorld employee. They will contact security or medical assistance and get the ball rolling towards a solution. There is a first aid station in a tent behind *Stingray Lagoon* in the North End of the park and another near *Shamu's Happy Harbor* in the South End.

Feeding Times

Feeding time is an especially interesting time to visit any of the aquatic habitats. Unfortunately, there is no rigid schedule. By varying feeding times, the trainers more closely approximate the animals' experience in the wild and avoid, to some extent, the repetitive behaviors that characterize many animals in captivity. However, you can simply ask one of the education staff at the exhibit when the animals will next be fed. If your schedule permits, I would recommend returning for this enjoyable spectacle.

Of course, at some exhibits — the dolphins, stingrays, and sea lions — you can feed the animals yourself — for a fee!

Keeping in Touch

If your spouse or teenager tends to wander off, you will appreciate the two-way radios for rent at the Information Desk in the Entrance Plaza. For $5 a radio, you can communicate with your errant family members and save the time wasted searching for them. A $100 refundable deposit is required to ensure you return the little gizmos.

Leaving the Park

You can leave the park at any time and be readmitted free the same day. Just have your hand stamped with a fluorescent symbol on the way out; when you come back, look for the "same day reentry" line and pass your hand under the ultraviolet lamp.

Lockers

Lockers are available just outside the main entrance and in the Entrance Plaza across from Cypress Bakery. The fee is $1 for small lockers, $1.50 for large (quarters only). Once you open your locker, you will have to insert another four or six quarters to lock it again. A change machine is located in the Entrance Plaza locker area.

Money

ATMs are conveniently located throughout the park. The one in the entrance area is just to the left of the ticket booths. All are connected to the Plus, Cirrus, and other networks. A foreign currency exchange window is located just past the ticket windows at Guest Relations; it is open from 10:00 a.m. to 5:00 p.m.

Pets

If you have pets, the toll booth attendant will direct you to the SeaWorld Pet Care facility, very near the main entrance, where Tabby and Bowser can wait for you in air-conditioned comfort. The fee is $6 per pet and you must supply pet food.

Sea Gulls

If you visit from November to February, you will be joined in the park by hordes of sea gulls. These are the New Yorkers of the avian world — loud, boisterous, often rude, but very clever and with the kind of raffish personality that can be endearing. Sea gull season brings with it the increased danger of aerial bombardment, which is unpleasant but not fatal. More amusing (if you're the observer rather than the victim) are the concerted attacks the gulls make on ice cream cones.

Smoking

Smoking is prohibited in all show and exhibit areas. The sit-down eateries have smoking sections; other restaurants have outdoor areas for smokers.

Special Diets

Vegetarians can stop at the Information Desk and request the Food Services staff's list of meatless dishes and the restaurants that serve them. Similar lists of seafood and low-fat selections and other dietary notes are available from the same source.

Splash Zones

All of the stadium shows give the adventuresome the opportunity to get wet — in some cases very wet. One advantage of the splash zones is that they are some of the best seats at SeaWorld. But the threat is very, very real.

I am a believer in splash zones for those who come prepared. Those inexpensive rain ponchos that are sold at every major park will hold the damage to a minimum (although there is probably no real way to guard against a direct hit from Shamu!). Kids, especially young boys, will enjoy the exquisite machismo of getting thoroughly soaked.

One word of warning: In the cooler periods of the year, a full soaking will be extremely uncomfortable, and may be courting a cold, or worse. Bring a big towel and a change of clothes, or be prepared to shell out for new duds at the SeaWorld shops.

Sailing the Sea: Your Day at SeaWorld

SeaWorld can be seen quite comfortably in a single day, without rushing madly around or otherwise driving yourself crazy. This is especially true if you've arrived during one of Orlando's slack periods or if you will be forgoing the thrill rides. But even during the most crowded times, SeaWorld is still more manageable than other parks in the area.

SeaWorld is not a large park, but its comfortable layout and the large Bayside Lagoon at its center make it seem larger than it is. Much of the North End of the park is lushly landscaped with large shady trees and bird-filled pools along the walkways. The South End, on the other side of the Lagoon, is open and airy with a gently rolling landscape. In look and feel, it is quite a contrast to the more tightly crammed spaces of the Magic Kingdom and Universal Orlando. Many parts of SeaWorld have the feel of a particularly gracious public park or botanical garden.

One of SeaWorld's key differentiators is the fact that the vast majority of its attractions are either shows that take place in large, sometimes huge, outdoor auditoriums or "continuous viewing" exhibits through which people pass pretty much at their own pace. My observation is that most people pass through pretty quickly so even if there's a line, the wait won't be unbearable. Once inside you can take your own sweet time.

Here, briefly, are the different kinds of attractions at SeaWorld:

Rides. There are just three "rides" at SeaWorld but they are doozies.

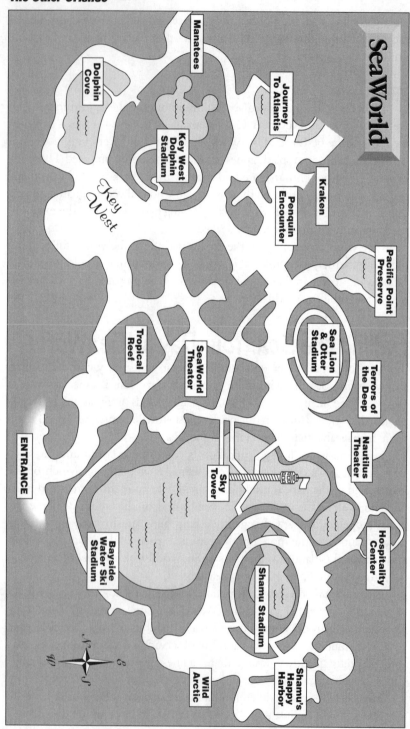

Outdoor Auditorium Shows. These are SeaWorld's primo attractions — Shamu, the sea lions, the dolphins, the water ski show, and some lesser events. There are plenty of shaded seats for these shows (anywhere from 2,400 to 5,500), but even in slower periods they fill up, which should tell you something about how good the shows are. It is possible to enter these auditoriums after the show has begun if they are not full.

Indoor Theater Shows. Some shows take place indoors, in darkened air-conditioned theaters. None of them involves sea mammals and none of them falls into the must-see category. When these shows begin, the doors close and latecomers must wait for the next performance. Be aware that it is difficult to leave these shows in the middle.

Aquatic Habitats. This is SeaWorld's term for its continuous viewing exhibits of live marine animals. The habitats range from huge tanks like those you may have seen at aquariums to elaborate stage sets the likes of which I can almost guarantee you've never seen before.

Guided Tours. These are small group experiences that operate on a limited schedule and charge a modest additional fee. They offer unique access to SeaWorld's "backstage" areas and a chance to learn a bit more about some of the park's most interesting inhabitants.

Catch of the Day

If you had very little time to spend at SeaWorld, I would venture to suggest that you could see just a handful of attractions and still feel you got your money's worth — if you picked the right ones. Here, then, is my list of the very best that SeaWorld has to offer:

The three major open-air animal shows — **Shamu, Clyde & Seamore**, and **Key West Dolphin Fest** — are the heart and soul of Sea-World. Anyone missing these should have his or her head examined.

Close behind are the major "aquatic habitats" — **Wild Arctic** (and the ride that introduces the experience), **Terrors of the Deep, Key West at SeaWorld**, and **Manatees: The Last Generation?** I have omitted **Pacific Point Preserve** and **Penguin Encounter** (both marvelous) only because you are likely to see their close equivalents elsewhere.

For thrill seekers, there is the stupendous roller coaster, **Kraken**. Finally, there is the water ski show, **The Intensity Water Ski Show**, worth a visit for the sheer athleticism and excitement of the amazing stunts.

The One-Day Stay

1. Get up early, but not as early as you would if you were heading for Disney or Universal. Remember, when SeaWorld says the park proper opens at 9, it means it. Get there a little earlier perhaps (you can get a bite to

eat or browse the shops in the Entrance Plaza starting at 8:30 a.m.), but no need to kill yourself.

2. After purchasing your tickets and entering the park, thrill seekers and ride freaks should head immediately to *Kraken*, followed by *Journey to Atlantis*. (Bear left after the entrance mall and follow the signs and the running kids.) Then plan on doing *Wild Arctic* and its exciting ride later in the day, preferably during a Shamu show when the lines for *Wild Arctic* tend to thin out.

If, for one reason or another you are taking a pass on the thrill rides, proceed immediately to *Wild Arctic*. (Just keep bearing right until you see the Lagoon and circle it in a counterclockwise direction.) If you're not interested in taking the ride, the line for the stationary version is always a good deal shorter, so coming later may be okay. Also, if you'd like to skip the ride portion altogether, it is possible to slip quietly in through the exit in the gift shop and just see the animals.

3. Now's the time to review the schedule printed on the back of the map you got when you entered. First, check the times of the "big three" shows — *Shamu*, *Clyde & Seamore*, and *Dolphin Fest*. Whatever you do, don't miss these. Don't try to see two shows that start less than an hour apart. Yes, it can be done but you will be making sacrifices.

Instead, schedule your day so you can arrive at the stadium about 20 minutes before show time, perhaps longer during busier seasons. That way you can get a good seat, like dead center for Shamu or in a splash zone for the kids. There is almost always some sort of pre-show entertainment starting 10 or 15 minutes before the show. It's always fun and, in the case of the warm-up to the sea lion show, often hilarious.

Arriving extra early for the water ski show is less imperative but a good idea if you really like this kind of show.

4. Use your time between shows to visit the aquatic habitats. Use the descriptions in the next section and geographical proximity to guide your choices. For example, you can leave the dolphin show and go right into the manatee exhibit. Or you can visit the penguins just before seeing *Clyde & Seamore* and visit *Terrors of the Deep* immediately after.

5. If you have kids with you, you will miss *Shamu's Happy Harbor* at your peril. Adults, of course, can give it a miss.

6. Fill in the rest of the day with the lesser attractions or return visits to habitats you particularly enjoyed. In my opinion, several of the non-animal shows and attractions can be missed altogether with little sacrifice. If your time is really limited (e.g. you got to the park late), I strongly urge you to take my advice. You can always come back another day and prove me wrong.

7. If you stay until the end, as I recommend, you will not want to miss *Shamu Rocks America* (otherwise what's the point of staying?). If you are visit-

ing during high season (which is the only time it is shown), you might as well see *Red, Bright and Blue Spectacular* if only because it's on your way to the exit.

This plan should allow you to see everything you truly want to see in one day and maybe even some attractions you wished you hadn't bothered with.

The Two-Day Stay

If you have the luxury of spending two or more days visiting SeaWorld (Discovery Cove visitors take note), I would recommend relaxing your pace, perhaps leaving the park early on one day to freshen up and catch a dinner show elsewhere. With two days, even a very relaxed pace should allow you to see everything in the park, several of them more than once.

Another strategy to adopt is to use the first day to concentrate on the shows and the second day to concentrate on the rides, the animal habitats and, perhaps, take a guided tour or two.

THE NORTH END

SeaWorld is not neatly divided into "lands" like some other theme parks I might mention (although the Key West area is a step in that direction). The only geographically convenient division of the park is provided by Bayside Lagoon. If you look at the map you collected on arriving at the park, you will notice that the vertical line formed by the *Sky Tower* effectively divides the park in two: the larger northern side ("The North End") is to the left of the Tower; the southern side including most of the Lagoon ("The South End") is to the right. By the way, although Bayside Lagoon is the official name of SeaWorld's artificial lake, many SeaWorld employees have never heard the term used.

For the purposes of describing the attractions at SeaWorld I have adopted this North End/South End division. Please remember that this is my terminology and not SeaWorld's. If you stop a SeaWorld employee and ask, "How do I get to the North?" you may be told to get on a plane and fly to Philadelphia.

The layout and open landscaping of the southern half, combined with the sheer size of the stadiums located there, make getting your bearings relatively easy. In the northern half, however, the layout and lusher landscaping, while pleasing to the eye, can be confusing. When traveling from Point A to Point B in the northern half of the park, use the map to get you started in the right general direction. Then rely on the directional signs, which are posted at nearly every turning, to guide you to your destination.

Often, you will be able to see the distinctive blue spire of the *Sky Tower* through the trees; use it to orient yourself. In almost every case, the fastest route between the northern and southern halves of the park will be via the wooden walkway across the Lagoon.

I begin with the northern half of the park for the simple reason that this is where you enter the park past the Shamu lighthouse in the artificial harbor that graces the airy entrance area. I describe the attractions in geographical, rather than thematic order. I begin with the *Tropical Reef* exhibit, the back of which you see past the flamingos as you walk through the Entrance Plaza into the park. From there I proceed in a roughly clockwise direction.

Tropical Reef

Rating:	★ ★
Type:	Aquatic habitat
Time:	Continuous viewing
Kelly says:	Best for fish lovers

There is no tropical reef in the *Tropical Reef* building. Instead of the sunny tropics, you enter a cool area of intense darkness. As your eyes adjust, you find yourself in a sort of art gallery of small aquaria set in the wall like paintings. Most of them showcase a single specimen or a single species and many of them are beautifully designed and lit.

One of the more intriguing species, swimming in a darkened tank, is the luminescent flashlight fish which sports a bright green spot used to send a fishy sort of Morse code to others of its species.

This is one of SeaWorld's older aquatic habitats and suffers, perhaps, in comparison to the newer and flashier attractions. Nonetheless, it has a quiet beauty of its own and will reward those patient enough to look closely and read the backlit identification signs.

Across from the entrance to the *Tropical Reef* is the Tide Pool exhibit, a shallow, open tank that mimics the rocky waters at the ocean's edge. Here you can take a close look at reef fish, starfish, anemones, and other creatures who depend on the tides to bring their meals.

Key West at SeaWorld

Key West at SeaWorld is not so much an attraction as a collection of related attractions wrapped in a single theme. Shades of Disney World! The attractions here are aquatic habitats featuring the denizens of warmer waters and the theme, of course, is the casual sophistication and good times atmosphere for which Key West has become famous. On both scores, SeaWorld acquits itself admirably.

Turtle Point

Rating:	★ ★ ★

Type:	Aquatic habitat
Time:	Continuous viewing
Kelly says:	Best when a staffer is present

Turtle Point is small by SeaWorld standards, a shallow sea water pool fringed by white sand beaches. It is home to four species — loggerhead, Kemp's ridley, hawksbill, and green sea turtles, all of them rescued animals.

Turtles, it must be said, are not the most lively creatures SeaWorld has on display. No leaps and twirls here. So, for most folks, this habitat will warrant no more than a quick look. Fortunately, SeaWorld staffers are often hanging out by the pool ready to answer questions. When a group of people gathers and starts exercising its curiosity, a visit to *Turtle Point* can be quite interesting.

Stingray Lagoon

Rating:	★ ★ ★ ★
Type:	Aquatic habitat
Time:	Continuous viewing
Kelly says:	Your best shot at touching a SeaWorld critter

Under a shading roof lies a long, shallow pool with a smaller "nursery pool" in one corner. Its edge is at waist height for easy viewing and interaction. Scores of stingrays lazily circle the main pool, while their "pups" navigate the nursery pool. The mature rays may look scary, but they are remarkably gentle creatures that will tolerate being petted (they feel a bit like slimy felt) and will almost always appreciate a free handout. Small trays of tiny fish called silversides can be purchased for $4 ($3 for annual passholders).

Once again, SeaWorld education staffers make regular appearances here, providing a steady stream of information about these fascinating creatures. The staffers are always ready to answer any questions you might have.

Thanks to the accessibility of the stingrays, this is a very popular attraction. If the pool edge is packed, be patient. Eventually you will be able to make your way forward where your patience is sure to be rewarded.

Dolphin Cove

Rating:	★ ★ ★ ★ +
Type:	Aquatic habitat
Time:	Continuous viewing
Kelly says:	A spectacular SeaWorld habitat

Dolphin Cove lets you get up close to these delightful creatures. This extensive Key West habitat allows petting and feeding on one side and viewing on the other, from both a raised platform and an underwater observation post. Most people start at poolside.

Dolphin feeding here is carried out by paying customers. A small paper cup of smelt-like fish is $4 ($3 for annual passholders) and there is sometimes a two-cup limit per person. Having fish to offer will definitely increase your chances of touching a dolphin, although they will occasionally swim close enough to the edge to allow a foodless hand to sweep along their flanks. But you can't just show up any old time and buy food. It's sold only at specified feeding times and only up to the quantity that SeaWorld's marine dietitians have determined is appropriate to keep the dolphin fit and not fat. If touching a dolphin is a priority for you or your child, I would advise checking out feeding times and arriving a bit early to get on line to purchase food. Otherwise, there is a good chance you will be disappointed.

A number of photographers associated with the Cove's photo concession roam the premises and snap just about everyone who makes it to poolside. The photos are posted in the concession just a few yards away. Two 5x7s or one 8x10 will set you back $20.

Tip: If you're going for a photo, have members of your party stake out a good spot on the edge of the lagoon well in advance of the posted feeding time. Then tip off a photographer as to your location (you'll recognize them by their cameras and headsets).

While touching these cousins of Flipper seems to be the first order of business for most visitors, don't overlook the underwater viewing area (as many people obviously do). It offers a perspective on these graceful beasts that you just don't get from above and, not incidentally, is a wonderful place to wait out those afternoon summer thunderstorms for which Orlando is famous. It will also give you a deeper appreciation of the skill and craft that went into designing the reef-like pool in which the dolphins live. To get there from the petting and feeding area, walk around the pool to your left.

As at all the habitats, SeaWorld staffers make occasional educational presentations. There is usually a staffer sitting on a life guard's raised chair on the beach across from the petting area. Feel free to hail him or her from the sidelines if you have any questions.

Entertainment at Key West

Rating: ★ ★ ★ ★
Type: Smorgasbord of live street performers
Time: Irregular and unpredictable
Kelly says: Great fun

Part of the Key West theme is a steady stream of live entertainment. At its most formal, it takes the form of live musical sets performed in a gazebo by Captain Pete's Island Eats, across from *Stingray Lagoon*. The music, light and easy, has an island slant, with Beach Boys and calypso standards much in evidence.

Near *Dolphin Cove*, a small, open-air performance area plays host to a slack rope walker, whose performance times are posted on a small sign. At other places in the Key West area, you may encounter fire-eaters, jugglers, or a comic prestidigitator luring you with card tricks or a unicyclist juggling. All of these performers observe the traditions of street performance. That is, they keep up a steady stream of amusing patter and shamelessly solicit applause and praise from the crowd. They also make effective use of pint-sized "volunteers" from the audience. If you enjoy the conventions of street performance, you are not likely to be disappointed here.

Performances take place on a somewhat irregular basis, more frequently in the afternoon hours. There is no posted schedule. However, there is a **Sunset Celebration** every day during which all of Key West's performers will be holding forth. Sunset time should be listed on the map and entertainment schedule you picked up at the park entrance.

Key West Dolphin Fest (at Key West Dolphin Stadium)

Rating: ★ ★ ★ ★
Type: Live show with pseudorcas and dolphins
Time: 25 minutes
Kelly says: A crowd-pleaser

This show, which rounds out the Key West experience, is Shamu in miniature. Instead of giant killer whales we have the far slimmer bottle-nosed dolphins and pseudorcas, or "false killer whales." The setting is also homier. Instead of the high-tech setting of Shamu Stadium, we have a smaller pool and a warm looking stage set with a casual Caribbean flavor.

The Key West flavor extends to the pre-show entertainment by a singer who turns out to be the show's host. One of the nicest touches of this show is the way it uses its audience volunteer — a four- or five-year-old, pre-selected before the show starts and waiting on the set. The lucky child gets to pet a dolphin, feed it, and give it some simple hand signals. The child is also invited to leap into the pool, where the dolphin will pick him (or her) up and carry him around the pool as he waves to the crowd. The audience knows it's a joke but, of course, the kid doesn't, and some kids show a remarkable eagerness to dive right in.

The stars of the show are the dolphins, of course, and they leap, dive, and propel their trainers about the pool, with great verve and agility. One segment of the show is given over to the false killer whales, long black tubular animals, and how anyone could mistake them for an orca is beyond me.

There is the usual deft mix of conservation education and entertainment here, although the accent is definitely on the graceful athletic agility of these charming marine mammals.

Tip: To reach the *Manatees: The Last Generation?* exhibit after the show, walk down the steps, toward the stage, and exit to your right, then bear left. To reach *Key West at SeaWorld*, walk toward the stage and exit to the left.

Manatees: The Last Generation?

Rating: ★ ★ ★ ★ ★
Type: Aquatic habitat
Time: 20 to 30 minutes
Kelly says: For everyone in the family

You don't expect a natural history exhibit to pack an emotional wallop, but this one sure does — and does it very deftly. It is unlikely that anyone in your family will emerge from this experience unaffected.

The manatee is a large, slow-moving marine mammal that favors the shallow brackish waterways along the Florida coast, the very same areas that have become a recreational paradise for boaters and fishermen. As man's presence in their habitat has increased, the manatees' numbers have dwindled. A sign in the entrance to this exhibit informs us that there are only about 2,000 manatees left in Florida and that about 10% of this number die each year. Far fewer are born. It doesn't take a mathematical genius to figure out that at this rate the manatee will be extinct (in the wild, at least) in the very near future.

The message takes on an additional poignancy when we realize that all of the small manatees in the exhibit are orphans and that some of the larger animals have been grievously wounded by their encounters with civilization. One has lost most of its tail, another a front flipper. One of the themes of this exhibit is SeaWorld's ongoing rescue efforts of manatees and other marine mammals. On video, we see a seriously wounded adult nursed back to health and released back into the wild. The news that at least one released manatee has reproduced in the wild cheers us like a major victory.

After viewing the manatees from above — in a pool that re-creates a coastal wetland, with egrets and ibises looking on — we pass into a circular theater for a short and highly effective film containing a plea for conservation and protection of the manatee. From there, we pass into the underwater viewing area where the majesty and fragility of this odd beast become even more apparent. Their slow, graceful movements and their rather goofy faces make the manatee instantly appealing. The aquatic setting is lovely too, shared as it is by a variety of native fish. There are glistening tarpon here and a variety of gar, including one large specimen of the alligator gar, a black beast that hovers just under the surface, the reasons for its name instantly apparent. In an interesting bit of verisimilitude, the pool contains tilapia, a fish that is not a native but imported from Africa. It competes with and threatens some native species.

Interactive touch-screen video monitors provide a self-guided wealth of additional information about manatees and the problems they face from habitat destruction and pollution. Staffers from SeaWorld's education center stroll the viewing area ready to answer your questions.

I found this a profoundly moving experience and one to which I returned eagerly. As you leave, you can pick up more information about how to be a responsible boater, diver, and snorkeler in manatee areas. You will also be challenged to make a personal commitment to help the manatee. What will you do?

Photo Op: As you leave the exhibit, look for the sculpture of the manatee cow and her calf floating artfully above the pavement. It makes an excellent backdrop for a family photograph.

Journey to Atlantis

Rating: ★ ★ ★ +
Type: Combination flume ride and roller coaster
Time: About 6 minutes
Kelly says: Wet and wild

It just goes to show you: always heed the warnings of crusty old Greek fishermen, no matter how crazy they seem. Of course, the tourist hordes ignore Stavros's sage advice and set sail on a tour of the ancient city of Atlantis which has mysteriously risen from the Aegean.

Rising some 10 stories, Atlantis looks gaudily out of place at SeaWorld, but it sure looks pretty in the golden glow of the setting sun. But it's not the architecture that draws us here. It's the dizzyingly steep water flume emerging from the city walls and the happy screams of those plunging down it to a watery splashdown. Wend your way through the Greek-village-themed waiting line and be entertained by the news coverage of the eerie reappearance of Atlantis as you wait for your boat.

The voyage gets off to a peaceful start, but after a benign and quite lovely interlude, the boat is seized by the evil Allura, who I gather is a vengeful ancient spirit of some sort. You are winched higher and higher before being sent on a hair-raising journey that combines the scariest elements of a flume ride and a roller coaster. It's a nifty engineering feat but most people probably won't care as they plunge down the 60-foot flume into a tidal wave of water. Another slow ascent gives you a chance to catch your breath before you zip through a fiendishly hidden mini roller coaster to another splashdown, as Allura cackles gleefully. It's all over quickly — too quickly for my taste — but you can always head immediately for the end of the inevitably long line for another go.

Tip: This is a very wet ride, especially if you are in the front row of the eight-passenger boat that serves as the ride vehicle. An inexpensive poncho (which you can get at any of the theme parks) provides pretty good protection. Expensive cameras and other items that might not survive a soaking can be checked as you enter the boat, but they are placed in unlocked lockers and no guarantees are provided. Pay lockers are available near the entrance to the waiting line; they cost 50 cents and if you don't have the change you will have to walk over to the nearby lockers for *Kraken*, where a change machine is available.

As you exit the ride, don't miss the lovely Jewels of the Sea aquarium, just off the inevitable gift shop. Hammerhead sharks and stingrays swim above you in a domed aquarium, while angelfish inhabit the aquarium beneath your feet. Around the walls, don't miss the moon jellyfish which glow enchantingly when you press the light button. Just outside the aquarium and gift shop, playful hidden fountains await to soak the unwary.

Photo Op: Just outside the Jewels of the Sea aquarium is a plaza with a splendid view of the 60-foot flume plunge. If you don't want to take your own pictures, shots of every boatload of happily terrified cruisers are on sale at the ride exit.

Kraken

Rating:	★ ★ ★ ★ ★
Type:	Roller coaster
Time:	2 minutes
Kelly says:	Aieeee!

I must confess I was less than thrilled when *Kraken* was announced. I have always felt that it is the animal shows that make SeaWorld so special and that thrill rides are beside the point here. And truth be told, *Kraken* is something of a distraction if you are watching the *Clyde & Seamore* show or visiting *Pacific Point Preserve* (see below). Of course, SeaWorld doesn't listen to me and coaster enthusiasts will be glad it doesn't. SeaWorld clearly set out to compete head to head with Universal and Disney for coaster bragging rights and, by Neptune, they've succeeded.

Kraken has several claims to fame. For starters, it is higher (at about 150 feet) and faster than any other coaster in Orlando. But the neatest (or scariest) thing about *Kraken* is that the seats are raised slightly so your feet dangle free. So even though the track is beneath your feet at all times, you don't have the same feeling of connectedness you get on other coasters. Nor do you have the comfort of the overhanging superstructure you get in an inverted coaster. The effect is subtle, yet undeniably terrifying.

For a coaster this fast (they claim speeds "in excess of" 65 miles per hour), *Kraken* is also remarkably smooth. Your head may be pressed against the headrest by the G-forces but it won't be buffeted about. Another thing you may notice (if you aren't screaming too loudly) is that *Kraken* is an unusually quiet coaster. Even if you are standing right next to the fence where *Kraken* dips underground at the end of its run, you can barely hear it. Farther away, it is only the shrieks of the riders you hear in the distance. Another item of note is that the ride designers have made a special effort to accommodate those with large upper torso measurements; specially modified seats in rows four and five of each car can handle those with chest measurements of up to 52 inches. There is also a minimum height requirement of 54 inches.

This is an extremely "aggressive" ride, to use the phrase preferred by the designers. They even have a sign urging those with prosthetic limbs to make sure they are securely fastened! So you will be well-advised to stow everything that's not firmly attached to your body in the pay lockers at the entrance to the ride. Smaller lockers cost 50 cents and a few larger ones are $1. A change machine is available.

Now you're ready for the experience itself. As you make the excruciatingly slow climb to the 15-story apex of the first hill, show off just how cool you are by taking in the panoramic view of the park you get from the top. It may be the last time on this ride you have your eyes open.

As you enter the first drop, you begin to fully appreciate the exquisite horror afforded by *Kraken's* unique design. The effect is less like riding in a roller coaster than like being shot through the air on a jet-propelled chair, all the while turning and twisting head over heels. There are seven loops — at least I think there are seven loops, because I keep forgetting to count — as the coaster soars over water and dips below ground along over 4,000 feet of torturous turquoise and yellow track.

The 119-foot vertical loop, the 101-foot diving loop, the zero-gravity roll and the cobra roll may all have their equivalents on other coasters, but experiencing them in *Kraken's* raised, exposed seats adds a heightened level of sheer terror that beggars description.

As astonishing as the engineering is, one of the best moments of the ride occurs thanks to the scenic design. It occurs when the coaster dives underground into what is described as the "monster's lair," a tunnel that appears to be on the brink of being totally inundated by a thundering waterfall. But before you have a chance to drown, you are whipped back above the surface and into a flat spin before returning to the starting point. Truly amazing!

On the downside, the experience is short, about two minutes altogether and a full minute of that time is consumed getting you to the top of the first hill and returning you to the starting point after the coaster brakes at the end.

If you'd like to get a preview of *Kraken*, perhaps to decide if you want to subject yourself to its special brand of terror, there are two good vantage points. The first is just to the left of the main entrance, where a viewing area has thoughtfully been provided for the faint of heart. This spot gives you a good view of the first drop and the end of the ride. Over at *Pacific Point Preserve*, you can get a good view of the main section of the ride.

Photo Op: If you have high speed film and a fast shutter speed, you might try for a shot in the viewing area near the large Kraken head where the cars dip underground, just at the ride's end.

And speaking of photos, you can pick up one of you and your terrified fellow riders at the exit to the ride for $16 or $23, depending on the mounting. Key chains and snow globes are slightly less.

For those who care about such things, *Kraken* takes its name from a mythical sea creature that, in SeaWorld's version at least, looks a lot like a giant dragon eel, a multicolored cousin of the moray. In a cave near the viewing area by the main entrance, you can see actual dragon eels pretending to be embryos in giant Kraken eggs.

Penguin Encounter

Rating:	★ ★ ★ ★
Type:	Aquatic habitat
Time:	Continuous viewing (5 to 10 minutes)
Kelly says:	Kids love this one

This is the only exhibit at SeaWorld that you smell first. It hits you the moment you enter but, for some reason, you get used to it very quickly. Soon you are facing a long glass wall behind which is a charming Antarctic diorama packed with penguins. If you bear to the right as you enter, you are funneled onto a moving conveyor belt that takes you at a steady pace past the viewing area; bearing to the left takes you to a slightly raised, and stationary, viewing area. Don't worry if you get on the conveyor belt and discover you want to dawdle; you can get back to the stationary section at the other end.

As you ride the conveyor, the water level is about at your chest, so you get an excellent view of the underwater antics of these remarkable birds as they almost literally "fly" through the water. On land, their movements are considerably less graceful, but their slow waddling has its own kind of grace, especially in the case of the larger king penguins with their yellow-accented faces. Overhead, artificial snow sprinkles down from hatches in the roof. The water temperature, an electronic readout informs us, is 45 degrees Fahrenheit, while the air temperature is maintained at 34 degrees. Chilly for us, perhaps, but these highly adapted creatures are used to a much deeper freeze, as we discover in the Learning Center immediately past the penguins.

Here, interactive teaching aids provide the curious with a wealth of additional information about gentoos, rockhoppers, and chinstraps. Here, too, you can watch informative videos about the hand-rearing of penguins and how they molt, the Antarctic environment and penguin predators, and Isla Noir, a Chilean island that is especially popular with penguins.

Just past the Learning Center is a smaller habitat featuring alcids, a group of birds, including the puffins and murres, that is the northern equivalent of the penguin. Unlike their Antarctic cousins, these birds fly in the air as well as beneath the sea. The alcid viewing area, like the penguin exhibit, is equally divided between land and sea and, if you're in luck, you will see murres "flying" to the bottom to scavenge smelt.

As you leave the exhibit, you will have an opportunity to circle back to the penguin viewing area for another look if you wish.

Xtreme Zone

Rating: ★ ★
Type: Interactive sports
Time: A few minutes
Kelly says: If you must

Opposite the entrance to *Penguin Encounter* is this open-air time killer. It has a temporary look and feel to it, but apparently it is here for the long haul. For $6 you can climb a simulated cliff face (with a helmet and safety harness) or bounce about on a trampoline while wearing a bungee cord harness. For $9 you can do both. Best of all, it costs nothing to skip it.

Pacific Point Preserve

Rating: ★ ★ ★ ★
Type: Outdoor aquatic habitat
Time: Continuous viewing
Kelly says: Don't miss feeding the sea lions

Over 50 sea lions roar and bark with delight in this two-and-a-half-acre, open-air, sunken habitat. SeaWorld's design team traveled to the Pacific Northwest to take molds of the rock outcroppings along the coast to build this remarkable re-creation. Adding to the verisimilitude is a wave machine, similar to those used in the water theme parks, that creates waves of anywhere from a few inches to two feet in height. The viewing area extends entirely around the exhibit, and while the sea lions (and a smaller number of harbor seals) are safely out of reach, it's almost as if you can touch them.

But if you can't pet them, you can feed them. Small trays of fish are available at certain times for $3 a tray ($2 for annual passholders) and their contents will very quickly disappear down a sea lion's gullet. It's all great fun and, if you aren't careful, you can very quickly squander your lunch money. The sea lions, for their part, have learned how to part you from your smelt and will bark furiously and even leap decoratively up onto the edge of the pool until their hunger is satisfied, which it never is. Fortunately, watching other people feed the sea lions is almost as entertaining as doing it yourself. The feeding stations are open regularly and it is only on extremely crowded days that the allotted ration of fish is sold out before closing time.

While their feeding behavior might lead you to believe these animals are tame, they are not. The sea lions you see perform in the *Clyde & Seamore* show just around the corner live separately from their cousins in Pacific Point. They have been trained for years and habituated to interacting with humans. The animals in *Pacific Point Preserve* are wild and like all wild animals unpredictable. In other words, don't dangle little Susie over the edge to get her within smelt-tossing range.

Tip: You might want to ask someone on the education staff when the main feeding will take place that day. While the public certainly helps with the feeding, the staff has to make sure that their charges are adequately fed. They do this by serving up fish by the bucketful at least once a day. This is a highly entertaining ritual so it's worthwhile to check the schedule. Also, the handlers have to hand-feed some of the older sea lions and seals who don't compete well for food with their younger rivals. You and your kids will undoubtedly find this part of the feeding particularly touching.

Clyde & Seamore Take Pirate Island (at Sea Lion & Otter Stadium)

Rating:	★ ★ ★ ★
Type:	Live water show with sea lions, otters, and walruses.
Time:	25 minutes
Kelly says:	The funniest show at SeaWorld

Forget about education. This one's all about high spirits and low humor and it's a sure-fire crowd pleaser. Clyde and Seamore are sea lion versions of Laurel and Hardy, or Ralph Kramden and Ed Norton, or maybe two of the Three Stooges. In any event, they're bumblers.

There's a plot about a search for gold (and fresh fish), a treacherous otter, and (of course) pirates, but it's almost beside the point. The real point of this show is watching Clyde and Seamore cavort up, down, and around the multilevel set and into and out of the pool that rings the lip of the stage. The humor is broad and the little kids love it. One thing that makes the show such a hoot is the slapdash way in which the human performers carry it off, bloopers and all. Some of the gaffes are due to the unpredictability of the animals but other boo-boos seem to be written into the script, although few will suspect as much unless they see the show several times.

If you are lucky, you might get to see a walrus or two make a cameo appearance. Walruses, I am told, are nowhere near as tractable as sea lions and, given their considerable bulk and potential for wreaking havoc, they only appear when they're in the mood. Even then, they may balk at performing, just like a Hollywood star, and the trainers know better than to argue with several tons of balky blubber. As usual, a small child is summoned from the audience to help out (and shake Clyde's flipper). And, of course, there are the usual dire warnings about splash zones, although the wetness quotient is far lower here than at the Shamu show.

Tip: If you arrive more than about 10 minutes early, you will be entertained by "The SeaWorld Mime." If you arrive fewer than 10 minutes before show time, you may become one of his victims. This is not mime in the cutesy Marcel Marceau tradition — there's no getting trapped inside an invisible box or walking against an imaginary wind. This is mime with an attitude, that mimics, mocks, and plays pranks on the steady stream of people arriving for the show. Those familiar with the work of David Shiner, the clown prince of this genre, will know what to expect. For others, I don't want to give too much away. This is, far and away, the best of SeaWorld's pre-show entertainments. It is an attraction in its own right and not to be missed.

Terrors of the Deep

Rating:	★ ★ ★ ★
Type:	Aquatic habitat
Time:	15 to 30 minutes
Kelly says:	Up close and personal with some scary fish

In *Terrors of the Deep*, SeaWorld has very cleverly packaged an aquarium-style display of some of the seas' scariest, ugliest, and most dangerous creatures. What kid could resist a title like that? They'll be so excited and grossed out that they won't even notice that they've learned a thing or two in the process. Adults will appreciate the ingenious and informative ways in which the specimens are displayed and explicated.

The tone and lighting of this exhibit is dark and foreboding, with appropriately ominous soundtrack music, but you needn't worry about any unpleasant surprises. When you get right down to it, it's fish in tanks and far too fascinating to be truly scary to any except perhaps the most suggestible kids. This is a very popular attraction and, with long lines in mind, the interior has been cleverly designed to offer space for the line to back up, while keeping the crowds entertained with informative videos and displays.

You enter this habitat via a bridge over a shallow pool in which some of the smaller and less threatening shark specimens are displayed. Here are small hammerheads and nurse sharks along with a variety of rays, including the jet-black bat ray. A long dark corridor, leads us to a clear acrylic tunnel through an artificial tropical reef. This is home to the moray eels — nasty-looking snake-like fish. The moray's coating of yellow slime over its blue flesh gives it a sickly green tint. At first all you see is the many varieties of reef fish swimming about, but closer inspection reveals the morays poking their heads out of their holes. The more you look the more you see. There are dozens and dozens of the creatures hidden in the crevices of the reef. From time to time one swims free, undulating its long body right overhead. Looking up you see the surface of the water. The tank has been designed to mimic the natural habitat as closely as possible; the lighting comes from a single overhead source, standing in for the sun.

The tunnel curves around and into a viewing area in which several tanks hold specimens probably best kept separate. First is the delicate and intricately camouflaged lion fish. Looks are deceiving here, because the lion fish's feathery appendages are actually poisoned spines which are highly toxic to swimmers unfortunate enough to come in contact with them.

Tried any fugu at your local sushi bar? You may want to reconsider after viewing the puffer fish on display here. Fugu, as the fish is known in Japan, is one of the world's most poisonous fish. The Japanese consider its edible portions a delicacy, and licensed fugu chefs carefully pare away the poisonous organs. Despite their precautions, several people die each year from fugu poisoning. Swimming unconcernedly with the puffer fish are surgeon fish, a pretty species that carries the marine equivalent of switchblades concealed near their tails. When attacked (or grabbed by unwary fishermen), they lash out with their hidden weapon, inflicting a nasty gash. Across the way are barracuda, looking every bit as terrifying as when I first encountered them while snorkeling in the Caribbean. Had I been to SeaWorld first, I would have known that an attack was unlikely and probably would have made less of a fool of myself.

As you walk down a sloping tunnel to the shark viewing area, videos and wall displays fill you in on little known shark facts. For example, did you know that a shark's liver takes up nearly 90% of its body cavity and accounts for nearly a quarter of its weight? Scientists theorize that, since the liver contains a great deal of oil and since oil is lighter than water, the shark's huge liver may contribute to its buoyancy.

The shark viewing area is large with three rows of benches for those who want to take a break and watch these spooky creatures float by the huge picture windows in front of them. Backlit signs identify the species in the tank: small sawtooth sharks, brown sharks, nurse sharks, bull sharks, lemon sharks, and sandpiper sharks. A video plays on a continuous loop, offering up shark facts and profiling some of the sharks on display. There are no giants here but what the specimens lack in size they more than make up for in number. If you ever encounter sharks in the wild, hopefully there will be nowhere near this many of them.

Your shark encounter is capped off by a ride on a conveyer belt through a 124-foot tunnel that takes you right down the middle of the shark tank. About a foot thick, the clear acrylic walls of the tunnel are supporting 450 tons of man-made salt water over your head. Don't worry, you're perfectly safe; the acrylic can withstand a tromping by 372 elephants (as you are informed on exiting).

Tip: You will pass one of the best viewing spots for the shark tank on your right as you exit. From here, you look back along the tunnel through which you just passed. This is also a great place to observe the twice-weekly shark feedings. At press time, they were feeding the sharks on Tuesdays and Thursdays, sometime between the hours of 10 a.m. and noon, but check with an attendant to get the latest information on the feeding schedule.

Cirque de la Mer (at Nautilus Theatre)

Rating: ★ ★ ★ ★
Type: Indoor stage show
Time: 45 minutes
Kelly says: One of the best of its kind

Why this show is called *Cirque de la Mer* is beyond me. It is neither a circus, of the sea, nor French. But why be picky? What we get, in fact, is a talented troupe that combines mime comedy, acrobatics, and ballet in an amiable vaudeville that, true to the genre, has something for everyone.

The sets and costumes draw on themes and imagery from Peru's Nazcan and Incan past but this show is pure twentieth century entertainment. Our master of ceremonies (who, by the way, is the show's creator) is an engaging, shaggy haired mime who uses a whistle much as Harpo Marx used his tooting horn. In his best bit, he creates a bizarre boxing match, using six volunteers from the audience to splendid comic effect. Two bare-chested acrobats perform a slow motion series of poses that highlight their sense of balance and superb physical conditioning. A lovely dance number showcases a lithe performer representing (I think) a condor who soars from above on wings of white cloth; it's a simple effect but mesmerizing nonetheless. He rescues a maiden about to be sacrificed and together they perform an intricate aerial ballet. This one's a real crowd-pleaser and deservedly so.

Sky Tower

Rating: ★ ★ ★
Type: Bird's-eye view of Orlando

Time:	Six and half minutes
Kelly says:	For those who've seen everything else they want to see at SeaWorld

Riding the *Sky Tower* will set you back an additional $3.00, unless you have an annual pass, in which case it's free. You'll have to decide whether the six-and-a-half-minute glimpse of Orlando from on high is worth the extra charge. I regularly see people answering that question in the negative.

The *Sky Tower* is a circular viewing platform that rotates slowly while rising from lagoon level to a height of 400 feet. From there you can see the dome of Spaceship Earth at EPCOT and Space Mountain at the Magic Kingdom, as well as some of the Orlando area's other high-rise buildings. Closer by, you will get a superb view of the layout of *Kraken*. If your timing is right you will get to see a load of terrified riders make a complete circuit on the awesome coaster.

There are two levels, each offering a single row of glassed-in seating that circles the capsule. You pick the level of your choice as you enter. The upper level would seem the better choice, and most people head that way, but it only gives you a 10-foot height advantage which doesn't really affect your enjoyment of the experience.

Riding the *Sky Tower* is an enjoyable enough way to kill some time if you aren't eager to see anything else and don't mind paying the extra charge. Seeing SeaWorld from the air can be fascinating, especially if the water ski show is going on at the time. You will also gain an appreciation for the cunning way the park is laid out and see why you've been having difficulty navigating from place to place in the North End.

The *Sky Tower* ride is at the mercy of the elements. Any hint of lightning in the area closes it down, as do high winds, which might buffet the top of the tower even when it's perfectly calm on the ground.

Pets Ahoy (at SeaWorld Theatre)

Rating:	★ ★ ★ +
Type:	Indoor theater show
Time:	25 minutes
Kelly says:	A must for pet lovers

If you saw *Animal Planet Live* at Universal Studios Florida, you might be tempted to skip this one. However, if you are a pet lover, you'll want to put this charming show on your list. It offers a pleasant break from the hot Florida sun.

The SeaWorld twist here is that almost all the animals in the show were found in Central Florida animal shelters and rescued from an uncertain fate. As a result, the cast list runs heavily to cats and dogs, although there is an amusing potbellied pig and even a mouse.

Ace trainer Joel Slaven (of *Ace Ventura: Pet Detective* fame) has done an amazing job here, especially with the cats. Not only do Slaven's pussycats do every doggie trick and do them better but there is a cat who does a tightwire act and one who bounds over the heads of the audience, jumping from one tiny platform to another.

Dolphin Nursery

Rating:	★ ★ ★
Type:	Small shaded outdoor pool
Time:	Continuous viewing
Kelly says:	Not much to see but hard to resist

This is where dolphin moms get to enjoy a little maternity leave with their newborns during the bonding process. A barrier fence prevents you from getting right to the pool's edge, so at best you will just be able to glimpse the little ones as they swim by in close formation with mom.

Still, even a glimpse of a baby dolphin is a hard lure to resist and you will probably want to pause here for a look. Education staffers are on hand to answer your questions. Feedings usually take place in the morning and late afternoon, making those the best times to visit.

Walk-By Exhibits

In addition to the larger, more formal aquatic habitats and stadium and theater shows, SeaWorld is dotted with a number of smaller, "walk-by" exhibits, typically showcasing the birds who live by the sea. They blend in so well with the landscaping that they seem almost like set decoration, and many people simply breeze by. Most of them are to be found in the northern end of the park.

Certainly some of them, like the sand sculpture exhibits, don't deserve more than a cursory look. Others, like the flamingo exhibit, will reward those who pause for closer inspection and perhaps a photograph. These exhibits are more elaborate and more thoughtfully designed versions of what you might see at the birdhouse of an old-fashioned zoo. In addition to the flamingos, you will find ducks, pelicans, and spoonbills. Signs identify each species and provide interesting tidbits of information about their habitat, range, and habits.

Eating in the North

Most of SeaWorld's eating establishments are located in this end of the park. I will describe them geographically, beginning in the Entrance Plaza and then proceeding in a roughly clockwise direction. In addition to the permanent establishments listed here, you will find outdoor stands and kiosks selling cool drinks and ice cream treats.

Polar Parlor

What:	Small ice cream parlor
Where:	In the Entrance Plaza
Price Range:	$

This compact, rather bare ice cream dispensary serves up some tasty sundaes in waffle cones (about $3.50). There is a small outdoor seating area. Or you can carry your sundae out into the park and take your chances with the dive-bombing sea gulls, who have obviously developed a sweet tooth.

Polar Parlor also serves up regular ice cream cones in the $2 and $3 range, as well as soft drinks, coffee, and ice cream floats ($3).

Cypress Bakery

What:	Compact bakery with outdoor seating
Where:	In the Entrance Plaza
Price Range:	$

Cypress Bakery, a perfect choice for that missed breakfast, serves croissants, muffins, cakes, pies, pastries, and enormous cookies along with coffee, tea, hot chocolate, milk, orange juice. Or try the Cypress Cooler ($2.50 or $2.95), a frosted concoction of espresso, chocolate, milk, and soft drinks. Seating is strictly al fresco at mostly shaded tables.

Captain Pete's Island Eats

What:	Outdoor fast-food eatery
Where:	In Key West, near *Stingray Lagoon*
Price Range:	$ - $$

This walk-up, window-service fast-food joint carries off its Key West theme deftly. Spicy conch fritters and sweet coconut and pineapple fritters are $3, hot dogs with fries $5, chicken fingers with fries about $7. You can wash them down with a nonalcoholic "Island Fruit Smoothie" in a variety of flavors ($3 each). There are also Bud, O'Doul's, and the usual range of soft drinks. On the sweeter side are funnel cakes (about $3), which can be had with hot fudge or strawberry toppings for about $4. Seating is outdoors, some of it shaded, near the gazebo where the musicians play (see *Entertainment in Key West*, above).

Mama Stella's Italian Kitchen

What:	Cafeteria-style Italian
Where:	Near *Penguin Encounter*

Price Range: $$ - $$$

One of the larger fast-food restaurants in the park, Mama Stella's offers pizza for about $5. For a buck more you can have fries with it. The rest of the menu is limited to three dishes: chicken parmesan (about $7) and for around $6 either a simple spaghetti with meat sauce or a chicken Caesar salad. A side will run you about $3. Just outside Mama Stella's, a walk-up window dispenses various ice cream offerings ($3 to $4).

Smoky Creek Grill

What: Barbecue joint
Where: Behind SeaWorld Theatre
Price Range: $$ - $$$

That mouth-watering smell that's been making you feel hungry ever since you entered the park comes from this barbecue stand. Here you can get succulent barbecued chicken and pork ribs that are comparable in quality, quantity, and price to the fare available in local barbecue restaurants. That makes Smoky Creek Grill one of the better deals at SeaWorld. Spareribs are about $7 or $8, depending on size, and the baby back versions about $10 or $13. The beef barbecue, when available, is about $8, with chicken slightly less. Kid combos for the tykes come in at $3 to a bit over $5 for Shamu Kid's Meal, which includes a souvenir lunch pail. The sides of cole slaw and baked beans are tasty, and if you still have room for dessert, you'll find the usual assortment on offer. You can wash it all down with soft drinks or beer.

All seating is outside in a patio protected from dive-bombing seagulls by thin wire string overhead or, if you prefer, in a sheltered seating area.

Chicken 'n Biscuit

What: SeaWorld fried chicken
Where: Across from the SeaWorld Theatre
Price Range: $$ - $$$

This is SeaWorld's version of KFC and other fried chicken fast-food chains. All chicken dinners come with french fries and a roll. The two-piece dinner is priced at about $6 and the three-piece at about $6.50. Corn on the cob or BBQ beans side orders are just under $2. Beer is available here in $2.99 and $3.79 sizes, along with the usual soft drink offerings. There is a smallish indoor seating area. Outdoor seating is in a sun-baked and rather charmless square, although some tables are shaded by umbrellas.

Waterfront Sandwich Grill

What: Fast-food burgers
Where: On Bayside Lagoon, near the *Sky Tower*

Price Range: $$ - $$$

This brightly painted eatery serves up standard burger and fries fare at fairly moderate prices. Burger platters, which include fries, are about $6 to $7. Sandwiches — Club and "California Light," featuring a smoked turkey breast — are served with potato salad and come in at about $7. Fries by themselves are about $2 or $2.50 depending on size. No alcoholic beverages are served here.

There is a largish indoor seating area; outside, the Waterfront Sandwich Grill shares a patio with the Dockside Cafe next door. The view looks out over the Lagoon and is charming.

Dockside Cafe

What: Walk-up stand
Where: Near *Terrors of the Deep* and the walkway
                 across the Lagoon
Price Range: $$

Sandwich platters are the prime fare here. Choices include club, barbecued grilled chicken, barbecued beef, and hot dogs for $5 to about $6, all accompanied by fries. Chicken strips with fries go for about $7, or $4 for a kid-sized portion. Fries alone are $2.50, and big cookies run about $2. Shamu, juice bars, and popcorn (all about $2.50) are also available. Only nonalcoholic beverages are served here.

Seating is all al fresco and the patio, which is shared by the Waterfront Sandwich Grill, can get crowded at meal times. If you can't find a seat outside, take your tray into the Waterfront Sandwich Grill next door.

Sunset Beach Tiki Bar

What: Full-service bar in outdoor gazebo
Where: Near the Beach Stage on Bayside Lagoon
Price Range: $

This is a real grown-ups' getaway serving Mai Tais, daiquiris, margaritas and other potent "island" drinks in day-glo souvenir plastic glassware. It opens sometime in the afternoon and a Jimmy Buffett-esque entertainer is often on hand to help the booze go down.

Bimini Bay Cafe

What: Caribbean-flavored sit-down eatery
Where: On Bayside Lagoon, near the flamingos
Price Range: $$ - $$$

The decor here evokes a breezy, pastel-drenched Caribbean bungalow, complete with a verandah. The restaurant service, however, is strictly indoors.

The verandah is used by strollers and patrons of the Tiki Bar next door.

The menu is short, simple, and tasty — and changes frequently, so it is hard to predict what will be on offer when you visit. Soup is $3 to $4, salads $8 to $9, and sandwiches $7 to $8. The sandwich menu here ranges from burger and chicken tenders to Grilled Mahi Mahi and a Bimini Veggie Wrap. All come with at least two side dishes. Kids meals featuring pasta, chicken fingers, or hot dogs are available for about $6.

Bimini Bay Cafe offers the widest selection of beverages in the park, including six beer choices and "homemade pink lemonade with unlimited refills during your meal."

The wait here can be daunting during the lunch time rush (usually about noon to 3:30). Reservations are not accepted but you can request priority seating at the Information Desk in the Entrance Plaza. This is almost as good as a reservation because it gets you the first table appropriate for your party size (two, four, etc.) that opens up at or after the time you request.

Bayside Oasis

What: Walk-up drinks and snacks
Where: Next to the Bimini Bay Cafe
Price Range: $

A simple stand offering soft drinks and coffee along with snacks, mostly of the ice cream variety.

Shopping in the North

Just as most of the restaurants are concentrated in the North End of the park, so are most of the shops. What follows are brief descriptions of these shops, beginning with those in the Entrance Plaza and continuing in a roughly clockwise direction. While the accent of the merchandise changes from shop to shop, the good folks at Fuji have made sure that you can get film everywhere. You will also find accomplished caricaturists scattered about; they will sketch you for $13 to $23, depending on size, color, and other variables.

Keyhole Photo

Photographers for SeaWorld's photo concessionaire roam the park, snapping visitors as they interact with the animals and enjoy the thrill rides. At this and other locations throughout the park, you can purchase the results in formats ranging for keychains to framed 8x10s ($10 to $45).

Shamu's Emporium

If you'd like to leave your souvenir shopping until the end of the day you can stop at this large shop on your way out of the park and be reasonably sure of finding something suitable for yourself and the folks back home. You have to pass right by it to get to the exit so don't worry about missing it.

There are several lines of marine animal sculptures, including some beautiful small sculptures by John Perry. This artist works in resin to depict dolphins, orcas, sharks, and other sea creatures which he then mounts on decorative burlwood bases. They range in size from small pieces depicting an individual to larger ones with several individuals of varying sizes. The price range is from about $16 to $100. Also in the art line are matted and framed photos of SeaWorld's stars ranging from $60 to $160.

Of course, the usual selection of t-shirts is to be found here, some of them quite stylish. Prices range from $15 for the standard variety to $28 for the fancy models. Also prominently displayed is a wide selection of plush toys in a variety of sizes at prices ranging from about $8 to about $40. Here your kids will find cuddly killer whales, seal pups, polar bears, sharks, walruses, manatees, even king penguins. In my opinion, the polar bears and penguins offer the best value for the dollar, although the $7 seal pup is sure to be a winner with any small child.

Before leaving, make sure to check out the selection of books and videos about some of the creatures you've visited during your stay.

Shamu's Souvenirs

Just a few paces away you will find this small square shop, hardly more than a kiosk really. It is aimed squarely at kids and features small toys, gifts, and t-shirts for tots ranging from about $16 to about $18. You can also pick up a hat and film here should you need either.

Bud's Shop

This small shop at the entrance to Key West features Budweiser gear in all its many guises.

Sandcastle Toys .n. Treats

Nearby and part of the Key West area is a somewhat larger shop with a larger range of merchandise and an emphasis on kids (there is a Sesame Street section here). Toys, caps, kid-sized clothing, and activity books can be found here and, true to the shop's name, there are treats in the form of candies and large lollypops.

Conch City Leather Work

This tiny kiosk at the entrance to Key West is crammed with leather items of all descriptions — key rings, belts, buckles, bracelets, hair ornaments, wallets, and very nice, multi-pocket shoulder bags ($25 and up).

Coconut Bay Trader

This is Key West's largest and poshest shop. There is a good selection of resort wear and swimwear for women, at moderate prices, as well as a small selection of tabletop sculptures. The shop also offers plush toys, pottery, and condiments, along with Fresh Produce clothing for women and girls and a nice selection of men's casual wear.

Gulliver's

This small kiosk is in a park-like setting near the back entrance to the Key West Dolphin Stadium. It features a representative cross-section of inexpensive SeaWorld merchandise, from desktop figurines to t-shirts and beach towels. There are also plush toys and hand puppets for kids.

Manatee Cove

This small circular shop is at the top of the ramp leading out of the manatee exhibit. Here you'll find a selection of t-shirts commemorating the sluggish sea mammal (kids $11 to $16, adults $18 to $31) and a large variety of manatee collectibles, including some very well executed small figurines. Manatee plush dolls range from $7 to $40. This shop has a good range of manatee books for all ages in case you or someone in your family would like to learn more about the endangered critter. This is also probably a good place to remind yourself that a portion of your purchase price will go towards helping rehabilitate injured manatees.

Golden Seahorse

You can't miss this large shop if you ride *Journey to Atlantis* or visit Jewels of the Sea Aquarium; you have to walk through it. The wares on display range from the ubiquitous t-shirts and dolphin sculptures to dolphin-themed photo frames, votive lamps, magnets, jewelry, and hair ornaments. You'll also find attractive, moderately priced clothing.

Kraken Gifts

This small kiosk, open on two sides and located hard by the exit to the eponymous roller coaster, has a surprisingly small selection of *Kraken* t-shirts, but it does have some rather nice beachwear for adults as well as a selection of floppy hats, plush toys, sunglasses, and jewelry.

Friends of the Wild

Near the exit to *Penguin Encounter* and just across from Mama Stella's, this spacious, airy store serves up a fairly representative cross section of Sea-World souvenirs.

Unique at this location is a jewelry section featuring moderately priced gold bracelets, earrings, brooches, and pendants, some bearing semi-precious stones and many with a dolphin or sea shell motif.

There is a nice selection of the John Perry art pieces described above as well as porcelain collectibles from Spain ($65 to $165). You will also find a variety of mugs and glasses, plus toys and books aimed at the younger crowd.

O. P. Otter's Souvenir and Gift Shop

This small kiosk, tucked away directly behind Chicken 'n' Biscuit, is pretty much limited to kiddie merchandise. You'll find plush dolls, toys, and t-shirts, as well as some other clothing.

Pearl Factory

You'll find this small shop behind SeaWorld Theater near the Smoky Grill Cafe. It sells Japanese cultured pearls in a variety of settings at prices that begin at about $20 and climb to $6,000. For $13 you can pick an oyster and, if you like the pearl you find inside, have it set in gold for $17 and up. Your setting choices range from rings to pendants, and silver settings are slightly less expensive.

Amazing Pictures

The photographer and props here let you transform yourself into a Shamu trainer or Hollywood star by inserting your face into the photo of your choice. Prices for the resulting photos range from $29.95 for a framed photo, t-shirt, or mug to $59.95 for a large poster.

Crosswalk Gifts

If you file out of the Clyde & Seamore show from the top of the auditorium, it will be hard to miss this small shop; it's just at the bottom of the hill. The accent here is on cuddly plush toys with a large selection at the usual prices ($7 to $30). You will also find clothing, mostly for girls and babies, as well as baby bottles, beach towels, and tiny backpacks ($25).

Ocean Treasures

Near the exit from *Terrors of the Deep* is one of SeaWorld's more upscale shops. Ocean Treasures carries men's and women's resort clothing, fossil shark teeth ($47), and shark-tooth pendants ($13 to $26), as well as some very attractive tote bags, sandals, and other accessories. There are also the usual plush toys.

Gulf Breeze Trader

A short walk away, on the way to the Nautilus Theater, you'll find this small shed-like store. The accent here is on moderately priced t-shirts, swimwear, and other clothing (including kids clothes) and accessories. Novelty photo frames were a big item here on a recent visit.

Cruz Cay Harbor

The emphasis here is on clothing, specifically the type of clothing that is usually referred to as "resort wear." Head here for Teva sandals and Tommy Bahamas sportswear for men and women (silk shirts $96) Cruz Cay also features decorative items for the home and a line of inexpensive jewelry, including earrings and pins, ($3 to $10).

Flamingo Point

The focus at this small kiosk is on t-shirts, most of them emblazoned with Budweiser logos. There are also hats and toys. Strangely enough, given its name, there were no toys or t-shirts featuring flamingos when last I visited.

Sweet Sailin'

With this colorful candy store we've come full circle, back to the Entrance Plaza and Shamu's Emporium. You can watch them make the creamery fudge, caramel apples ($2.50), and some of the chocolates sold here in bulk (about $2.50 a quarter pound). You can also get a fancy cup of coffee ($2 to $3).

Exit Gifts

Just in case you have second thoughts after leaving the park, SeaWorld has thoughtfully provided this vest-pocket shop just outside the gates for your convenience. Unfortunately, you'll have to make do with a limited selection of souvenirs.

THE SOUTH END

The southern half of SeaWorld lies to the right of the *Sky Tower* on the map, most of it across the wooden walkway that takes you over Bayside Lagoon to Shamu Stadium. The whole feel of this side of the park is quite a bit different, with its large open spaces between huge modern stadiums and buildings.

Once again, I describe the attractions in geographical rather than thematic order, beginning with the *Hospitality Center* and continuing in a clockwise direction around Bayside Lagoon.

Clydesdale Hamlet & Anheuser-Busch Hospitality Center

Rating:	★ ★ +
Type:	Horse stables and free beer
Time:	As long as you want
Kelly says:	For horse lovers and Bud fans

Since Anheuser-Busch, the brewing giant, owns SeaWorld, you probably can't hold it against them for blowing their own horn a bit. And even if you find this sort of blatant self-promotion distasteful, you'll probably have to admit they do a pretty good (and fairly tasteful) job of it.

There are really two attractions here, *Clydesdale Hamlet*, the home of Budweiser's trademark Clydesdale beer wagon team, and the *Anheuser-Busch Hospitality Center. Clydesdale Hamlet* is actually a very upscale stable, impeccably clean and not in the least aromatically offensive. This is where the impressive Clydesdales hang out between appearances elsewhere in the park and where you can meet and pet them at times posted in the daily calendar.

These steeds, from Scotland, were originally bred for the heavy work of hauling man's stuff from place to place, and while they may not have the magnificent grace of their racing cousins they are pretty impressive in their own right — all 2,000 pounds of them. They are also pampered, beautifully groomed, and obviously well-cared for. There are stable attendants always close at hand to make sure you don't slip them a sugar cube or a contraband carrot and to regale you with horse lore. Did you know, for example, that if you hold down the jaw of a supine Clydesdale, it will be unable to stand up? Seems they have to be able to raise their heads off the ground first before they begin the process of standing up.

Next door is the *Anheuser-Busch Hospitality Center*, a large, airy pavilion whose architecture reflects that of the stable. It's a lovely building surrounded by immaculate lawns. A comfortable outdoor seating area overlooks a crystal clear lake, fed by a babbling waterfall. It's the nicest place in the park to just sit and take your ease.

Inside you'll find The Deli (a fast-food restaurant) and the Label Stable (a souvenir shop), which are described at the end of this section. The centerpiece of the Center, however, is the free beer dispensing area that faces the main entrance and is backed by huge copper brewing kettles. That's right, free beer. The cups are on the small size (about 10 ounces) and there's a limit (one sample at a time, two per day), but it's still a gracious gesture. Most of Anheuser-Busch's brands are available, including the nonalcoholic O'Doul's.

Here at the Hospitality Center, several times a day, you can attend **Budweiser Beer School**, a pleasant enough way to kill 45 minutes and perhaps get answers to those questions that have been tormenting you for years. Why is it called Budweiser? Who was Anheuser? However, I suspect most people are lured here by the beer tasting that follows some videos about the history of Anheuser-Busch and the art of brewing beer. At the end you get a certificate attesting to your newfound status as a "Beermaster."

Arcade and Midway Games

Rating: ★ +
Type: Video and "skill" games arcades
Time: As long as you want
Kelly says: For video game addicts

Here, in addition to electronically screeching video games, you will find a collection of the sort of "skill" games that are a staple of state fairs, traveling carnivals, and seaside boardwalks. Brighter and shinier than the originals, it's true, but almost exact copies nonetheless. My feelings about these money-siphoning operations, located near the Shamu Stadium, can be summed up pretty easily — why bother? The main reason you paid good money to come to SeaWorld is just paces away and everything you can do here, you can do elsewhere for less money. That being said, these venues are clean and attractive and the prizes at Midway Games are better than most.

The Shamu Adventure

Rating: ★ ★ ★ ★ ★
Type: Live stadium show
Time: 25 minutes
Kelly says: The acme of the SeaWorld experience

Could there be a better job than being a killer whale trainer and being shot 30 feet into the air off the nose of a 5,000 pound orca? You won't think so after seeing this razzle-dazzle demonstration put on by the dashing young SeaWorld staffers who spend their time teaching the Shamu family some awesome tricks (although the trainers prefer the term "behaviors").

Actually, they aren't "tricks" at all in the common sense of the term. They are simply extensions of natural behaviors that have been reinforced by the whales' trainers with patient attention and liberal handfuls of smelt. Nor is *The Shamu Adventure* to be confused with mere entertainment. In keeping with SeaWorld's commitment to conserving the marine environment and saving endangered marine species, this show teaches important lessons about the realities of nature (including its darker sides) and the importance of the marine mammal husbandry practiced at SeaWorld Orlando and its sister parks around the country.

The stars of the show are members of the family *orsinus orca*, commonly known as killer whales and affectionately known by nearly everyone who visits SeaWorld as Shamu. The first killer whale ever captured was named Namu after a town in British Columbia. Shamu means "mate of Namu" in the language of British Columbia's native people. Of course, different whales appear in different shows, so the mammoth performers in this show are, in a sense, playing the role of Shamu.

The "stage" is a huge seven million-gallon pool filled with man-made salt water kept at a chilly 55 degrees (although the whales are used to much chillier water in their natural habitats) and completely filtered every 30 minutes. At the back is a small island platform for the trainers, above which looms "Jumbotron ShamuVision," a large screen on which a film and live video of the show in progress are displayed. The front of the stage is formed by a six-foot high Lucite wall, which gives those in the first several rows an underwater view. Downstage center is a shallow lip which allows Shamu to "beach" herself for our enjoyment.

On film, TV's "animal expert" Jack Hanna introduces us to killer whales in their natural habitats around the world, but the real focus of the show is the awe-inspiring and absolutely delightful interaction of the whales and their trainers. The whales leap, glide, dive, and roll with a grace that belies their huge size. The trainers ride on their charges' bellies, surf the pool on their backs and, in the most breathtaking moments, soar high aloft, propelled off a whale's snout.

One of the show's more amusing moments comes when the trainers attempt to answer the burning question, "Who make better trainers, men or women?" A male and female volunteer are selected from the audience and, as so often happens in battles of the sexes, the man completely loses his dignity and gets wet.

And speaking of getting wet, the warnings that precede the show's grand finale are in deadly earnest. If you're sitting in the first 14 rows, you'll likely get very, very, very wet. Actually, it's possible to sit in this section and escape a drenching — I've done it. But if you happen to be in the direct line of one of the salvos of chilly salt water hurled into the audience by the cupped rear fluke of a five-ton whale, you will be soaked to the skin. It's pretty much a matter of luck. Some of the biggest laughs come when people who have fled the "splash zone" for the higher ground of the first promenade get nailed anyway by a particularly forceful fluke-full of water.

The best seats in the house. Many kids (especially 9- to 13-year-old boys) will insist on sitting in the splash zone and will feel cheated if they don't get soaked. But adults should consider sitting here as well. If you wear a rain poncho (which you may already have from a visit to another park) you can protect yourself relatively well, and these seats do offer an excellent view, especially underwater. But the seats higher up, where you are assured of staying dry, offer excellent sightlines and the video coverage of the show assures that you won't miss anything.

Shamu Rocks America

Rating: ★ ★ ★ ★ ★
Type: Live stadium show
Time: 20 minutes
Kelly says: Shamu and trainers at play

This is the last show of every day in Shamu Stadium. It is somewhat shorter and different in tone but no less exciting and enjoyable. In fact, they seem to save the best for last.

This time around, there's little or no attempt to "educate" you. Instead, the focus is on fun and the amazing feats of which these sea-going behemoths are capable. For fun, there's a showing of *SeaWorld's Funniest Home Videos* featuring stunts that didn't quite go off as planned. For amazement, there's the wonderful spectacle of watching the trainers romp and play with their multi-ton partners. Also, whereas the daytime shows tend to showcase the female trainers, the men tend to take over at night. Maybe they're just trying to make up for the male-bashing of the earlier shows, but whichever gender takes the stage at night expect the highest leaps and the biggest splashes in this version of the Shamu show.

Some things don't change, however. The show still ends with a barrage of water to the lower seating area. Why tamper with success?

Tip: During the busy seasons when the park is open well after dark, the *Red, Bright and Blue Spectacular* show is usually scheduled to begin about 20 minutes after *Shamu Rocks America* ends. If you sit to the left-hand side of the stadium, near an exit, you'll be well positioned for the dash over to the Bayside Water Ski Stadium that inevitably follows.

Shamu: Close Up!

Rating: ★ ★ ★ ★
Type: Aquatic habitat
Time: As long as you wish
Kelly says: For everyone in the family

Before or after the stadium show, why not pop backstage and visit with the stars in their dressing room? That's essentially the opportunity afforded by *Shamu: Close-Up*. While it's not as elaborately decorated as some of SeaWorld's other "aquatic habitats," this large pool with its underwater viewing area gives you a chance to observe these graceful beasts as they relax and unwind between shows.

There's usually not a great deal to see on the surface, unless it's feeding time or the trainers are performing some "husbandry" procedures. At these times, the trainers will appear on the other side of the pool from the public viewing area and, using microphones, explain the procedures they are carrying out, such as washing the whales' teeth, drawing blood, or collecting a urine sample (now there's an attraction for you!). During these presentations, they will also have the whales do a few "tricks" for your amusement, like swimming around the pool waving at you. A member of the education staff will usually be prowling the area to answer any questions. If nothing's happening when you come by, ask this person when the staff is likely to be doing something next. Schedules are erratic, but the education staffer may be able to suggest a good time to return.

During sea gull season (roughly November through February) you may get to see the whales hunting for these pesky birds. They bait the surface of the water with chewed up bits of fish and when an unwary gull swoops down for a free morsel, the whale strikes from below. They seldom actually eat the birds but tend to "play" with their injured prey much as a cat will with a mouse. The battered gulls are fished out of the water by the training staff and are, we are assured, carefully nursed back to health by the aviculture staff. Sometimes, the staff will place a whale sized version of a "tubby toy" in the water for the whales to play with, which also tends to make surface viewing more interesting.

If nothing is happening up top, you can still get a great look at the whales through the three large underwater viewing windows. Just follow the edge of the pool in a clockwise direction to locate the ramp to the Underwater Viewing Area. This is a not-to-be-missed perspective on these magnificent creatures. Especially enchanting is the opportunity to watch Shamu and her much smaller calf, Baby Shamu, swimming gracefully in tandem. The whales are rotated through this viewing pool, so there's no guarantee that a specific whale will be there when you drop by. There are benches in front of the acrylic picture windows and if the crowds are thin enough you can watch while you rest. During presentations upstairs, the trainers will sometimes give a whale the "go see the people at the viewing window" signal. It consists of forming a large rectangle in the air.

Photo Op: Plastic replicas of killer whale snouts and dorsal fins poke out of the asphalt near the pool as if it were the Pacific Ocean. They make good props for photos of your little ones.

Shamu's Happy Harbor

Rating:	★ ★ ★ ★ +
Type:	Play area
Time:	30 minutes to an hour

Kelly says: Great for young kids, toddlers, and their long-suffering parents

If *Wild Arctic* (below) represents an attempt to reach out to the thrill-seeking segment of the tourist population, *Shamu's Happy Harbor* seeks to appeal to the youngster too antsy or uninterested to sit still for a fish — no matter how big it is. Here is a way for even very young children to be entertained in that most effective of ways — by doing things for themselves.

Shamu's Happy Harbor is dominated by a four-story, L-shaped, steel framework painted in bilious shades of sea green and pink. At first glance it looks like a construction site gone very wrong. Closer inspection reveals it to be an intricate maze of cargo netting, plastic tubes, and slides that kids can climb up and through to their heart's content. Some chambers in this maze contain tire swings, just like the ones in backyards across America, except that these are two stories above ground level. The cargo netting is completely enclosed in smaller-mesh black netting. While there's no danger of falling, the upper reaches of the structure are quite high and some smaller children may become frightened.

It's not just for kids, either. Adults can join in, too, although some of the parents I watched obviously wished they weren't allowed. While the corridors of netting are big enough to accommodate anyone, the tubes are designed with smaller people in mind. Thus, the average sedentary grown-up will get quite a workout going through them. You're allowed to climb up but stairs are provided for the trip down. Too many middle-aged sprained ankles is my guess.

The larger structure of *Shamu's Happy Harbor* is complemented by any number of lesser activities, called "elements," all of them action-oriented. These will keep kids busy for hours unless you can drag them away to the next show at the Sea Lion and Otter Stadium. There are four-sided, canvas "mountains" that kids can climb with the help of knotted ropes and then slide down, "ball crawls" that are rooms filled with small plastic balls to a depth of a few feet in which children can jump and "swim," and large inflated rooms in which kids 54 inches and shorter can bounce and tumble. There is also an area featuring remote-controlled cars and tugboats. Nearby vending machines dispense tokens (one token for $1, six for $5) that yield two minutes of play.

Standing in front of it all is a kid-sized schooner, the **Wahoo Two**, just waiting to be explored. Nearby, **Pete's Water Maze** offers a jumble of tubes and netting which is constantly splashed with jets of water. On the far side of the Harbor from the entrance is **Boogie Bump Bay**, a play area within a play area which has been very specifically designed for kids shorter than 42 inches. Here the little ones can do most of the activities available in the larger area but on a scale of their own and without having bigger kids to intimidate them and hog all the fun. One unique feature here is a "fence maze," tall enough to keep little ones perplexed but short enough to allow parents to track their progress. Also in Boogie Bump Bay is a fabulous sandbox area, the kind you wish you had at home. At the other end of the Harbor, you'll find **Shamu's Splash Attack**, where you can pay to sling water bombs at a friend. Buckets of five water-filled balloons are two for $5, and **Op's Beat**, where kids can bang on hanging steel drums to their heart's content.

Shamu's Happy Harbor is an ideal place for parents to take the squirmy baby of the family when he or she gets restless with the more grown-up attractions at SeaWorld.

Photo Op: Just opposite *Shamu's Happy Harbor* is a made-to-order photo backdrop. It's a life-sized model of Shamu and Baby Shamu perfectly posed under a sun awning (to protect your shot from that annoying glare). Place your kid on Shamu's back and click away.

Wild Arctic

Rating:	★ ★ ★ ★ ★
Type:	Simulator ride plus a spectacular habitat
Time:	5 minutes for the ride; as long as you want for the habitat
Kelly says:	A SeaWorld must-see

That large, techno-modern, warehouse-like building near Shamu Stadium houses one of SeaWorld's most popular attractions — a devilishly clever combination of thrill ride with serene aquatic habitat. All in all, this is one of the most imaginative attractions in Orlando. Mercifully, the waiting line snakes through an area that is shielded from the blazing sun, because the lines can get long.

Tip: To avoid long waits, you will be well advised to see *Wild Arctic* early in the morning. Another option is to visit during performances at nearby Shamu Stadium. But time your visit carefully; the waiting line fills up very quickly when the Shamu show empties out.

During our wait, we are entertained by a fascinating video presentation on the lifestyle of the Inuit peoples who inhabit the frozen realm of the Arctic. And during our slow journey through the line, we are asked to make an important decision: Do we want to take the helicopter ride to the base station or do we want to go by land? It's a choice between "motion" and "non-motion" and it can be important.

The Wild Arctic Ride

If you choose to take the helicopter, be prepared for a whale of a simulator ride (you should pardon the expression). We begin our journey by crossing a metal bridge into the vehicle itself. Once all 59 voyagers are strapped in, the staff exits, the doors close, and the "helicopter" takes off.

The ride, which lasts all of about five minutes, simulates a flight aboard an amphibious (not to mention submersible) helicopter to a research station deep within the Arctic Circle. Despite the gale warnings crackling over the radio, our friendly pilot can't help doing a little sightseeing, including putting the rotors into "whisper mode" so we can drop in on a polar bear family, and dipping below the waves for a glimpse of a narwhal. But his unscheduled detours exact their price and soon we are caught in that gale. At first the pilot prudently puts down on a glacier to await a better reading on the weather but the glacier gives way and we plummet headlong towards the icy waters below.

At the last second, the pilot gets the rotors whirling and we zoom away from certain death. Next, he decides we'll be safer flying through a crevasse, away from the howling winds, but we fly straight into and through an avalanche. Finally, we break through into the clear and the Arctic base station lies dead ahead.

It's a real stomach-churner and remarkably realistic. As I write these words I realize that I'm becoming a little queasy just remembering it all. The action is fast, abrupt, and violent. You'll find yourself being tossed from side to side as you grip the armrests and scream — in excitement or terror, depending on your mood.

Those who choose the "non-motion" alternative for their voyage to the *Wild Arctic*, are escorted past the three simulators to a stationary room where they watch the same video, before entering the Arctic base station.

Tip: The non-motion line moves much, much faster than the line for the simulator ride. If you are pressed for time, you might want to consider making the ultimate sacrifice (or use this as an excuse for missing what can be a very scary ride).

Note: You may want to take an over the counter medication before you head for the park if you are prone to motion sickness but would like to experience the ride.

The Wild Arctic Aquatic Habitat

Once you wobble off the simulator ride, you enter SeaWorld's most elaborately conceived aquatic habitat, one that would have been a five-star attraction even without the exhilarating thrill ride that proceeds it.

The conceit here is that scientists have discovered the wrecked ships from the expedition of John Franklin, a real-life British explorer who disappeared in 1845 while searching for the nonexistent Northwest Passage. The wreck, it seems, has drawn a wide variety of wildlife seeking shelter and prey, so the scientists "stabilized" the wreck and constructed their observation station around it.

The first "room" of the habitat simulates an open-air space, with the domed ceiling standing in for the Arctic sky. A sign informs us that we are 2,967 miles from SeaWorld in Florida. Gray beluga whales (the name is derived from the Russian word for "white") are being fed in a pool directly in front of us. Thankfully, SeaWorld has not attempted to mimic Arctic temperatures.

Next, we enter the winding tunnels of the research station proper. The walls alternate between the ancient wood of the wrecked vessels and the corrugated steel of the modern structure. We view the animals through thick glass walls; on the other side, temperatures are maintained at comfortably frigid levels for their Arctic inhabitants.

Art imitates reality here in the form of the SeaWorld research assistants, clad in their distinctive red parkas. They are here to answer guests' questions but they are also carrying out valuable scientific research by painstakingly recording the behavior patterns of the polar bears and other animals in the exhibits in an attempt to find ways to short-circuit the repetitive motion patterns that befall many animals in captivity. One strategy has been to hide food in nooks and crannies of the habitat, encouraging the animals to use true-to-nature hunting behaviors to find their food. By the way, the fish swimming with the polar bears usually avoid winding up on the dinner table, although the younger bears sometimes just can't resist taking a swipe at them.

For most people, the highlight of this habitat will be the polar bears, including the famous twins Klondike and Snow, born in the Denver Zoo, abandoned by their mother, nursed through infancy by their zookeepers, and then placed with SeaWorld as the facility best equipped to nurture them to adulthood. Klondike and Snow alternate in the main viewing area with two adult bears. Polar bears are solitary animals so the two pairs are kept separate to avoid any unpleasant scenes. As brother and sister, Klondike and Snow enjoy playing together and, thanks to being raised in captivity, they may never have to be separated.

There are also enormous walruses swimming lazily in a separate pool. Harbor seals are represented only via a video presentation showing the animals in their natural habitat. The narration is cleverly disguised as the radio transmissions of the scientists gathering the footage for research purposes.

After viewing the animals on the surface, we walk down a series of ramps to an underwater viewing area for a completely different and utterly fascinating perspective. Video monitors show what's happening on the surface and simple controls allow visitors to move the cameras remotely to follow the animals when they climb out of the pool. The set decoration below the surface is every bit as imaginative as it is above, simulating the Arctic Sea beneath the ice shelf.

There's much to explore here, including displays that let kids crawl through a simulated polar bear den or poke their heads through the ice, just like a seal. Dotted throughout the exhibit are touch-sensitive video monitors that let us learn more about the animals we are viewing and the environment in which they live. Just before the exit ramp, a small room offers a variety of interactive entertainments.

One lets you plan a six-week expedition to the North Pole, selecting the mode of transportation, date of departure, food supply, and wardrobe. Then you get to find out how wisely you planned. Another computer offers up a printout that tells, among other interesting facts, how many people have been born since the date of your birth.

Tip: The exit is through the Arctic Shop and a prominent sign says "No Re-Entry." However, late in the day, it appears to be easy to sneak back in through the back door if you'd like another peek at this fabulous habitat.

The Intensity Water Ski Show

Rating: ★ ★ ★ +
Type: Outdoor water ski show
Time: 25 minutes
Kelly says: Super stunts

Twenty of the best water skiers the country has to offer go mano a mano in a hypercharged competition played out to the accompaniment of the kind of pulse-pounding rock anthems that are a staple of the modern sports arena. (Bring earplugs if you are sensitive to loud noise.)

Sea-Doo racers speed through a slalom course of buoys, and barefoot skiers scorch their soles at 40 mph. The long-distance jumpers hit the ramps at twice the speed of the boats pulling them and leap more than 120 feet before splashing down. Best of all are the wakeboarders, who zip across the wake of the boats pulling them to perform dizzying aerobatic feats of skill and daring. If this is the only water ski show you get to see on your Florida trip, you will be more than satisfied.

Note: I am told that this show is the result of the water skiers' complaints that they didn't have enough to do in earlier versions of the water ski spectaculars staged here. We owe them a vote of thanks.

The best seats in the house. This show benefits from some height. The best seats are on the upper level, dead center, in the small section just below the show's control room.

Red, Bright and Blue Spectacular
Rating: ★ ★ ★

Type: Nighttime multimedia show

Time: 15 minutes

Kelly says: A rousing finale

If you are visiting during the high season, *Red, Bright and Blue* is the grand finale to your day at SeaWorld. It is shown just once a day and takes place at the Atlantis Bayside Stadium about 45 minutes before the park's scheduled closing time. Since it's scheduled immediately after *Shamu Rocks America* and is on the way to the park exit, most people check it out and I would recommend that you join them.

The show is an odd multimedia mixture of elements with no spoken narration, making it ideal for non-English speakers. One of the neatest elements of the show is a curtain of water spray that rises from the Lagoon to serve as a screen on which film is projected. Most of the show, however, consists of bursts of laser light from behind the audience and from across the lake, cute cartoons projected in the same laser light against the ski show backdrop, and (best of all) copious fireworks.

All of this is accompanied by a loud up-tempo medley of all-American music celebrating all-American themes and motifs — from Broadway musicals like *West Side Story* and *On The Town* to "Orange Blossom Special" and "Pop Goes the Weasel." The show ends with a rousing gospel rendition of "God Bless America." Hear, hear!

Paddle Boats
Rating: ★ ★ +

Type: Just what it says

Time: As long as you want, one half hour at a time

Kelly says: Can be skipped

In Bayside Lagoon, off the wooden walkway, you can rent large, pink, flamingo-shaped paddle boats for a leisurely outing on the lagoon. The boats seat two adults comfortably and rent for $6 a half hour. If you have the time and enjoy this sort of activity, you may want to give them a go.

Life jackets come with your rental and are required wearing. You must be at least 56 inches tall to ride and you must be 16 or older to take a boat out alone. Check the park's daily calendar for opening hours, which vary.

Eating in the South
Only three of SeaWorld's eateries are located in the South End of the park. I will describe them in geographical order, starting with The Deli and continuing clockwise around the Bayside Lagoon.

The Deli

What:	Cafeteria-style sandwiches
Where:	In the *Anheuser-Busch Hospitality Center*
Price Range:	$$

Tucked into a corner of the *Anheuser-Busch Hospitality Center,* The Deli serves up thick sandwiches in the $5 to $7 range. Among them are roast turkey, top round of beef, German sausage, and the Hospitality Club sandwich. All are served with potato salad.

Interestingly enough, no beer is served here, but you can take your tray to the lovely outdoor patio and walk back in to the free sample line to pick up a small plastic cup of frosty brew.

Coconut Cove Snack Company

What:	Quick snacks with kids in mind
Where:	At *Shamu's Happy Harbor*
Price Range:	$

This walk-up stand is dedicated to the proposition that what a kid playing at *Shamu's Happy Harbor* needs is a sugar rush, not healthy food. Churros, the sugared fried dough from Mexico, are about $2. Apple juice for little ones is a little less. There is also a variety of sugary snacks, drinks, and ice cream bars, all in the $2 to $3 range.

Mango Joe's Cafe

What:	Cafeteria-style fajitas and sandwiches
Where:	Near *Wild Arctic*
Price Range:	$ - $$

Chicken and beef fajitas or fajita sandwiches are featured here for about $7.50 and very tasty they are indeed. There are also sandwich platters (among them a fish sandwich and a veggie wrap) for about $6 to $6.50. Mango Joe's serves some specialty salads, too, including one of crab meat and tiny bay shrimp and a fajita salad served in a tortilla "bowl" (both about $7). In addition to the usual soft drinks and iced tea (about $2), Bud is served here in $3 and $4 sizes.

Shopping in the South

There are a limited number of shopping opportunities in the South End of the park, but if you're a Bud fan or a polar bear fancier, you are sure to find a lot of nice merchandise that suits your fancy. What follows are brief descriptions of the South's shops, starting with Label Stable in the *Anheuser-Busch Hospitality Center* and continuing in a clockwise direction around Bayside Lagoon.

Label Stable

This vest-pocket souvenir shop is in the *Anheuser-Busch Hospitality Center* and, naturally, is aimed at those who want to wear their beer on their sleeve. T-shirts run from about $11 to about $28, with caps in the $10 to $20 range. Beyond that there is the usual assortment of logoed key rings, mugs, refrigerator magnets, and such, along with figurines ranging from $60 to $19,000.

Shamu Stadium Gift Shop

This shop is literally a hole in the wall of the massive Shamu Stadium. The wares here are mostly Shamu oriented and mostly for kids. They include a line of Shamu clothing for infants and toddlers (about $6 to $20), Shamu inflatable pool and plush toys, plus postcards, film, and key chains.

Wild Arctic Gift Shop

The *Wild Arctic* attraction is sure to put you in an upbeat mood, so hang on to your wallets as you pass through the gift shop on your way out. This shop has some of the most attractive (and most expensive) stuff you'll see at SeaWorld. The clothing is especially good looking, with shirt prices approaching $60 and windbreakers for about $77. Even t-shirts can be on the pricey side here, coming in at around $18 to $31. Collectibles such as pewter thimbles and spoons ($4 to $7) are on offer, as are books and videos about the animals of the frozen north. Kids and parents may be equally drawn to the book-plus-plush-toy packages devoted to the Arctic's inhabitants ($10 to $17). Put out by the Smithsonian Institute, each focuses on a single creature — puffin, polar bear, seal, and so on. Art lovers may want to check out the polar bear sculptures by John Perry ($50 to $80).

OTHER ADVENTURES

SeaWorld offers a number of "Behind the Scenes" guided tours, as well as animal interactions, and educational activities. The guided tours carry a nominal additional charge, over and above your admission price. The other activities range from moderately pricey to downright expensive but offer some opportunities to interact with or learn about the animals here that you'd be hard-pressed to find elsewhere.

Guided Tours

If you have the time and interest, these can be fascinating. The guides are members of the education staff and are all extremely knowledgeable, personable hosts. At this writing three guided tours are offered on a regular basis.

Each lasts approximately one hour and costs $7.95 ($6.95 for children 3 to 9), including tax. Annual passholders get a 50% discount. The schedules are somewhat erratic depending on the number of people expected to visit the park that day and other factors.

Since all tours limit the number of participants, signing up early is advisable. To enquire about schedules and availability, head for the tour desk when you arrive. You'll find it almost directly ahead as you pass through the entrance turnstiles. When you purchase your tours, you will be given a yellow card with the name and time of your tour. This serves as your "ticket" and lets the guide know who belongs to the tour and who doesn't. Tours begin at different points in the park. The meeting points are marked with signs. You will be given directions to them when you sign up.

Polar Expedition

This tour has three stops. The first two take you "backstage" at *Wild Arctic*. The first stop is the beluga whale holding pool, where you may be lucky enough to see "off- duty" whales relaxing. Also in this area are some of the seals that keep the belugas company in the exhibit. Then it's off past the huge filtration tanks that keep the artificial salt water in the attraction sparkling clean, to the hidden "den" of the polar bears.

Whether you will actually see any bears depends on your luck with timing. Nothing happens on a rigid or even regular schedule with these animals. Their keepers don't want them to become habituated to a set routine and, so, try to keep the daily sequence of events as it is in the wild — fairly random.

Even if you don't get to see bears through the glass in their den, you can see them on the remote video camera that is focused on their public habitat. You will also get a wealth of fascinating information about polar bears in the wild and the behind-the-scenes world of *Wild Arctic*. You might be told, for example, that the water in the exhibit is kept at 45 to 55 degrees Fahrenheit, just warm enough to prevent ice from forming on the bears' fur. When keepers must enter the water, they wear three wet suits and then can only stay in the water ten minutes before hypothermia starts to set in. You'll even get to pet polar bear fur (courtesy of a deceased bear whose pelt remains behind for its educational value).

The next stop, after a short bus ride, is the chilly confines of the Avian Research lab, where you will have a chance to pet a Magellanic penguin (two fingers only, please!). Penguin mothers have a spotty record when it comes to parenting skills. Abandoned or abused chicks are brought here to be reared in a more caring environment. The center even hatches orphaned eggs. Depending on when you visit, you may see young chicks covered in their downy gray baby coats or molting into the more recognizable sleek black and white of their mature feathers. Penguins are gregarious and curious birds and they will take great interest in your visit, waddling over for a closer look and eyeing you with apparent curiosity. Careful of your fingers!

Predators!

Here's a great chance to pet a shark and find out more about these cartilaginous carnivores we all love to hate. For those who don't like to read, taking this tour can serve as an alternative to reading all that informational signage in the *Terrors of the Deep* exhibit.

You also get to visit the inner workings of the shark tank, where you can gain some appreciation of the water filtration system. Then comes a chance to examine shark jaws, shark skins, and sawfish bones up close. The piece de resistance is a close encounter with a shark — a small, docile critter, but a shark nonetheless. Reach out your hand and enjoy bragging rights back home.

To The Rescue!

SeaWorld is far more than "just" a theme park. This engrossing and entertaining tour highlights SeaWorld's role as a major rescuer and rehabilitator of aquatic — and other — animals. What you see on this tour will depend on which animals are currently in the park's care. You will likely get to see manatees and sea turtles that have been injured, typically by the carelessness of Man. You may see some dolphins, but they are usually here for reasons other than injury. Thanks to its reputation, SeaWorld is sometimes given injured animals that are not part of its usual stock in trade — like snakes, rabbits, and exotic birds. These, too, are on display.

The areas you visit also include SeaWorld's "hospital," where surgery can be performed on walruses and dolphins, as well as tanks used to quarantine sea animals that are new to SeaWorld before they are introduced to the exhibits. If you've ever wondered how to rid sea animals of parasites, this is the place to find out. (Answer: Dip them in fresh water for a few seconds.)

Animal Interaction Programs

Yes, you can interact with the animals at SeaWorld — if you have the money and are at least 13 years old, 52 inches tall, and can climb a flight of stairs and lift 15 pounds. SeaWorld offers three interaction programs, ranging in price from $200 to $349 including tax. One lets you swim with Shamu's cousin, the pseudorca dolphin, and learn some training commands. The others give you a taste of the caregivers' and trainers' regimens, along with a share of their work.

Despite the high prices, the programs are very much in demand and arrangements have to be made well in advance of your visit. Registration is by mail or fax only; you cannot register by phone. You can, however, make a reservation and request a registration form and brochure in person at the tour desk in the park or by calling (800) 432-1178 or (407) 370-1382 and leaving your name and address on the answering machine. Alternatively, write SeaWorld Adventure Park, ATTN: Interactive Programs, 7007 Sea-World Drive, Orlando, FL 32821. The program fee is non-refundable and must accompany your registration.

False Killer Whale Interaction Program

This is your chance to get up close and personal with the half-ton black dolphin known as the false killer whale (Pseudorca Crassidens), whom you may already have seen diving and leaping in SeaWorld's *Key West Dolphin Fest* (see above). For $200 per person including tax, four guests a day get to don wetsuits and interact with these creatures after learning a bit about their physiology and training. The program lasts from 10 a.m. to noon and includes a post-interaction lunch at Mango Joe's Restaurant, a t-shirt and souvenir photo, and a seven-day pass to SeaWorld.

Animal Care Experience

Think you'd like to rescue injured manatees or care for beluga whales, seals, and other marine mammals? If you've got $389 ($350 for annual pass-holders) and can get yourself to the park by 6:30 a.m., here's your chance to find out. Up to four guests per day get to work with SeaWorld's caregivers, helping to prepare the mammals' food (each species has a special diet) and feed and care for them. The experience lasts eight hours (6:30 a.m. to 2:30 p.m.) and includes lunch, a t-shirt and souvenir photo, a career book, and a seven-day pass to SeaWorld.

Trainer for a Day

Every day starting at 9 a.m., six lucky (and well-heeled) people have the opportunity to spend seven hours following around and helping a real, live SeaWorld trainer. You'll have to do some of the grunt work of food preparation and cleaning up after the animals, but you'll be rewarded with the opportunity to learn some training techniques and, best of all, interact with dolphins, sea lions, and whales. Unfortunately, you don't get to be shot into the air off Shamu's snout, but then for $389 you can't have everything. The program includes lunch with the trainers, a waterproof disposable camera, and a t-shirt.

Family Adventures

SeaWorld offers a smorgasbord of special activities, day camps, and sleepover programs for kids from kindergarten through the eighth grade (roughly ages 5 through 13). Birthday parties with a variety of themes range from $318 to $675 (including tax) for groups of up to 20 people and typically include invitations, food, favors, a visit by a character, and the same backstage access offered by the guided tours.

Camp SeaWorld is the umbrella name for a series of single-day and week-long programs for kids of various ages. A variety of age-appropriate programs are offered during the year. They typically run from 9:00 a.m. to 5:00 p.m. (programs for younger kids end earlier). Prices, including tax, range from $50 for single-day programs to $265 for the week-long sessions. After-camp care, until 6:00 p.m., can be arranged for an additional fee. Annual passholders receive a 10% discount on these programs.

Year round sleepover programs offer bonding experiences for kids and their parents, including such treats as a Father's Day fishing trip and Halloween outings to *Terrors of the Deep.* These overnight events cost about $65 per person (including tax).

For more information on these programs call (800) 406-2244 and request a brochure, or visit www.seaworld.org. Overseas callers can dial (407) 363-2380. The email address is educationres@seaworld.org. The brochure spells out the registration process in some detail. A complete health history and medical release form must accompany all registrations.

CHAPTER THREE:

Discovery Cove

As I write these words, the newspaper carries a short piece about a 14-year-old Italian boy saved from drowning in the Gulf of Manfredonia by a dolphin. The lad, a non-swimmer, fell off a sailboat and was sinking under the waves when he felt something pushing him upward. "When I realized it was Filippo, I hung on to him," the boy was quoted as saying. One can only assume that Filippo is Italian for Flipper!

This is only the latest example of a tale that has been told since antiquity. The frescoes of the ancient Minoan civilization of Crete are alive with playful dolphins, and Greek literature is peppered with accounts of dolphins saving wrecked sailors. So humankind's fascination with this playful and occasionally lifesaving creature has a long and honorable pedigree. And as the story about the boy from Manfredonia illustrates, *Flipper*, the hit TV show about a preternaturally precocious dolphin and his towheaded sidekick, clearly has a hold on the world's imagination long after its original prime-time run.

The marketing geniuses at SeaWorld were not blind to this intense fascination with the stars of their animal shows and some years ago instituted the Dolphin Interaction Program (now discontinued) that allowed a small number of guests to duck backstage at SeaWorld and actually meet and swim with the stars of the show. Out of this somewhat makeshift idea, SeaWorld has created Discovery Cove, a whole new class of theme park, the first one to be designed specifically for one-to-one human-animal interactions. At Discovery Cove you can not only swim with dolphins but cruise with stingrays, have tropical fish nibble at your fingers, and let exotic birds perch on your head and shoulders while you feed them by hand.

Because of its unique mission, Discovery Cove has been carefully de-signed to accommodate a limited number of visitors. Only 1,000 people can come to Discovery Cove each day and only 750 of them will be able to swim with the dolphins. Consequently, reservations are mandatory, whether you will be swimming with the dolphins or not. Discovery Cove will admit walk-ups for its "non-swim" program (i.e. you don't get to interact with the dolphins) *if* there is room. That is a very iffy proposition during the warmer months, but your odds of getting in on short notice improve dramatically in the winter.

This limited-capacity policy is, first and foremost, for the protection of the animals, but it has undeniable benefits for the human visitor. The park clearly has room for more than a thousand, so there is plenty of space to spread out on the expansive beaches. No scrambling for lounge chairs, no shoulder-to-shoulder sunbathing and only the very occasional traffic jam at prime snorkeling spots.

Before You Come

Because of its limited capacity and obvious popularity, a visit to Discov-ery Cove demands advance planning. Reservations are mandatory and mak-ing reservations six months or more in advance is not such a silly idea. Some-what to the surprise of Discovery Cove's marketing people, more visitors (over 50%) want to swim with the dolphins than had been anticipated. So if a dolphin interaction is your goal, the sooner you book, the better your chances.

While it is extremely unlikely that you will be able to book a dolphin swim on short notice, it can happen, especially if you can be flexible on dates. Cancellations do occur. If you want to visit Discovery Cove and not swim with the dolphins, your chances of getting in at the last minute are only slightly better.

The best plan is to phone regularly before your visit and drop by in per-son once you have reached Orlando. Obviously, the more people in your party who want to swim with the dolphins, the less likely it is you will be successful. It is also possible that there will be openings for just two people when you have a party of four.

There are two ways to make reservations, by phone or on the Internet. The toll-free reservation line is (877) 434-7268. The Internet address is www.discoverycove.com. You can make a reservation for the day you visit but you cannot reserve a specific time to swim with the dolphins until you arrive at the park, which is a good incentive to arrive early on the day of your visit. More on this later.

When's the Best Time To Come?

Although I don't generally recommend coming to Orlando at the height of the summer if you can possibly avoid it, the tropical island beach resort ambiance of Discovery Cove makes it a delightful place to spend a blistering hot summer's day. The salt water pools are kept nice and cool for the animals and make for a bracing dip. Of course, summer brings with it the increased likelihood of stormy weather. Dolphin interactions will be held in the rain, but will be cancelled if there is lightning in the area.

In late spring and early fall, the weather should be closer to ideal. Winter in Orlando can range from the pleasant to the chilly. At this time of the year, the weather may not be ideal for lounging on the beach but the water temperature may be warmer than the air temperature. On the other hand, crowds are generally smaller during the cooler months and the non-swim package is discounted in January and February (see below). Wet suits are available to ease any discomfort of in-the-water activities.

Getting There

Discovery Cove is located just off I-4, near SeaWorld, on Central Florida Parkway so the driving directions are similar. From the south (i.e. traveling east on I-4) use Exit 27A and you will find yourself pointed directly toward Discovery Cove; it's a little more than half a mile along on your right, a short distance past the SeaWorld entrance on the left.

From the north (i.e. traveling west on I-4), get off at Exit 28, onto the Bee Line Expressway (Route 528). Take the first exit and loop around to International Drive. Turn left and proceed to Central Florida Parkway and turn right. The Discovery Cove entrance will be on your left, almost immediately after turning.

Arriving at Discovery Cove

Self-parking is free and just a short walk from the entrance, or you can drive right up to the front door and opt for valet parking for $10 (plus a tip, which will be expected). These options are clearly marked as you drive in.

Opening and Closing Times

The official opening hours are 9:00 a.m. to 5:30 p.m. but since the first dolphin swim begins at 8:50, the doors are open earlier. It is also possible to linger until 6:00 before you are politely pointed to the exit. My personal recommendation is to arrive early, about 8:00 or 8:15, if you are participating in the dolphin swim. I provide some more advice on timing your dolphin swim later. On the other hand, if you are coming in winter, when the first dolphin swim isn't until 10:00 a.m., you can afford to sleep in a bit.

The Price of Admission
Prepare yourself for a shock. Discovery Cove is probably the most expensive theme park you will ever visit. But before you flip immediately to the next chapter, read on. On closer examination, Discovery Cove offers extremely good value for your investment. At press time, prices (including tax) were as follows:

All-Inclusive Package (includes the dolphin swim):
> Adults and children over 6: $210.94
>
> *Non-Swim Package:*
> Adults and children over 3: $126.14
> Children under 3 are **free**.

Discounts
Hah! Discovery Cove is booked solid months in advance, so there is no compelling need for Discovery Cove to discount admission. Even if you show up at two in the afternoon and they just happen to have an opening for the non-swim package, you still won't get a discount. They did run a "Grand Opening" special for the non-swim package, but I don't expect to see any further discounts in the foreseeable future.

Cancellation Policy
Because the number of daily visitors is carefully controlled, a visit to Discovery Cove is more like a tour package or a cruise than a visit to a "regular" theme park. The advance reservation and cancellation policies reflect this fact.

All reservations must be prepaid 45 days prior to your visit, or immediately if your planned visit is less than 45 days away. If you have to cancel your reservation you may incur a penalty. Cancellations made more than 45 days before the reserved date get a full refund; between 44 and 30 days, a 75% refund; between 29 and 7 days, 50%. If you cancel fewer than seven days out, you forfeit the entire amount.

Is It Worth It?
The simple answer is, "Absolutely!" The more considered answer is, "That will depend on your own very personal cost/value analysis."

For many people, just the dolphin interaction would be worth $210. I heard one woman say, after patting a dolphin's tail fluke, "If that's all I got to do, it would have been worth it." For quite a number of people I met at Discovery Cove, swimming with a dolphin is an almost spiritual experience and questions of cost are beside the point. Others will have a far more jaundiced approach to the subject and I suspect you know who you are.

For those who may be uncertain, let me attempt to persuade you of what a good value Discovery Cove really is. Just understand that I am a bit prejudiced because I love the place.

First, Discovery Cove is far more than swimming with the dolphins (which, I must point out, occupies less than 30 minutes of your stay there). A day at Discovery Cove is like a visit to a very posh resort on a faraway tropical island. The only reminder that you are still in Orlando is the top of the SeaWorld *Sky Tower* peeking over the top of the palm trees. You get to snorkel with stingrays and along a coral reef populated with more colorful fish than you're likely to see in the Caribbean itself; plus, you're virtually guaranteed a shark sighting. You will also have a chance to visit a jungle paradise where gaudily plumaged birds perch on your shoulder and eat from your hand. A day here can be a much-needed escape from the hustle and bustle of tourist Orlando and that, surely, is worth something.

And Discovery Cove's admission price is pretty much all-inclusive. Parking is free (other parks typically charge $6 or $7). A very good lunch is included (approximately a $20 value). The food you feed the dolphins, rays, and birds is also on the house (SeaWorld charges $4 for a small tray of fish). Lockers are free, too (other parks charge several bucks for the same in and out locker access). Towels, snorkels, masks, and wet suits are also included; most water parks charge a rental fee for 'extras' like these.

Remember, too, that not every member of your family has to swim with the dolphins; in fact, some may have no interest at all. Sometimes wives will swim while husbands look on or kids will frolic while grandparents videotape the action from the shore. And since the non-swim package is about $85 less than the all-inclusive option, the savings can be considerable.

Best of all, admission to Discovery Cove includes seven consecutive days admission to SeaWorld. If you are not swimming with the dolphins, the price of admission gives you eight days of theme park fun for less than $16 a day! Even with the dolphin swim you are looking at a per day cost of just over $26. Not too shabby.

Here is another comparative exercise: If you take a cruise to the Bahamas, you can purchase a shore excursion that lets you snorkel and swim with dolphins and stingrays. The total cost for this experience through one cruise line (minus the expertise of Discovery Cove's trainers, of course) was recently $173. The cost of the cruise, needless to say, is not included.

Of course, there's no way of escaping the fact that $210 is a lot of money. Otherwise, why would I have to go through this lengthy explanation to justify the cost? Unfortunately, the price will put Discovery Cove out of reach for many families. Still, the fact that Discovery Cove is booked solid many months in advance is proof that, so far at least, there are plenty of takers.

Staying Near the Park

The hotels listed in the SeaWorld chapter are also fairly close to Discovery Cove, although the only one that might reasonably be considered within walking distance is the Renaissance Orlando Resort, and it's a fairly long walk. From the other hotels and motels, the most direct route to Discovery Cove is down busy International Drive, which has no sidewalk along this stretch, making for a long, dangerous (and perhaps muddy) walk. Besides, walking to the park doesn't save you any money since parking at Discovery Cove is free.

Good Things to Know About ...

Access for the Disabled

Discovery Cove has provided ramps with handrails into many of the water areas. Those who can maneuver themselves into the shallows of the Dolphin Lagoon, will be able to experience the dolphin swim. Special wheelchairs that can negotiate Discovery Cove's sandy beaches are available and work is under way to provide a "platform" that will enable guests to get around in their own wheelchairs. Eventually, Discovery Cove plans to introduce special "flotation chairs." Phone ahead to see what will be available when you visit.

Dolphins

Dolphins have such a wonderful public image as cute and cuddly critters that it's easy to forget that they are, in fact, large, powerful, and unpredictable wild animals. The dolphin PR machine likes to play down the fact that, in their natural state, they vie for dominance by biting, scratching, and fighting. Those scrapes and scars and nicks you'll see on your dolphin friend bear mute testimony to this fact of life in the big bad ocean.

I mention this not to frighten or dissuade you — it's not like you'll be diving into a pool of man-eating sharks — but to encourage you to approach these magnificent creatures with the respect they deserve. Follow your trainer-host's directions and you'll do just fine. Do something stupid and you run the slight but very real risk of injury.

Emergencies

The park is dotted with fully certified lifeguards, but any nearby attendant should be your first stop in an emergency. A first-aid station is located near the Tropical Gifts shop not too far from the front entrance.

Getting Oriented

Discovery Cove does not hand you a paper map as other parks do. Since the park is quite compact, there's really no need. The main axis of the park is a paved walkway, with lockers, changing rooms and restaurant to your right (as you walk from the main entrance) and the beach, lagoons, and river to your left. It's hard to get lost but, just in case, mosaic tile maps called "Points of Discovery" are dotted about on low-slung rocks to help you get your bearings.

Leaving the Park

You may leave the park and return during the day. Just make sure to have your hand stamped as you leave.

Lockers & Changing Rooms

Lockers are free and plentiful. There are two locker locations. The one nearest the Dolphin Lagoon seems to be the one most people find first. The other is located between the dolphin and stingray pools. You will find it down a path that turns left off the park's main artery. Both locker areas are next to spacious and well-appointed changing rooms complete with showers, extra towels, hair blowers, and toiletries.

Money

The best way to handle money at Discovery Cove is not to. The laminated ID card you receive on arrival bears a bar code that can be linked to your credit card. If you prefer the old-fashioned way, all the shops and refreshment stands accept cash and credit cards.

Pets

Discovery Cove does not have its own kennel facilities. If you arrive with a pet, staffers will escort you to SeaWorld's kennels nearby, where the boarding fee is $6 per animal (bring your own food).

Sunscreen

Don't bother lathering yourself with sunscreen prior to your visit. You'll just be asked to shower it off. Discovery Cove provides its guests, free of charge, a special "dolphin-friendly" sunscreen. Take care when applying it, because a little goes a long way. It doesn't seem to disappear as readily as most commercial sunscreens, so if you use too much you'll look a bit like you've dipped your face in flour. If you like it, you can pick up more in the gift shops.

Dive Right In: Your Day at Discovery Cove

At first blush it may seem there are only a few things to "do" at Discovery Cove, but they somehow manage to add up to a very full, relaxing, and rewarding day. Think of your day at Discovery Cove not as a visit to a mere theme park but as a day spent at a very exclusive tropical resort with some highly unusual amenities and you will not only approach the experience with the right attitude but increase your odds of getting the most from your investment.

Even if you are not planning to swim with the dolphins, I recommend arriving early. And if you *are* swimming with the dolphins I strongly advise being among the first to arrive. That's because your appointment to meet and swim with a dolphin will not be finalized until you arrive (you can request a morning or an afternoon swim when you make your reservation). The earlier you arrive, the more choice you will have.

My personal feeling is that you are better off being in one of the first dolphin swims of the day. The theory is that in the morning the dolphins are more active and curious, because they've had a night to rest and haven't yet spent a day with overexcited tourists. I'm not actually sure how accurate this theory is. After all, the dolphins have been specifically trained for this duty and each dolphin is limited to just six sessions a day. What's more, if a dolphin shows signs of losing interest, the trainers will simply call for a replacement. Still, I find the theory has a certain appeal. Besides, by doing the dolphin swim first thing, you get your day off to a smashing start and you can relax for the rest of the day, without keeping one eye on your watch for fear of missing your appointment with dolphin destiny. And in the summer, a morning swim slot means you will avoid the afternoon thunderstorms that are an Orlando trademark.

So, assuming you are arriving early, here's how your day at Discovery Cove might play out.

My first bit of advice is to arrive dressed for the water. This is Orlando, remember, and no one at your hotel will think it odd that you are strolling through the lobby dressed in a swim suit, t-shirt, and sandals. If you like, you can bring along "regular" clothes to change into at the end of the day.

Arriving at the main entrance is a bit like arriving at a nice hotel, especially if you have opted for valet parking. The large airy lobby, with its exposed wooden beams and a peaked, thatched roof, is what you might expect at a Polynesian resort. Suspended above you, sculpted blue dolphins frolic amid schools of tiny fish. Around the rather spare lobby some ten check-in counters are arranged. Head for the one with the shortest line.

Your host will find your reservation and check you in. Your photo will be taken with a digital camera and put on a laminated plastic ID card that you can wear around your neck. The card has a bar code that can be linked to your credit card. That way, you can "pay" for anything in the park with your ID card and settle a single bill on leaving the park. It's a terrific convenience and highly recommended.

If you are booked for a dolphin swim, you will also pick a swim time and be assigned to one of three cabanas. The cabanas are not changing rooms, as the term might suggest, but staging areas where you will be briefed prior to your dolphin encounter. It is your responsibility to arrive at your assigned cabana at the appointed time.

Once checked in, you will join a group of eight or so other guests to be escorted into the park itself. Your guide will tell you a bit about what to expect during your stay and direct you to the lockers and cabanas. During this brief introduction, each family group will pose for a picture, which is included in the cost of admission; you can pick it up later in the day or as you leave the park.

The first stop in the park is the Swim Gear counter where you will be issued a mask and snorkel. The snorkel is yours to keep, the mask must be returned. You will also be issued a blue and neon-yellow neoprene vest that is a cross between a wet suit and a flotation device. The vest is required wearing in the water. It is actually a clever way to keep you buoyant and visible (and therefore safe) without making you feel dorky. And, like a wet suit, it provides some comfort in the chilly waters of the Dolphin Lagoon and Coral Reef.

Tip: If the Swim Gear counter near the front of the park is crowded, head for the other one which is located at the back of the park past the dolphin swim lagoons. There are also more lockers in this area.

If you'd like more wet suit warmth, you can request an actual wet suit, very much like those worn by the trainers. This one comes to mid-thigh and offers more coverage than the vest alone. For non-swimmers and little ones, stiff yellow life-vests are also available. Towels are issued at Swim Gear and if you mislay yours during the day, replacements are readily issued.

Your next stop will most likely be the lockers. They are simple wooden affairs located in shaded palapas. The doors of unclaimed lockers will be open and inside you will find the key, which is on a lanyard so you can wear it around your neck. (The ID card and key, by the way, tuck neatly inside your vest, so they don't get in your way during the day.) Near each locker area is a changing room, should you need it.

If you have followed my advice and arranged an early dolphin swim, it will now be time to head to your assigned cabana to begin your experience. If you have time before your appointment, you may want to use it to scope out the beach area and choose a lounge chair or two to accommodate your party. Take your time and pick a spot that offers the ideal combination of sun and shade to suit your tastes.

After your dolphin encounter, you might want to head straight for the stingray pool. This is because the rays will be hungriest in the morning. Trying to feed a full stingray in the afternoon can be a daunting challenge.

Otherwise, you can pretty much take things easy for the rest of the day, basking in the sun, swimming in the river or saltwater pools, visiting the Aviary, or eavesdropping on the later dolphin swims as the spirit moves you.

Attractions at Discovery Cove

Discovery Cove has a limited number of "attractions" but they are some of the best to be found in the Orlando area. They are enjoyable enough that you may be surprised to find a very full day seems all too short.

Swim with the Dolphins

Rating: ★ ★ ★ ★ ★
Type: Animal interaction
Time: About 30 minutes
Kelly says: An unforgettable experience

Your dolphin encounter begins when you arrive at your appointed cabana at the appointed hour for a briefing. This is primarily an exercise in heightening your anticipation with a brief video, but a trainer does put in an appearance to offer some pertinent safety tips, such as keeping your hands away from the dolphin's blow hole. ("It'd be sorta like me sticking my finger in your nose," she points out helpfully.)

Following the briefing you and your "pod" of anywhere from six to nine people will be led to the lagoon. I have heard conflicting reports on the maximum group size for the dolphin encounter. Nine people is said to be the maximum and seven or eight the preferred number. There were six in my group.

At water's edge you meet the two trainers who will guide your encounter. Your first challenge is getting used to the chilly water, which is kept between 72 and 76 degrees Fahrenheit for the comfort of the dolphins.

The dolphins make a splashy entrance, zipping from their holding pen and leaping into the air in greeting before splitting off to head to their respective human pods. Eagerly, you wade to the edge of a sharp drop-off to meet your new dolphin friend. The dolphin you meet may have been specially trained for duty at Discovery Cove or may be an old pro. I swam with Capricorn, an aging movie star of sorts who was 36 and had appeared in *Jaws III*.

Here at the edge of deep water you and the other members of the group will get to rub down your dolphin, a tactile interaction the dolphin obviously enjoys. Then you take the plunge into deep water for the main part of the experience. How many people go out at one time is a function of the size and makeup of your group. Our trainers said they usually take people out as couples, but since there were two singles in our group we went out in threes.

Exactly what you do with your dolphin will depend to some extent on what behaviors the dolphin has been trained to perform, but you will almost certainly be able to give some hand signals to which the dolphin will respond by chattering excitedly or spinning in a circle. The interaction is carefully planned so that every member of your group gets equal access to the dolphin and no one feels cheated of one-on-one time with their frisky friend. You will also have a chance to feed your new friend several times in the course of the interaction. This tends to keep the dolphin interested, but don't be surprised if your dolphin decides to take an unscheduled break to check out something of greater interest elsewhere in the pool. This is normal apparently and if your dolphin shows sufficient lack of interest in the proceedings the trainers will simply call in an understudy.

For most people, the highlight of the interaction comes at the end when they place one arm over the dolphin's back and cup their other hand over a flipper and get towed back to the shallows. There they pose in a sort of hug with their new-found friend for the photographer who has been carefully documenting the entire dolphin interaction for posterity and profit.

Tip: Bring a face mask, minus the snorkel, along for your encounter. The snorkel is not really necessary but the mask will give you an interesting perspective on the dolphin. When not in use, it can be pushed up to your forehead.

Back ashore, you are led to another palapa where a series of iMacs have been set up for you to view the photos of you and your family. The technology is impressive and so are the prices should you decide to purchase a print. It's $16 a pop for five-by-seven inch prints in an inexpensive cardboard frame. There's no discount for quantity purchases and, since you'll have from 10 to 12 photos to choose from, it's very easy to spend over $100, as at least one person in my group did. Most people contented themselves with a single souvenir shot, while I went only moderately crazy. Key chains and snow globes are also options, but the prints make the nicest and most practical souvenirs. Another option is a 60-minute video of your dolphin encounter. The first half hour is pretty much the same video you saw during your preswim briefing, but the second half stars you. The cost is $60. Of all the elements at Discovery Cove, the pricing of the photos and video was the only thing I heard the slightest complaint about.

Tip: You collect your photos later, at Adventure Photo, next to the main gift shop. Pick them up early and stash them in your locker. A line starts forming at around 3:00 p.m. and it gets longer as the day wears on.

Unfortunately, you are not allowed to take those nifty disposable underwater cameras along with you — the dolphins might pinch them and do themselves an injury, we were told. But if a non-swimming member of your party is an accomplished photographer with a telephoto lens, he or she may be able to get some great shots from the shore.

Tropical River

Rating:	★ ★ +
Type:	Circular river
Time:	Unlimited
Kelly says:	Best for the Aviary

If you've visited a water park, you've probably experienced a variation of this attraction. It's a circular fresh water "river," varying in depth from three to 12 feet, with an artificial current that will bear you lazily along. The river rings the ray pool and the *Coral Reef* and takes about 20 minutes to circumnavigate at an easy pace. This is strictly a one-way river; swimming against the current is discouraged by the lifeguards stationed along the route and it is virtually impossible to be out of sight of a lifeguard. The river is kept several degrees warmer than the saltwater pools. After visiting a saltwater pool like the Coral Reef, the river will feel like a warm bath.

Most people bring along their snorkels, although there are no fish in the river and very little to see. An attempt has been made to add visual interest by studding the bottom with chunks of Mayanesque ruins and visitors seem to have created their own decorative touches by arranging stones on the bottom in the form of peace symbols, smiley faces, and hearts.

The edges of the river are attractively landscaped with lush tropical foliage but the banks are high and rocky and there are only four places to enter or exit. The main entrance, between the Dolphin Lagoon and the ray pool, broadens out into a large lagoon-like pool backed by a very pretty waterfall.

The best section of the *Tropical River* is the one that passes through the *Aviary*. Heavy waterfalls at either end prevent the birds from escaping. Inside is a tropical paradise and you may be surprised at how closely you can approach birds perched at the water's edge. You can step out of the river here and visit the birds at even closer range.

Aviary

Rating:	★ ★ ★ ★ +
Type:	Animal interaction

| *Time:* | Continuous viewing |
| *Kelly says:* | Discovery Cove's best-kept secret |

Imagine a jungle paradise where the birds are so tame they'll eat out of your hand and foot-high deer peek about the blossoms as you pet them. This is what you'll find if you step out of the *Tropical River* into the very special world of Discovery Cove's jungle aviary.

The *Aviary* is populated with some 200 exotic birds representing 100 species from the four corners of the world, many of them so intriguingly colored that they look more like products of the vivid imaginations of folk artists than creatures from the natural world. Since many of the birds found here have been hand-raised by Discovery Cove trainers, they are completely tame and will happily eat out of your hand. Food is readily available from some of those same trainers, who can also answer your questions about which bird is which. Typically there are one or two examples of each species, but in some cases, like the gaudily colored conures, you will see a small flock flying through the trees or perching on the branches. There are actually three aviaries here. There is one on each side of the river and the far aviary has a smaller aviary within it housing tiny birds like hummingbirds.

The type of food you choose — grain pellets, fruit, or meal worms — will determine which birds you attract, and unlike the dolphin encounter, your time here is unlimited. You can also feed the tiny muntjac deer, which have their own special diet.

If you'd like to develop your bird-watching skills, ask one of the attendants for a laminated chart that identifies the species in the *Aviary*.

Tip: Most people discover the *Aviary* while cruising down the *Tropical River,* but there are two unmarked land entrances. You will find them just past the stingray pool. They make visiting the *Aviary* several times during the course of the day a very tempting option.

Ray Lagoon

Rating:	★ ★ ★
Type:	Animal interaction
Time:	Continuous viewing
Kelly says:	Little kids love it

This shallow saltwater pool seems only slightly larger than the concrete ray pool over at SeaWorld. But instead of hanging over the edge, here you can wade right in and snorkel with these intriguing little critters whose scary look belies their sweet and docile nature. What's more, you don't have to pay a small fortune to feed them here; food is freely available at regular intervals from the attendants, who are extremely knowledgeable sources of information about their charges.

Tip: If you have your heart set on feeding a stingray, come early in the day. Unlike some of us, stingrays are smart enough to stop eating when they are full.

Coral Reef

Rating:	★ ★ ★ +
Type:	A swim-through aquatic habitat
Time:	Continuous viewing
Kelly says:	A great snorkeling experience guaranteed

Having been disappointed on several snorkeling outings in the real tropics, I was impressed by the variety of multicolored tropical fish on display in this clever re-creation of a coral reef. It's not real coral, of course, but a thin film of algae encourages fish to nibble at the simulated coral outcroppings very much as they do on the real thing.

Here you can snorkel to your heart's content without worrying about visibility being lessened by churning surf. Nor do you have to worry about those nasty little things — jellyfish, fire coral, and moray eels — that frequent real reefs. And the sharks and barracudas are thoughtfully kept behind thick (but virtually invisible) sloping glass walls. You get the illusion of swimming above them without the bone-chilling fear that typically arrives with the realization that you are swimming a few feet from something that might eat you.

The fish are fed periodically, and when the water around you is swirling with bits of food, it will also be alive with a kaleidoscope of fish. Put out your hand and the bolder among them will nibble hopefully at your fingertips as large manta rays cruise the depths below.

Dining at Discovery Cove

Your lunch is included in the price of admission and is served cafeteria-style from 11:00 a.m. to 4:00 p.m. at the **Laguna Grill**, another imposing Polynesian-style structure about halfway into the park. Although the service style may bring back memories of your high school lunch room, the food is surprisingly good if somewhat limited in choice.

This is not an all-you-can-eat buffet but a set meal that includes an entree, a side salad, a soft beverage, and a dessert. Your entree can be either a warm dish or a cold salad, with just a few simple choices in each category. The salads are the fairly standard chef's, chicken or seafood, while the hot entrees tend to be simple pasta combinations or stir fry dishes, the sorts of things that can be served up easily from a steam table. Made-to-order burgers are also available. I found the quality to be quite good although not exceptional. All seating is outdoors, most of it well shaded.

Care is taken to assure you get only one "free" meal; an attendant swipes the bar code of your ID card when you pick up your food. If you want seconds or crave another meal later in the day, you will have to pay for it. For those with hearty appetites, entrees are in the $9 to $11 range and an extra dessert will set you back about $3 or $4. Refills on drinks cost about $2.

There are two **beach bars** located elsewhere in the park, one near the Dolphin Lagoon and the other near the stingray pool and Aviary. Here you can get soft drinks, iced tea, fruit punch, and lemonade for about $2. More elaborate fruit smoothies and similar concoctions are about $3.

For those who crave something alcoholic, the Cove offers a range of "tropical frozen specialties" for about $5. Budweiser beer is on draft for about $3. Wine is just over $3. The snacks are pretty unimaginative and include nachos ($4), soft pretzels ($1.25), and Shamu Bars ($2.50). Fresh fruit for those who insist on snacking healthily costs $1. Those with deep thirsts might be attracted to the huge refillable mugs with Discovery Cove logos ($3.50), which come with free refills all day long. Coffee mugs are smaller and more expensive ($10) but they are insulated and quite handsome.

Shopping at Discovery Cove

The relentless merchandising that characterizes virtually all theme parks is mercifully muted at Discovery Cove. The major shopping venue, **Tropical Gifts**, is strategically located near the main entrance, so you can pick up the bathing suit you desperately need as you enter and the high-priced souvenir you almost certainly do not need as you leave.

The shop is located in an airy Polynesian-style building complete with peaked, thatched roof. The merchandise is as airy and high-class as the surroundings. Here you will find the kind of upscale resort wear for men and women that will tempt you even if you didn't forget to pack your bathing suit or outerwear.

For those who want something more tangible in the way of a souvenir, there is a large variety of dolphin figurines and sculptures in all price ranges; the more elaborate sculptures can range up to $20,000. You will also find some very nice jewelry in dolphin, sea turtle, stingray and other deep sea motifs at moderate prices. Somewhat more expensive are artsy glassware pieces that may or may not appeal to your taste.

On a more practical level, you can find things like film and more of that dolphin-friendly sunscreen you got when you arrived. I would recommend picking up one of the inexpensive disposable underwater cameras. You won't be able to take it with you to meet the dolphins, but you'll find plenty of use for it elsewhere in the park.

Next to Tropical Gifts is **Adventure Photo** where you come to claim the complimentary family photo that was snapped on your arrival and any dolphin photos you ordered earlier.

A smaller open-air kiosk farther into the park wisely concentrates on more affordable t-shirts, sandals, reef socks, inflatable toys, magazines, and the kind of trashy novels we love to take to the beach.

CHAPTER FOUR:

Cypress Gardens

This is where it all began. Yes, it's true, Silver Springs was running glass bottom boats before the turn of the century, but that was simply a matter of capitalizing on a ready-made attraction. In the opinion of many, the Central Florida theme park phenomenon actually began when Dick Pope carved a man-made paradise out of a patch of swampy cypress forest along the east shore of Lake Eloise to create Cypress Gardens in 1936. Today, Cypress Gardens is world-renowned for its spectacular botanical gardens and its innovative water ski spectaculars. As theme parks boomed in the 1970s, Cypress Gardens added other attractions to meet the competition, but it still retains the easygoing, leisurely air that has characterized it since its early days.

The story of Cypress Gardens' development and of Dick Pope's single-minded boosterism is almost as entertaining as the park itself. When he launched his enterprise on little more than a dream and a hunch, most people thought he was nuts. One newspaper called him "the Swami of the Swamp." Opening day brought in gate receipts of $38. Hardly a propitious sign. Fortunately, Pope, whom the *Orlando Sentinel* calls "the flamboyant father of Florida tourism," was blessed with an instinct for publicity that P.T. Barnum would have admired. Within five years, Cypress Gardens was drawing half a million visitors a year.

Pope did it with publicity — free publicity. He staged photo shoots of pretty girls in his picture perfect park and mailed copies by the thousands, in gardenia-scented envelopes, to newspapers and magazines throughout the country. The media took the bait. One photograph of a skyborne water skier appeared in 3,670 publications. Of course, Cypress Gardens was mentioned in the caption. Pope lured filmmakers and television stars to Cypress Gardens. Esther Williams, Mike Douglas, and scores of others used Cypress Gardens as a backdrop. He staged outrageous stunts like playing the piano for a ballerina while both of them were being towed behind a speedboat, she on water skis, he on a piano-sized platform. Taking a cue from the Miss America pageant, he started crowning a new queen of something or other on an almost daily basis. All of it became grist for Pope's voracious publicity mill. Pope and his wife were also inspired improvisers, creating new marketing strategies on the spur of the moment. Some of Cypress Gardens' most revered traditions, like the water ski shows and the Southern Belles, came about almost by accident.

When Dick Pope's health began to fail in the mid-eighties, Cypress Gardens was sold, first to the publisher Harcourt Brace Jovanovich, then to the Busch Entertainment Corporation (of SeaWorld and Busch Gardens fame). It is now owned by a group of former Busch executives who are preserving Pope's legacy.

Cypress Gardens has long had a reputation as a park for senior citizens. While that perception may not accurately reflect the breadth and scope of the park's appeal, the fact remains that on the typical day you will see a majority of silver-haired guests. I wouldn't let that dissuade younger readers from coming and bringing the kids. There's plenty here to enchant visitors of all ages, just so long as they don't come expecting another Universal Orlando or SeaWorld.

Before You Come

If you'd like to get advance information on what will be going on at Cypress Gardens during the time of your visit, give them a call at (800) 282-2123 or (863) 324-2111. They'll be happy to fill you in on the floral calendar or send information. Cypress Gardens also maintains a colorful web site at www.cypressgardens.com.

When's the Best Time to Come?

Cypress Gardens' high season extends from fall into spring, the months when "sunbirds" flock south from cooler climes. Generally speaking, you will find more activities happening during the winter than during the torrid summer months. The size of the crowds, however, is never a factor in picking the date of your visit; Cypress Gardens is rarely mobbed. And thanks to the wizardry of the horticultural staff, there's always something to see.

If you're a true gardening buff, you may want to call ahead for the "Floral Calendar" to help guide your planning. Simply dial (863) 324-2123 and ask for extension 297. Otherwise, I recommend spring and fall. The floral festivals at these times are spectacular and the weather is close to ideal; the summer can be stifling and winter is unpredictable, with temperatures ranging from pleasant to quite chilly. If you visit between November and April, the park will be open late enough for you to enjoy the spectacular sunsets over Lake Eloise.

Getting There

Cypress Gardens is a leisurely one-hour drive from Orlando (less, if you drive like the locals who take the 65 miles per hour speed limit as a suggested minimum). The easiest way to get there is to follow I-4 to Route 27 South. Turn right off Route 27 at State Route 540 (it is well marked). Cypress Gardens is a bit less than four miles along on your left.

Parking at Cypress Gardens

Cypress Gardens' general parking is $6, on grass, in an area dotted with shade trees. Parking for motorcycles costs $4, for RVs and trailers $8. You will never be terribly far from the front gate, so no transportation is provided. Parking is free for annual passholders.

"Preferred Parking" is also available for $7 ($6 for annual passholders). This allows you to park in a two-tiered, sunken circular lot formed by a sinkhole. The Preferred Parking lot is close to the main gate but it is still possible to be parked in this area and be farther from the gate than the early birds who snared the best spots in the general parking area.

Opening and Closing Times

Reflecting the laid-back tempo preferred by its core clientele, Cypress Gardens does not open early and boogie late. The park opens every day of the year at 9:30 a.m. During the torrid summer, the park closes at 5:00 p.m. Periodically, there will be special nighttime events that require a separate admission and may run later. In the milder months of November through April, the park stays open until 8:00 or 9:00 p.m. Only in January does closing revert to 5:00 p.m. On July 4, the park stays open until 10:00 p.m.

It's a shame Cypress Gardens never offers early admission since the early dawn hours would be an ideal time to avoid the heat of a stroll through the botanical gardens.

The Price of Admission

Cypress Gardens sells admission by the day and by the year. At press time, prices (including tax) were as follows:

One-Day Pass:
Adults: $37.02

Children (6 to 17): $21.15
Ages 5 and under **free**.

Annual Pass:
Adults: $79.45
Seniors (55+): $71.50
Children (6 to 17): $52.95

The annual pass carries a number of benefits, including a 10% discount at all shops and restaurants, 15% off tickets for friends and family, a frequent diner and shopper program, and a quarterly newsletter.

Considering the discounts, the annual pass pays for itself if you visit the park more than once during the year. Still, the pass will probably make the most sense for Florida residents or others who find themselves in the Winter Haven area on a regular basis. If you decide you want one, step into Guest Relations; they will have your pass ready when you leave the park.

Discounts

The Cypress Gardens' web site, www.cypressgardens.com, offers a coupon good for $5 off on each of up to six admissions, and you will find dollars-off coupons for it in all the usual places (see *Chapter 1: Introduction & Orientation*). The park also runs frequent promotions — kids free with an adult, Moms free on Mothers' Day, and so forth — so you may want to call ahead to see what's available. Discounted tickets are often available from hotel Guest Services desks and ticket brokers in the Orlando area. Active duty members of the military and members of AAA and AARP receive a 10% discount at the gate on daily admission.

Staying Near the Park

If Cypress Gardens is your primary destination, or if you just want to spare yourself the drive back to Orlando, you may want to stay just outside the main gate.

Best Western Admiral's Inn
5665 Cypress Gardens Boulevard
Winter Haven, FL 33884
(800) 247-2799; (863) 324-5950; fax (863) 324-2376
Standard mid-range motel.
Price Range: $$
Amenities: Pool, restaurant, lounge
Walk to Park: 2 minutes
Other moderately priced motels can be found three to four miles west

along Route 540 (Cypress Gardens Boulevard) in the town of Winter Haven. None is within walking distance.

Special Events

Cypress Gardens offers a growing number of themed special events throughout the year. Most of these elaborate floral displays fill the International Gardens section and are geared to the changing seasons. Here are the major events, with their approximate dates. A recorded message at (800) 324-2123 offers a listing of upcoming events. A complete list can be obtained by calling (863) 324-2111 and asking for extension 213, 215, or 290.

Spring Lights (February to April). A twinkling extravaganza involving over 100 animated pieces bedecked with lights and displayed beside the moss-draped oaks, babbling brooks, and waterfalls of Cypress Gardens.

Spring Flower Festival (Mid-March to mid-May). Huge topiary animals covered in bright flowers fill the lawns of the park for this salute to the resurgence of life in the spring.

Victorian Garden Party (year round). Nearly 100 ivy-covered topiary figures with floral accents recreate the ambiance of 1860s America, complete with a topiary riverboat at the lake's edge.

Fourth of July. Celebrate the nation's birthday with special water ski shows and the largest fireworks display in Polk County. There is a nominal additional charge for admission after 6:00 p.m.

Mum Festival (November). Mum's the word — chrysanthemum, that is — in this cornucopia of autumn flowers. More than two and a half million blooms are displayed in cascades, columns, cones, spheres, even bonsai trees.

Ghostly Gardens (October). For three days around Halloween the park takes on a not-too-scary aspect. There is a separate admission for this after-hours event.

Garden of Lights (November 28 to early January). Get in the Yuletide spirit with this riot of lights on just about everything in the park, including animated displays. Every year the number of lights seems to increase. It's now five million and counting.

Poinsettia Festival (Late November to early January). A huge indoor display of this delicate and lovely Christmas favorite helps celebrate the holiday season.

Cypress Gardens also plays host to some major musical acts, with the accent on swing. Among the acts playing two-day stands during recent years were the Glenn Miller Orchestra, Guy Lombardo and His Royal Canadians, the Lettermen, and Bobby Rydell. Each act performs several times a day. Call for details.

Dining and Shopping at Cypress Gardens

Your dining choices at Cypress Gardens are limited. Fortunately, the one full-service restaurant is a winner, especially when you choose to dine al fresco, overlooking the main floral display area. In addition to the eateries reviewed in this chapter, there are a number of small refreshment stands that operate seasonally. For those who keep track of such things, soft drinks are $1.75, $2.00, and $2.25 for small, medium, and large sizes.

Like the dining, the shopping is not a reason in itself to visit the park. There are some nice things to be found at the Butterfly Shop and if you need to stock up on decorations for your Christmas tree, the Santa Claus shop offers a wide selection of tasteful tree ornaments along with decorative accessories for the rest of the house.

Good Things to Know About...

Access for the Disabled

Almost all of the park is wheelchair accessible, although some of the inclines are best negotiated with the help of a companion. The exceptions are the boat rides which may not be able to accommodate all disabled guests. Both wheelchairs and electric carts can be rented at the Bazaar Gift Shop in the entrance arcade. Wheelchairs are $6.50 per day. Electric carts are $32 for the day. A brochure, *All Are Welcome*, containing "helpful hints for guests with special needs" is available at Guest Relations in the main entrance arcade.

Babies

Strollers can be rented at the Bazaar Gift Shop. Single strollers are $6.50 per day, doubles are $10. Diaper changing stations can be found in most restrooms, men's and women's.

Emergencies

Medical personnel are available during park hours. If you or someone in your party has a problem, contact the nearest park employee. If you lose a child, do the same; park staffers are far better able than you to comb the underbrush for your little ones.

Leaving the Park

You may leave the park and return during the day. Just make sure to have your hand stamped as you leave.

Lockers

Coin-operated lockers (50 cents for each use) can be found in the entrance arcade near the Resort Wear gift shop.

Mail

A tiny branch post office is located just outside the main gate, but plan to get there early. The window is open only from 9 a.m. to 10 a.m., Monday through Friday. Otherwise, stamps can be purchased at the Bazaar Gift Shop. Cards and letters posted here will receive a special "Cypress Gardens" postmark. If you're there when the window is open, ask them to use the hand cancellation stamp; it's easier to read.

Money

There is an ATM located in the entrance arcade, just before you reach the ticket windows. It is connected to the Plus, Cirrus, Honor, and Exchange networks. It will also provide cash advances on Visa and MasterCard.

Pets

A self-service pet kennel will be found near the main entrance to the park. The small, glass-fronted lockers (which look a bit like wall-mounted microwave ovens) cost $1.50 while the larger, dog-sized ones below cost $2.00. Quarters are required; change can be obtained from the parking lot toll booth. Disposable food bowls and a wash-up sink are also provided.

Safety

Cypress Gardens is open to all the birds and animals who take it into their minds to pay a visit. The park warns people not to feed the birds or other little critters because they are wild and unpredictable and may become aggressive. That's good advice, but the squirrels are hard to resist. It's unlikely that you'll see an alligator during your visit but, if you do, remember that feeding wild alligators is not only stupid but illegal.

Special Diets

If you have special dietary needs, your best bet is the Crossroads Restaurant, which offers a number of special meals on request.

Weddings

More than 300 weddings are performed at Cypress Gardens each year, and once you've seen the place you'll understand why. If you'd like to hold your nuptials in this lush and lovely setting, call (863) 324-2111 and ask for extension 383 or 273. Receptions for up to 200 people can be arranged. Prices for wedding packages start at $900.

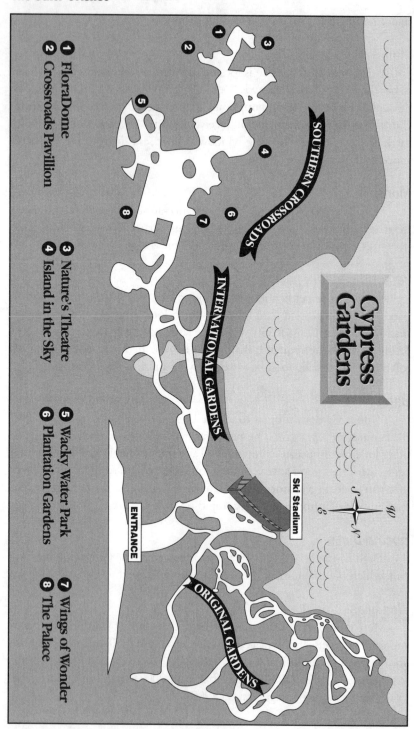

Cypress Gardens

SOUTHERN CROSSROADS

INTERNATIONAL GARDENS

ORIGINAL GARDENS

Ski Stadium

ENTRANCE

❶ FloraDome
❷ Crossroads Pavillion

❸ Nature's Theatre
❹ Island in the Sky

❺ Wacky Water Park
❻ Plantation Gardens

❼ Wings of Wonder
❽ The Palace

Smelling the Flowers: Your Day at Cypress Gardens

Cypress Gardens can easily be seen and appreciated in a day. You may not see everything, but as you read through the descriptions that follow, you will probably find there are some things you won't mind missing.

Cypress Gardens' fame rests primarily on its flowers and spectacular gardens. Many guests are also attracted by its reputation as the Water Ski Capital of the World. But the park has developed an eclectic blend of attractions. The major themes are:

The Gardens. Not only are "the original gardens" (so called to distinguish Pope's original creation from later innovations) still growing, but there are also regular floral festivals, the formal *Plantation Gardens*, and special garden-themed presentations.

Water Skiing. The Cypress Gardens water show is the original and, in the opinion of many, still the best.

Variety Entertainment. Cypress Gardens presents a regular schedule of family-style entertainment, from singers in the *Cypress Gazebo*, to magicians, to an ice show.

Nature Shows. In addition to the gardening shows already mentioned, Cypress Gardens presents show-and-tell presentations starring some of nature's most interesting birds and reptiles.

Rides. Cypress Gardens is not and never has been a "ride" park. Yet there are some rides, most of them for little ones.

This is not a large park, although when you take into account the meandering paths through the many garden areas, you can walk a fair distance during your visit. The park comprises 200 acres and runs north to south along the shore of Lake Eloise; it is divided into three areas, the "original" gardens, International Gardens, and Southern Crossroads (see map, page 102).

The One-Day Stay

As you enter the park, pick up a copy of *Cypress Gardens Entertainment & Attractions*, a large one-sheet flyer with a map of the park and a schedule of shows and events. Scan this for the show times of the entertainments you most want to see and plan accordingly. In my opinion, the water ski show and the ice skating show are must sees. You should also try to catch the animal show in *Nature's Theater.*

If you arrive at opening time, the Southern Crossroads area won't be open yet and the first water ski show will be a few hours away. So a visit to the nearby botanical gardens is a logical first step. This is also a good time to

101

see them, before the heat of the day. Depending on how long it takes you to see the gardens, you may have time for both the *Botanical Boat Cruise* and the half-hour *Southern Breeze Lake Cruise.* If so, you may finish up just in time to catch the first performance of the water ski show. If you have a little time to kill, visit International Gardens and check out the current floral show.

Now you have the afternoon to tour the attractions in Southern Crossroads and enjoy a leisurely lunch. In addition to the shows recommended above, don't miss *Wings of Wonder. Island in the Sky* is a fun diversion that can be squeezed in just about anytime you like; it only takes five minutes.

Another option is to save your visit to the botanical gardens for late in the day. Photographers, especially, may find the afternoon sun and the lengthening shadows a plus. You can linger until the staff starts to shoo you out at closing time.

"The Gardens"

At the north end of the park, where you enter, is what I call "The Gardens," which comprises what the management refers to as "the original gardens" and the water ski arena. Proceeding south, you enter the International Gardens, a gentle valley that extends from the water ski arena to the entrance to Southern Crossroads. This is the area of the park in which most of the major floral festivals are held. (The other is Crossroads Pavilion, a large tent-like structure at the south end of the park.) In International Gardens you will find the lovely Italian Fountain and the Mediterranean Waterfall. The waterfall is artificial and fed by thousands of gallons of recycled lake water; the stream that flows from its base to the lake marks the approximate centerline of the park. Finally, there is Southern Crossroads, a melange of shops, eateries, and attractions arranged along a pleasant tree-shaded promenade that evokes the antebellum Deep South. Most of the park's attractions are located here.

For this survey of Cypress Gardens attractions, I will start at the north end of the park, describing the "original" botanical gardens and their surrounding attractions, and then move directly to Southern Crossroads at the opposite end. I have not attempted to describe International Gardens because the displays there change constantly. See the list of Special Events above to get an idea of what you will find there at the time of your visit.

For those with sufficient time, starting at the north end of the park and slowly wending your way southward is a highly efficient way in which to see the entire park. Assuming that there will be a few attractions you will pass up, the entire tour can be done in a day. Those who want to be absolutely thorough will probably have to return a second day to complete their survey.

The Gardens area contains relatively few attractions but they are the ones for which Cypress Gardens is justly famous. The two marquee attractions, the ski show and the botanical gardens, are doozies.

The water ski show area with its twin stadiums is the first thing you see as you enter the park, so we'll start there.

Ski Stadium: "2001 Ski Odyssey"

Rating: ★ ★ ★ ★ ★
Type: Water ski spectacular
Time: 20 minutes
Kelly says: The original and still the best

An entire industry was born here at Cypress Gardens when Dick Pope inaugurated regular water skiing shows. The story goes something like this: During the early forties, Pope staged a water skiing exhibition for a photographer as part of his ongoing campaign to get free publicity for his park. This time he got something else. A group of soldiers was touring the park after the photo appeared and asked, "What time's the water ski show?" Thinking quickly, Pope quoted a show time that gave him just enough time to round up some water skiers and put on the first show.

Since then the water ski shows have become a Cypress Gardens trademark, one Pope promoted tirelessly. In a never-ending effort to improve the shows and stay one or more steps ahead of the inevitable copycats, Pope and his crew kept dreaming up new, bigger, and better stunts. As a result, Cypress Gardens boasts 51 world-record water skiing firsts, the most recent (an eight-man flip off a single ramp) in 1994.

One result of all this striving is that Cypress Gardens doesn't have to resort to gimmicks to put on a good show. They simply showcase talented athletes who, by dint of hard work, have become the best in the world at what they do. The show has a theme, of course — currently it's outer space, complete with skiers in space suits — but the structure of the show remains the same in all its incarnations — a display of water skiing artistry that moves deftly from the pretty nifty to the truly amazing.

True to the Pope tradition, the show doesn't ignore the possibilities of attractive young women (none dare call them girls) in bathing suits. The Cypress Gardens AquaMaids specialize in looking pretty but they are a lot more than cheesecake. These women are accomplished athletes who combine balletic grace with impeccable balance and split second timing in a series of appearances that punctuate the show.

The heart of the show is the stunt skiing, and that is the province of the men. Barefoot water skiing seems amazing enough to me but these guys do it in more ways than you'd imagine possible, from starting out face down and backwards in the water to jumping off regular water skis at 45 miles an hour.

On a variety of skis and ski boards, they twist and flip and dismount spectacularly at the foot of the stands.

There is also an interlude of "adagio" skiing, male-female teams on a single pair of skis who engage in a series of graceful lifts as they speed along at 40 miles an hour. The form was borrowed from ice skating and adapted to water skis in the early seventies; I can't help feeling it's a lot harder on water.

In the guise of "The Rampmasters," four guys put on a display of gutsy ramp jumping that involves aerial spins over the heads of their colleagues, back and front flips in unison, and something called a "gainer," a sideways flip at nearly 50 miles an hour. Corky, a wonderfully corny circus clown, provides an opportunity for some good-natured high jinks and derring-do that may not be pretty but is still pretty amazing.

As a sort of bonus, they throw in something that has little to do with water skiing, except perhaps that the hang glider involved gets his initial lift by being towed behind a boat. The announcer points him out off in the distance and then, via a wireless mike, the high flying daredevil narrates his own descent and pinpoint landing on the shore between the two stadiums. Pretty neat if you've never seen it done before.

The climax of the show is one of Cypress Gardens' famed human pyramids — a four-level extravaganza in which a bottom row of six men hoist six AquaMaids aloft, the top one waving Old Glory as they zoom in review past the stands. Cypress Gardens skiers have actually created a five-level pyramid (there are photographs to prove it) but the trick is apparently too dangerous to attempt in public.

The best seats in the house. In this case there are two houses, twin stadiums separated by a grassy slope. You can also sit on the grass and, if you do, the park provides simple cardboard mats to protect your tush from grass stains. My feeling is that the best seats are in the right-hand stadium. The hang glider zips right past you and the human pyramid heads directly towards you on its final run.

The stadiums' overhangs offer some protection from the sun, although the lower seats become exposed about midday. Seating is on simple aluminum benches. Signs painted on them warn that the first five rows may become a splash zone, but there seems less of an effort made here to soak you than at, say, SeaWorld. A splash or two does find its way into the seats but it's usually fairly localized.

Extra added attraction: If you have at least some level of water skiing experience, why not take advantage of your presence at Cypress Gardens to get some tips from the pros? Thanks to **Extreme Experience** you can. For $50, plus tax, you get a behind-the-scenes tour of the ski arena, a coaching session with a certified instructor, and the thrill of skiing in the show arena of the

"Water Skiing Capital of the World." There is also a $25 option that omits the backstage tour and some of the bells and whistles. You must be at least six years old. Sessions fill up on a first come, first served basis. Call (863) 324-2111 or inquire at the Information Booth in front of Landings Snack Bar near the ski stadium.

Botanical Gardens

Rating: ★ ★ ★ ★ ★
Type: Beautifully landscaped gardens
Time: 40 to 45 minutes or as long as you wish
Kelly says: Among the best of its kind in the world and
                a photographer's paradise

By definition, botanical gardens are a sort of museum. Most botanical gardens seem to strive for order. Succulents here, pines there, palms over there. Tropical plants in this area, temperate plants in that area. That way people can study them better. Completeness is also a goal, trying to have more epiphytes than the next botanical garden, for example. The aesthetics of display, while important, often seem to be a secondary concern, except in the more formal gardens.

The designers of Cypress Gardens, however, seem to have started by asking a simple yet powerful question — "How can we produce the most stunning visual spectacle possible?" — and letting everything else follow from there. The result is a remarkable blend of over-the-top landscaping hyperbole and serene beauty.

These 16 acres contain over 8,000 different kinds of plants, trees, and flowers collected from 90 different countries. There are over 60 varieties of azaleas alone. I have no idea whether that means the collection is unusually complete (I mention azaleas only because it's a flower I recognize). Nor do I know if the designers have carefully segregated tropical plants from the temperate varieties (I suspect they have not). I don't know if the Oriental Gardens contain only oriental plants or the French Garden only flowers indigenous to France. But I can't imagine anyone will care.

Here the purely aesthetic experience is paramount. A leisurely stroll, with open eyes and a receptive soul, will yield abundant treasures. And if you're a typical vacation photographer, bring along a few more rolls of film than usual. You'll find ample use for them.

As large as it is, the garden is not a maze and there's little likelihood of getting lost. The map on the *Cypress Gardens Entertainment & Attractions* sheet that you picked up at the park entrance, while schematic, is adequate and the trails are well marked. Real gardening enthusiasts may want to invest in a copy of *Cypress Gardens Botanical Walking Tour* (about $4), which can be purchased in the Bazaar Gift Shop in the entrance arcade and at other shops in the park. It contains a somewhat better map with a suggested route through the gardens marked in red arrows. It also contains a reference to some of the many plants and flowers to be found in the gardens, including tips on which ones make good house plants.

Many plants in the gardens are identified by marker signs. The colored dots on the signs correspond to sections in the *Walking Tour*, although it's probably faster to look up the plant name in the index. The book contains close-up pictures of the plants it describes but unfortunately doesn't include any panoramic views of the garden's many stunning vistas.

Tip: The garden is dotted with wooden benches. Bring a handkerchief or paper towel, as many of them are wet in the morning hours, before the sun has had a chance to dry them off.

As you enter the gardens, you cross a bridge onto a chain of man-made islands. To your left is Lake Eloise, its shore often guarded by stately cypress trees emerging from the shallow water. To the right is a man-made canal. Must-see sights along this archipelago are the **Big Lagoon**, across which you will see a pretty Southern Belle gracing one of Cypress Garden's loveliest vistas. At the end of the island is a typical Dick Pope inspiration, the **Florida Pool.** This is a swimming pool in the shape of the state of Florida, nestled right against the lake shore. It's fenced off now and used primarily for publicity shots. Its main claim to immortality is its appearance in the 1953 Esther Williams film, *Easy To Love.*

The **Oriental Gardens** are an oasis of cool serenity presided over by a towering gold Buddha. A wooden "Japanese tea house" offers a place to sit in the shade and survey the scene. Even those seemingly immune to Nature's wonders will be startled by the massive **banyan tree.** This behemoth began its tenure at Cypress Gardens as a 50-pound sapling in a bucket. Today it's larger than your average castle, with its aerial root system creating a charming maze of paths through its very heart.

There are two formal gardens nestled here, the **Rose Garden** and the **French Garden.** The former pays homage to two saints: St. Francis of Assisi, better known as an animal lover, was also a devoted gardener. St. Fiacre, a seventh-century Irish monk who created a renowned monastery garden outside Paris, is the patron saint of gardeners. Interestingly, he is also the patron saint of taxi drivers, because in the 17th century the horse-drawn carriages that ran between Paris and his suburban shrine were nicknamed fiacres. The French Garden is a charming sunken brick oval with a perfectly symmetrical floral arrangement and a wooden bench under the spreading arms of a red silk cotton tree.

Tip: Near these two gardens is **Banyan Terrace**, a rental facility for meetings and banquets. When it is not otherwise engaged, the place is pretty much deserted, but you can find a bench on the broad terrace overlooking Lake Summit (where the ski team practices). It makes a nice quiet getaway from the heat and the sun.

Perhaps the most beautiful spot in the entire gardens is the **Gazebo**. This is no rustic wooden affair but a resplendent white-domed structure supported by eight fluted Greek columns and flanked by gently bubbling fountains. Also known as the "Love Chapel," it is the site of the over 300 weddings that take place at Cypress Gardens each year. The Gazebo stands at the top of a rise that looks down across the Big Lagoon and out to Lake Eloise; the view from here is as fine as the reverse view from below. An ingenious **photo op** has been provided near the French Garden. You stand facing a large mirror with your back to the Gazebo. Place your camera on the small platform (also facing the mirror), set the timer, and smile. You'll get a lovely shot of yourself with the Gazebo in the background and the words "Cypress Gardens" floating on the mirror.

The gardens are dotted with a rotating display of **wildlife sculpture**. Some are on permanent display but most are on loan from the artists. The display changes once a year, in November. If you take a fancy to one of these works of art, you can buy a copy. The smaller ones are almost cheap ($2,500 or so) but the larger pieces cost tens of thousands of dollars. If it makes the buying decision easier, 5% of the proceeds goes to support the work of the National Wildlife Federation.

The Southern Belles

The Southern Belles deserve a special note. Although the botanical gardens seem to be their "natural habitat," they will be seen in all areas of the park. The story of their origins is another example of the wonderfully ingenious and utterly benign hucksterism that characterizes the history of Cypress Gardens.

It seems that in 1940 a devastating winter freeze killed the colorful but delicate flame vines that framed the entrance at that time. The interior of the park had been saved by the heat of many oil heaters and looked just fine. Visitors didn't know this, however, and when they saw the wilted entrance they assumed the worst and kept on driving.

Noticing this, Julie Pope, Dick's wife, rounded up a bevy of local high school girls and outfitted them in colorful antebellum hoop-skirted gowns. She then placed them strategically in front of the damaged flame vines to wave at approaching cars. Not only did attendance pick up, but the visitors were so enchanted by the girls that another Cypress Gardens tradition was born. Today, the Southern Belles take turns sitting decorously in the hot

Florida sun to serve as beautiful props in tourists' photos. In typical Cypress Gardens hyperbole, they are billed as "the most photographed women in the world." Their bright and fanciful gowns are another Cypress Gardens trademark. All of them are made by hand at the park. Each one takes some 13 yards of fabric, 5 yards of lining, over 63 yards of lace, and more than 45 hours to complete. Since that moment of inspiration in 1940, over 800 of them have been created. Thanks to the Junior Belle Program (see *Shopping in Southern Crossroads*, below), visiting moms and daughters can live out this cheerful fantasy.

Botanical Boat Cruise

Rating: ★ ★ ★ ★
Type: Guided boat tour
Time: 15 minutes
Kelly says: Another angle on these magnificent gardens

Near the entrance to the botanical gardens you will spot a lakeside landing for the boat cruise. This is a leisurely, short guided tour past the lake shore cypresses and back through the gardens' man-made canal aboard an 18-passenger motor launch. It is not, I hasten to add, a substitute for a stroll through the gardens themselves but it does offer a different perspective and a few sights you can't see from the land.

As you cruise north along the shore and enter the canal that links Lakes Eloise and Summit you will see to your left a patch of untouched, dense cypress swamp that stands as a sort of "before" to the botanical gardens' "after." It makes you appreciate the magnitude of Pope's accomplishment.

Then you enter a man-made canal laboriously dug out of the muck by dollar-a-day laborers between 1936 and 1938. Later, you can see photos of the canal under construction in the *Cypress Roots* display at the other end of the park. Cruising through the canal you will pass the **Chairman of the Board**. With an estimated age of 1,600 years, it is the oldest cypress tree in the gardens. The canal cruise also offers an excellent look at the gardens' 27 varieties of palm trees, including a "one-in-a-million" two-headed palm tree. This botanical rarity is one of just four in the entire state of Florida.

The tour is capped off by a brief stop in the Big Lagoon for yet another look at the beautiful, flower-fringed greensward sloping up to the Gazebo.

Southern Breeze Boat Cruises

Rating: ★ ★ ★ ★
Type: Boat cruise on the lake
Time: 30 minutes to 1 hour
Kelly says: Bird watching and real estate envy

There is an additional charge for these relaxing excursions aboard a two-level paddlewheeler, but it's worth the price. Tickets can be purchased at a booth in front of the Landings Snack Bar. You will be given a specific departure time; seating is limited so you may not always be able to get on the next sailing.

The regular Lake Cruise ($6, $4.50 for annual passholders) takes you on a counterclockwise, seven-mile circumnavigation of Lake Eloise, never getting more than a few dozen yards off shore. The Southern Breeze evokes the paddle steamers that once plied the Mississippi; downstairs is glassed in and air conditioned, while the shaded upper deck allows the breeze to blow through your hair.

Aside from the warm sun and the cool breeze, there are two major attractions of this ride. The first is nature itself. Be prepared to see lots of birds, or at least their nests. Ospreys have established a prominent place among the lakeside birds and their large nests and distinctive markings make them readily identifiable. You will also most likely see heron, cormorants, and anhinga, all of which your tour guide will point out. Depending on the time of the year, you may glimpse a gator or two or three, some sunning themselves placidly on residents' boat docks. One reason for the increase in raised sun decks around the lake was the gators' penchant for pulling themselves up alongside startled sunbathers. You'll also no doubt be treated to local lore about the 200-odd gators who call Lake Eloise home — the 14-footer that was captured and relocated to a remote area, the rogue gator that was shot and whose belly yielded nine dog collars.

The tour also serves as a ready-made real estate tour for those in the market and those who wish they could afford to be. Homes by the lake start at about $500,000 for places that would be hard to sell elsewhere to several million for the grander manses, including one that is a replica of Tara from *Gone with the Wind*. On a recent tour, a large house complete with mother-in-law apartment over the boathouse was on the market for $1.2 million. You'll learn that those huge screened-in pools and patios, called "Florida rooms," keep out not just the bugs but alligators as well. Apparently, once a gator gets into your pool, the fire department will have a tough time hauling him out.

The cruise usually lasts between 30 and 45 minutes, but in the high season, when there are more people in the park, Lakes Lulu and Summit are added to the itinerary and the cruise stretches to 45 minutes to an hour. These lakes are reached via narrow canals which link a total of 14 lakes in the Winter Haven area. On Lake Lulu you can glimpse the spring training home of the Cleveland Indians and on Lake Summit a section of Cypress Gardens that is open to the public only for special events.

Eating in "The Gardens"

Aside from the Dinner Cruises (described below), your dining choices here are strictly fast-food and strictly of the sweet and salty snack variety. All of these stands are conveniently located in or near the ski stadiums. Feel free to carry your snacks in to sustain you as you watch.

Baker's Dozen

This bakery and coffee shop is a place to stop for breakfast on the way into the park or to load up on goodies for the drive back to the motel or for tomorrow's in-room breakfast. Turnovers, muffins, Danish, and giant cookies are $2 to $3. You can also pick up Cypress Gardens' award-winning key lime pie by the slice or, better yet, pick up a whole pie for about $12. There are stools and a counter inside and shaded outdoor tables.

SuperCone

This ice cream parlor specializes in waffle cone sundaes with your choice of hot fudge, strawberry, or caramel topping for under $4. Chocolate-dipped cones are a bit more. There is also the usual range of beverages. A picture window lets you watch the ski show in air-conditioned comfort.

Lakeview Terrace

This stand is actually in the left ski stadium, up at the top of the stands. The featured snack here is a jumbo chocolate chip cookie ($3). Muffins, cookies, cotton candy, and soft pretzels are about the same price. There are a few small tables but most people eat in their seats.

Landings Snack Bar

Located between the right ski stadium and the boat landing, this snack bar features funnel cakes (fried dough) with powdered sugar ($3) or fruit ($3.50). Also on hand are cookies, strudel, and muffins, all for about $2, along with the usual array of beverages. Seating is outdoors at small tables with awnings.

Dinner Cruises

The Southern Breeze paddlewheeler turns restaurant at night offering dinner cruises with a view. Cruises take place daily from October to May and on Friday, Saturday, and Sunday the rest of the year. Since there aren't any four-star restaurants to rush off to, it makes a nice way to end your day at Cypress Gardens.

The food is served buffet style in the narrow confines of the Southern Breeze's lower deck. Typically three meat courses are offered — prime rib au jus, chicken, or fish — with all the trimmings. You are called by table to serve yourself, but servers are on hand to bring you drinks and dessert. The food is plentiful and, considering the setting, very reasonably priced. Dinner cruises are $30 for adults and $15 for children 6 to 12. On Sundays at about 1:30 p.m., there is a brunch cruise costing $20 for adults and $12 for kids. Monday night is Country Night and the regular menu gives way to barbecued chicken and ribs. Reservations are required. Call (800) 282-2123, ext. 45.

Shopping in "The Gardens"

There's really only one shop in "The Gardens." That is Resort Wear. All the other shops described here are in the entrance arcade, before you get to the ticket booths. So you can visit them without paying admission to the park.

Resort Wear/My Gallery II

At Resort Wear you'll find an extensive selection of t-shirts, polos, and sweats in a variety of styles, patterns, and colors, from kiddie models at about $10 to more elaborate adult styles for about $40. Most are in the $14 to $20 range. There is also a goodly selection of ladies swim wear and a variety of straw hats for both men and women. A portion of the shop is given over to a display of work by local Florida artists. Prices on these pieces range from about $50 to several hundred dollars. These artists would probably be classified as amateur, but if you find a piece you like, the prices are very attractive.

Bazaar Gift Shop

Perhaps the largest gift shop at the park, the Bazaar focuses on items that feature the Cypress Gardens name and logo on every imaginable surface, from shot glasses to t-shirts. There's also a kids' section and a nice assortment of collectible figurines and wall hangings. You will find some beautifully elaborate old-fashioned dolls with prices to match.

Photo Memories

This photo shop, with a small collection of period costumes, sells film and frames and also offers "olde time" photos. Its main business, however, is providing the photographic support for the **Junior Belle Program** (see below).

Sweet Creations

This is a standard-issue candy store featuring eight varieties of fudge ($4 for half a pound), honey, and an assortment of candies ($5 a pound).

Crystal Etc.

Small, delicate glass sculptures and other decorative objects are featured in this shop. Prices start at about $10 and go up from there.

Southern Crossroads

At the South end of the park, Southern Crossroads evokes a make-believe antebellum Southland that probably never existed in quite this quaint a form. The long promenade (which dead-ends at the park's southern extremity) is accented by flowers and shaded by oaks dripping theatrically in Spanish moss. Off this central corridor is artfully arranged a collection of shops, restaurants, and entertainments in gracious white clapboard buildings. The area is actually quite compact, yet it seems wonderfully spacious and contains a multiplicity of things to see and do.

The following attractions are described in roughly the order in which you will encounter them as you walk through Southern Crossroads:

The Palace: "Skate The States"

Rating: ★ ★ ★ +
Type: Ice show
Time: 25 minutes
Kelly says: Glitzy and fun

The Palace evokes an old Southern playhouse, complete with faux marble columns at the entrance. Inside is an 800-seat auditorium with a standard proscenium stage. The stage area has been converted into an ice rink but, given the shallowness of the performing area, some compromises have been made. Don't expect the electrifying leaps you may have seen in other ice shows where the skaters have the advantage of larger arenas.

That being said, the Russian performers who grace this show do the most with the space available as they present this rousing tribute to the good ol' USA. After a poetic ballet under black light that features a skater who goes airborne thanks to a harness, the show takes us on a whirlwind tour of the states with each vignette serving as an excuse for another display of skating grace and athleticism.

First stop is the international gateway city of Miami (although why they chose the ghastly rap accompaniment is beyond me). From there it's off to New Mexico for some fiery juggling and baton twirling, to Detroit for a salute to Motown and to Hollywood for a hymn to show biz razzle dazzle. The show also evokes a New York City complete with derelicts and purse snatchers (Wait'll Michael Bloomberg hears about this!) before visiting Broadway for a "Chorus Line" reprise. It all ends in the nation's capital with a rousing finale to the strains of "God Bless America."

To top it all off, the designers have contributed some lovely costumes and exciting visual effects. *Skate the States* performs about four shows a day. If this sort of thing appeals, check the schedule to make sure you don't miss it.

Wings of Wonder

Rating: ★ ★ ★ ★ +
Type: Butterfly-filled conservatory
Time: Continuous viewing
Kelly says: One of Cypress Gardens' best

What an inspired idea this is! Build a 5,500 square foot Victorian style glass conservatory and run a stream through it. Keep the glass walls and roof sparkling clean. Plant the conservatory with the kinds of trees, plants, and flowers that butterflies love. Then fill the space with over 1,000 free-flying butterflies, exotic waterfowl, and a few iguanas.

The result is pure enchantment and an experience that will reward patient viewing. The more you look, the more butterflies you will see. Some of them are so ingeniously camouflaged, it may be many minutes before you realize they are there at all. A looping path takes you through this wonderland, past babbling waterfalls and quiet ponds as butterflies flutter all about you. At the back, you can see butterflies in the pupal stage, just before they emerge in all their splendor; with a bit of luck, you may see one break through to the light. Somewhere between 700 and 1,000 butterflies are hatched each week in this fashion to keep the conservatory well stocked.

Plantation Gardens

Rating: ★ ★ ★
Type: Formal gardens
Time: Continuous viewing
Kelly says: Best for serious gardeners

Past *Wings of Wonder* a large open area with a stunning view of the lake has been set aside to showcase themed formal gardens. The **butterfly garden** has been designed to attract the local species. The **herb and scent garden** invites you to touch, rub, and taste. If you've never seen a vegetable in the wild, you may spot one of your favorites in the **vegetable garden**. The **rose garden** offers another chance to display this perennial favorite. Looking back you will have a lovely view of Magnolia Mansion (see "Shopping in Southern Crossroads," below). Or stroll across the lush green lawn to the lake's edge, a spot rarely visited by guests.

Crossroads Gazebo

Rating: ★ ★ +
Type: Live solo entertainers
Time: About 20 minutes per show
Kelly says: Hit or miss

The gazebo in question is a small structure in the middle of the Southern Crossroads promenade. Here, about every hour throughout the afternoon, earnest young singers accompanied by a synthesized rhythm section attempt to entertain an audience of resting seniors old enough to be their grandparents. It's got to be the toughest job in show business.

Carousel Cove

Rating:	★ ★ ★
Type:	Kiddie rides
Time:	As long as you (and junior) can stand
Kelly says:	Head here with squirmy kids

You enter *Carousel Cove* near the *Crossroads Gazebo*. On your right is the colorful carousel with its gaily painted wooden horses. The gaudy carousel seems to appeal to kids up to about 10 or 11. The other rides are standard mechanical amusement park rides for the toddler set and will probably seem déclassé to anyone much over five. At the very back of *Carousel Cove* is a regular old playground with a climb-up, crawl-through, slide-down structure in wood and plastic, a welcome refuge for tired moms and dads (or grandparents) with active kids.

Wacky Water Park

Rating:	★ ★ ★ ★
Type:	A seasonal mini-water park for young kids
Time:	As long as you want
Kelly says:	One of Cypress Gardens' most popular spots

Here's another of Cypress gardens' great ideas. Into the underutilized *Carousel Cove* area, Cypress Gardens plopped a scaled-down, kid-sized version of a water park. The result is that this has quickly become the only part of the park that regularly boasts crowds.

There are two parts of this park within a park. Near the entrance is a shallow round wading pool that slopes from zero depth at the edge to about two feet in the middle, where a rocky tropical island serves as a base for two tiny water slides. A lifeguard stands watch, while a sign warns "No Rock Climbing!" Around the perimeter of the pool, three animal-themed stations squirt and spray water and invite little ones to play.

At the back, arrayed along a small artificial hill, are a series of water slides that all spill into a common pool at the hill's base. To the left, a broad blue flume takes a lazy dogleg into the pool, while in the center twin white slides head straight down. It's the closest *Wacky Water* gets to a "speed slide" and kids like to race one another to the bottom. Also in the middle is a U-shaped slide, two-thirds of which is a covered tube.

The largest slide, Typhoon Twister, is on the right. It has a higher starting point than the others and after a slow curve it corkscrews quickly to the bottom. This one uses inflatable tubes, small ones for those under 48 inches and larger and double ones for taller people. From beneath Typhoon Twister, a smaller slide heads straight to the water with two small drops along the way.

There is nothing too extreme here and all slides end in a narrow "slow-down" lane that prevents anyone from getting dunked in the shallow pool. My guess is that the park will seem pretty tame to any kid over 11. Of course, that leaves a lot of kids (plus their parents and grandparents) who will think the park is just great.

Lockers and simple changing facilities (no showers, sinks, or toilets) are provided in the arcade area just outside the *Wacky Water Park* entrance gate. Lockers rent for $6.18 and $3 of that is returned when you bring back the key. Picnic tables with umbrellas fill the spaces around the wading pool and the water slides and many families bring food. A small refreshment stand at the entrance sells soft drinks and slushies ($2) along with candy bars and cookies ($1).

This is a seasonal attraction, open weekends in April and then daily from May 1 to September 30.

Cypress Junction

Rating:	★ ★ ★ ★
Type:	Model railroad exhibit
Time:	Continuous viewing
Kelly says:	A treat for the model railroad buff

Maintained by a volunteer staff of locals, the HO-gauge train set on display here is one of the nicest I've seen. Others may be larger or have more trains, or more "miles" of track, or more levels and tunnels and switchbacks, but surely there are few that are as exquisitely designed as this. Especially enthralling are some of the smaller touches, like the airliner flying past the thunderstorm (complete with thunder and lightning). The trains travel through "six identifiable areas of the United States" beginning in what looks like Miami Beach, visiting the Southwest and Chicago before ending in the "mountains of Maine." Be sure to pick up the one-page flyer in the small wooden box near the entrance for all the facts and figures on this astonishing labor of love.

Kodak's Island in the Sky

Rating:	★ ★ ★ ★
Type:	Aerial platform ride
Time:	5 minutes
Kelly says:	A too-short bird's eye view

Tucked away behind Magnolia Mansion is a 370-ton counterbalance which is used to loft a circular platform 153 feet in the air (roughly 16 stories high), where it rotates to give its passengers a panoramic view of Cypress Gardens and Lake Eloise. Off in the distance, you can see the silhouette of stately Bok Tower, 11 miles away (see *Chapter 15*). Seating is single-file around the edge of the platform and once the platform is airborne, you can stand and move to the rail for a better look.

This is a fun way to get another perspective on the park, and the lofty vantage point offers photographers many wonderful **photo ops**. At five minutes from start to finish, this ride is a bit too short for my taste, but it's free and you can ride as often as you wish (or until your film runs out). The location of this attraction and the mobile platform itself have been cleverly hidden behind trees and buildings. You can see the raised platform from elsewhere in the park, but you could spend all day in Southern Crossroads and never suspect it was there.

Antique Radio Museum

Rating:	★ ★
Type:	Exhibit
Time:	Continuous viewing
Kelly says:	A blast from grandpa's past

This hodgepodge display of old radios and radio components will probably appeal most to people who will experience a wave of nostalgia when they see the very console on which they listened to FDR's fireside chats or the old crystal set on which they heard news of the Hindenberg disaster. I had that very experience with a snazzy 1950s plastic Westinghouse table model on which I heard the first, seminal chords of rock and roll. For younger visitors these may be the first radios they've seen outside a car or a Walkman.

Cypress Roots

Rating:	★ ★ +
Type:	Exhibit
Time:	Continuous viewing
Kelly says:	Cypress Gardens memorabilia, and worth a peek

This small exhibit houses bits and pieces of Cypress Garden's family album, everything from vintage water skis to a "celebrity wall" of stars who have visited (there's a key in case you don't recognize Tiny Tim). A vintage television console plays clips from movies and TV shows that were shot at Cypress Gardens. Photos and newspaper clippings provide a fascinating, if somewhat spotty, history of Cypress Gardens and its founder's prodigious penchant for publicity.

Check out one of Dick Pope's gaudy sports jackets, a flowered model looking like it was cut from upholstery fabric. Pope explained his eye-popping sartorial style by pointing out that he was a short man. Unless he dressed conspicuously, he claimed, people might mistake him for "a short fire plug."

Gardens Theatre: Mystical Magic

Rating:	★ ★ ★
Type:	Magic show
Time:	25 minutes
Kelly says:	Neat tricks and easygoing humor

It's the standard magic show formula: a personable magician performing card tricks, plucking coins from the air, and doing odd things to his lovely blonde assistant in strange looking metal contraptions, but this act is a cut or two above the usual standard.

Fred, the magician, is charming company and he keeps up a running patter that has the audience chuckling happily through his act. His assistant Kelly (no relation) handles her much smaller role with aplomb. Most important, the tricks are clever and original — I can't remember seeing any of them performed elsewhere — and extremely well executed. The show and the tricks change from time to time, just to keep things fresh.

FloraDome

Rating:	★ ★ ★
Type:	Floral display
Time:	As long as you wish
Kelly says:	A feast for the green-thumb set

The spirit of the original gardens comes to Southern Crossroads in this over the top display of seasonal flowers accented with fountains, pools, waterfalls, and babbling brooks.

Starting in March, the *FloraDome* serves up luscious and lavish displays of begonias and fuchsia in more colors than you thought possible. This is followed in May with a summer show highlighting impatiens, ferns, and mosses. July and August features caladiums and exotic Siam tulip gingers.

In fall, the display turns to hauntingly beautiful orchids and bromeliads. Rounding out the year is the Poinsettia Festival mentioned earlier under Special Events. Those who lovingly tend windowsill, sun porch, or backyard gardens will be enchanted. Those who never bother to stop and smell the flowers may be convinced to do so here.

Nature's Way

Rating:	★ ★ +
Type:	Small zoo
Time:	Continuous viewing
Kelly says:	Worth a stroll-through en route to the shows in *Nature's Theatre*

This vest-pocket zoo is tucked away in a corner of the park under an attractively shaded canopy of moss-draped oaks. Most animals are held in roughly circular sunken pits, eliminating the need for bars.

Most of the animals are Florida natives (although there is a growing collection of "exotic" animals such as rheas, emus, and wallabies). Best of all are the injured birds of prey for which Cypress Gardens cares; some of them appear in the presentations in *Nature's Theatre* (see below). There is also a magnificent Indian rock python, all 17 feet and 225 pounds of him.

Along the shores of Lake Eloise you will find **Nature's Boardwalk**, a charming area offering a chance to feed the emus and such (50 cents for a small handful of food pellets) and delightful views across the lake. Then you can toss turkey franks to five-foot alligators and gawk at Mighty Mike, a stunning 13-foot specimen in **Gator Gulch**. Also in this area is the **Birdwalk Aviary**, a walk-in exhibit of birds and a few tiny Muntjac, or barking, deer. The big draw here are the chattering, multi-hued lorys and lorikeets which you can feed ($1.50).

With the possible exception of the python, you can see more, larger, and better displayed specimens elsewhere in the Orlando area. Still, this makes a pleasant time-killer as you wait for the nature shows to begin.

Nature's Theatre: "Calling All Animals"

Rating:	★ ★ ★
Type:	Nature show
Time:	15 minutes
Kelly says:	Too short

Nature's Theatre is a simple tarp-covered amphitheater that serves as the venue for a series of educational nature shows hosted by Cypress Gardens' staff members, who show off some of their more intriguing charges. Check the schedule for show times.

Exactly what you will see is hard to predict, but generally the show includes at least one raptor, such as a horned owl or red-tailed hawk. The raptors are Cypress Gardens' lineup of injured birds of prey that can never be released back to the wild and are living out their lives in the comfort and security of the Gardens. They earn their room and board by posing for your photos during this informative presentation. You may also see macaws, baby alligators, and a snake or two. For each animal, the handlers present a fascinating sampler of natural history tidbits. Some of the critters are paraded in front of the audience for those who wish to touch or take close-up photos.

The reptile portion features the show's true star, an albino Indian rock python with the rather cruel nickname "Banana Boy." The snake retains the camouflage markings of his species but with a pronounced yellow hue. It's a beautiful animal.

On The Wild Side

Rating: ★ ★ ★
Type: Tour
Time: 30 to 45 minutes
Kelly says: A treat for animal lovers

After each presentation at *Nature's Theatre*, a limited number of people (15) can take a backstage guided tour of the Nature's Way Research Center. In some ways, the tour is a repeat of the theater presentation, except you get a better view and are more closely involved with the animals. You will get to feed and perhaps handle some of the adorable little critters, including tortoises, possums, gators, and even a pygmy marmoset. Photos are allowed and this is a great chance to get some terrific shots of your kids. The length of the tour is determined to some extent by the curiosity of the group; more questions means a longer tour. There is an extra charge for this special experience, but at $3 for adults and $2 for kids, it is modest.

Eating in Southern Crossroads

While "The Gardens" offers only snacks, Southern Crossroads offers more substantial fare. Here you will find a small but good selection of eateries. I describe them in roughly the order you encounter them on entering this section of the park.

Crossroads Restaurant & Terrace

What: Full-service restaurant with lovely terrace
Where: Near entrance to Southern Crossroads
Price Range: $$ - $$$

This is Cypress Gardens' only full-service restaurant and, given its moderate pricing, it shouldn't disappoint. The interior decor is simple and tasteful but, on a fine day, the better choice is to dine al fresco. The tree-shaded outdoor Terrace overlooks the International Gardens area where the seasonal flower festivals are held. Overhead fans keep the air circulating. All in all, it's a perfectly delightful dining experience.

The food may not win any awards (the exception is noted below), but it is fresh and attractively presented in generous portions at modest prices. Among the appetizers, the sumptuous basket of light and feathery Diablo onion rings ($4) and the seafood stuffed mushroom caps ($5) are good choices.

Entrees are in the $9 to $10 range and include standbys like carved roast beef au jus and roast turkey. I particularly liked the creamy chicken in puff pastry and the Alpine chicken with cheese and mushrooms. All entrees come with a small side salad and a choice of french fries or rice pilaf. Main course salads — chicken, seafood, and tuna — are $8 or $9, as are the sandwiches, which include Cypress Gardens' version of a club sandwich, a French dip sandwich, and the usual burgers.

The desserts ($2 to $3) are special. In fact, the key lime pie was chosen as the best in the region by a local newspaper. Treat yourself to a dessert on the Terrace.

Carousel Ice Cream

What:　　　Ice cream stand
Where:　　At entrance to *Carousel Cove*
Price Range:　$

A basic walk-up ice cream stand dispensing cones and floats in the $3 range, along with the usual range of beverages.

Cypress BBQ

What:　　　Fast-food BBQ
Where:　　In the plaza near the *Crossroads Gazebo*
Price Range:　$$

Barbecue ribs and chicken (about $7 to $8) are the featured items here. The BBQ is quite good actually, although the takeout style presentation doesn't tend to raise one's expectations. Key lime pie is also available here at about $2.50 the slice.

Service is fast-food style at a walk-up window and the eating area is largely out of doors. Time your meal to one of the regular shows at the *Crossroads Gazebo* and you can be entertained as you eat.

Ice Cream Parlor

What:　　　Ice cream specialties
Where:　　Near *Island in the Sky*
Price Range:　$

Delicious, homemade, deep-dish fruit cobblers with ice cream are the specialty here, along with the usual sundaes, for about $4. There is very little indoor seating available.

Village Fare Food Court

What: Selection of fast-food windows
Where: Near exit of *Island in the Sky*
Price Range: $$

Village Fare is a large circular eatery with a semicircular array of fast-food windows along the back wall. The number of windows operating at any given time is a function of the crowds the park is drawing.

Choices range from deli sandwiches, to roast beef or fried chicken dinners, to burger platters and baskets with fries. The typical main course will run about $6 to $7. Beer is served here for about $3, along with the usual array of soft drinks.

Shopping in Southern Crossroads

The shops in Southern Crossroads are less cluttered with Cypress Gardens souvenirs than one might expect. Instead, there is a nice selection of craft-type gifts and gardening paraphernalia, along with some more touristy fare.

Ole Woodcutter

This small shop specializes in die-cut wooden names. You have your choice of plain ($6) or mirror-coated ($11) wood. Names mounted on themed wooden backgrounds cost up to $45.

The Bear Bungalow

There is a bewildering variety of teddy bears on display here, from simple little bears, to elaborately dressed up Southern Belle bears, to truly humongous bears that will dwarf a small child. Prices range from about $12 all the way up to about $350. Also available are bear figurines and bear prints.

Cracker Creek

Across the street is this laser version of an old-fashioned shooting gallery. About a dozen laser rifles are pointed toward targets arrayed around Aunt Fanny's Cabin, a dilapidated backwoods Florida shack, complete with moonshine still. You can test your skill for $1 in quarters. A change machine is available.

Butterfly Shop

Located at the exit to *Wings of Wonder*, this shop is impossible to miss. Not surprisingly, the theme is butterflies. There are butterfly stickers, pins, magnets, books, t-shirts, jewelry, even a little motorized butterfly that will flutter tirelessly around your potted plants.

Magnolia Mansion

Since Magnolia Mansion evokes a Tara-like antebellum mansion, it is perhaps fitting that it is devoted entirely to *Gone With The Wind* souvenirs and memorabilia. One room contains a private collection, but most of what you see here is for sale, everything from $2 bumper stickers that say "Frankly my dear, I don't give a damn" to $200 dolls decked out in southern finery. GWTW fans will probably enjoy this; others may find it plain silly.

Legend of Santa Claus

Far more interesting than this shop of Christmas-related merchandise is the walk-through exhibit that leads into it. Using ten life-sized mannequins, the display traces the origins of Santa Claus, from St. Nicholas, the fourth century "boy bishop" of Myra in Asia Minor, to the jolly old elf we know today. It's an interesting survey of how numerous folk and religious beliefs from Siberia, Russia, and central Europe coalesced to create a popular contemporary commercial myth. The merchandise on sale is not half bad either. Most of the stuff here, from carved wooden statuettes to stuffed dolls, has a country crafts feel to it that's rather charming.

Junior Belle Boutique

This is headquarters for the **Junior Belle Program**, a brilliant gimmick of which Dick Pope would have most assuredly approved. For $47.62 (tax included) you can have your daughter dolled up and dressed just like one of Cypress Garden's *real* Southern Belles, complete with a pint-sized parasol, for a two-hour stroll through the park grounds and a free photograph. Perfect! Cypress Gardens gets more adorable atmosphere and you pay for it! On top of that, they give you a press kit to send to your local newspaper along with a picture of your little angel, the perfect Pope touch.

Cynicism aside, the results are absolutely adorable and you might find it hard to resist. In fact, the program has proved so popular that it is now open to "girls of all ages," Moms and Grandmoms included, at the same price. Annual passholders receive a 10% discount. Call (863) 324-2111, ext. 300, to make a reservation. You can also ask them about ordering custom made Junior Belle dresses, but sit down while you do — prices start at $250.

Historical Research, Inc.

This shop is one outlet in an international chain with over 500 locations. For about $18 their computer will spit out a history of your family name on acid-free paper in ink that will not fade in the light. You can gussy it up with framing and a variety of coats of arms if you wish. If you can't rein in your family pride, you can easily spend several hundred dollars here.

CHAPTER FIVE:

Gatorland

Those born during World War II or earlier, may remember the roadside attractions that dotted the tourist landscape. Half carnival sideshow, half shanty town, these entrepreneurial "attractions" served as living proof of Mencken's maxim that "no one ever went broke underestimating the taste of the American public." Trading on actual freaks of nature ("See the two-headed calf!") or objects of less certain provenance ("Mummified Indian chief!"), the typical roadside attraction tended to spread incrementally along the highway as the owner figured out new ways to lure the passing parade of cars with stranger wonders or larger souvenir shops featuring the latest in joy buzzers and whoopee cushions. Each year, it seemed, the advertising budget would finance a few more garish billboards, a few more miles away, until tourists knew hundreds of miles in advance that something extraordinary lay ahead. The old roadside attractions were a blight on the landscape. They were tacky, lowbrow, often smelly, and altogether marvelous. They represent one of the most cherished memories of my youth and I wish they were still around.

At Gatorland, they still are — in a way. Gatorland is a modern and evolving nature-themed attraction. It is well-run, clean, and in spite of the 5,000 alligators crammed into its 110 acres, remarkably smell free. But its roots are firmly in the roadside attraction tradition. In fact, that's how it started out back in 1949.

Owen Godwin was a local cattle rancher — Florida was once America's second-biggest cattle producer, after Texas — who decided to turn a liability into an asset. Alligators were the Florida cattleman's nemesis. They would hunker down in water holes and kill unsuspecting calves. This intolerable loss of income prompted a vendetta against the gator, and cattlemen became adept at capturing and killing the scaly predators. Godwin realized not only that there was a market for the hides and meat of the gators he killed but that few of the tourists who whizzed past on highway 441 had ever seen an alligator and might pay for the privilege. So Godwin rounded up some gators and a passel of the snakes that thronged his property and the "Snake & Reptile Village" was born, beckoning to the southbound tourist traffic. Even today, in spite of Orlando's phenomenal post-Mickey growth, Gatorland's location seems a bit out of the way. In 1949, it really must have seemed in the middle of nowhere.

Gatorland has come a long way since its early days, not so much in its look and feel as in its focus and attitude. For a while Godwin followed the pattern of many roadside attractions. As he prospered, he traveled farther afield, adding "exotic" animals to his collection. Those days are past and only a few holdovers from that era remain.

For many years, Gatorland was a working alligator "farm," sending over 1,000 gators to market each year. So successful was the Gatorland model that it sparked a renaissance in alligator farming across the American south. So Gatorland phased out its farming operation to concentrate on the zoological side of the operation and the conservation of Florida species. Gatorland is also a partner with the University of Florida in alligator research and is the only place on earth where alligators are bred through artificial insemination.

Compared to the big attractions in town — Disney, Universal, and Sea-World — Gatorland is downright modest. Many of the exhibits are made of simple cinder block construction painted white and green, and I'm sure the appearance of much of the park hasn't changed a whole lot since the sixties. Rather than a being a drawback, I find this homey quality to be a large part of Gatorland's charm. If you don't come with exaggerated expectations fueled by Hollywood scenic artists and are willing to accept the park on its own low-key terms, you won't be disappointed.

Before You Come

There is no pressing need to do in-depth research prior to a visit, but if you'd like to check prices or hours you can call Gatorland at (800) 393-5297 or (407) 855-5496. The web site is www.gatorland.com.

When's the Best Time to Come?

Even at the height of the tourist seasons, Gatorland will be far less mobbed than the larger attractions. The best time to visit, then, is dictated more by the patterns of the animals than those of the people who come to see them.

Alligators are cold blooded and derive their warmth from the sun and surrounding atmosphere. Thus, in the winter they tend to be slow moving and sluggish, not that they're particularly lively in the best of circumstances. April and May is breeding time and if you visit then you will be entertained by the bellowing of amorous males attracting their mates. It sounds a bit like a lovesick Harley if you can imagine such a thing. Alligators lay hard-shelled eggs in nests on the ground. So by June you may be able to see nests in the *Alligator Breeding Marsh*. The hatchlings emerge in late August and early September, when visitors will be treated with dozens of joyous events in the **Gator Grunts Nursery**. Birds have their own migratory and mating patterns. Nesting in the *Breeding Marsh* begins in January or February, hits its peak in April and May, and continues through the summer, as various species arrive to hatch and raise their young.

Regardless of when you come, don't arrive too late in the day. If you arrive mid-afternoon, you may miss some of the shows.

Getting There

Gatorland is located at 14501 South Orange Blossom Trail, also known as US Routes 441, 17, and 92, in the southern fringes of Orlando. It is seven miles south of the Florida Mall and 3.5 miles north of US 192 in Kissimmee. To reach Gatorland from I-4, take either the Bee Line Expressway (SR 538) or Central Florida Parkway east to Orange Blossom Trail and turn right.

Gatorland will be on your left as you drive south, made prominent by its trademark alligator jaws entrance. There is parking for about 500 cars, which gives you an indication of the size of the crowds they expect. Parking is free and all spaces are a short walk from the entrance.

Opening and Closing Times

Gatorland is open from 9:00 a.m. until dusk. In winter that means until 6:00 p.m., in spring and fall 7:00 p.m., and in summer 8:00 p.m. The park, which is largely out of doors, operates rain or shine, 365 days a year.

The Price of Admission

At press time, admission prices (including tax) were as follows:

Adults:	$19.01
Children (3 to 12):	$8.99

Annual passes are $30.72 and $16.94 (tax included), for adults and kids, respectively. You can upgrade to the annual pass before leaving the park on the day of your visit. If you think you will return within a year, this is a good deal. I suspect it will appeal most to bird watchers and nature photography buffs, who will find plenty to keep them occupied at various times of the year. Gatorland's annual pass is good only for admission to the park. It does not give you a discount on food or at the gift shop, nor does it allow you to bring in guests at a discount.

Discounts

Members of AAA, CAA (the Canadian Automobile Association), AARP, and the military receive a 20% discount on admission. These discounts cannot be combined with any dollars-off coupons.

Good Things to Know About . . .

Access for the Disabled

The entire park is accessible to the disabled (with the exception of the third level of the Observation Tower in the *Alligator Breeding Marsh*) and wheelchairs are available on a rental basis for $3.71 (plus tax) per day, plus a $10 refundable deposit.

Babies

Strollers are available on the same terms as those for wheelchairs. Diaper changing facilities will be found in all restrooms.

Leaving the Park

When you pay your admission, your hand will be stamped with a gator symbol. It allows you to leave (for lunch perhaps?) and return on the same day.

Money

An ATM hooked up to the Cirrus, Plus, AFFN, and Honor systems is located in the gift shop.

Safety

Alligators may look like they never move a muscle but they can move with surprising speed when a meal is in the offing. And to an alligator your toddler looks an awful lot like lunch. The railings over the alligator lake have been fitted with green mesh guards to discourage leaning over the sides. Nonetheless, I have seen people lift their children onto the railings and lean them over for a closer look or to help them feed the gators.

DON'T DO THIS! You will not only give people like me heart failure but if your child wriggles loose and falls he or she could very well be killed.

Special Diets

Gatorland's eateries are not equipped to handle special diets. However,

Gatorland welcomes picnickers, so feel free to bring your own meals. In fact, feel free to bring an entire cooler. There are several nice areas to eat your own meals; just ask a park employee. No alcoholic beverages are permitted and Gatorland requests that you do not bring any glass containers into the park.

Swamp Thing: Your (Half) Day at Gatorland

Gatorland has trademarked the phrase "Orlando's best half-day attraction." That seems about right to me. Many people stay for a shorter period and it's doubtful you will stay longer unless you are an ardent bird watcher or a wildlife photographer willing to wait for that perfect shot. In any event, you can take your time here. There is never any need to rush madly from place to place to avoid long lines or crushing crowds.

As I mentioned before, Gatorland is modest in both scale and execution. Unlike the bigger parks, it's not filled with attendants and hosts; you are pretty much on your own, although you can certainly feel free to collar one of the "gator wranglers" with your questions. These guys take turns wrestling gators, handling deadly snakes, and allowing themselves to be hunted by hungry crocs. They are knowledgeable, charming, and maybe just a little nuts. They are one of Gatorland's major assets. You will recognize them by their distinctive swamp explorers' outfits that grow wetter and sweatier and dirtier as the day wears on.

The park is an elongated rectangle divided lengthwise into three main parts. The first is a huge alligator-clogged lake that stretches the entire length of the park. When you enter the park from the Gift Shop after paying your admission you step onto a large wooden platform over this lake. The platform is honeycombed with open areas filled with sunbathing and swimming gators. One of these openings is the site of the *Gator Jumparoo* show, Gatorland's signature attraction. Also on this platform is a space set aside for children's birthday parties.

Across the wooden platform, you will find *Alligator Alley*, the second major area of the park. It is a long, narrow, shaded concrete walkway that runs north and south through the middle of the park. It is instantly recognizable by the wavy, blue-green, snake-like line down its middle. Along this walkway you will find a variety of displays, animal pens, and scientific work areas, as well as (at the southern end) the *Gator Wrestlin'* arena and Pearl's Smokehouse.

On the other side of *Alligator Alley* is the third major area, a 10-acre *Alli-*

gator Breeding Marsh, with its wooden walkway and Observation Tower, and behind that the crocodile exhibits. The *Swamp Walk*, reached through a gate at the south end of the park, comprises a separate fourth area.

The Half-Day Stay

When you pay your admission you will be given a sheet of paper with a Gatorland map on one side and a schedule of the day's shows on the other. Check to see the starting time of the next show. If you have more than half an hour before show time, spend it gawking at the huge gators in the main pool. This should whet your appetite for what's to come.

Your first order of business should be the live shows. It doesn't much matter in which order you see them. You may want to consider seeing the wrestling show twice. In between shows, you can check out the smaller exhibits dotted along the spine of the park.

Give yourself at least 20 uninterrupted minutes or more to take in the *Alligator Breeding Marsh and Bird Sanctuary*, more if it's nesting season. You'll probably want to spend some time at the highest level of the **Observation Tower** for a great bird's-eye view and then take a leisurely stroll along the water level walkway for a closer look. The *Swamp Walk* is restful but not a must-see unless you're a bird watcher. Remember to bring along your binoculars for a closer look at the wildlife.

Attractions at Gatorland

There are four live shows at Gatorland, each presented several times a day, and they form the heart of the Gatorland experience. The shows let us get close — but not too close — to critters that alternately fascinate and repel us. Since alligators, crocodiles, and other reptiles are a natural source of curiosity for most of us, it's easy for these shows to jump right in and start answering our unasked questions about these scaly creatures. The result is that staple of the modern-day theme park: effortless "edutainment."

A group of about five young men, all Florida natives, takes turns starring in these exhibitions. They have mastered an easy, laid back, aw-shucks, country boy style that is most ingratiating. The humor — and there's lots of it — is self-deprecating while at the same time letting us city slickers know who's got the really cool job. These guys are the living embodiment of Gatorland and I think you'll find it hard not to like them.

Gator Jumparoo

Rating: ★ ★ ★ ★
Type: Outdoor show

Time: 15 minutes
Kelly says: As close as it gets to performing alligators

This show is simplicity itself. The scene is a large open square in the wooden platform over the alligator lagoon. A walkway leads to a small platform in the middle where our host stands and dangles plucked chicken halves from a metal cable over the shallow waters below. The audience stands at a railing along the sides of this watery alligator pit.

Alerted by the clanging of a large bell, mammoth gators swim lazily into view. Slowly, they zero in on the morsels over their heads. They begin to lunge upwards at the bait, urged on by cheers from the crowd. Alligators jump by curling their tails on the shallow bottom and thrusting upwards. A successful leap is something to see and will make a great snapshot for the photographer with good timing.

One thing this show teaches is that alligators are none too bright. They have brains the size of a lima bean (about the size of the tip of your thumb, the host tells us, knowing perhaps that we are probably as familiar with vegetables in the wild as we are with gators). Their aim is none too good either. They regularly seem to over- or undershoot their targets.

After the gators have snared the half chickens, the host ups the ante by grabbing whole chickens and hand feeding them to the now-excited gators. The thick leather belt around his waist, attached to a thick chain, ensures that while a gator might get an arm, the rest of the host will be spared.

This show appeals to some of our most primordial fascinations with animals and it's an appeal that's hard to deny. Most people find this show very entertaining. Precisely how exciting the show is will depend to some extent on when you visit. During the cooler months, alligators tend to be sluggish. Under optimum conditions, the gators leap lustily, flashing their pale undersides and gaping maws as they snare lunch.

The best seats in the house. First of all, there are no seats, just a railing. If you're not in the first row, your view will be somewhat impaired. The best view is to be found along the side directly facing the small gazebo in which the host stands. Arrive about ten minutes early to secure a spot by the rail.

Gator Wrestlin'

Rating: ★ ★ ★ ★ ★
Type: Outdoor show
Time: 15 minutes
Kelly says: Best show at Gatorland

Gatorland's best show takes place in an open-air arena next to Pearl's Smokehouse. Covered bleachers face a sunken sandy platform surrounded by a small moat and a raised border which (we hope) keeps the gators from getting out. Twelve gators, about seven or eight feet long, lie on the sand sunning themselves.

This is a two-man show. Ostensibly one is the host and the other the gator wrangler but I suspect the second man is there in case the wrangler gets in trouble. This show is obviously for real and there's no disguising the fact that it's hard work. ("I never finished school," the wrangler says. "So you kids out there study real hard or you might wind up doin' this.")

Alligator wrestling began, we are told, as a matter of necessity. Alligators would hide in water holes and take the occasional calf. The cattle boss would order the hands to get that gator out. Their courage bolstered by a little moonshine, the ranch hands would oblige. Eventually, the practice became a competitive sport that gave young men a chance to show off their courage and prowess. Which is exactly what happens in this show.

The show begins with the wrangler kicking the gators off their sunny perch into the moat. They hiss their annoyance. Then a kid picked from the audience carefully picks out the biggest one for the wrangler to wrestle. Resigned to his fate, the wrangler drags the wriggling, hissing, and none too cooperative beast onto the sandy platform.

Along with an informative patter about alligators, often made breathless by the exertion of keeping a 150-pound gator motionless, the gator wrangler shows off a few of the tricks of the trade — like pulling back the gator's head and placing his chin across its closed jaws. Despite his assurance that it doesn't take much pressure to hold a gator's jaws closed, you respect and admire his gumption. At one point, the wrangler pries the gator's jaws apart to show us his teeth. "If this works, it's gonna make you a pretty nice little snapshot," he says and then adds with perfect backwoods sang froid, "If this don't work, it's gonna make you a pretty nice little snapshot."

Maybe there's less to wrestling gators than meets the eye, but I wouldn't bet on it. The casual machismo and sly good humor with which these fellows put their charges through their paces makes for a thoroughly entertaining 15 minutes. After the show, the stage area is mobbed with audience members eager to ask questions ("Didja ever get bit?") and shake the hand of someone with the guts to wrestle a gator.

Jungle Crocs Show

Rating:	★ ★ ★ ★ +
Type:	Outdoor show
Time:	15 minutes
Kelly says:	As unpredictable as its stars

The jungle crocs section (described below) has its own show, or perhaps I should say "shows." Each day a different species of croc is showcased and the main order of business is lunch, so the entertainment is something of a moveable feast. Which species is spotlighted on any given day is left up to the discretion of the keepers, so it's impossible to pick and choose which crocs you will see perform on the day you visit.

Crocodiles are more aggressive than alligators and when a snack is in the offing they move with startling rapidity. Much of the entertainment value of these shows comes from the awareness that the crocs are, in essence, hunting the gator wranglers who put themselves at some risk to feed the crocs while amusing us. Perhaps the most entertaining is Dundee, a humongous "saltie" or Australian salt water crocodile. The goal of this show is to get Dundee to stand up for his supper, revealing his considerable length and heft.

Tip: There are four separate show areas in the crocodile area, but only one of them (by the Cuban croc enclosure) has bleacher seats; all the others are standing room only. So it's a good idea to arrive early, ask a gator wrangler where the show will be, and stake out a good spot.

Up Close Encounters

Rating: ★ ★ ★ +
Type: Outdoor show
Time: 15 minutes
Kelly says: Poisonous snakes and other creepy-crawlies

If this show is less spectacular than the others, it probably has to do with the fact that while snakes may grow to be 12 feet long they never weigh much over six or seven pounds. Snakes, of course, have their own fascination, especially the ones on display here.

Actually, this show might more accurately be called Poisonous Snakes of Central Florida. The state is host to 69 species of snakes, of which only six are dangerous, of which only four are to be found in the Central Florida region around Gatorland. Which snakes are profiled in the show will depend on availability. The host meticulously takes visitors through his repertoire of both poisonous and nonpoisonous snakes (the yellow rat snake, we are told, makes an excellent pet). Most of the stars of the show are paraded in front of the audience, hanging decorously from a metal snake handler's hook. Sit in the front row if you'd like to get good photos.

Gatorland Express Railroad

Rating: ★ ★
Type: Swamp train ride
Time: 15 minutes
Kelly says: Easy intro to gator lore

The *Gatorland Express Railroad* leaves about every 20 minutes from a small station behind *Lily's Pad*. It's a scaled-down steam engine that takes you on a lazy loop circling the *Alligator Breeding Marsh* and crocodile exhibits (see below). While not the most exciting of experiences, it provides a painless introduction to Gatorland and alligator lore. There is, however, an additional $1 charge for this attraction, which is probably not worth it unless your kids insist. On the other hand, the charge lets you ride as often as you wish.

The engineer/narrator is a gator wrangler taking a break from his more strenuous chores at the live shows. He points out sights of interest along the route and fills you in on Gatorland's purpose and the range of its attractions. The train makes a stop by Pearl's Smokehouse, near the entrance to the *Jungle Crocs*; you can get off here but can't get on.

Alligator Breeding Marsh and Bird Sanctuary

Rating: ★ ★ ★ ★ +

Type: Observation platforms and walkways through a wildlife sanctuary

Time: As long as you wish

Kelly says: Bring your binoculars

This is one of Gatorland's more recent attractions and one of its most successful, in its own low-key way. The concept was ingenious: Build a natural setting in which some 100 female and 30 male alligators would feel free to do what comes naturally and provide a steady stream of new alligators to enthrall visitors and serve the growing market for gator meat and hides. But because birds like to nest over alligator holes for the protection they provide against predators like raccoons, opossum, snakes, and bobcats, Gatorland hoped for a bonus population of wild birds. They built it . . . and they came.

Today there are over 1,000 bird nests in active use at Gatorland. Here you will find the magnificent, bright white great egret with its majestic plumage alongside the more dowdy green and blue herons. There are also snowy egrets, cattle egrets, and tricolor egrets. With a bit of luck you might also spot an osprey perched high in a pine tree, surveying the alligator pool below and weighing his chances for a fish dinner.

The *Alligator Breeding Marsh* has three entrances. To the north near *Lilly's Pad* and to the south near Pearl's Smokehouse you can gain access to the wooden walkway that runs the length of the alligator lake. In the middle of the park is a bridge that takes you directly to the Observation Tower. Starting in June you will be able to see alligator nests, some remarkably close to the walkway. Shortly after the eggs have been laid, Gatorland staffers remove them to an incubator to insure hatching. Signs left behind document the date of laying and the number of eggs.

Large, shaded gazebos with wooden benches offer a chance to rest, relax, and contemplate the serenity of the preserve. It's hard to believe some of Florida's scariest critters are basking just feet from where you sit. You'll see plenty of gators from the walkway. They wallow in the mud, float almost submerged in the water, and sun themselves on logs and the opposite shore. But for a really great look, you'll want to climb the Observation Tower.

The **Observation Tower** is a three-story affair located in the center of the walkway. It is accessible from the walkway, of course, but you can also reach the second level via a bridge directly from the park's central spine. An elaborate zigzag ramp next to the bridge makes the tower's middle level accessible to wheelchairs.

If you brought binoculars to Florida, don't forget to bring them to Gatorland. Climb to the top level, where signs point out the direction and distance to major Florida landmarks. Look straight down at the alligator lake and you will see dozens of 10-footers clustered around the base of the platform.

Look across at the opposite shore and you will see more gators amid the foliage; the longer you look, the more you'll see. Look at the trees in spring and you will see dozens of egrets tending their nests. Look closer and you will see the drabber species well camouflaged amid the leaves. A quarter will get you a brief look through a telescope mounted on the railing but when a hawk appears in the high branches, the line gets long.

Jungle Crocs

Rating:	★ ★ ★ ★
Type:	Walk-by animal exhibit
Time:	Continuous viewing
Kelly says:	Come for the shows

It's not quite equal time but this exhibit gives the alligator's crocodilian cousins a chance to bask in the sun. Down a wooden walkway at the southern end of the *Alligator Breeding Marsh*, Gatorland has assembled one of the largest collections of crocodiles, which can be distinguished from alligators by their pointy snouts and snaggly, protruding teeth. There are saltwater crocs ("salties") from Australia and Southeast Asia, Nile Crocs from (where else?) the Nile, as well as a representative cross section of American and Cuban crocodiles.

Tip: It's best to time your visit to one of the regular feeding sessions. These critters are more active feeders than alligators and the sound of their two-inch teeth slamming down on 30 pounds of red meat is really something to hear.

Walkabout Tours

Rating:	★ ★ ★ ★

Type:	Guided tour
Time:	About 45 minutes
Kelly says:	The inside info from a gator expert

Twice a day, you can take a guided tour of Gatorland hosted by a knowledgeable animal expert. This is an excellent way to turn a visit to Gatorland into a genuine learning experience for your kids (not to mention yourself). The guide fills you in on gator lore and Gatorland history. A feeding may be included and the tour concludes with an encounter with a baby gator, which is remarkably strong considering its small size.

There is an additional charge for this tour, but the $6.36, including tax, seems quite reasonable to me. If you'd like to give your family a private tour, you can arrange one for up to ten people for $50.

Swamp Walk

Rating:	★ ★ ★
Type:	Wooden walkway through a cypress swamp
Time:	Five minutes or as long as you like
Kelly says:	Best for bird watchers

Through an iron gate, across a heavy swinging wooden bridge over an algae-tinged moat with yet more alligators, lies what Gatorland bills as the headwaters of the Everglades. From here, so the sign says, water flows through the Kissimmee lake system to Lake Okeechobee and, thence, to the Everglades.

What we see on this leisurely walk is a wilderness setting with a quiet calm and a very special type of beauty, made all the more enjoyable because, thanks to the raised wooden walkway, we don't have to wade through the muck and the cottonmouth moccasins and the poison ivy to appreciate it. Most folks walk through at a brisk pace, but if you linger you are likely to be rewarded with glimpses of birds and other wildlife that more hurried tourists miss out on.

Much of the Orlando area looked just like this before people started draining the wetlands to farm and, later, build shopping malls. Only the soft whoosh of traffic on nearby highway 441 reminds us that we are in modern, not primordial, Florida.

Giant Gator Lake

Rating:	★ ★ ★ ★
Type:	Huge alligators in huge observation area
Time:	As long as you wish
Kelly says:	Rewards patient viewing

This is the huge lake that lies right next to the Gift Shop and park entrance. The place is home to Gatorland's largest specimens, giant 12-footers who are truly awesome, whether in catatonic repose in the sun or cruising ominously through the murky waters.

Other than feeding them (see below), there's not much to do here except watch. At first it will seem that there's nothing much going on. It may even seem that some of these critters are statues. But your patience will be rewarded. As you continue looking you will be able to sort the alligators from the crocodiles and start to notice those nicely camouflaged gators lurking in the shadows or lying submerged and motionless.

Photo Op: If you've got a video camera try for a shot of a white heron hitching a ride on the back of a floating gator. Also, look for a large plaster model of an alligator on the boardwalk; it makes a good prop for a photo of your fearless kids.

Feed the Gators

Rating:	★ ★ +
Type:	Audience participation
Time:	A few minutes
Kelly says:	Fun for the kids

Near the *Gator Jumparoo* platform is a stand selling four turkey hot dogs for $2.50 to those who'd like to feed a gator. Don't expect to be able to dangle your hand down like the gator wrangler in the Jumparoo show. The trick to feeding gators is to loft your hot dog gently so it lands to either side of the gator's head. They can't see directly in front. Many of the dogs wind up in the beaks of the ugly wood storks that patrol this area. Resist the temptation to hand feed these scavengers; their beaks can draw blood.

Tip: Take your hot dogs over to the *Alligator Breeding Marsh* and feed the gators from the Observation Tower. The gators over here are not as well-fed as those in the Giant Gator Lake and will show more interest in your free handouts.

Alligator Alley Animal Exhibits

Rating:	★ ★
Type:	Zoo-like walk-by exhibits
Time:	15 to 30 minutes
Kelly says:	Worth a stroll by; kids will enjoy feeding the lorikeets, goats, and deer

Alligator Alley is lined with a hodge-podge of cages, pens, and glass-walled displays that hearken back to the days when Gatorland was building its collection of "exotic" animals. Today, most of the animals on display are Florida natives like "Judy" the black bear and a small collection of emus, along with a variety of turtles, gators, and crocs.

The **Snakes of Florida** display is one of the more elaborate, housing a representative sample of Florida's 69 snake species behind glass windows and accompanied by helpful bits of written information. The walk-through **Very Merry Aviary** houses a scruffy band of lorikeets whom you can feed ($1 with two refills); it is open for half-hour periods on a regular schedule posted on the door.

Many of the animals, like the macaws and emus (not Florida natives), and the farm animals in **Allie's Barnyard** can be fed. Convenient dispensers contain appropriate treats (at 25 cents a modest handful) for the kids to feed to their favorites. Like the aviary, Allie's Barnyard opens up for half-hour up close sessions about four times a day.

Lilly's Pad

Rating:	★ ★ +
Type:	Kiddie play area
Time:	As long as you wish
Kelly says:	For toddlers unimpressed by alligators

Located just a hop, skip, and a jump away from the *Gator Jumparoo* arena, *Lilly's Pad* offers refuge for squirmy toddlers. There are two separate play areas here, wet and dry. For cooling water play, there is a large rubberized mat with sprinklers, fountains, and surprise spritzes. The adjacent playground is filled with colorful wooden, plastic, and metal play structures and is carpeted with a layer of soft wood chips. In between, a small shaded area gives parents some relief from the sun.

Eating at Gatorland

Pearl's Patio Smokehouse

What:	Fast-food stand featuring BBQ gator ribs
Where:	At the south end of the park, next to *Gator Wrestlin'* arena
Price Range:	$ - $$

Pearl's Smokehouse is a wood-sided, tin-roofed, Florida-style fast-food stand. Nearby is a screened-in smokehouse where the signature dish is prepared in a big black oven. You get your food at one of several serving windows and eat at umbrella-shaded picnic tables. There is a white sand play area with a rustic cabin for little ones to climb in, around, and over under Mom and Dad's watchful eyes. A few steps away is a covered seating area, closer to the *Alligator Breeding Marsh*. Here you can sit at a small counter facing a pen holding a white-tailed deer buck who will cruise by looking for a handout.

The featured attraction at Pearl's is alligator served up in two ways: as breaded, deep-fried "nuggets" or (my personal choice) as barbecued ribs, both for about $6 a serving. Or you can get a sampler platter, which features both, for $7. It would really be a shame to come to Gatorland and not try this local delicacy. The ribs are lightly sauced and succulent. They look a lot like small pork ribs but the bones are much lighter, some no bigger than fish bones. So nibble with care. The taste lies an indefinable somewhere between pork and chicken. The gator nuggets are chewier versions of the chicken nuggets you get at McDonalds. Any gator-y taste is pretty well masked by the breading, spices, and deep frying. There is barbecue sauce available for those who want to mask the taste even further. Whichever version you choose, my advice is to go for it. At these prices you can afford the gamble. At least get one order for the members of your group to sample — if they dare! Who knows, you may turn out to be a gator fan.

My observation, however, is that many people are not yet ready to take the plunge. If you are one of them, you needn't worry about going hungry. Good old reliable hot dogs are about $2 and turkey subs, ham and cheese, and smoked chicken breast sandwiches are about $4. A side order of fries is under $2 and a variety of soft drinks are served for $1.50 and $2 in small and large sizes only. Beer is $3. Desserts, mostly of the ice cream bar variety, are all $2 or less. Coffee, tea, and milk are under a dollar. You can eat hearty at Pearl's for well under $10 a head.

Tip: Pearl's is right next door to the *Gator Wrestlin'* arena. Consider taking your lunch over there and eating while you grab a good seat and wait for the show to begin.

Ice Cream Churn

What:	Snack and sandwich bar
Where:	Near the *Gator Jumparoo* attraction
Price Range:	$

The name pretty much says it all. In addition to ice cream treats in the $2 to $3 range, you can get the same sandwiches available at Pearl's (no gator though) at the same prices. A full range of drinks is also available here. Two smaller snack stands, one near *Lilly's Pad* and another near the entrance to the *Alligator Breeding Marsh* Observation Tower, are open seasonally as the crowds warrant. They serve a limited selection of snacks and drinks.

Shopping at Gatorland

No self-respecting theme park would be complete without offering its visitors regular opportunities to part with their cash in the name of souvenir hunting. Gatorland is no exception, although the number of shops and kiosks is mercifully limited.

Gator-Themed Souvenirs

What better way to commemorate your visit to Gatorland than with a photo of yourself with a real, live alligator. No, you don't get a chance to pose with any of the 12-foot whoppers you saw in the pool, but you can have your picture taken while holding a small gator whose jaws have thoughtfully been taped shut. If gators aren't your cup of tea, you can also have a boa constrictor draped decoratively over your shoulders. The cost is about $6 and the stand can be found right next to the *Gator Jumparoo* area.

The Gift Shop

For such a modest park, Gatorland has a surprisingly upscale gift shop. The big attraction, as you might expect, is the extensive range of alligator skin products. The price tags are truly heart-stopping but if you've done any serious comparison shopping you will realize there are some real bargains to be had here.

Full alligator boots, which retail for $2,000 and up in places like New York, are available here for $1,100. Men's loafers, handmade in Italy, are $598 here; they cost $900 in downtown Orlando. Alligator "vamp" boots (that is, half alligator, half leather) are $550; they can be found for $800 at the boot outlets in Kissimmee.

Nice wallets for men and women cost $129 to $290. Women's purses are in the $825 to $1,800 range. Men's and women's belts range from about $130 to $180. If you're really cheap, you can settle for an alligator key chain ($12.50) or money clip ($35). Less expensive than alligator skin is snake skin. Wallets run from $90 to $260.

A very nice line of denim shirts with embroidered logos runs about $50. Rather showy men's hats with a country-western look range from $42 to $105. The usual array of t-shirts is in the more economical $15 to $25 range. There are also some intriguing "natural history" gifts including skulls and mounted rattlesnakes in strike position, as well as books and videos about reptiles, most aimed at a younger audience.

In addition to the pricier items, the gift shop carries a full assortment of standard tourist souvenirs, from mugs and refrigerator magnets to alligator claw backscratchers and games for kids. There's lots to see here and you can always return to shop another day without paying admission to the park.

CHAPTER SIX:

Splendid China

A s you drive up the landscaped but strangely deserted boulevard that leads to Splendid China you might think you were headed for a new subdivision of luxury homes. In fact, if you drive past the Splendid China entrance, you will find several are sprouting in the immediate area. But nestled in this nursery of suburban developments is one of the Orlando area's oddest attractions.

Coming up with the perfect label for Splendid China is difficult. While there, I overheard a bewildered, towheaded moppet whine, "Mummy, I thought this was a theme park."

"It is a theme park," Mum replied, a bit testily.

But if you think of a theme park as a series of rides, with long lines and furry-costumed critters circulating amongst the crowds, you will be disappointed.

Splendid China might more accurately be called "Miniature China." It is, in fact, a travel agent's brochure sprung to life — or at least rendered in three dimensions. Not too surprising considering that this outdoor museum park is a collaboration of a Hong Kong-based travel company and the government of the People's Republic of China.

According to its founders, Splendid China seeks to provide "Americans and overseas visitors the most extensive and authentic close-up of China possible without actually visiting China itself." It does this through two primary media. First, there are the more than 50 miniature reproductions of China's most popular natural and man-made tourist attractions. These are no tabletop dioramas but ambitious outdoor re-creations, almost photographic in their detail, rendered in one-third to one-fifteenth scale. Many of them are impressive, indeed. The miniature Great Wall of China stands five and a half feet tall in places and snakes along for more than half a mile. Less obvious, but just as effective in promoting China as a destination, are the entertainments and cultural shows that take place throughout the park on a regular basis during the day. For many people, the shows will be the highlight of the visit.

Who then is most likely to enjoy Splendid China? On several visits, the crowd has been heavily weighted towards senior citizens, who seem to like the leisurely pace and gentle entertainments. There are also young children in evidence, usually in groups, suggesting that they have been brought here for "cultural enrichment." Beyond that, Splendid China should appeal to serious photographers. The extreme detail with which the models are executed offers many opportunities for cunning trompe l'oeil photos. A telephoto lens and a good selection of filters will probably come in handy in heightening the illusion of having traveled to China for these shots.

Before You Come

A recorded message at (407) 396-7111 provides current hours, admission prices, and information on special events. To reach the park's main switchboard, call (800) 244-6226. Local or international callers can dial (407) 396-7111. The web site address is www.floridasplendidchina.com.

When's the Best Time to Come?

The short answer is whenever you're in town. Crowds are not an issue at Splendid China. However, if you're a photographer, I would advise waiting for a nice, sunny day. If you'd like to maximize your chances of seeing all the shows, visit Thursday through Sunday.

Getting There

To reach Splendid China, take I-4 to Exit 25B and drive 3.3 miles west on US Route 192 (Irlo Bronson Highway). The entrance sign to the park will be on your left, two golden dragons rampant around a circular sign that says "Splendid China." The park entrance is a little more than half a mile up this side road. Parking is free.

Opening and Closing Times

The main part of the park opens every day at 9:30 a.m. and closes at 7:00 p.m. The 90-minute stage show, *Mysterious Kingdom of the Orient*, plays from 6:00 p.m. to 7:30 p.m. The Suzhou Street shopping and dining area, which is free of admission charges, remains open until 8:30 p.m.

The Price of Admission

At press time, admission prices, including tax, were as follows:

Adults:	$28.88
Children (5 to 12):	$18.88
Seniors (with AARP):	$25.99

Children 4 and under **free**.

You may purchase separate admission to the evening show, *Mysterious Kingdom of the Orient*, which is included in the above prices. The show-only prices, including tax, are:

Adults:	$16.00
Children:	$10.65
Seniors:	$13.85

Children 4 and under **free**.

An annual pass is available for $37.05 including tax ($21.15 plus tax for children). You may upgrade to an annual pass on the day of your first visit. To do so, you must pay the full price and then take your original admission receipt to Guest Services for a refund. Annual passholders receive complimentary admission tickets to distribute to friends and family. They also get unlimited admission to the *Mysterious Kingdom of the Orient* show (described below), which makes this an option worth considering if you live in the Orlando area. Splendid China runs frequent promotions featuring discounts. Two-for-one promotions crop up with some regularity. In addition, you should be able to find dollars-off coupons in the usual places as well as on Splendid China's web site.

Special Events

During January or February of each year, Splendid China celebrates the Chinese lunar New Year with a week-long celebration that includes special performances and special menus in the restaurants. For news of other special events, call (407) 396-7111.

Good Things To Know About...

Access for the Disabled

The entire park is wheelchair-accessible. Wheelchairs can be rented for $5 a day. Electric scooters are available for $30 a day.

Babies

Strollers are available at Guest Services, to your right as you enter the park. Single strollers are $5 a day, double strollers $7.50. You will find diaper changing stations in the restrooms.

Guest Services

Guest Services is located at the end of Suzhou Street next to the turnstiles where you enter the park proper. It provides most of the services outlined in this section as well as reservations to the Suzhou Pearl Restaurant. This is also the place to check should you need first aid.

Lockers

A limited number of small storage lockers are available for 50 cents. If you add to your stash during the day, it will cost you another 50 cents to relock your locker.

Tours

Guided tours can be arranged through Guest Services subject to availability. The one-hour tours use motorized golf carts and cost $9.63 per person, tax included. This is an easy way to see the park's highlights without hiking under a hot Florida sun.

Scaling the Wall:
Your (Half) Day at Splendid China

Splendid China has perhaps more than its fair share of detractors. Some have ideological bones to pick with the Chinese government. Others simply find the park "boring." True, the serene spectacle of acre upon acre of meticulous scale model buildings that is the park's centerpiece seems oddly out of place in hyperkinetic Orlando, but the park also offers some of the best live entertainment to be found in Central Florida. It may not be to everyone's taste, but I would urge you not to dismiss Splendid China out of hand. Even if you only come for the wonderful evening show, *Mysterious Kingdom of the Orient,* this park is worth a look.

You enter Splendid China through a spectacular traditional archway 44 feet high and 82 feet wide. It is apparently the largest such structure ever built outside China. Through this gate lies Suzhou Gardens a 63,000-square-foot re-creation of the legendary gardens of the city of Suzhou as it looked some 700 years ago. The square is dominated by a lovely water garden accented with dramatic Taihu stones. These gnarled and weathered limestone rocks were prized by the ancient Chinese for their ability to mimic mountains in miniature. The setting is airy and peaceful and forms a lovely backdrop for martial arts and tumbling demonstrations. Suzhou is one of China's "water cities" which, like Venice, are crisscrossed with canals. A more extensive model of a water city can be seen elsewhere in the park (number 42 on the map provided by the park).

The Suzhou Gardens section contains all of Splendid China's souvenir shops as well as two restaurants, and Guest Services. Best of all, Suzhou Gardens is open free of charge to all comers. You only have to ante up the price of admission if you decide to pass the turnstiles at the far end of Suzhou Gardens to explore the scale models and gardens beyond. A visit here can help you make up your mind about visiting the whole park or serve as a pleasant interlude in its own right, especially in the evening when the area is illuminated with thousands of tiny lights.

Most of the park's 76 acres are beyond the turnstiles and are given over to models of China's man-made wonders (with a few examples of nature's handiwork thrown in for good measure). Through the use of clever landscaping and strategically placed trees and shrubbery, the designers have created a constantly changing scenic experience that unfolds artfully as you stroll the grounds, allowing each exhibit to be appreciated on its own. This large "back" area of the park is also dotted with performance venues, but the emphasis is squarely on the scale models that await you around each turn.

The (Half) Day Stay

When you purchase your tickets, you will be given a map of the park with a schedule of the day's entertainments. My suggestion would be to construct your visit around the show schedule, taking in the sights between performance venues as you move from show to show. Not every show will be to everyone's taste. Use the descriptions below to guide you. However, I can't imagine anyone not liking the acrobatic and magic shows. These are definite must-sees.

The map you receive names and numbers each scale model exhibit. If you follow the map in numerical order, you will make a leisurely, spiraling circumnavigation of the park, ending up approximately in the middle of the large back section. A notation on the map estimates that it will take about four hours to view the park in this fashion and I have found this to be a reasonable estimate. For others with less time and patience, the map thoughtfully highlights twelve "must-see" exhibits.

Diehard tourists may want to jump right in and do it all, but others may want to get a quick overview first by catching the **tram ride** that runs regularly from in front of the Stone Forest at the front of the park. While not precisely a tour, there is a host who will point out some of the highlights of the park along the way. The tram ride circles the park in a clockwise direction and the whole trip takes about 20 minutes.

In summary, then, I would advise seeing most if not all of the shows and as many of the scale model exhibits as you have either the time or inclination for. It is quite possible to spend a full, unhurried day at Splendid China with a leisurely lunch thrown in. Most people, however, spend about four hours touring the park.

Attractions at Splendid China

In a sense there is only one attraction at Splendid China with nearly 60 variations on the theme.

Scale Models

Rating:	★ ★ ★ ★
Type:	Self-guided outdoor museum/park
Time:	As long as you wish; at least two hours for a good look
Kelly says:	Great phun for photogs

The original Splendid China is in Shenzhen, a city near Hong Kong. It was conceived as "a 10,000 mile journey through 5,000 years of Chinese history and culture." Florida Splendid China is a near carbon copy of that park. It was constructed over three years at a reported cost of $112 million. The models were painstakingly created by a team of 125 artisans brought over from China and assisted by 280 Americans. The models range in scale from one-fifteenth to one-third the size of the originals.

The attention to detail is astonishing. The **Great Wall of China** re-creation, for example, contains some six million tiny bricks, each laid by hand using real mortar. The miniature versions of the distinctive Chinese roof tiles were all individually cast and glazed. The scale model streets were paved in precisely the same manner as the originals. Even the trees have been carefully crafted by bonsai artists to match the scale of the model they are decorating.

Most models incorporate small porcelain figures giving each scene a charming "lived in" look. At various points along the Great Wall we can observe tiny workmen busy constructing the only man-made object visible from space and, a little farther along, an invading army undertaking the considerable challenge of attacking this mammoth defensive system. At Beijing's **Forbidden City** we see an elaborate official ceremony under way, and at the fabled **Shaolin Temple** we see the monks in the courtyard practicing their kung fu. One model even features some modern-day tourists sporting video cameras!

The brochures boast of more than 60 scale models. I only count 56, but no matter. What's here is impressive enough. These little scenes are spread out over an ingeniously landscaped park-like setting. You observe these miniature marvels from broad avenues that wind their way through the park and, thanks to the cunning of the landscapers, you seldom find your attention to one diorama distracted by another in the distance. The avenues you follow are thoughtfully punctuated by "shade structures," long roofed benches decorated with Chinese lanterns and hanging plants, their superstructures cooled by nearby foliage and climbing vines. Here and there you will find a kiosk at which you can slake your thirst.

At each display you will find a sign containing a brief description of the site and a map of China pinpointing its location. The signs also tell you the date of completion and the scale of the model. Especially interesting is a time line at the bottom of the sign that tells you what was happening elsewhere in the world. For example, the **Temple of Confucius** was completed about the time Hippocrates was born in Periclean Athens. When the magnificent golden-roofed **Yellow Crane Tower** was built, Christians were being persecuted by the Romans. It's a wonderfully effective way of putting the accomplishments of Chinese culture in perspective for a Western audience.

Near each sign is a green metal box with two buttons. Push them and you can hear the text on the sign read in either English or Spanish. Don't be afraid that people will think you can't read. These spoken signs let you peruse the model while being told about it. I found it a very enjoyable way to take in the sights. They are also a ready-made sound track for your home video camera.

A closer examination of the variety of scale models reveals that there are several different types. Most successful are the single buildings and temple groups. There are also scenes of entire villages depicting the distinctive architecture of China's various ethnic minorities. Somewhat less successful are the grottoes grouped near Suzhou Gardens. They reproduce statues and temples carved out of living rock. They never quite match the realism of the buildings modeled elsewhere. An exception is the **Midair Temple**; a good photograph of this fairy-tale temple will convince people you actually traveled to Shanxi for the shot. Least successful are the re-creations of natural scenery. The **Stone Forest**, while a lot of fun, has an unfortunate way of reminding us of the mountains of one of the many miniature golf courses that dot the Orlando landscape.

Carping aside, many of the exhibits are truly beautiful. The **Summer Palace**, viewed across an artificial lake, is especially evocative. And the **Terra Cotta Warriors** of Xian will have you plotting a trip to see the originals. Reproduced in one-third size here are just a fraction of the more than 8,000 life-sized sculptured soldiers created to accompany the Qinshihuang emperor to the afterlife. Each sculpture is different, reflecting a very specific individual with a very identifiable personality. When all this was happening in far-off Xian, Rome was busy conquering the lands that would later become Spain.

One of the more controversial displays, but nonetheless arresting, is the **Potala Palace** of Tibet. When the park opened, this model drew protests over China's brutal occupation of Tibet and suppression of the Tibetan people and their religion. Like the original, this one-fifteenth scale model sits high on a landscaped hill. Photographed against the blue Florida sky, it looks remarkably real.

Photo Op: Splendid China offers opportunities for the amateur and professional photographer that are ... well, splendid. Through careful framing and composition, it is possible to capture some remarkably realistic views of a China you have never visited. In many cases it is possible to set your subject against a backdrop of blue sky creating an almost perfect illusion. A telephoto lens and the artful use of filters will enhance the shots you take here. One of the nicest angles can be found in the shade structure behind the **Lijiang Scenery** model (number 39 on the Splendid China map). From here you can shoot through the greenery and the sculpted mountains of Lijiang to the Potala Palace in the near distance.

Entertainment at Splendid China

Just as fascinating as the scale models — perhaps more so for some people — are the various entertainments offered throughout the park during the course of the day.

Performances take place at venues scattered around the grounds, ranging from large theaters, to covered amphitheaters, to tents, to intimate pavilions, to the great outdoors. The major venues are the $2 million Golden Peacock Theater; the Temple of Light Theater, a covered amphitheater with open sides; and the tent-like Pagoda Garden show area.

Note: What happens at which venue and when is subject to change. Not all shows are presented every day. You are most likely to be able to see all the shows if you visit on a weekend.

Since most of the entertainment involves live performances by artists from China, and since these folks like to get home every now and then, exactly what you will see when you visit is hard to predict. However, even though the performers may rotate, the general shape of the entertainment provided remains much the same. What follows, then, are descriptions of the shows I have seen on my visits. They will give you some flavor of the entertainment experience that awaits you. Just be aware that when you visit the lineup may be somewhat different.

Chinese Folk Dance and Costume

Rating: ★ ★ +
Type: Theater presentation
Time: 20 minutes
Kelly says: Lovely to look at

This show gets off to a slow, if colorful, start as the cast members appear in a variety of traditional and ethnic costumes. They parade about the stage and strike poses reminiscent of socialist realism posters of the fifties and sixties. The regions and ethnic groups represented by the costumes are not identified. If your curiosity is aroused, the small costume display in the theater may satisfy you after the show.

The pace picks up with a selection of dances from various ethnic groups. Whatever rough edges these dances might have in their home settings seem to have been smoothed with a polite balletic quality and the dances remain picturesque without ever becoming truly exciting.

Chinese Martial Arts

Rating: ★ ★ ★
Type: Theater presentation
Time: 20 minutes
Kelly says: More of a dance recital

Don't look for any chop-socky violence in this show. Here a series of experts demonstrate China's major martial arts schools as you watch. Tai-chi, kung-fu, and qi-gong (and perhaps a few others) are represented. No one fights; instead solo performers go through what look like practice routines combining a series of moves or stances. In the case of tai-chi, it is a slow, stately, and rather lovely process. With qi-gong, the motion is much faster and more furious. Sometimes the performers flash swords or slap long wooden poles on the ground.

Unfortunately, there is no narration to explain what you are seeing, so unless you are a devotee of the martial arts, this show will be vaguely unsatisfying. Of course, no explanation is needed for the fellow who presses a spear into his throat until the spear shaft bends and then lies down on a bed of nails with a block of stone on his stomach which a colleague pounds on with a sledgehammer. It's sort of kung-fu master meets circus strongman.

Imperial Bells Music Show

Rating: ★ ★ ★
Type: Chamber concert
Time: 20 minutes
Kelly says: Enchanting

This enjoyable show offers a painless introduction to Chinese music offered up by a gracious ensemble playing a variety of traditional instruments. Most prominent are the eponymous bells, cast in bronze and forming a sort of giant xylophone.

A representative selection of Chinese tunes is played on Chinese versions of the hammered dulcimer, wooden flute, and lute. Oddest of all are the two-stringed fiddles with their small snakeskin-covered sound boxes. The eerie high-pitched notes they produce are a hallmark of Chinese music. The ensemble ends the show with a spirited rendition of "Oh, Susanna," which proves to be a real crowd-pleaser.

Splendid China Acrobats

Rating: ★ ★ ★ ★ +
Type: Acrobats and jugglers
Time: 30 minutes
Kelly says: Fabulous

This show features a number of brief turns presented in almost kaleidoscopic fashion. What exactly you see will depend on Splendid China's current roster of performers at the time of your visit. The combination of acts and skills represented changes frequently, but in the years I have been visiting, the show has never been less than compelling.

You might see a young girl balancing glasses of water in increasingly unbelievable ways while twirling a hula hoop and two fans. Or two "foot jugglers" who lie on their backs and tumble large pots and tables overhead. Or a hoop dancer who twines his body through increasingly intricate patterns formed by 20 some iridescent red hoops. Or eight young women spinning eight plates apiece on long slender poles while they go through a graceful acrobatic routine in perfect unison. Or an acrobat who stands on his head on a swinging trapeze while spinning hoops. All very impressive.

Mysterious Kingdom of the Orient

Rating: ★ ★ ★ ★ ★
Type: Stage spectacular
Time: 90 minutes
Kelly says: Not to be missed

Missed the acrobat shows in the park during the day? Not to worry. This spectacular stage show, which plays every evening except Monday at 6:00 p.m. in the 750-seat Golden Peacock Theater, reprises most of the best acts. In fact, it adds new layers of complexity to many of them — something that hardly seems possible. On top of that, it showcases even more astonishing feats of skill and balance.

Once again, the precise combination of acts you see will depend on who's on the bill at the time of your visit. There may be aerialists performing high overhead atop tall poles balanced on the stout shoulder of a man below. Or a foot juggler who juggles not only a large pot but a tiny girl on top of it. You may see 6 agile men and women doing handstands on a teetering tower of chairs, or a bicycle built for 12. Whatever it is, it will doubtless be jaw-dropping. And the acrobatic acts are just one element of this extravaganza.

Mysterious Kingdom of the Orient provides a framework on which to string a series of lavish costume spectacles, lively or graceful dance routines, and displays of acrobatic, juggling, and magic skills.

The dancing is vaguely balletic with martial arts grace notes. At its most energetic, the choreography leans heavily to heroic poses, dashing leaps, and waving banners which make for some startlingly beautiful stage pictures. In its more reflective moods, it features beautiful women, gorgeously costumed, floating across the stage as water lily blossoms or courtesans of the Imperial court.

Usually, saying that the costumes are one of the best things in a show is a decidedly backhanded compliment. Not in this case. Even better is that many of these costumes are worn by some of the most beautiful women China (or any other country) has to offer.

The show changes about every six months or so, which means that the shape, length, and quality varies somewhat. The shows I have seen have varied from the truly astonishing to the merely wonderful. Still, this is quite simply one of the best shows to be seen in Orlando. Anyone who pays the price of admission to Splendid China and misses this show should have his head examined. The separate admission charged for the show alone makes it an attractive option for those who have no particular interest in visiting Splendid China itself. And if you paid full price for your park or show admission, Splendid China will throw in a free (if somewhat uninspired) meal at the nearby Seven Flavors restaurant. Or you can opt for a 25% discount off the already moderate prices at the more elaborate Suzhou Pearl restaurant. These two options make *Mysterious Kingdom of the Orient* a serious contender in Orlando's dinner attraction sweepstakes.

Eating at Splendid China

Splendid China misses a sure bet in the food department. While you certainly won't starve on a visit to the park, neither will you get a chance to savor the best of what China's culinary tradition has to offer. The limited food choices are located in the Suzhou Gardens section; once past the turnstiles, in the main section of the park, your choices are limited to soft drinks and the occasional ice cream sandwich from vending machines.

Suzhou Pearl Restaurant

What:	Elegant full-service restaurant
Where:	Suzhou Gardens, by the koi pond
Price Range:	$$ - $$$

This is Splendid China's attempt to bring fine Chinese dining to Central Florida. There is an emphasis on seafood, Hong Kong style, with only a few nods to the cuisine of other regions. While the food may not be the finest, the prices are moderate with entrees ranging from $9 to $17. Specialties like Peking Duck ($35) and seasonal fish dishes are more expensive. Some of the dishes, like Crispy Shrimp with Honey Walnuts, have the virtue of being adventurous and the extensive menu offers Chinese specialties, such as Crispy Jelly Fish, that you are not likely to find elsewhere in the area. The wine list features some American varietals at prices ranging from $16 to $30 a bottle.

Since Suzhou Pearl is open late and you don't have to pay park admission to eat here, you might want to keep it in mind if you have a hankering for "fancy" Chinese food at reasonable prices. Hours are 3:30 p.m. to 8:30 p.m daily except Mondays; the phone number is (407) 397-8835.

Seven Flavors

What:	Fast-food Chinese style
Where:	In Suzhou Gardens
Price Range:	$ - $$

If you've ever had Chinese food at a shopping mall food court, you know what to expect here. The food is undistinguished but cheap. "Combos," which offer a choice of entree and varying side dishes are priced between $6 and $7. On a recent visit, the entrees offered were Buddha's Delight (a vegetarian dish), General Tso's chicken, and beef broccoli. Ordered separately, entrees are about $6. Yang-Zhou fried rice and Beijing lo mein are about $5. Soft drinks are available in three sizes from about $1 to $1.50, while imported Tsingtao beer is served for a little over $3. All seating is indoors in a setting devoid of atmosphere. No credit cards are accepted.

Shopping at Splendid China

All of the shopping at Splendid China is cleverly and conveniently located in the Suzhou Gardens area at the front of the park, to your left as you enter the main gate. The shops, all fairly small, are interconnected so (assuming all the shops are open) you can enter at one end of the courtyard and shop 'til you drop out at the other. Unfortunately, that's not always a valid assumption. The retail operation at Splendid China has been in flux almost since the day it opened, so much so that it is becoming increasingly difficult to predict what will be on offer when you visit. Although the various shops have separate names, those names do not always jibe with the merchandise on display.

Rather than attempt a shop-by-shop description, I will offer an overview of what was available at various shops on some recent visits and attempt to reassure you that you will probably be able to find something for those on your gift list at prices you are unlikely to match elsewhere. Those of you who like Chinese style pottery and decorative items will find it especially hard to resist some of the bargains you'll find here. Best of all, you can visit the shops for free, without paying the admission to the miniature displays.

Several shops were recently combined to form the **Chinese Art Gallery** offering Chinese scrolls and furniture pieces. Most of the scrolls (about $50) are in traditional style, but some of them are modern takes on ancient forms. There are also some very nice reproductions of Chinese antique furniture here at what strike me as very moderate prices. Especially nice are the larger multi-drawer chests and the high side tables.

If you took a fancy to the lilting Chinese music piped throughout the park, you can pick it up on cassette or CD for about $8. You should also be able to find a small selection of books from and about China. Cookbooks are prominently displayed as you might expect, but there are also translations of the great Chinese philosophers and upscale guidebooks to China.

Some of the best buys to be found at Splendid China are the decorative objects and ceramic pieces. There are few actual antiques; these are mostly reproductions. The prices seem quite reasonable and it's unlikely you'll be able to cut a better deal back home, unless perhaps home is in China.

Large pottery vases are a standout here. Elaborately decorated pieces standing four feet high and adorned with gaily colored birds and flowers are $300. Smaller vases and urns can be had for less than $200 and occasional half-price sales can create some terrific bargains.

A small selection of jade objects features a pretty bowl for just $130 and pendants for $120, while bracelets go for $1,000. Dong Yang yellow wood carvings, which are amazingly light for their size, depict elaborate scenes such as a group of horses galloping across what look to be sea waves. A lovely four-piece nested set of black lacquer tables with mother-of-pearl figures set under glass is just $450 while an elaborate four-panel dragon screen is about $1,000.

Be on the lookout for artificial floral arrangements executed in glass. They are very attractive and very cheap ($20 to $40). I can guarantee that Aunt Martha will be convinced you spent much, much more. Look too for figurines at surprisingly low prices. Some very attractive porcelain figures of Chinese fishermen are just $7 to $15. There are also imitation jade Buddhas, calligraphy sets, and willowy white porcelain Guan Yin statuettes for under $40. A beautiful waist-high rosewood altar table on display on a recent visit was just $450.

The usual theme park souvenirs are the order of the day in other shops. A selection of magic tricks that comes with a demonstration and personal instructions is $25. Bamboo boats, some of them quite large, range from $10 to $130. Abacuses are $7 to $11. A martial arts section features a good selection of books on the subject, kids' kung fu outfits ($20), and toy num chuks and other martial arts implements, some of them quite nasty looking.

Splendid China t-shirts in a variety of colors and styles (some of them quite nice) are always on offer, but beyond that the selection can be unpredictable. Most of what you find will be for women with a to-be-expected emphasis on Chinese styles. Some of these can be excellent buys. Among the items you might find are traditional Manchu qi pao dresses, ankle length and close-fitting, in a variety of colors for about $60. A very pretty white woven nightgown is $76. Colorful women's robes with gaily embroidered dragons are just $22.

There is a jewelry store with most selections in the inexpensive to moderate category. There you will also find some very pretty lacquerware jewel boxes and cabinets. Along with the usual array of gold chains, jadeite and amethyst beads, cloisonné, and costume jewelry, you will find Chokin 24 karat gold metal carvings on small plates for just $20 and more elaborate ladies' fans from $36 to $72.

You should also be able to find a small selection of imported teas here, ranging from Special Relaxing Tea, to Ginseng-Oolong, to Chrysanthemum, to the more familiar Jasmine and green teas. Gift-boxed assortments are available.

CHAPTER SEVEN:

The Holy Land Experience

When The Holy Land Experience, Orlando's newest theme park, opened in February of 2001 it garnered worldwide publicity, much of it tinged with controversy. It received hoots and sniggers from secularists for whom religion is, at best, a quaint anachronism. It also took flak from some religious leaders who took exception to the very idea of the new park.

Aside from referring one and all to the First Amendment of the U.S. Constitution, I do not wish to get involved in whatever controversy there may be about The Holy Land Experience. I would, however, like to report that, taken on its own terms, it is a remarkably successful endeavor.

Using popular media for religious messages has a long and honorable tradition, from the mystery plays of medieval Europe, that sought to teach Bible stories to the illiterate, to the Mitzvah-Mobiles of modern day New York that reach out to lapsed Jews. So why not a theme park that seeks to bring to life the Jerusalem of the time of Jesus Christ and teach, nay preach, a religious message to those who come to gawk? It may not be for everyone but the medium just might get the message across to people unlikely to pull out and dust off that Gideons Bible in their motel room.

Reflecting the Jewish heritage of its founder, Marvin Rosenthal, The Holy Land Experience places considerable emphasis on the Jewishness of Jesus and his milieu. He was a rabbi, as the park's explicators point out. Much is made of the historical and archaeological accuracy of the exhibits and biblical text is often linked with historical fact. Many of the park's "cast members" (to use a Disney turn of phrase) are dressed as priests of the Herodic Temple, who blow the shofar, the ceremonial ram's horn, to announce show times, and everyone on the park staff greets you with a hearty "Shalom!" Ancient Hebrew hymns highlight some of the live performances, several of the exhibits pay homage to the Judaic traditions of the Old Testament, and Jewish prayer shawls and menorahs are sold in the gift shops. Indeed, reflecting the ongoing Christian connection with the Holy Land, 80% of the merchandise sold in the shops is imported from Israel.

The Holy Land Experience is not a large park, just 15 acres, about the size of a small "land" at one of the major Orlando parks. It is also worth noting that, scenically, The Holy Land Experience is extremely well executed. The lead design firm was ITEC Entertainment Corp., the same outfit responsible for much of the theme-ing of Islands of Adventure over at Universal Orlando. They've also done work for Disney and their experience shows, although they were obviously working with a more limited budget here. Still, the results are impressive and The Holy Land Experience compares favorably with other "minor" parks in the Orlando area.

My guess is that The Holy Land Experience will appeal most to true believers. Indeed, church groups of one sort or another were much in evidence on my visits. Those drawn to the Christian message might also find a visit enlightening. But religious belief or religious yearning are not prerequisites for admission and non-believers should not dismiss The Holy Land Experience out of hand. Anyone with a shred of intellectual curiosity will find much of interest here even if they remain unconverted.

Before You Come

If you would like current information about operating hours and schedules, you can call, toll-free, (866) USA-HOLYLAND (872-4659). The local number is (407) 872-2272. The web site for the park, www.theholylandexperience.com, contains basic information and is a good place to check for late-breaking developments.

If you haven't already read the Bible, it's unlikely you'll do so just to prepare for a theme park visit, but here's a fairly painless assignment anyway. Pull out the Bible in your hotel room and glance through the closing chapters of Exodus, starting at Chapter 36, to learn a bit about the construction of the wilderness tabernacle. If you like, continue on into the first several chapters of Leviticus to learn about the practice of blood sacrifice. One of the more interesting presentations at The Holy Land Experience is based on these sections of the Good Book.

Getting There

The Holy Land Experience is located at 4655 Vineland Road at the corner of Conroy Road. It is just off Exit 31A on I-4 and can be clearly seen from the highway. Coming from the south (that is, traveling east on I-4), turn left at the top of the exit ramp, cross the bridge, and take the first right. Coming from the north (west on I-4), keep turning right from the top of the exit ramp. This will take you into the parking lot of The Holy Land Experience. Parking is $3 for all vehicles.

Opening and Closing Times

The Holy Land Experience is every day of the year except Thanksgiving and Christmas. Normal operating hours are as follows:

Monday to Thursday, 10:00 a.m. to 5:00 p.m.; Friday and Saturday, 9:30 a.m. to 7:00 p.m.; Sunday, 12:00 noon to 6:00 p.m. During holiday periods hours may be changed or extended. Call for information.

The Price of Admission

The Holy Land Experience has several ticket options. Because it is a not-for-profit ministry, no taxes are levied on the admission charges.

One-Day Pass
Adult: $22
Child (4-12): $17
Children under 4 are admitted **free.**

Jerusalem Gold Annual Pass
All ages $59

Group Rates

If you have a group of 20 or more, you can qualify for reduced rates, but only if you reserve ahead and put down a deposit of $100 or 50% of the total cost (whichever is greater) within a month of making the reservation. The remainder of the total cost must be paid in full three weeks prior to your visit. Your tickets will be held at Guest Services pending your arrival. The group rates are:
Adult: $19
Child: $15

Which Price Is Right?

For most people, a one-day pass will suffice. The $22 rate will no doubt seem very fair to committed believers, but I suspect it will discourage the merely curious. The annual pass will appeal most to those who live in the Orlando area although, if you plan to attend three or more days of Bible lectures, the annual pass becomes cost-effective.

Good Things To Know About....

Access for the Disabled

All of The Holy Land Experience is wheelchair accessible. Wheelchairs may be rented in the Old Scroll Shop, which is directly in front of you as you enter. Wheelchair rental is $5.

Babies

Strollers are available for rent in the Old Scroll Shop. Single strollers are $3, doubles are $5. Diaper changing areas are available in all the restrooms in the park.

Dress Code

The Holy Land Experience expects its guests to dress appropriately. While recognizing that most people are here on vacation, the management draws the line at halter tops, short-shorts, and other forms of dress deemed (in their opinion) to be immodest. They also refuse entry to those who arrive "in costume."

First Aid

First aid facilities are available in the Guest Services office near the front.

Leaving the Park

If you wish to leave the park during the day, make sure to retain your ticket. You can use it to regain admittance later in the day. Leaving for lunch is an option, although nothing is within walking distance.

Pets

The Holy Land Experience has no pet boarding facilities, and no animals (other than seeing-eye dogs) are allowed in the park. Plan accordingly.

Prayer & Religious Activity

The management of The Holy Land Experience expects some exhibits to move visitors to prayer. However, they reserve the right to eject those whose religious activity (in their sole opinion) is creating a disturbance.

Sun

Much of The Holy Land Experience takes place outdoors under the broiling Florida sun. Many of the best shows take place in the Plaza of the Nations, an uncovered marble square that can get brutal on the warmest days. Head coverings and sunscreen are highly recommended.

The Pilgrim's Route: Your Day at The Holy Land Experience

The Holy Land Experience is recommended as a three- to five-hour experience, although to fully absorb all the park has to offer will require the better part of a day. When you arrive, you will be given a fold-out map that contains information about the park's amenities and services. In the map is a small schedule of live shows and other events that you can use to plan your day.

There are two types of attractions: **Featured Presentations**, indoor, theater-style shows, about 20 to 30 minutes in length, that operate on a continuous schedule, and **Live Performances**, outdoor musical shows with a more limited performance schedule.

I found the most workable strategy was to arrive early and see all the live performances first. The schedule is such that you have a comfortable amount of time to move from one show to the next and get a good seat. When you have seen all the shows, it will be time for lunch. Then, during the hottest part of the day (for you summer visitors), you can see the indoor presentations.

This touring strategy will take you into the late afternoon. If you wish, you can linger and see some of the shows again while waiting for nightfall. You can also have dinner at the Oasis Palms (see below). But even if you leave early, you might want to return after dark (remember to save your ticket). The Plaza of Nations, with its torches lit, is especially nice at night.

Attractions at The Holy Land Experience

As I mentioned, there are two types of attractions. I will begin with a description of the Live Performances and then move on to the Featured Presentations.

Garden Tomb Music and Drama

Rating: ★★
Type: Songs and testimony
Time: 25 minutes
Kelly says: More earnest than artful

The historical and biblical accuracy of the rest of the park gives way to religious fervor in the live performances and this show is a perfect case in point. Using Calvary's Garden Tomb (see below) as a backdrop, three people give their testimony in song and speech. There are several versions of the show; what follows will give an idea of what to expect.

First a woman sings, in ululating Hebrew, "Hear me, O Lord!" Then she tells us her story. She is a Canaanite woman, a worshipper of idols, whose daughter was possessed by demons. The distraught mother turned to Jesus and found redemption. She is followed by one of the women who discovered the empty tomb on the third day. Finally, a man appears to sing a stentorian hymn of praise to his "Savior God."

The conviction of the performers is undeniable. I was especially impressed by the anguish of the Canaanite woman. But, for me, the music was less than compelling.

Today's The Day

Rating:	★★+
Type:	Mini-musical drama
Time:	20 minutes
Kelly says:	Heartfelt and effective

This show is a step up in both dramatic and musical quality. It takes place in the Plaza of the Nations, before the Temple, and begins when three young hotheads come to the Temple steps talking of rebellion against the Roman occupation, a sort of Judean Liberation Front in the making. Simeon, an older, wiser man counsels patience and reminds them of the prophecies of the Messiah. Joseph and Mary arrive with the infant Jesus and Simeon immediately recognizes the Messiah. Simeon sings a moving hymn of praise as, one by one, the onlookers have their own moments of revelation.

This is a heartfelt mini-pageant that will hit home for believers. Others, I fear, will remain unconverted.

Tip: When watching shows in the Plaza of the Nations, take a seat on the far right (as you face the Temple). From here it is a straight shot to the line for the film *Seed of Promise* in the Theater of Life (see below).

Revival in the Land!

Rating:	★★★
Type:	Contemporary gospel music
Time:	20 minutes
Kelly says:	Good of its type

This was my favorite live show, perhaps because it is the most straightforward and tuneful. Six young performers, three men and three women, dressed casually in tones of black and white, sing a half dozen or so contemporary gospels songs on the steps of the Temple in the Plaza of the Nations.

Many of the songs aspire to an Andrew Lloyd Webber-ish quality which I confess is not a style to which I respond well. I much preferred the more traditional songs like "Gather By The River," which was artfully arranged and put across with real conviction. Many of the numbers had the audience clapping along with fervor.

Tip: The Plaza of Nations can get hot and uncomfortable on sunny days. Since there are truly no bad seats here, you may want to arrive early to stake out a spot in the few scraps of shade around the edges. Many people take the folding chairs that serve as seating here and move them to whatever shade is available.

Seasonal Pageants

Rating: ★★★
Type: Multi-location musical dramas
Time: 40 minutes
Kelly says: Large-scale expressions of faith

During the Christmas and Easter seasons additional live performances with an appropriate holiday theme will almost certainly be added, often-times displacing one or more of the shows already mentioned. Some, but by no means all, special holiday shows may require an additional charge.

During the Christmas season, you might see *Caravan of Kings*, while at Easter you might see *The Kingdom, the Power, and the Glory.* These shows are more elaborate versions of *Today's the Day* (see above). The Christmas show I saw, for example, involved five separate locations around the park and used real camels for a dramatic entrance by the three wise men. The music is in the quasi-operatic, Andrew Lloyd Webber mode (which may be to your taste) and many of the vocal performances are quite accomplished.

Typically, there will be two shows a day, one in the early afternoon and one just before the park closes in the evening. However, if you are planning on visiting during a holiday period, it's a good idea to call ahead or visit the web site to find out what will be playing when you arrive.

The Wilderness Tabernacle

Rating: ★★★+
Type: Stage show with special effects
Time: 25 minutes
Kelly says: Interesting evocation

Of all the attractions at The Holy Land Experience, this is the most theme-park-like. In a darkened theater, we see a dramatized recreation of the tabernacle God commanded Moses to build in the wilderness after the exodus from Egypt. As a voiceover narrator tells the history of the tabernacle an actor representing Aaron, the very first High Priest, mimes the rituals and sacrifices being described. Because the Bible (Exodus Chapter 36ff) gives fairly complete instructions for building the tabernacle, the recreation is remarkably evocative.

The presentation progresses from the sacrificial altar and bronze laver (or purification bath) outside into the tabernacle itself. There we see the Holy Place, an antechamber with three ritual objects, and the Holy of Holies itself where the Arc of the Covenant resided and into which the High Priest entered just once a year. The presentation ends with a "Shekinah Glory" special effect that is straight out of "Raiders of the Lost Arc."

All in all, I found this show a fascinating use of theme park show biz to teach a religious and archaeological lesson.

Calvary's Garden Tomb

Rating:	★★★
Type:	Re-creation of Christ's tomb
Time:	Continuous viewing
Kelly says:	Best as a stage set

In a sunken garden setting, the approach lined with white lilies at Easter time, lies this imaginative reconstruction of Christ's tomb. The huge circular stone door is rolled aside as it was on the third day when the women who came to anoint Christ's body discovered he was risen. If you step inside you see a typical tomb of the period, the winding cloths in disarray, and a small sign that says. "He is not here for He is risen."

Benches in front of the tomb allow a place for quiet contemplation. Above the tomb rise the three crosses of the crucifixion. The tomb makes a compelling backdrop for live performances.

Note: Many of the plants on the grounds of The Holy Land Experience have signage explaining their biblical connections. Here at the tomb, for example, a sign in front of an aloe plant tells us that the plant was often used for embalming and offers a Bible verse (John 19:39) in which the plant is mentioned.

Temple of the Great King and Plaza of the Nations

Rating:	★★★
Type:	Historical recreation
Time:	Continuous viewing
Kelly says:	A fitting setting for the shows

The Temple of the Great King is a half-scale re-creation of the Herod's Temple which stood on Jerusalem's Mount Moriah in the first century A.D. What we see is actually just the Temple's facade and a courtyard in front of it surrounded by 30 Corinthian columns with golden capitals. Supposedly, this is all archaeologically accurate, although the model of Jerusalem (see below) seems to differ on the matter of column style.

Be that as it may, the Plaza of Nations, as this space is called, is a dazzling centerpiece for The Holy Land Experience. Add a high priest in white robes and bulbous turban, blowing a shofar to summon the faithful, and a uniformed Roman solider striding purposefully about and you have a nice, if pared down, evocation of ancient Jerusalem.

It is here that many of the live performances take places, using the semicircular steps to the Temple as a stage. Seating is provided by folding chairs arranged in a semicircle facing the Temple.

The Seed of Promise (in the Theater of Life)

Rating: ★ ★ ★
Type: Religious film
Time: 30 minutes
Kelly says: Well-done

A 150-seat theater hidden away behind the facade of the Temple of the Great King is used for the screening of a devotional film that speaks directly to believers. This handsomely produced film, shot on location in Israel in high-definition video, encapsulates the religious message of The Holy Land Experience. Beginning with a depiction of the Roman sack of Jerusalem in 70 A.D., the film travels back in time to the Creation, where we see Adam and Eve in the Garden of Eden, and forward again to the almost sacrifice of Abraham atop Mount Moriah. The film ends with Jesus, arisen from the dead, visiting the lands around Jerusalem and making Himself known to His followers. The official stance of The Holy Land Experience is strictly non-denominational, but if there is an underlying theological point of view to the place it is no doubt encapsulated in this brief and compelling presentation.

I can't help commenting on the way Hollywood cliché has of trumping historical accuracy in films of this sort. Eve is shown as a blonde (with tan lines, yet!) and Jesus, always shot from the back, appears to have used blonde highlighter in his tawny hair. At least Abraham and Isaac appear to be of their time and place.

The film is shown on a regularly repeating schedule with a showing always scheduled for immediately after a performance in the nearby Plaza of the Nations. A high priest blows the shofar to announce each show.

Jerusalem Model A.D. 66

Rating: ★★★★
Type: Large city model
Time: Continuous viewing
Kelly says: Come for the informative talks

A large room in a building past the Plaza of the Nations houses a fascinating scale model of Jerusalem as it existed in 66 A.D. Why 66 A.D.? Because, with the completion of the northern wall, this was the largest the ancient city ever grew. Four years later, it was obliterated by the Romans in retaliation for Jewish uppityness.

The model, which measures 45 feet by 25 feet, is historically accurate with one exception. The houses have been enlarged to show detail. The housing was actually six times as dense and the streets 15 times as narrow as depicted. In fact, the houses were packed so closely together that in Jesus's time you could leap from roof to roof and traverse the entire length of the city without ever touching the ground.

That last tidbit, was gleaned from the fascinating half-hour talks that are given here. I strongly urge you not to miss these entertaining mini-lectures. Without them, the display is merely interesting, but the talks make this the best attraction at The Holy Land Experience.

Every hour on the hour, a knowledgeable biblical scholar (most if not all of them are preachers) steps onto a small open space next to the Temple Mount and, with the aid of a laser pointer, conducts a guided tour of the Jerusalem that Jesus knew. In a fascinating blend of Bible stories with historical records and archaeological excavation, he brings oft-told stories of the work and especially the Passion of Jesus, to life. I was fascinated to learn, for example, that Jesus' description of Gehenna (Hell) was a direct reference to the trash heap that burned ceaselessly outside Jerusalem's walls. His contemporary listeners would have known immediately what He was talking about.

By the time you visit, a video version of this talk may be available for purchase. If so, it would make an excellent souvenir of your visit.

Bible Lecture (in the Shofar Auditorium)

Rating: Decide for yourself
Type: Classroom-style lecture
Time: One hour
Kelly says: For the serious student of the Bible

Behind the model of Jerusalem lies the 510-seat Shofar Auditorium. Here, one-hour lectures on a variety of Bible-related topics are given by recognized experts in the field.

The schedule is somewhat erratic. At one time, lectures were given only on Friday and Saturday. During a recent visit, they were also being offered on Monday and Wednesday.

From what I observed, these talks follow the tradition of close Bible reading and explication that is the hallmark of contemporary evangelical Christianity. If this is something that would interest you, call ahead to find out what will be on tap during your visit.

Dining at The Holy Land Experience

For the moment, your dining choices are limited since there is just one restaurant open. A coffee shop is shown on the map, but no opening date has been set.

Oasis Palms Café

What: Cafeteria style restaurant
Where: To the left of the entrance to Plaza of the Nations
Price Range: $$

This small cafeteria seats just 120 people, half of them outside at tables overlooking the Oasis Lagoon and its towering jet-like fountain. Given the crowds that the park attracts, lines get long at lunch time. Fortunately, the kitchen has its act together and the line moves quickly. Lines are virtually nonexistent at dinner time since most guests have left by then.

The food is billed as American and Middle Eastern and in true theme park style they even serve "Goliath Burgers," which are traditional American fare, as are the Sahara Fries you can get to accompany them. Other entrees include a Grilled Chicken Persian Pita Stuffer and the vegetarian Jaffa Felafel Pita. These can be ordered a la carte or as a platter that includes a four-bean Mediterranean salad and couscous. Soft drinks and coffee are also served. Prices are extremely reasonable, with a typical combination platter and soft drink costing just $8.

Brownies, cookies, and apples ($1) are the only desserts offered here but outdoor stands sell Milk and Honey Ice Cream and other treats for about $2 to $2.50.

Shopping at The Holy Land Experience

There are no money changers in the Temple but there is shopping nearby, most of it near the front entrance. **Methuselah's Mosaics Village Gallery** features framed original art with religious themes at prices (up to $5,000) that might make you say a quick prayer. Less expensive are handsomely framed Bible verses in raised gold letters against a suitably ancient background. Next door, the **Old Scroll Shop** offers a much wider range of merchandise. It varies from the expected t-shirts ($13), polo shirts ($40), and fanny packs ($20) — all with The Holy Land Experience logo — to Jewish religious articles such as prayer shawls and menorahs. Much of the merchandise is from Israel including some lovely Havdalah candles, cups and plates, and Nativity scenes carved from olive wood. You can also find Bibles and a variety of devotional books, audio tapes, and videos, although not as many you might expect. Indeed, the proselytizing seems decidedly muted.

Outside, the **Jerusalem Street Market** occupies a narrow passageway to the park proper. It sells a small sample of what you found in the Old Scroll Shop. In the park itself, behind the Jerusalem model, a small shop offers much the same selection as the Old Scroll Shop.

Words of the Prophets

God created the world in seven days. It's taking The Holy Land Experience a little longer. The most spectacular coming attraction is **The Scriptorium**, scheduled to open in summer of 2002, which will house the world's largest private collection of Biblical papyri, manuscripts, and books, including first editions of most Bibles ever printed and autograph manuscripts of major figures of the Protestant Reformation. Guided tours of the collection will be offered. It will surely be the crown jewel of The Holy Land Experience.

The **Qumran Dead Sea Caves** greet you as you enter, but the exhibit itself is not scheduled to open until mid or late 2002.

Finally, **The Sycamore Tree**, a coffee shop in the Jerusalem Street Market area, is still on the drawing boards.

CHAPTER EIGHT:

Kennedy
Space Center

About an hour from Orlando (and Disney's Tomorrowland) is a place where the fantasy drops away, replaced by awe-inspiring reality. It is here, at the John F. Kennedy Space Center, smack in the middle of a wildlife refuge, that real people, riding real live spaceships, are blasted into outer space on a variety of scientific missions. Nearby Cape Canaveral handles military and commercial launches. On the fringes of this very serious enterprise, the Kennedy Space Center Visitor Complex (a separate entity) lets us earthbound types get a peek at this very special world and imagine — just for a moment — what it must be like to be on the cutting edge of tomorrow. If you time your visit just right, you can even see the actual space shuttle roaring into the heavens towards another rendezvous with the future.

The Kennedy Space Center (or "KSC" for short) is immense, one-fifth the size of the state of Rhode Island. Only 6,000 of its 140,000 acres are used for operations; the rest is a wildlife refuge. Most people are amazed to learn that this monument to high-tech is home to more endangered species (15) than any other place in the United States except the Everglades. There are also 310 types of birds flitting between the launch pads. Yet over the years, the complex has logged some 3,000 launches. As you might expect, you will only get to see a small sliver of Kennedy Space Center's vastness but the access you are granted is remarkable.

For those who care about such things, I should note that no taxpayer money is used to support the visitor facilities, tours, or other tourist activities at Kennedy Space Center. All of these are run by a private company, Delaware North Parks Services, and are entirely self-supporting.

Before You Come

Doing homework for your visit to Kennedy Space Center is not absolutely necessary, but it helps if you have at least some background knowledge of the space program. A painless way to get that background is to head down to the video store and rent *The Right Stuff* and *Apollo 13*. Both films are a lot of fun to watch and offer great insight into the human as well as the technical dimensions of the space program. Somewhat harder to find but worth looking for is the Discovery Channel special, *The Space Shuttle*.

For information about the Kennedy Space Center Visitor Complex itself, call (321) 449-4444. Ask for brochures and they will patch you into a voice mail system where you can record your name and address. The brochures are free and take about one week to arrive.

The Visitor Complex brochure, with its schedule of tours and films, can help you plan out your day in advance. Readers with an Internet connection can log on at www.kennedyspacecenter.com and follow the prompts.

Another way to get an advance look at the Center is to call either the (321) number above or (800) 621-9826 and order the *Kennedy Space Center Visitor Complex* tour book. It is $5.95, plus $4 shipping and takes about a week to arrive. It doesn't provide tour and film times but it will certainly whet your appetite and help you decide how to focus your time during your visit.

When's the Best Time to Come?

To a great extent, attendance at KSC reflects the seasonal ebb and flow of tourists described in *Chapter 1*. However, attendance is also greatly affected by the launch schedule at the Kennedy Space Center.

The days before and after a launch tend to be busier than usual as excitement builds in anticipation of the big event. The day of a launch, the Visitor Complex closes for the six hours preceding the blast-off. If the shuttle launches before 9:00 a.m., the center is open all day. Given the fact that launches are frequently delayed, however, the six-hour pre-launch closing can mean that the Visitor Complex will be open for just a few hours or not at all on a launch day.

So even though seeing a launch is one of the neatest things to do while you're in Florida, a visit to Kennedy Space Center at that time may not be an ideal choice — unless you don't mind missing some things or will be able to spend more than a day on the Space Coast.

For a recorded message giving dates and other information about upcoming shuttle launches dial (321) 867-4636. If you are interested in seeing a shuttle launch, see the discussion on getting tickets and the best view at the end of this chapter.

Getting There

The easiest way to reach KSC from Orlando is to get on the Bee Line Expressway (SR 528) headed east. The tolls will set you back $2.50 each way but it's the fastest route (about an hour or so). Turn off onto SR 407 North, and then onto SR 405 East, which will lead you directly to the Visitor Complex. You can also take SR 50 (Orlando's East Colonial Drive) to route 405. It takes a bit longer but it's free.

Once you get on SR 405, don't be misled by the *Astronaut Hall of Fame*, which you will pass on the right. This is a separate attraction (described in *Chapter 12: Another Roadside Attraction*) and not part of KSC. The Kennedy Space Center is farther along, also on the right, and also graced with a life-size replica of the space shuttle.

Parking, in lots with sections named after shuttle craft, is free.

Opening and Closing Times

Hours for the Visitor Complex vary throughout the year. Opening time is invariably 9:00 a.m. but the closing time changes to keep pace with sunset. The earliest closing time is 5:30 p.m. and the latest is usually 7:00 p.m. However, you should call for exact times.

Tours and IMAX films begin at 9:30 a.m. Tours stop departing about three hours prior to the closing time of the Visitor Complex. The last showing of the IMAX films is usually about one or two hours prior to closing. Some attractions at the Visitor Complex also close early.

The Price of Admission

You enter the Kennedy Space Center Visitor Complex through the Ticket Plaza which is themed to evoke the International Space Station. The ticket booths take the form of space station modules, while the overhead shading is provided by large solar panels. A few space-walking astronauts float above, adding to the effect. There are about 20 ticket windows, with the Will Call windows located to your far left as you approach the Ticket Plaza.

Kennedy Space Center offers a single admission, which includes access to all the exhibits at the Visitor Complex, the Kennedy Space Center bus tour, and admission to the IMAX films. Prices, before tax, are as follows:

Kennedy Space Center Visitor Complex Admission:
Adults:	$26
Children (3 to 11):	$16

KSC also offers two special interest tours: *Cape Canaveral Then & Now* and *NASA Up Close*, described later. These tours cost an additional $20 (for both adults and children) and purchase of the regular admission is required. In other words, you can't show up just to take one of these tours.

The *Cape Canaveral* and *NASA Up Close* tours have only two or three departures each day and each tour is limited to 28 people. The ticketing procedure is also somewhat cumbersome. You must first purchase your tickets at the Ticket Plaza, then proceed to the Information counter in Information Central to make your reservations for a specific departure time. Failure to follow these procedures can result in confusion at tour time; you may even be denied boarding.

Annual Pass

The Kennedy Space Center Visitor Complex offers an annual pass option as follows (prices do not include tax):

Adults:	$44
Children (3 to 11):	$28

The annual pass allows unlimited access to the Visitor Complex, the KSC bus tour, and the IMAX films, plus priority purchase of tickets to view shuttle launches. Annual passholders also get a discount of $3.50 on tickets for each of up to six guests as well as a subscription to the quarterly Visitor Complex newsletter. Passholders must show the pass and a photo ID each time they enter.

The annual pass will appeal, first and foremost, to space junkies, but since it costs less than two separate one-day admissions it may be attractive to those who: want to take the time for a more leisurely visit to KSC, travel to Florida more than once a year, or might want to see a launch or two.

Good Things to Know About . . .

Access for the Disabled

All of KSC Visitor Complex is wheelchair accessible. Free wheelchairs may be obtained at the Information counter in Information Central, the first building you enter after paying your admission. The IMAX films are equipped with devices for the hearing impaired.

Audio Tours

Audio tours of the Visitor Complex are available at the Information counter in Information Central. The cost is $5, tax included. In addition to English, audio tours are available in Spanish, French, German, Italian, Portuguese, and Japanese. In fact, these tours seem to be most popular with non-English speakers.

Babies

Stroller rentals are free at KSC (at the Information counter in Information Central). Diaper changing tables are located in some restrooms, including the men's room at the Orbit Restaurant.

Cameras

Forgot your camera? No problem. Stop at the Information counter in Information Central and exchange two forms of ID for a free loaner 35mm camera to use during your visit. Film is not included but is readily available in shops at the Visitor Complex.

First Aid

There is a well-equipped first aid station with a nurse on duty from 9:00 a.m. to 5:00 p.m. It is located near the bus boarding area.

Leaving the Park

Since the Kennedy Space Center is far from any population center, it is unlikely you will want to leave during your visit but if you decide to do so, just get your hand stamped at the exit and you will be able to reenter.

Money

You will find ATMs to the right of the Ticket Plaza, on the wall of the Space Shop across from the *Astronaut Encounter*, and at the Apollo/Saturn V Center. They are connected to all the major bank systems and credit cards.

Pets

Pets will be boarded free of charge during your visit. The pet kennel is to your right as you approach Information Central.

Security

Security is exceptionally tight. All visitors must pass through metal detectors and a battery of additional security personnel stands ready to conduct more detailed searches. Coolers and backpacks are banned and no lockers are available, so plan on leaving your excess stuff in the car and traveling light.

Blast Off:
Your Day at Kennedy Space Center

I have found that it is impossible to see everything at Kennedy Space Center in one day. It is, however, possible to see most of it — including one of the special tours — if you get there early and step lively for the next 8 to

10 hours. Even a delay of a few hours will decrease your chances of seeing everything.

When you arrive at the Visitor Complex, your first stop is the Ticket Plaza where you collect your access badge. Once you have your badge, you proceed through a building called Information Central. This is really just a spacious antechamber containing the Information counter, which doubles as Lost and Found. Pass through this building and you are in the Visitor Complex itself. Kennedy Space Center and the adjacent Cape Canaveral Air Force Station cover a great deal of territory. The Visitor Complex, by contrast, is quite small; you can walk from one end to the other in about five minutes. Your visit to Kennedy Space Center will be centered here — except when you leave on the bus tour.

The One-Day Stay

Getting the most out of a one-day visit to Kennedy Space Center requires early arrival and careful planning.

When you purchase tickets, you will be handed a map of the Complex and a schedule of tours, IMAX film showings, and other events. Pause a moment in the coolness of Information Central to orient yourself with the map and plan your day with the schedule. You will notice that the bus tour of Kennedy Space Center, called simply *KSC Tour*, has continuous departures, while the *Cape Canaveral Then & Now Tour* and the *NASA Up Close Tour* have only a few. So if you have paid the heavy premium to take either of the latter tours (you can realistically take only one), plan your day around it. Seeing both IMAX films in one day may prove tricky, too, since *L5: First City in Space* has only a few showings each day. I recommend seeing *The Dream Is Alive* and catching *L5* only if time permits.

If you plan on doing all or most of the major, scheduled attractions, you will discover that once you have mapped out your schedule, you will have a half hour or an hour here and there during the day to see what's left and eat. I suggest grabbing your food on the run if you want to maximize your touring time. There are plenty of freestanding kiosks scattered about, making this a viable strategy.

You can use the descriptions below and your own taste to determine which of the "what's left" will most appeal to you. I strongly recommend the *Launch Status Center* and the *Astronaut Encounter*.

The Two-Day Stay

If you have more than one day to allocate to visiting the Kennedy Space Center Visitor Complex your task becomes much easier, and only slightly more expensive. Purchase an annual pass, then on the first day take one of the special tours. On the second day, take the other and see the exhibits or films you didn't have time for the first day.

Special Note: During times of heightened security, the two special bus tours, *NASA Up Close* and *Cape Canaveral Then & Now*, both described below, may be cancelled. In that case, it will be very easy to see KSC in a single day.

Attractions at KSC Visitor Complex

Most of the attractions at the Visitor Complex are available for continuous viewing, except the IMAX films and the *Astronaut Encounter* which have frequently scheduled showings throughout the day. The exhibits range from the compelling to the easy to miss. They are described here starting from Information Central and proceeding in a roughly clockwise path to the back of the Complex. Since distances are short, see the ones that appeal most first, then visit the others as time permits.

Robot Scouts

Rating:	★ ★ ★
Type:	Walk-through presentation, with animated displays
Time:	20 minutes
Kelly says:	A well-done introduction to unmanned space exploration

Our host for this clever overview of current unmanned space exploration missions is Starquester 2000, a robot himself who has been temporarily grounded by a faulty navigational system. As we walk along a twisting, darkened corridor, we pause at six windows where we get a quick and painless overview of the Voyager, Viking, Cassini, and other missions, as well as the Hubble Space telescope. These robot scouts attempt to determine if life exists elsewhere in the solar system, whether humans can survive on the various planets and moons they have visited, and in general just how the universe works.

It's a reminder of how many stunning discoveries have been made in the last few decades by these remote controlled "trailblazers for human exploration," as Starquester never tires of calling them. And even though this attraction looks forward to a human presence on Mars, it is also a reminder that unmanned space exploration will be standard operating procedure for the foreseeable future.

Universe Theater: "Quest for Life"

Rating:	★ ★ +

Type: Film
Time: About 20 minutes
Kelly says: An okay time-killer

On the other side of the Information Central building, a comfortable theater specializes in showing short films on various aspects of space and the space program. These films run continuously, with a short break between showings. The current offering is *Quest for Life*, an earnest but not terribly compelling film that surveys the latest scientific theories about the origins of life on earth and then speculates on the likelihood of life existing elsewhere in the universe. The filmmakers use extremely optimistic odds in making their calculations, odds that have been challenged by some scientists, although the controversy on this point is not noted in the film.

Nature & Technology

Rating: ★ ★
Type: Diorama
Time: Continuous viewing
Kelly says: Can be skipped

Tucked around the corner from the Universe Theater is this small display about the Merritt Island National Wildlife Refuge. It consists of an "immersive" diorama depicting the wildlife and natural scenery that surround the Space Center.

Early Space Exploration

Rating: ★ ★ ★ +
Type: Space program museum
Time: Continuous viewing
Kelly says: An eye-popping encounter with history

A portion of the original control room from the Mission Control building used during the Mercury and early Gemini missions has been transported here from its original home on Cape Canaveral. I found this small room, which looks a bit like a set from a low-budget 1950s television series, absolutely entrancing. It bears mute testimony to the speed at which our technology is exploding. The view you get is the same President Kennedy once enjoyed when he came to the Cape to witness a launch.

Otherwise, this is a once-over-lightly history of the early space program. Sometimes, the Beatles seem to get equal billing with the Mercury astronauts, but if you take the time to read the signage, you'll learn quite a bit. And the few artifacts on display, actual Mercury and Gemini capsules prominent among them, are fascinating.

Rocket Garden

Rating:	★ ★ ★
Type:	Outdoor display of rockets
Time:	Continuous viewing
Kelly says:	Great photo backdrops

This may remind you of a sculpture garden at a museum of modern art. Indeed, some of the rocket engines on display look just as arty and a lot prettier than some modern art. The stars of the show, however, are the big rockets. A plaque gives the vital statistics for each object for the technically inclined, but most people will be content to gawk and have their pictures taken in front of these amazing machines.

The Rocket Garden can be appreciated from a distance, but the Apollo-Saturn service arm, once part of the gantry that served the giant Saturn rockets, is worth a visit. Armstrong, Aldrin, and Collins walked down this metal walkway en route to the moon. Also worth a closer look is the mammoth Saturn 1B rocket lying on its side on the far side of the garden; this behemoth generated a thrust of 1.3 million pounds as it lofted Skylab astronauts into orbit back in the seventies.

Guided tours of the area are available twice daily, with the schedule posted on a sign. This is a great chance to hear some stories that illuminate the human dimension of the space program.

Mad Mission to Mars 2025

Rating:	★ ★ ★
Type:	Live show
Time:	About 30 minutes
Kelly says:	Aimed squarely at the kids

Just opposite the Universe Theater is another show venue, this one showcasing a half-hour of up-tempo silliness hosted by two twenty-something rocket scientists, one of whom is just a little madder than the other.

Using a variety of props, gimmicks, audience volunteers, and an animated 3-D floating robot named WD-4D (get it?), the two provide an overview of the serious science behind a hoped-for mission to explore the Red Planet. There's even a hip-hop rendition of Newton's Laws of Motion. It's virtually incomprehensible, of course, but it is mildly diverting which, I suppose, is the point. The kids love it.

Exploration in the New Millennium

Rating:	★ ★ +
Type:	Displays on Mars and beyond
Time:	Continuous viewing

Kelly says: On and off fun, if you have the time

This walk-through grab bag of displays and short films links the explorers of old with those yet unborn, with the vastness of space substituting for the oceans crossed by the Vikings and Columbus. To keep kids interested, you can pick up an Exploration Passport that can be stamped at various stations throughout the exhibit.

You'll find a nifty mock-up of the Viking Mars lander in a simulated Martian landscape. Nearby, a three-screen video presentation on the **Exploration of the Solar System** is perhaps the most informative display here. Farther along you will find a small display on Mars featuring an opportunity, so we are told, to touch an actual piece of Mars. But this is not a sample brought back from Mars by one of those robot scouts. It's a slice of a meteorite which scientists say originally came from Mars, which to my way of thinking is not quite the same thing. A better idea here is a place where you can leave your signature electronically so it can be transported to Mars on a future mission. Another simple, but fascinating, touch is a curving wall on which the sun, planets, and moons of our solar system are painted to scale to illustrate their relative size.

At the end of the exhibit is a small theater showing *Space Race 3000,* a fanciful TV broadcast from the far-distant future about a race to Proxima Centauri to test three very different forms of interstellar propulsion — an antimatter engine, a light sail, and a ram scoop.

Astronaut Encounter

Rating: ★ ★ ★ ★
Type: Meet a real live astronaut
Time: About 20 minutes
Kelly says: Best for the astronaut Q&A

This is one of the Visitor Complex's more inspired attractions, despite some unnecessary padding. A perky host warms up the audience with some space program trivia and then clowns around with two young volunteers from the audience. That's the unnecessary part. But about ten minutes into the show, a real live veteran of the space program shows up and things get considerably more interesting.

All the astronauts who appear in this show are the real McCoy, with at least one space flight to their credit, and some of the big names of the space program have appeared on this stage. The astronaut chats for a bit and then segues effortlessly into a question and answer period that can be great fun. The host circulates through the audience with the mike so everyone can be heard. For some reason, the show always seems to end with a kid asking how the astronauts go to the bathroom in space. Just like a space mission, this show is planned to the last detail. After the Q&A, the astronaut hangs around for **photo ops**.

IMAX Theater Exhibits

Rating: ★ ★ +
Type: Various displays
Time: Continuous viewing
Kelly says: If you have the time

A number of exhibits and displays are scattered about the large building that houses the IMAX film theaters (see below). If you have a few moments to spare before or after the show — or have ducked inside to escape a rain shower — you might want to take a quick look around.

At one end of the building is an art gallery featuring works commissioned by NASA to commemorate the space program. They range from hyperrealism to the surreal to the completely abstract and are worth at least a quick look. At the other end is a space used for temporary or traveling displays; these can range from the excellent to the merely interesting. In a passage between the two theaters you will find a small display explaining the process whereby shuttles are prepared, launched, retrieved, and prepped yet again for flight.

Astronaut Memorial (Space Mirror)

Rating: ★ ★ ★
Type: Memorial to fallen astronauts
Time: Continuous viewing
Kelly says: Intricate, intriguing, and moving

At first this monument to those who have lost their lives in the space program struck me as a bit of overkill. But as I examined the intricate mechanism that uses the sun's beams to illuminate the 16 names on this massive memorial, I came to realize how fitting it is to blend the high-tech and the heavenly to honor these special people. The entire memorial tilts and swivels to follow the sun across the sky as mirrors collect and focus the sun's rays onto clear glass names in a huge black marble slab. From the opposite side the effect is startling. The memorial is handsomely sited at the end of a large pool at the back of the IMAX Theater; a small kiosk on the side of that building houses computers that offer background information on the astronauts honored on the memorial.

Shuttle Plaza/Explorer

Rating: ★ ★ +
Type: Full-scale shuttle model

Time:	Continuous viewing with the possibility of long waits
Kelly says:	If you have time

The full-scale model of the space shuttle is certainly impressive. But don't be surprised if you find a visit a bit of a let down, especially if you've had to wait 40 minutes or an hour for a glimpse inside. The line spirals up an elaborate exterior superstructure (which also contains an elevator for the disabled). You can step in on two levels — the cockpit and, immediately below it, the crew compartment. To your left is the huge empty cargo bay. What stuck me most was how cramped the space allotted to the crew is. Not even a New York landlord would have the gall to call this a studio apartment. This attraction closes down when lightning is spotted within 30 miles of the Visitor Complex. Guided tours of the Shuttle Plaza area, which also contains two booster rockets, are offered from time to time.

Launch Status Center

Rating:	★ ★ ★ ★ +
Type:	Live briefings and educational displays
Time:	Briefings last about 20 minutes
Kelly says:	The best thing at the Visitor Complex

The modest looking, almost anonymous, white geodesic dome near the Explorer mock-up in Shuttle Plaza houses what is, in my opinion, the best thing at the Visitor Complex. There are models and displays here of the retrievable solid rocket boosters and their motors, a manned maneuvering unit, even an outer-space soft drink dispenser. Perhaps the most fascinating artifact is an actual solid rocket booster nose cone from the 66th shuttle mission; usually these sink to the bottom of the ocean and are replaced, but this one remained afloat long enough to be retrieved.

The main attractions here, however, are the live briefings that occur every hour on the hour from 11:00 a.m. to 5:00 p.m. Held in front of a set of simulated mission control panels like those used in astronaut training, they feature a live "communicator" and live shots from remote video cameras strategically stationed around the working heart of the Space Center, including the Vehicle Assembly Building and the launch pad itself.

No matter when you visit, there will always be something going on at the Space Center and this is your opportunity to get the inside scoop. Obviously, the most interesting time to come here is in the days and hours before a launch and during an actual mission, when you'll get to see the live video feed from the shuttle itself. However, a visit is worthwhile no matter where they are in the launch cycle. The communicators are veritable encyclopedias of information about the space program, and I would urge you not to be shy about asking questions once the formal briefing is over.

Center for Space Education

Rating: ★ ★ ★
Type: Hands-on science displays open to public
Time: Continuous viewing
Kelly says: For teachers and budding astronauts

On the opposite side of the Visitor Complex grounds from Shuttle Plaza, set well away from the other attractions, this large building houses the educational outreach component of the Kennedy Space Center. Inside, teachers will find a library and resource center just for them. Special programs for visiting school groups are also held in this building. The Exploration Station is open to the general public. It is a largish room filled with hands-on, interactive exhibits that demonstrate basic principles of science. This will probably most appeal to younger kids.

The Bus Tours

The only way to see the working end of the Space Center is by taking a guided bus tour. Three tours are offered, representing the past, present, and future of the space program. The main tour, included in the price of admission, visits the Kennedy Space Center on Merritt Island. This is where the shuttle launches take place; you will get a fairly close look at the major sites in the vast complex and get an awe-inspiring close-up look at the largest rocket ever built.

The *KSC Tour* is quite clearly the star of the show, with continuous departures starting at 9:30 a.m. and continuing until about three hours prior to closing. There are two stops on this tour and you can stay as long at each of them as you wish because the buses run continuously. This system has obvious advantages but the downside is that crowds can build up, making the bus loading process slow and chaotic. So it's best to take this tour early in the day.

Cape Canaveral: Then & Now, visits the site of the original U.S. space program. On this tour, you get to enter sites where history was made. Unfortunately, this tour runs only a few times a day, costs a hefty $20 extra, and is frequently curtailed or even unavailable because of the steady stream of commercial launch activity at Cape Canaveral. Unlike the main Kennedy Space Center tour, the Canaveral tour requires that you stay with the same group on the same bus.

NASA Up Close covers some of the same territory as the *KSC Tour* but is much more in-depth. Like the Canaveral tour, it costs $20 extra and operates on a limited schedule. Realistically speaking, on a one-day visit you will be able to take only one tour in addition to the *KSC Tour*, not both.

Special Note: During times of heightened security, the two special bus tours, *NASA Up Close* and *Cape Canaveral Then & Now*, may be cancelled.

All tours leave from an efficient bus terminal at one end of the Visitor Complex. The buses are much like regular city buses except they have much larger windows. No food is allowed aboard the buses and the only beverage allowed is bottled water, which is available for purchase at the Visitors Complex and each stop of the *KSC Tour*. It's not a bad idea to bring some, especially in the warmer months.

Both Kennedy Space Center and Cape Canaveral Air Force Station are working spaceports, which means that these tours may be modified, curtailed, or even cancelled, to accommodate launch and other activities. This is much more likely to happen with the Cape Canaveral tour since the Cape has more launches, some of which are top secret military missions.

Another unpredictable element, in terms of what you will see, is the wildlife at the Center. Alligators, sometimes jokingly referred to as part of the security system, are sighted frequently and there are bald eagle nests along the tour routes.

The standard narration on the tours will be supplemented — or interrupted — whenever the driver feels it's time to add his or her own commentary or release a late-breaking news bulletin ("Wild hogs on the left!"). Foreign language narration, in French, German, Spanish, and Portuguese, is available on tape on a first-come, first-served basis.

Kennedy Space Center Tour

Rating: ★ ★ ★ ★ ★

Time: 2 to 3 hours

Kelly says: The next best thing to becoming an astronaut

Now that the Apollo/Saturn V Center is open, the bus tour of Kennedy Space Center has become yet another "must-see" stop on the Central Florida tourist circuit. And no wonder. This tour takes you to the sites where the space shuttle is prepared and launched. It also gives you an opportunity to gape and gawk at an actual Saturn V rocket. It's as close as you'll come to being launched into space without joining the astronaut corps.

There are two stops on this tour — the LC-39 Observation Gantry and the Apollo/Saturn V Center. You will also get to drive by the Vehicle Assembly Building, where the space shuttle is mated with its immense fuel tanks prior to each launch.

The **LC-39 Observation Gantry** ("LC" stands for "launch complex") is a four-story tower that offers a bird's-eye view of launch pads 39A and B, from which all shuttle flights depart. If you visit close to a launch, you'll see the support structure that completely surrounds the shuttle. It is only removed a few hours prior to launch. You may also get a chance for an up-close photo of the massive crawler transporters that carry the shuttle from the **Vehicle Assembly Building** (VAB) to the launch pad. These six-million-pound vehicles roar along at one mile per hour when fully loaded and get an incredible 35 feet per gallon.

You'll also get close to the VAB itself. One of the largest buildings in the world, its roof covers five acres. It encloses so much space that it has its own atmosphere and it has actually rained inside. It was here that the gigantic Saturn V rockets used in the Apollo program were assembled. The shuttles seem tiny by comparison.

The undisputed highlight of this tour is a visit to the **Apollo/Saturn V Center**. The building is massive — and it has to be to house a refurbished, 363-foot-tall Saturn V moon rocket, one of only three in existence. Before you get to see the star of this show, you enter the **Firing Room** where the actual mission control consoles used during the Apollo missions form a backdrop for a video and audio re-creation of the launch of Apollo VIII, the first manned lunar mission.

Then you step into the massive building that houses the Saturn V, suspended horizontally in one long open space. No description can prepare you for just how immense this thing actually is. The word "awesome" moves from hyperbole to understatement. Arrayed around, alongside, and under the rocket are interpretive displays filled with astounding facts about this magnificent achievement.

Before you leave, be sure to visit the **Lunar Theater** where you will see a re-creation of the first landing on the moon and be reminded of just how touch-and-go this mission was up to the very last second. After the show, you step into the **New Frontiers Gallery** for a preview of space missions yet to come.

If you don't linger at the various stops, you can complete this tour in about one and a half hours, but rushing through is a mistake. Take your time, invest two or three hours and enjoy yourself. There are places to eat at each stop and the Apollo/Saturn V Center even boasts the **Moon Rock Cafe,** the "only place on earth where you can dine next to a piece of the moon."

Between stops a taped commentary plays on ceiling-mounted video monitors. Although it provides some interesting background information, it is most memorable for the annoying way it plugs the merchandise available at the inevitable souvenir shops. But that is a minor quibble. This tour is an exciting experience for anyone. For Americans, it should be a source of deep patriotic pride.

Tip: Try for a seat on the right side of the bus as you shuttle from stop to stop.

Cape Canaveral Then & Now Tour
Rating: ★ ★ ★ +
Time: Approximately 2 hours
Kelly says: Stirring history for true space buffs

First, the bad news: This tour costs $20 extra for both adults and children (although I've seen few children on the tour). It has only two or three departures a day. It has a limited capacity of just 28 seats on a smaller bus. This tour is very often changed or modified to accommodate launch activity, making it difficult to predict what you will actually see on the day of your visit. It also requires a much greater exercise of the imagination than does the *KSC Tour* (although that's probably a good thing).

Still, I suspect there will be those who will slightly prefer this tour to the other. The main reason is that on this one you actually get to enter the places where space history was made, even if those places are now mere empty concrete spaces where towering launch gantries once stood.

It was from Cape Canaveral that the first Americans were launched into space. You can walk through the blockhouse that housed mission control for the early Mercury missions and stroll out to the pad from which puny looking Redstone rockets launched the first Americans into space using a gantry jury-rigged from an old oil drilling rig. The room-sized computer used for these launches could be replaced by a modern laptop, with plenty of room left over on the hard drive for games. Next door is a small museum with a collection of artifacts relating to the early days of the space program.

Much of the launch pad area has been turned into a sort of outdoor sculpture garden displaying two dozen or so rockets and missiles, including my personal favorite, the sleekly magnificent and rather sexy Snark.

Cape Canaveral entered the space age in 1950 with tests of captured German V-2 rockets. But it is far from being a dusty museum or a monument to the past. It is a bustling modern spaceport from which a wide variety of unmanned military, scientific, and commercial satellites are launched into orbit, including many of the satellites that provide our telephone communications and weather forecasting. As you drive around, you may catch glimpses of preparations for upcoming launches. Yet much of the land here has been leased back to the farmers who occupied the area before the space age; now orange groves and launch pads sit side by side in incongruous harmony.

The narration for this tour is handled by both the driver and a guide, who banter back and forth much in the style of co-hosts on a morning news program. Their knowledge is considerable and their devotion to their jobs and the history entrusted to them apparent. Either side of the bus is okay since you get to walk up to and into the most interesting sights.

NASA Up Close

Rating: ★ ★ ★ +

Time: 90 minutes

Kelly says: In the footsteps of the astronauts

Like the Cape Canaveral tour, this one carries a hefty $20 additional fee for both children and adults. But I suspect that the *KSC Tour* will convince a lot of people that paying the extra bucks for a closer look at what they've just seen will be well worth it.

In a sense *NASA Up Close* begins where the *KSC Tour* leaves off, offering you extra special access to places you glimpsed from afar on the main tour. With the expert guidance of a space program expert who is a gold mine of little known facts, you get to visit **Launch Pads 39A and B**, a stop that offers one of the best **photo ops** to be had at KSC. With the towering pads to one side and the Atlantic Ocean to the other, you'll get a terrific view of the rotating service structure that swings away for the actual launch, the flame trench that harnesses and channels the inferno created by the shuttle's rockets, and the massive lightning rods that protect the shuttle from Florida's stormy weather.

A favorite stop is the **Launch Countdown Clock**. If you've ever seen a launch on television, you've seen this landmark. Now you'll get a chance to have someone snap your picture as you stand next to it. You also get closer to the **Vehicle Assembly Building**. It looks immense from the vantage point offered on the *KSC Tour*, but now it is positively awe-inspiring.

Every mission begins with an inch-by-inch journey on the **Crawler Transporter**, which you'll revisit on this tour. And since all space missions must come to an end, the **Shuttle Landing Facility** looks after the longest and widest landing strip in the world, giving returning astronauts plenty of margin for error because the gliding space shuttle gets only one shot at landing. Perhaps the most stirring moment comes when the tour guide takes you along the same route the astronauts travel on launch day. On your way from the crew's preflight quarters to Pads 39 A and B, you'll be briefed on the orbiter processing facility, the parachute refurbishing center, and the flight training facility where Apollo astronauts earn their wings.

The IMAX Films

If you've never seen an IMAX film, this is an excellent place to remedy that situation. IMAX is an ultra-large film format, ten times larger than standard 35mm film and three times the size of the 70mm films you see at your local movie theater. It is projected on a screen some five and a half stories high and 70 feet wide. The sound system is equally impressive, producing bass tones you will feel in your bones.

The IMAX Theater at the Visitor Complex contains two back-to-back IMAX theaters, the only such IMAX "multiplex" in the world. The auditoriums are small relative to the size of the screen, so I would recommend showing up early so you can grab a seat towards the back of the house. There are doors on five levels and I find the seats in the middle of the third level to be just about ideal.

Of the films reviewed below, *The Dream Is Alive* will almost certainly be playing when you visit. The other films change from time to time.

The Dream Is Alive

Rating: ★ ★ ★ ★ +
Time: 37 minutes

This film offers a fascinating overview of what the shuttle program is all about. It takes you step by step through the process of refurbishing and readying a shuttle for the next mission. It features spectacular footage of the shuttle in action, including enthralling sequences on the training of astronauts to service an orbiting satellite and the subsequent successful completion of the mission. Best of all are the sequences shot by the astronauts themselves far above the planet's surface. Walter Cronkite narrates with his trademark aplomb. If you can see just one of the IMAX films, I recommend this one.

L5: First City in Space

Rating: ★ ★ ★
Time: 33 minutes

3D is the gimmick in this short film fantasy about a space city of the future that captures a comet to serve as a source of water and other useful raw materials. Some of the footage is fun, especially the sequence in which an intrepid astronaut lands a small craft on the comet to repair the robot engines that will power this chunk of space ice back to L5. But for the most part this film is a disappointment. IMAX seems to work far better in recording actual reality than in creating computer animated fantasy.

Eating at Kennedy Space Center

While you won't have to subsist on the powdered drinks and squeeze-tube dinners that were once standard fare for astronauts, neither can you expect a gourmet dining experience at KSC Visitor Complex. The eateries here are geared to processing hundreds of generally young diners in a quick and efficient manner, and the food quality seldom rises above fast-food or cafeteria level, although the desserts in The Orbit are delicious. One of the management's best inspirations has been to dispatch dozens of freestanding food carts to various points in the Visitor Complex. They offer everything from ice cream snacks to fruit to more substantial fare like hot dogs. Given the difficulty of squeezing everything into a one-day visit to the Center, it makes a lot of sense to eat on the run from these carts and save the big sit-down meal for later in the evening.

The only full-service restaurant at the Visitor Complex is **Mila's Road-house**, overlooking the *Space Mirror*. The decor is vaguely fifties or sixties in feel (there are a few outdoor tables) and the menu runs to home-cooked meat-and-veg meals, burgers, and beef and chicken sandwiches. Hot dogs and spaghetti are offered to the small fry. Most entrees cost less than $10, desserts are under $4. Wine is served by the glass ($4) and bottle ($14 to $22).

Next door is **The Orbit**, a large, noisy fast-food emporium with a modern metallic high-tech decor. Service is cafeteria style, with a large central carousel dispensing beverages, salads, sandwiches, and desserts. On one side of the carousel, you can get pizzas and pasta dishes for about $6 to $8. On the other side, a steam table offers roast beef, turkey, chicken, and fried fish dinners with a choice of vegetables. Prices range from $6 to about $10. Beer and wine is served here ($4).

Another cafeteria, **The Lunch Pad**, is located near the bus depot. This is the place to come for breakfast first thing in the morning or for burgers and fries or a variety of sandwiches later in the day. There is also a decent grilled chicken Caesar salad available here, one of the healthier food choices to be found at the Visitor Complex. A standard meal of sandwich, fries, and soft drink should cost well under $10.

Food is also to be had on the *KSC Tour*. The LC-39 Observation Gantry and the International Space Station Center both have hot dog stands where a quick meal will cost about $5. The Apollo/Saturn V Center features the **Moon Rock Cafe**, a cafeteria where you will find hot dogs, Polish sausage, and cheeseburgers served with fries for $4 to about $6. Individual pizzas are about $5 and desserts are in the $2 to $3 range. If you are trying to pack as much as possible into a one-day visit, grabbing a hot dog on this tour and eating it while waiting for the bus is a good strategy.

Beyond these sit-down eateries, the Visitor Complex offers a number of walk-up windows dispensing a variety of fast foods and desserts. **Planetary Pizza**, near The Lunch Pad, offers pizzas and calzone for about $5 to $6. The **New Frontier Café**, opposite the *Astronaut Encounter*, serves up beef, pork and chicken sandwiches for about $7. The **Milky Way Parlor**, near the *Universe Theater*, sells Comet Cones ($2 to $3) and Solar Sundaes ($3). There are a number of even smaller freestanding kiosks selling drinks and snacks; these open and close as the crowds ebb and flow.

Shopping at Kennedy Space Center

The largest selection of KSC souvenir and outer-space themed merchandise to be found anywhere is yours to browse through in the mammoth, two-level **Space Shop**, which lies between the ticket pavilion and the bus depot. Here you will find everything from t-shirts priced well under $20 to leather bomber jackets with the NASA logo for over $200. There are also buttons, badges, patches, and medallions commemorating every shuttle mission. Some of these collectibles are issued in limited editions of just one million copies, so snatch yours up before they're gone!

Among the best souvenirs are the videos (available in all international formats) and the space shuttle and rocket model kits. A video version of *The Dream Is Alive* (about $25) makes a nice memento. The official Kennedy Space Center tour book (about $6) also makes an excellent (not to mention inexpensive) souvenir. The video version of the tour is about $20. Other souvenirs include packets of bona fide space food and sew-on mission patches.

Tip: For a nifty (and cheap!) souvenir or gift, buy a postcard and stamp and mail it here. It will arrive with a special Kennedy Space Center cancellation. Philatelists take note.

The Right Stuff shop is located at the Saturn V facility that is visited on the main bus tour. It contains much the same assortment of goods as the Space Shop, although there is much more of an Apollo/Saturn V/moon mission focus.

Space Shop II, a much smaller shop with a much smaller selection, is located just by the exit in case you have a last-minute change of heart. If you want stuff but don't want to spend your time at the Visitor Complex shopping, call the mail order department at (800) 621-9826 and wade through the automated answering service.

Seeing a Launch

You've probably seen film clips of shuttle launches on TV. You've probably seen them dozens of times. But, to quote Al Jolson, you ain't seen nothin' yet! Seeing a shuttle launch live and in person is one of the truly great experiences a Florida vacation has to offer. Catching at least a glimpse of a launch is surprisingly easy. On a clear day, the rising shuttle is visible from the Orlando area. Getting a closer look, however, requires a bit of planning.

First, you must understand that you don't have to be close to the launching pad to get ringside seats. In fact, no one can be close to the launching pad. The greatest danger a launch poses to bystanders is, surprisingly, the noise generated by the awesome engines. It is, I am told, the loudest manmade sound next to the explosion of a thermonuclear device. An elaborate sound suppression system clicks in at launch time, spewing 300,000 gallons of water on the escaping gases from the rocket engines. Were it not for this system, the observers in the press and VIP section, some three and a half miles away, would permanently lose their hearing.

Unless you're a credentialed reporter, a relative of an astronaut, or have some inside pull at NASA, you will be a good bit farther way. But you can still have an excellent view and an experience you will remember for the rest of your life.

The best viewing venue for the general public is along the NASA Causeway that runs from Merritt Island to Cape Canaveral Air Force base across the Banana River. This puts you approximately six miles from the launch pad. There's nothing fancy about the viewing area; KSC buses you to the Causeway and lets you sit or stand on the grassy area between the road and the river. No seating is provided but you can remain aboard the air conditioned bus if you prefer. The shuttle will be visible to the naked eye across the water to the north; a pair of binoculars will allow you to see the vapor pouring off the fuel tanks.

Viewing a launch requires a modest investment and some advance planning. The Kennedy Space Center Visitor Complex sells approximately 5,000 tickets for its buses to the viewing area. The cost is $15 for all ages, in addition to regular admission. Tickets may be purchased by calling (321) 449-4444 or on the Internet at www.kennedyspacecenter.com. (See below for a free alternative.)

The demand for these tickets is unpredictable. On at least one occasion, they sold out within an hour of first being offered. For other launches, typically those scheduled during the wee hours of the morning, the demand has been considerably less intense. If you find that the launch is sold out, there is still a slim chance you may be able to get tickets. Very occasionally a few tickets go back on sale on launch day. So if you arrive bright and early that morning, you just may be able to buy a ticket. No guarantees, of course, but for a sold-out launch it's your best bet. Given the uncertainty of the actual launch date, you will have to check back regularly to plan your visit. A recorded message at (321) 867-4636 provides the latest information.

On Launch Day

If you're headed to NASA Causeway via the KSC buses, plan on pulling on to SR 405 (from the west) or SR 3 (from the south) several hours before the scheduled launch time. Park your car in the Visitors Complex parking lots and head for the buses that will shuttle you to the viewing area. Once there, remember you are on government property and in a wildlife refuge to boot, so there are a few simple rules. Cooking and fires are prohibited, as are alcoholic beverages. You are not allowed to fish, wade, swim, or feed the wildlife (there are some manatee holding pens along the causeway viewing area). If you have a pet, you'll have to make arrangements to leave it behind.

The atmosphere at the viewing area is infectiously cheerful and friendly. People seem to instantly become one happy family. At the launch I attended, a professor of astronomy from a nearby university was letting passersby take a peek at the shuttle through his eight-inch telescope. Dotted along the viewing area are NASA Exchange trailers selling snacks and souvenirs. The prices for food and drink are surprisingly cheap, especially considering you are a captive audience.

A public address system mounted on poles carries live announcements from NASA mission control. As launch time approaches, you will hear the actual conversations between mission control and the shuttle crew. A few minutes before the launch, several local radio stations begin live coverage. Among them are 580AM, 90.7FM, and 107.1FM.

At the actual launch, you will see a flash of light a second or two before blast-off. Then the shuttle disappears in a towering cloud of white exhaust only to emerge a moment later, its engines spewing a blinding flame. The shuttle will be well up into the air before you hear the sound, but when it arrives at your viewing point you will feel the land tremble beneath your feet as well as hear the throaty rumble of the booster rockets. As it continues its eight minute journey to orbit, arcing gracefully to the east, the shuttle looks like a tiny toy atop a massive column of white clouds.

About two and half minutes into the flight, the booster rockets drop away. (If you have binoculars, you may be able to spot the parachutes that lower them to the sea for recovery by NASA ships.) At this point, the shuttle becomes a star-like point of light hurtling into the history books. I was lucky. The launch I observed went up on the dot. But you should be aware that, more often than not, the shuttle doesn't go up on schedule. If there are delays for weather or technical glitches, you will be kept posted. If the launch is scrubbed (that is, canceled) you can still enjoy the Visitor Complex.

Seeing a launch for free

If you'd rather not pay the KSC admission fee and the $15 extra charge to be bussed out to the NASA Causeway, you can still get an excellent view of the launch from Space View Park in nearby Titusville. Take Exit 80 from I-95 (SR 406, Garden Street). The park is two blocks south of SR 406. Nearby Veterans Memorial Park often has a loudspeaker broadcasting the audio feed from NASA. Get there early.

CHAPTER NINE:

Busch Gardens Tampa

Busch Gardens is a somewhat schizophrenic mixture of zoological park and amusement park, with a dash of variety show thrown in. Given the seemingly disparate demands of these elements, the designers have done an admirable job of creating an attractive whole. Aesthetically, a stroll through Busch Gardens is one of the most pleasing in Central Florida.

Like any good theme park, Busch Gardens has one. In this case it's Africa, the mysterious continent so linked in the popular imagination with wild animals and adventure. Borrowing a page from the Disney manual, the park is divided into nine "lands," or as Busch calls them, "themed areas." With few exceptions, they take their names from countries or regions in Africa. The metaphor works wonderfully for the zoo side of things, although it results in the occasional oddity (Bengal tigers in the Congo? Dolphins in Timbuktu?). It is largely extraneous to the park's other elements. A roller coaster is a roller coaster, whether it's named after an Egyptian god (*Montu*) or in a Congolese dialect (*Kumba*). Switch the locations of these giant coasters and no one would know the difference. On the other hand, who cares?

Since this book focuses on Orlando, the question naturally arises: Why schlep to Tampa for another theme park? There are two main answers: the animals and the roller coasters. Disney's Animal Kingdom has created some competition to Busch's great apes and white Bengal tigers, but it has no mammoth roller coasters. There are other reasons, as well. For early risers at least, Busch Gardens is a very doable day trip from Orlando. The participation of Busch Gardens in the Orlando FlexTicket program (see "The Price of Admission," below) adds just another incentive to make the trip.

Finally, Busch Gardens has a personality and an allure all its own. The innovative animal habitats temper the frenzy of the rides, and the rides give you something to do when just sitting and watching begins to pale. The park is beautifully designed with some absolutely enchanting nooks and crannies. While it's a great place to do things, Busch Gardens is also a delightful place simply to be.

My only caution would be that the amusement park side of the equation can tend to overshadow the zoo. Many of the animal exhibits reward quiet, patient observation, but the excitement generated by the smorgasbord of giant roller coasters and splashy water rides will make it hard to cultivate a contemplative state of mind, especially for the younger members of your party. Perhaps the best strategy is to use exhibits like the *Myombe Reserve* (great apes), the walk-through aviary, and the air-conditioned koala habitat to cool out and cool down between bouts of manic activity. Another approach is to devote one visit to the amusement park rides, another to the zoo exhibits.

Gathering Information

By dialing (800) 4ADVENTURE (423-8368) you can hear some very general information about the Busch family of theme parks and short sales pitches about individual parks. You can also leave your name and address to have general information about all their parks sent to you (in about two to three weeks). You can reach a real live person by calling (888) 800-5447. In Tampa, call (813) 987-5082 for a series of recorded messages that provide current operating hours and admissions prices for one-day tickets, the various annual pass options, and other information. This recording tends to be rather general.

For the latest on Busch Gardens' zoo animals, you can check out the park's animal information site at www.buschgardens.org.

Another web site provides information for the amusement park side of Busch Gardens Tampa. The address is www.buschgardens.com.

When's the Best Time to Come?

Plotting the best time of year at which to visit is less of a consideration than with the other major theme parks of Central Florida. According to the trade paper *Amusement Business*, Busch Gardens gets half the visitors Universal hosts each year and less than a third of those who show up at the Magic Kingdom. On the other hand, attendance continues to grow and on several recent visits large groups of foreign tourists and American high school kids were much in evidence.

Getting There

Busch Gardens is roughly 75 miles from Universal Orlando, about 65 miles from the intersection of I-4 and US 192 in Kissimmee. You can drive there in about one and a quarter to one and a half hours depending on where you start and how closely you observe the posted speed limit. Drive west on I-4 to Exit 6B (US 92 West, Hillsborough Avenue). Go about 1.5 miles and turn right on 56th Street (SR 583); go another two miles and turn right on Busch Boulevard. Busch Gardens is about two miles ahead on your right.

Shuttle Bus Service

If you'd rather not drive from Orlando, you can take advantage of the shuttle bus service that Busch operates from SeaWorld. The fare is $5 per person, but if you have a 5-park FlexTicket the service is free. There are five pick-up points conveniently located along Orlando's I-4 corridor, including Universal Orlando, SeaWorld, and Old Town in Kissimmee. Buses depart between roughly 8:00 a.m. and 9:00 a.m. with return journeys timed to the current closing hours at Busch Gardens Tampa, which vary seasonally (see below). Reservations are required. To make one, or check the latest schedule and pick-up points, call (800) 221-1339.

Parking at Busch Gardens Tampa

You know you're almost at Busch Gardens when you see the giant roller coaster *Montu* looming overhead. You'll probably also hear the screams as you pull into the parking lot. Actually, there are a series of parking lots with room for 5,000 vehicles. Lots A and B are near the park entrance and are reserved for handicapped and preferred parking, respectively. There is much more parking across the street, which is where you will most likely be stowing your car. Trams snake their way back and forth to the entrance, but if you're in A or B it's just as easy to walk.

Motorcycles and cars park for $7, campers and trailers for $8, tax included. If you have any Busch Gardens annual pass, parking is free. Preferred Parking, in Lot B, costs $11 ($6 for annual passholders).

Opening and Closing Times

The park is usually open from 10:00 a.m. to 6:00 p.m. every day of the year. However, during the summer months and at holiday times the hours are extended, with opening at 9:00 a.m. and closing pushed back until 7:00, 8:00, or 9:00 p.m. The Morocco section stays open a half-hour or so later than the rest of the park to accommodate last-minute shoppers. Call Guest Relations at (813) 987-5212 for the exact current operating hours.

The Price of Admission

Busch Gardens sells only one-day admissions, but you can get a discount for the next day's admission if you buy it while you are still in the park. The following prices include tax (which is slightly higher than in Orlando).

One Day Admission:

Adults:	$53.45
Children (3 to 9):	$43.82
Seniors (55+):	$50.23

Children under age 3 are admitted **free**.

After 3:00 p.m., admission is discounted as follows:

Adults:	$42.74
Children (3 to 9):	$33.11

Visa, MasterCard, and Discover credit cards are accepted. While you are in the park, you can purchase a ticket for admission the next day for $11.68, including tax. This makes a two-day visit to Busch Gardens a very good buy.

A ***Value Ticket*** that lets you spend one day at Busch and one day at its water park, Adventure Island, is $64.15 ($53.45 for kids). A ***Value Pass*** good for one day each at Busch and SeaWorld is $88.34 ($72.37 for kids).

Orlando FlexTicket

Busch Gardens participates in the Orlando FlexTicket program described in *Chapter 1: Introduction & Orientation*. The 5-Park, 14-Day pass grants admission to Universal Studios Florida, Islands of Adventure, SeaWorld, and Wet 'n Wild (all in Orlando), as well as to Busch Gardens. It is priced as follows:

Adults:	$215.46
Children (3 to 9):	$175.12

Annual Passes

Busch Gardens Tampa offers a variety of annual pass options, called "Passports," which take the form of a credit card sized photo ID. Silver Passports are valid for one year and Gold Passports for two. If you are at the park, you will find the Pass Center located to your right as you approach the main ticket windows. In the following list of prices, which include tax, the Silver Passport price is given first, followed by the Gold Passport price. Seniors are those 55 years or older.

Busch Gardens Passports

Unlimited access to Busch Gardens Tampa.

Adults:	$90.90 / $139.05
Children & Seniors:	$80.20 / $128.35

Busch Gardens – Adventure Island Passports

Annual pass to both Busch Gardens and Adventure Island, the nearby

Busch water park (see *Chapter 10: Water Parks*).

Adults: $123.00 / $171.15

Children & Seniors $112.30 / $160.45

Busch Gardens - SeaWorld Passports

Annual Pass to both Busch Gardens and SeaWorld Orlando.

Adults: $138.40 / $186.32

Children & Seniors: $127.75/ $175.67

Busch Gardens - SeaWorld - Adventure Island Passports

Annual Pass to Busch Gardens, Adventure Island, and SeaWorld.

Adults: $170.61 / $218.48

Children & Seniors: $159.85 / $207.82

The amount of a one-day admission can be applied to these passes, but only if you upgrade on the day you buy it.

EZpay

Busch offers the option of paying for your Passport in equal monthly installments over the 12- or 24-month term of the Passport. Payments are charged to your credit card and no finance charges or fees are added. This option makes an annual pass almost irresistible.

Discounts

You can get a 10% discount on single-day admissions tickets by ordering them on the Busch Gardens web site, www.4adventure.com. Once you're in Tampa, you will find dollars-off coupons for Busch Gardens in all the usual places (see *Chapter 1: Introduction & Orientation*). Discounted tickets are also available from hotel Guests Services desks and ticket brokers in the Orlando area. In addition to the discounts accorded to senior citizens purchasing annual passes, AAA cardholders can get a 10% discount on one-day admissions at the ticket booths, while handicapped guests (blind, deaf, mentally handicapped) receive a 50% discount. Special deals are offered to Florida residents during the off-season (fall to spring); call for details. Annual passholders receive a 10% discount on merchandise in park shops and at the larger eateries as well as a 15% discount on admission to other Busch theme parks.

Buying Tickets

Tickets can be purchased as you arrive, at ticket booths immediately in front of the park entrance. However, you can save yourself a bit of time by purchasing your tickets the day before, in the afternoon, when there are no lines. If you are based in Orlando, you can purchase a discounted combination ticket when you visit SeaWorld. You can also purchase Busch Gardens tickets at SeaWorld even if you are not visiting SeaWorld.

Busch Gardens tickets are available through several local Tampa hotels, so you might want to check with the concierge or the front desk if you are staying nearby. Other options are to purchase tickets through your travel agent before you leave home or on the Busch Gardens web site (see above).

Staying Near the Park

If you'd like to spend a few days at Busch Gardens or just want to avoid doing the roundtrip from Orlando in one day, you may want to consider staying at one of the motels within walking distance of the park. Other, more upscale hotel choices are available just a short drive away.

Howard Johnson

4139 East Busch Boulevard
Tampa, FL 33612
(813) 988-9191; fax (813) 988-9195

> A standard mid-range motel.
> *Price Range:* $ - $$$
> *Amenities:*   Pool
> *Walk to Park:*   10 minutes

Days Inn

2901 East Busch Boulevard
Tampa, FL 33612
(813) 933-6471

> A standard mid-range motel.
> *Price Range:* $$ - $$$
> *Amenities:*   Pool, restaurant
> *Walk to Park:*   15 minutes

Baymont Inn & Suites

9202 North 30th Street
Tampa, FL 33612
(813) 930-6900; fax (813) 930-0563

> Newly built mid-range hotel.
> *Price Range:* $$ - $$$
> *Amenities:*   Pool
> *Walk to Park:*   15 minutes

Red Roof Inn

2307 East Busch Boulevard

Tampa, FL 33612
(813) 932-0073; fax (813) 933-5689
A nice, clean budget motel.
Price Range: $$
Amenities: Small pool
Walk to Park: 20 to 30 minutes

Special Events

Busch Gardens hosts a growing number of razzle-dazzle themed events timed to the calendar. The oldest of these is an alcohol-free New Year's Eve celebration for young people and families. Halloween shenanigans are in evidence during October. These are typically after-hours affairs that require a hefty separate admission if purchased separately (a recent Howl-O-Scream event was $35). However, if you "upgrade" while you are in the park, or have an annual pass, discounts are substantial.

During the Christmas season there are nightly tree lighting ceremonies and in the fall the park hosts a series of big band concerts. A patriotic July Fourth celebration was in the planning stages at press time. To learn more about what events may be planned during your visit and to get the latest on ticket prices, call toll-free (888) 800-5447.

Dining at Busch Gardens Tampa

On the whole, the dining experience at Busch Gardens is a step down from that at its sister park, SeaWorld, in Orlando. However, the single full-service restaurant (Crown Colony House) has some very tasty dishes and, if you can wangle a window seat, the views are spectacular. Also worth noting is that the barbecue at Stanleyville Smokehouse is on a par with that served up at SeaWorld. Most disappointing is that Busch Gardens has not chosen to extend its African theme to its restaurant menus. I found myself wishing for something akin to the first-rate Moroccan restaurant at EPCOT.

For those who keep track of such things, the prices for soft drinks are $1.59, $1.99, and $2.39 for small, medium, and large sizes. (An interesting note: No straws are served at any of the park's restaurants or fast-food outlets in deference to the safety of the animals.)

Shopping at Busch Gardens Tampa

The souvenir hunter will not leave disappointed. There are plenty of logo-bearing gadgets, gizmos, and wearables from which to choose. The t-shirts with tigers and gorillas are especially attractive. Tiger fanciers will also be drawn to the beach towels with the large white Bengal tiger portrait.

Best of all are the genuine African crafts to be found here and there around the park. Look for them in Morocco, Crown Colony, and Timbuktu. The prices can be steep for some of the nicer pieces, but there are some very attractive (and attractively priced) smaller items to be found.

Most of the shops offer a free package pick-up service that lets you collect your purchases near the front entrance on your way out, so you needn't worry about lugging things about for half the day. You can avail yourself of Busch Gardens' mail order services by dialing (800) 410-9453 or (813) 987-5060. Souvenirs are also available on the Busch Gardens web site at www.buschgardens.com.

Good Things To Know About ...

Access for the Disabled

Handicapped parking spaces are provided directly in front of the park's main entrance for those with a valid permit. Otherwise, physically challenged guests may be dropped off at the main entrance. The entire park is wheelchair accessible and companion bathrooms are dotted about the park. Some physically challenged guests may not be able to experience certain rides due to safety considerations. An "Access Guide" is available at Guest Relations near the main entrance.

Wheelchair and motorized cart rentals are handled out of a concession next to the Jeepers and Creepers shop in Morocco. Wheelchairs are $9 a day (which includes a refundable $2 deposit). Motorized carts are $35 (including a $5 deposit). Motorized carts are popular, so plan to get there early to be sure you get one.

Animal Observation

Busch Gardens does an excellent job of displaying its animals in natural settings. One consequence of that is that they can sometimes be hard to see. So if spying out elands or catching a glimpse of a rare rhino baby is important to you, consider bringing along a pair of binoculars. They will come in handy on the *Skyride*, the *Trans-Veldt Railroad*, and even at lunch in the Crown Colony House restaurant.

Babies

Diaper changing tables are located in restrooms throughout the park. A nursing area is located in Land of the Dragons.

If you don't have your own, you can rent strollers at the concession next to Jeepers and Creepers in Morocco. Nifty looking Jeep Strollers are $11 for the full day, which includes a $2 refundable deposit. Double strollers are $15, which also includes a refundable $2 deposit.

Drinking

As a reminder, the legal drinking age in Florida is 21 and photo IDs will be requested if there is the slightest doubt.

First Aid

First aid stations are located in Timbuktu behind the Das Festhaus restaurant and in Crown Colony in the *Skyride* building. If emergency aid is needed, contact the nearest employee.

Getting Wet

The signs say, "This is a water attraction. Riders will get wet and possibly soaked." This is not marketing hyperbole but a simple statement of fact. The water rides at Busch Gardens are one of its best kept secrets (the mammoth roller coasters get most of the publicity), but they pose some problems for the unprepared. Kids probably won't care, but adults can get positively cranky when wandering around sopping wet.

The three major water rides, in increasing order of wetness, are *Stanley Falls Log Flume, Congo River Rapids*, and the absolutely soaking *Tanganyika Tidal Wave*. (The *Mizzly Marsh* section of Land of the Dragons can also get tykes very wet.) Fortunately, these three rides are within a short distance of each other, in the Congo and Stanleyville, allowing you to implement the following strategy:

First, dress appropriately. Wear a bathing suit and t-shirt under a dressier outer layer. Wear shoes you don't mind getting wet; sports sandals are ideal. Bring a tote bag in which you can put things, like cameras, that shouldn't get wet. You can also pack a towel and it's probably a good idea to bring along the plastic laundry bag from your motel room.

Plan to do the water rides in sequence. When you're ready to start, strip off your outer layer, put it in the tote bag along with your other belongings, and stash everything in a convenient locker. There are lockers dotted throughout the Congo and Stanleyville. A helpful locker symbol on the map of the park will help you locate the nearest one. Now you're ready to enjoy the rides without worry.

Once you've completed the circuit, and especially if you rode the *Tidal Wave*, you will be soaked to the skin. You now have a choice. If it's a hot summer day, you may want to let your clothes dry as you see the rest of the park. Don't worry about feeling foolish; you'll see of plenty of other folks in the same boat, and your damp clothes will feel just great in the Florida heat. In cooler weather, however, it's a good idea to return to the locker, grab your stuff, head to a nearby restroom, and change into dry clothes. Use the plastic laundry bag for the wet stuff.

The alternative is to buy a Busch Gardens poncho (they make nice souvenirs and are readily available at shops near the water rides) and hope for the best. This is far less fun and you'll probably get pretty wet anyway.

Lost Children

If you become separated from your child, contact the nearest employee. Found children are returned to the Security Office next to the Marrakesh Theater in Morocco.

Leaving the Park

Just have your hand stamped at the exit for readmittance on the same day. Your parking stub will get you back into the lot free.

Money

Busch Gardens has thoughtfully dotted ATMs around the park, just in case you run out of cash. You will find them just outside the main entrance, as well as in Morocco, Stanleyville, and Timbuktu, conveniently located near the shops. They are connected to the Plus, MoneyStation, and Cirrus systems. In addition, you can get cash advances on your American Express, Visa, MasterCard, or Discover card.

Pets

There is a free Pet Care Center located between parking lots A and B. The simple facility has large and small chain-link-fence kennels. They provide locks for the kennels — if you're lucky enough to find an attendant on duty when you arrive. Food bowls and a wash-up sink are also available.

Special Diets

A "Dining Guide" is available at Guest Relations just inside the main entrance. It will alert vegetarians to restaurants in the park where they can request special meals. Those with other dietary needs (low-fat, no-salt, etc.) will have to use their judgment to pick and choose from the standard menus.

Walkie Talkies

Near the front entrance is a small kiosk renting two-way radios for use in the park. If you have a spouse or kid who tends to wander off, this might be of interest. The rental rate is $10 a day. A deposit of your driver's license, $100 in cash, or a credit card imprint is required.

On Safari: Your Day at Busch Gardens

The bad news is that it's difficult — probably impossible — to see all of Busch Gardens in a day. The good news is that most people will be happy to forego some of the attractions. The more sedate will happily pass up the roller coasters to spend time observing the great apes, while the speed demons will be far happier being flung about on *Montu* than sitting still for a sing-along in Das Festhaus.

In many respects, Busch Gardens is a "typical" theme park. Each area of the park is decorated and landscaped to reflect its particular "theme," which is also reflected in the decor of the shops and restaurants (although not necessarily in the merchandise and food being offered). The attendants wear appropriate uniforms and a variety of rides, exhibits, attractions, and "streetmosphere" compete for your attention. If you've been to any of the other big theme parks in Central Florida, it's unlikely you'll find anything radically different about Busch Gardens.

As I noted earlier, Busch Gardens combines a number of seemingly disparate elements into an eclectic whole. Here, then, are some of the elements in the Busch Gardens mix:

The Zoo. Home to 3,000 animals, representing 340 different species (the numbers will probably have risen by the time you visit), Busch Gardens is one of the major zoological parks in the nation. It is also a highly enlightened zoo, embodying the latest thinking about how animals should be housed and displayed to the public. You will receive an understated but persistent message about the importance of conserving and protecting the planet's animal heritage. Like its sister park, SeaWorld in Orlando, Busch Gardens boasts a zoological staff that is friendly, visible, approachable, and more than happy to answer questions.

Meet The Keeper. One way in which the staff helps spread the conservation message is through regular "Meet The Keepers" shows built around feeding and caring for the animals. The presence of food means that the animals are usually at their most active during these shows; the attendants also attempt to coax their charges into appropriate poses for those with cameras. The schedule for these Meet The Keeper events is printed on the back of the large Busch Gardens map you pick up just inside the main entrance.

Roller Coasters. Busch Gardens boasts one of the largest concentrations of roller coasters in the nation. They range from the relatively modest *Python* to the truly awesome *Montu*. Even the smallest of these rides features elements, like loops, that are not to be found on just any roller coaster. You will be well advised to take advantage of the coin-operated lockers located near every roller coaster to store your loose gear. Anyone who is serious about their roller coasters will definitely want to put Busch Gardens on their must-see list for their Central Florida vacation.

Water Rides. Busch Gardens is also home to a group of water rides that are designed to get you very, very, very wet. They are great fun, but require some planning and strategizing. Unless, of course, you're a young boy, in which case you simply won't mind walking through the park sopping wet from the top of your head to the toes of your $100 sneakers. See *Good Things to Know About ... Getting Wet*, above.

Live Shows. There is a regular schedule of entertainment throughout the day in open-air amphitheaters and indoor, air-conditioned theaters. A few are animal-oriented, but most are pure variety entertainment shows that change periodically. Most shows don't gear up until 11:00 a.m. or noon. Thereafter, they run pretty regularly until closing time. The show schedule is printed on the back of the large Busch Gardens map you pick up at the main entrance.

Orientation to Busch Gardens

Your very first step on any visit to Busch Gardens Tampa is to pick up a copy of the park map at the main entrance. One side contains a full-color map of the park; the other side is packed with helpful information, such as the "Entertainment Guide," which lists performance times for the park's stage shows and the "Meet The Keepers" schedule, which lists times of the various "animal enrichment" programs scheduled for the day of your visit. You will also find information about any special or seasonal events that may be happening that day.

As you will see by perusing the map, Busch Gardens is divided into nine "themed areas," most of them named after a country or region of Africa. Each area is relatively compact but the entire park is quite large (335 acres) making covering the entire place a bit of a challenge, especially on foot.

In describing the nine areas, I will start with Morocco, the first area you encounter as you enter the park, and then proceed clockwise around the park, ending with the newest themed area, Egypt. I am not suggesting that you tour Busch Gardens in this order (although it would be the most direct route if you were to walk the entire park). Use the descriptions that follow, along with the suggestions given above, to pick and choose the attractions that best suit your tastes and that you can comfortably fit into the time available. Remember that you can use the *Skyride* between the Congo and Crown Colony and the *Trans-Veldt Railroad* with its three stops to cut down on the walking.

In addition to the attractions listed below, Busch Gardens features a number of strolling musical groups playing peppy music designed to put a

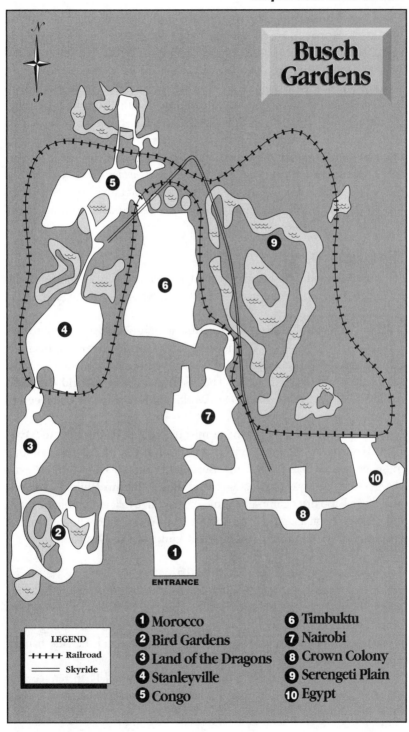

Busch Gardens

LEGEND
+++++ Railroad
═══ Skyride

ENTRANCE

❶ Morocco
❷ Bird Gardens
❸ Land of the Dragons
❹ Stanleyville
❺ Congo
❻ Timbuktu
❼ Nairobi
❽ Crown Colony
❾ Serengeti Plain
❿ Egypt

bit of bounce back in your step as you stroll the grounds. The **Mystic Sheiks of Morocco** are a brass marching band outfitted in snappy red and black uniforms that make them look like a military band from a very hip African nation. They are most frequently sighted in Morocco and Crown Colony. **Sounds of Steel**, a four-man steel drum band, marches through Stanleyville and the Congo from time to time, and the **Men of Note** offer up the kind of close harmony, a capella doo-wop music more associated with the streets of Philadelphia than the souks of Morocco. Still, they can often be found entertaining departing guests there.

There are two television series — the new *Captain Kangaroo* show and the syndicated *Jack Hanna's Animal Adventures* — that film segments at Busch Gardens. Hanna's set is located in Bird Gardens and shoots on an erratic schedule from fall through early spring.

Big Game

For those with limited time or who just want to skim the cream of this multifaceted park, here are my selections for the trophy-winning attractions at Busch Gardens:

For coaster fans, **Montu** and **Kumba** are musts and you'll want to ride **Gwazi** just to be complete. Of the water rides, **Congo River Rapids** is my favorite and the **Tanganyika Tidal Wave** is highly recommended for those who want to get totally drenched. The best theater show is **World Rhythms on Ice**. If you won't be going to SeaWorld, add **Dolphins of the Deep** to the list.

Animal lovers will not want to miss the chimps and gorillas in **Myombe Reserve** or the tigers on **Claw Island**. **Edge of Africa** is another must-see animal habitat, but the **Serengeti Safari Tour** (for an extra charge) is the best way to get close to the animals. **Rhino Rally** is a fun way to get an all-too brief glimpse of some other veldt dwellers combined with a mild thrill ride on a raging river. And finally, if you have preschoolers in tow, you will not want to miss the spectacular **Land of the Dragons**.

The One-Day Stay for Ride Fans

1. Plan to arrive at the opening bell. As soon as the park opens, grab a map just inside the turnstiles and proceed directly to *Montu* in Egypt (keep bearing right). If *Rhino Rally* is on your list, try to get there first thing in the morning, before you ride *Montu*; lines form quickly and the ride handles many fewer riders per hour than the coasters.

2. After *Montu*, walk back through Morocco to *Gwazi*. Then, retrace your steps to Crown Colony and take the *Skyride*, a shortcut to the Congo. Once there, head for *Kumba* and then cool off with a ride on *Congo River Rapids*.

3. Now head south, pausing to admire the tigers on *Claw Island* and ride *Stanley Falls* and the *Tanganyika Tidal Wave*. By now, you will be soaking wet. It may also be close to noon. Check the Entertainment Guide on the back of your map. The Stanleyville Theater and the dolphin show are nearby, or you could catch the *Skyride* again and head back to the Moroccan Palace Theater to catch the ice skating show.

4. After lunch, you have several choices. You can hit your favorite rides again, try the lesser rides, or (my personal suggestion) visit the various zoo attractions, perhaps catching another show at some point in the afternoon. Don't forget to check the schedule of Meet The Keeper shows.

The One-Day Stay for the More Sedate

1. If you are not a ride fanatic you don't have to kill yourself to get there at the minute the park opens, although a full day at Busch Gardens, taken at a moderate pace, is a full day well-spent. For now, I'll assume you are arriving early. Grab a park map and the Entertainment Guide and bear to the right as you stroll towards Crown Colony. En route, peruse the times for the variety shows and the Meet The Keeper sessions.

2. If you plan to take the *Serengeti Safari Tour*, sign up now. After a leisurely tour of *Edge of Africa*, and if you're interested and the lines aren't too long, you might want to walk to Egypt and pop into *King Tut's Tomb*. Otherwise, stroll to Nairobi for a visit to *Myombe Reserve* and the *Nairobi Nursery*. Don't dismiss *Rhino Rally* out of hand. Although it is touted as a "thrill ride" the thrills are very muted and the wildlife worth a look.

3. Now board the *Trans-Veldt Railroad* at the Nairobi Station for the journey around the Serengeti. Disembark in the Congo and visit the tigers at *Claw Island*. You may even be able to grab a quick barbecue lunch at Stanleyville Smokehouse.

4. Now you're ready to see some shows. You can walk to Timbuktu for the dolphin show and *International Celebration* at Das Festhaus (and have lunch if you haven't grabbed a bite yet) or you can take the *Skyride* again to catch the ice skating show at the Moroccan Palace.

5. Round out your day with a visit to Bird Gardens and the *For The Birds* show. If you have little ones in tow, don't forget to let them have their own special time in Land of the Dragons.

Morocco

There's only one entrance to Busch Gardens and Morocco is your first stop in the park, so some of the available space is given over to housekeeping. Here you'll find Guest Relations and, just around the corner to your right, the stroller and wheelchair rental concession. Since Morocco is also the exit to the park, a fair amount of space is given to souvenir and other shops, the better to lure those on the way out.

Otherwise, the main business of Morocco is stage shows of one sort or another. There are two theaters and an outdoor stage here, all reviewed below. There is also an **alligator pond**, where several times a day a Meet The Keeper show takes place. It's a zoologically correct version of the more popularized shows you get at Gatorland or other gator-themed attractions in the Orlando area.

Moroccan Roll (Marrakesh Theater)

Rating: ★ ★ ★ +
Type: Live stage show
Time: 25 minutes
Kelly says: Rock with a North African roll

On a thrust stage with Moorish arches and purple curtains, this peppy revue pays homage to the Morocco theme using a succession of rock standards with North African overtones. If tunes like "Rock the Casbah" and "Walk Like an Egyptian" ring a bell then you get the idea.

A Jim Carrey-esque master of ceremonies in peddler's robes and a fez cracks jokes as ancient as any pyramid and coaxes "volunteers" from the audience between numbers. The performers are attractive young singers and dancers, along with a trumpeter and electric guitarist. Sometimes the theme gets a little lost as "Midnight at the Oasis" segues into "Living La Vida Loca." By show's end all pretense disappears in rousing renditions of "Old Time Rock and Roll" and "The Heart of Rock 'n Roll." There are some very competent pop voices in the ensemble and the dancing makes up in show-biz pizzazz what it lacks in precision. After the show, some of the performers mingle with the audience for **photo ops**.

The Marrakesh Theater is a shaded area across the plaza from the Zagora Cafe, which means you can escape the sun but not the heat.

World Rhythms on Ice (Moroccan Palace Theater)

Rating: ★ ★ ★ ★ ★
Type: Indoor theater show
Time: About 30 minutes
Kelly says: A terrific ice show

The 1,200-seat Moroccan Palace Theater is a nice re-creation of those movie palaces of the distant past which often drew on exotic locales for the inspiration for their lavish interiors.

Currently holding forth here is an inspired tour of the world in song and ice-borne dance. After a rhythmic visit to Africa that makes liberal use of black light effects, the show visits England, Brazil, China, Germany, and the good old U.S.A. with an Arctic fantasy thrown in for good measure. All of the numbers are inventive in both costume and design, and the skaters (a Russian troupe) are first-rate. Standouts include the China segment, which features an enormous flying dragon that seems to fill the entire theater, and the African scenes that make enchanting use of puppets to back up the skaters. And the rousing red, white, and blue finale is a real crowd-pleaser. All in all, this is one of the best theme park shows in all of Central Florida.

Sultan's Tent

Rating:	★ ★
Type:	Open air snake show
Time:	About 10 minutes
Kelly says:	Much ado about touching a snake

A belly-dancing snake charmer holds forth in the plaza around the corner from the Zagora Cafe on a regular schedule. After a brief and wordless introduction in which she shimmies and drapes a python over her head, she gets down to the main order of business which is sitting at the edge of the stage and letting you touch and photograph her slinky friend. If your kids are snake fanciers, it's worth a look should you happen on a show in progress.

Eating in Morocco

Sultan's Sweets

What:	Fudge, ice cream, and baked goods
Where:	On the way to the Moroccan Palace
Price Range:	$ - $$

If you forgot breakfast, or just want a sugar rush before pressing into the park interior, this is a good place to stop. The limited menu features sweet baked goods like turnovers and awesomely syrupy cinnamon rolls. There are also croissants and muffins, along with coffee. Baked goods are all in the $2 to $4 range. Coffee, cappuccino, and espresso is $1 to $3.

Later in the day, you can pick up a soft serve sundae in a waffle cone for about $4 or choose from a wide variety of fudge and candy. Fudge in all its varieties is about $10 a pound. Some fancier candies are a bit more. There is a small section of indoor seating, but the best seating is outdoors under canopies; it's a very pleasant place to sit and take in the passing scene.

Zagora Cafe

What:	Fast-food burgers and sandwiches

| *Where:* | Across from Sultan's Sweets |
| *Price Range:* | $ - $$ |

This spacious fast-food eatery looks out across a lovely palm-accented plaza to the Marrakesh Theater. About half of the seating is under a large colonnaded porch decorated with the stuffed heads of African game animals, including a trumpeting elephant. The plaques identifying each beast take care to note that the specimen in question died of natural causes. The other half of the seating is outdoors on a semicircular terrace.

The menu is basic: turkey sandwiches, burgers, and fajita sandwiches for about $6 to $7. Kids' safari meals (a hot dog and fries) are about $4. Desserts — carrot cake, chocolate cake, strawberry and blueberry cheesecake — are quite good at about $3.

Ice Cream Parlor

What:	Just what the name says
Where:	Near Marrakesh Theater
Price Range:	$

This is a small fast-food style ice cream parlor that gets crowded when shows at the next-door Marrakesh Theater let out. Single and double scoops are about $2 and $2.50 respectively. A waffle cone sundae will set you back about $3 to $4. The usual range of soft drinks is also served here.

Shopping in Morocco

Casablanca Outfitters

There is some nice travel attire here but most of the merchandise on offer consists of inexpensive t-shirts and miscellaneous souvenirs. Best of all is the selection of men's and women's safari and sun hats, some of them quite stylish. Another good souvenir is the video "Safari Adventure," the official souvenir of Busch Gardens ($15).

Tangiers Taffy House

This vest-pocket candy store sells wrapped candy and saltwater taffy by the pound or the piece for $1.99 or $2.25 for half a pound. A variety of candies and large, gaudily-colored lollipops is also available.

Rabat Label

This is a much larger version of the small Label Stable at SeaWorld. You will find Anheuser-Busch logos on a wide variety of clothing and other merchandise. If your bowling ball positively must have the Bud logo on it, this is the place to come.

Old Time Photo

Turn of the century style photos in period costumes run from $20 to $45 depending on the size of the print and the number of people. Also available is a safari-themed backdrop, complete with jeep.

Safari Central

Despite the name, there's little in the way of safari gear here. Instead, it's a good place to come for a wide selection of branded souvenirs, everything from key chains, mugs, and refrigerator magnets to t-shirts. The best buy in t-shirts (in my opinion) are the black shirts with the large brooding portraits of gorillas, white tigers, and other wildlife stars (about $12 to $17). In the same vein are beach towels with the white tiger ($17) and a large selection of plush toys ($7 to $40).

Jeepers and Creepers

Actually an extension of Safari Central, this kids' store has a wide variety of clothing and toys for the younger crowd. At one end is a play area where you can park your fidgety child in front of a TV monitor showing cartoons.

Nature's Kingdom

Located near Sultan's Sweets, this shop has an environmental theme and features rocks and crystals, mounted butterflies, wood crafts, rustic baskets and pottery, and the obligatory t-shirts.

Sidi Kacem African Curios

One of the nicer touches, shopping-wise, in Morocco is the way in which the designers have evoked the souks of Fez and Marrakesh. Sidi Kacem's is actually a mini-Moroccan bazaar comprising an indoor shop and a number of outdoor stalls that surround it.

Here you'll find crafts such as soapstone carvings and boxes, pottery from the Moroccan city of Safi hand-painted in traditional patterns ($8 to $450), carved wooden animals from Kenya ($10 to $1,500), hand-crafted Moroccan leather goods ($40 to $100), and brassware ($10 to $500). You may even get to meet some of the actual craftspeople responsible for these attractive wares; they staff the stalls on an irregular schedule.

Inside you'll find a goodly selection of African-style baubles, bangles, and beads ($20 to $40) along with some very attractive women's clothing.

Safari Trader

This shop is actually just outside the entrance to the park, allowing for those all-important last-minute purchases. There is a small and somewhat haphazard selection of souvenir t's and merchandise here. However, the Safari Trader also unloads discontinued and overstock merchandise at discounts of up to 50%. Depending on when you visit, you might find some real bargains here.

Bird Gardens

As the name suggests, Bird Gardens houses most of the birds in the Busch Gardens zoo collection. In addition to the few larger bird displays mentioned below, the area is dotted with flamingos and other exotic water fowl, their wings obviously clipped, in beautifully landscaped open settings with ponds and streams. They are joined by a rotating group of visiting Florida species. Some of the walkways are lined with gaudy parrots in free-hanging cages. Over all, the effect is enchanting, rather like the private gardens of a rich and tasteful eccentric.

Bird Gardens is also home to *Gwazi*, a mammoth twin-track wooden roller coaster that greets you as you enter. Near *Gwazi*, you will find **River Rumble**, a water game, and **Xtreme Zone**, where you can climb a simulated cliff or bounce on a trampoline. There is an additional charge for these activities.

Gwazi

Rating:	★ ★ ★ ★ +
Type:	Dueling wooden coasters
Time:	About two and a half minutes
Kelly says:	Up-to-date nostalgia

For those who remember the days when all roller coasters were made of wood, *Gwazi* will be like a stroll down memory lane — until the first drop reminds you that this isn't your father's coaster.

The "gimmick" here, of course, is that there are two separate coasters, each holding 24 passengers, one representing a tiger, the other a lion. As you snake your way to the departure platforms, you get to choose which one you'll take on and each route has its own themeing — the lion territory evokes the an African desert environment, while the tiger territory is reminiscent of the jungles and streams of Asia. The dueling trains depart simultaneously and "race" to the finish with six "fly-bys" along the way. The close encounters may not be quite as scary as on some of the dueling steel coasters — the realities of wooden coasters mandate a decent amount of space between the rail and the edge of the superstructure — but they are pretty scary nonetheless. Likewise, the ride itself may seem tamer. After all, it's hard to do an inversion on a wooden coaster. But the rumble and rattle of wood makes

Gwazi seem faster than its 50 miles per hour and on some of the turns the cars seem to be at right angles to the ground. Wooden coasters also have a liveliness that steel coasters don't. Coaster enthusiasts would say "it's alive!" which is another way of saying that the give in the wood makes each ride seem different from the last.

Tip: Any serious coaster buff will want to ride at least twice, once on each track. After many rides, coaster mavens seem to agree: the lion coaster has the steeper first drop, but the tiger coaster is, over all, the more intense experience.

There are some other good things to be said about *Gwazi*. It lasts longer than some of its zippier competitors and because the height restriction here is only 48 inches, more members of the family will get a chance to ride. *Gwazi* is also quite beautiful, in a way in which the more modern steel coasters aren't. The wood is weathered rather than the more traditional white and blends in nicely with the African conical thatched roof motif of the entrance. And from the top you get a fascinating (but brief) glimpse of one of the park's "backstage" areas, as well as the surrounding terrain.

Even if you don't choose to ride, *Gwazi* is worth checking out if only to marvel at the way a million board feet of lumber have been put together to create this behemoth. It has a delightfully scary way of looking rather flimsy in spite of its massive size. One good vantage point is to be had just inside the exit, where riders can purchase pictures ($10 to $16) to commemorate the experience. Another place to get a fairly good look is further into Bird Gardens, near the eagle display and the Clydesdale statue.

For The Birds (in Bird Theater)

Rating: ★ ★ ★ +
Type: Live amphitheater show
Time: About 30 minutes
Kelly says: Fascinating birds and lore, awful comedy

This show is perfect theme park edutainment. A parrot talks and even sings on cue. A variety of multicolored parrots and raptors fly through hoops, swoop low over the seats, and land on volunteers brought up from the audience. The odd-looking South American serijama, nicknamed the lizard smasher, demonstrates its unique meal preparation technique. Some neat raptors, including a bateleur eagle from Africa and a magnificent bald eagle from the land of the free and the home of the brave fly in for guest appearances. All of this is accompanied by a steady flow of fascinating facts and lore about the birds on display. At show's end, some of the birds are brought to the front of the stage to give you a closer look and a chance for snapshots.

Unfortunately, the show is marred by a wrong-headed and totally unnecessary attempt at comedy, so steel yourself for some truly awful "jokes." Fortunately, the birds are so fascinating that this is still one of the best animal shows in the park.

Hospitality House Stage

Rating:	★ ★ +
Type:	Live music
Time:	About 20 minutes
Kelly says:	Diverting with lunch

On a small outdoor stage near the Hospitality House (see below), a cheerful ragtime band holds forth on a regular schedule. The selections are all likely to be familiar and they are all certified toe-tappers put over with a great deal of good-humored élan. If you find yourself near here at show time, why not grab a free beer inside and give a listen?

Budweiser Beer School

Rating:	★ ★
Type:	An edutainment commercial
Time:	45 minutes
Kelly says:	Best for the air conditioning

This is a pleasant enough way to kill some time and perhaps get answers to those questions that have been tormenting you for years. Why is it called Budweiser? Who was Anheuser? However, I suspect most people are lured here by the beer tasting that follows some videos about the history of Anheuser-Busch and the art of brewing beer. At the end you get a certificate attesting to your newfound status as a "Beermaster."

Koala Habitat

Rating:	★ ★ +
Type:	Animal habitat
Time:	Continuous viewing
Kelly says:	Cute and cuddly

A long, snaking walkway leads across a bridge over a pond filled with a variety of water fowl (bird feed dispensers thoughtfully provided) to a vaguely Chinese-style building with a series of antechambers. The building originally housed pandas and was designed to accommodate large crowds. The current occupants, while cute and cuddly in their own right, obviously don't have quite the same cachet, so it's unlikely you'll find a line here.

Inside is a spacious and wonderfully air conditioned two-level viewing area. The lower level is a conveyor belt that takes you at a stately pace past the animals; the upper level allows for more leisurely contemplation.

The display area features koalas at one end and Dama wallabies at the other. The koalas, about the size of a large, tubby housecat, calmly munch eucalyptus leaves, while the wallabies (equally small) are a bit more lively. If there's a new "joey" (or baby) in the koala family, a sign will direct you to the *Nairobi Nursery* (see the Nairobi section). Compared to other habitats in the park, this one seems a bit under-decorated. If you've never seen one of these little critters up close, it's worth at least a quick visit.

Aviary

Rating:	★ ★ ★ +
Type:	Walk-through animal exhibit
Time:	Continuous viewing
Kelly says:	A lovely place to pause

This is a smallish habitat compared to others in the park, but its size belies its enchantment. Essentially a large tent made of a dark mesh fabric, the aviary lets you visit a wide variety of tropical birds in a remarkably realistic setting, instead of peering at them through the bars of a cage. Benches allow for long and leisurely viewing and a large illustrated guidebook lets you tell one species from another. Some, like the roseate spoonbill, may look familiar but others, like the odd Abdim's Stork and a beautiful blue Victoria Crowned Pigeon that thinks it's a peacock, will probably be new to you.

I have discovered that the longer you sit and relax here, the more the mesh tent fades from your consciousness. What remains is a charming encounter with some very lovely birds.

Eating in Bird Gardens

The Watering Hole

Riding *Gwazi* can work up a serious thirst, so this small kiosk at the exit to the dueling wooden coaster is a welcome sight. There are the usual soft drinks plus popcorn and frosted lemonade ($3).

Hospitality House

What:	Deli sandwiches and free beer
Where:	Near the Bird Show
Price Range:	$ - $$

Like its counterpart at SeaWorld, the Anheuser-Busch Hospitality House is a beautiful modern building in a knock-your-socks-off setting. The main draw is the free (albeit small) beer samples. The limit here is one at a time per person and two per person per day. There is also a small fast-food counter, the Hospitality House Cafe, featuring sandwich platters and pizza for about $7. Salads and desserts are both about $3.

Your best seating choice is outside on the two-tiered terrace overlooking the duck-filled pond. The vista is, quite simply, one of the loveliest at Busch Gardens. Also outside is an area where kids can try their skill at piloting remote-controlled tugboats. A token (one for $1, six for $5) gives you about two and a half minutes of play.

Bird Garden Refreshments

Next to the entrance to the Bird Theater, this little kiosk sells popcorn for a bit over $3, plus the usual selection of soft drinks.

Shopping in Bird Gardens

Gwazi Gift Shop

This small open-sided shop near the exit to the coaster sells the expected "I Survived *Gwazi*" t-shirts ($13 to $25) as well as beach towels ($17) in case you spilled something (like breakfast) on the ride.

Bird Gardens Gift Shop

If you visit the koalas, it will be hard to miss this shop which is right by the exit. It carries a broad range of cuddly plush toys including, inevitably, some koalas. A good sized version of the cuddly marsupial runs about $25. The rest of the shop is given over to figurines, frames, kids' toys, and other miscellaneous souvenirs, all at moderate prices.

The Pearl Factory

This small shop sells Japanese cultured pearls, in five basic colors and 120 shades, in a variety of settings at prices that begin at about $20 and rise sharply from there. For $13 you can pick an oyster and, if you like the pearl you find inside, have it set in a variety of gold settings for $17 and up. Silver settings are slightly less expensive.

Caribbean Breeze Gifts

Wind chimes in a variety of fanciful designs are the main stock in trade of this shop housed in a rustic looking wooden hut near Bird Theater. Wooden chimes are about $20 and tinkling metal tube chimes run from $12 to $20. Best of all are the ceramic chimes in a wide variety of styles ($35 to $55). You will also find outdoor flag "sculptures" here if you are looking to add a festive note to your yard or patio ($20 to $25).

Land of the Dragons

Sandwiched between Bird Gardens to the south and Stanleyville to the north, is a play area just for the preschool set. Other theme parks in Central Florida have similar kiddie areas but nowhere will you find the concept pulled off with as much wit and verve as the Land of the Dragons. Here, the clever design of *Fievel's Playland* at Universal and the size of *Shamu's Happy Harbor* at SeaWorld come together to create the only five-star kiddie attraction in this book.

There are animals to be seen here, too, of course. At one end are the iguanas, monitor lizards, and komodo dragon that give the area its name. At the other, in a separate circular area, is *Lory Landing* described below. But the emphasis is on fun in the Land of the Dragons and the little ones will not be disappointed.

Interactive Play Areas

Rating: ★ ★ ★ ★ ★
Type: Hands-on activity
Time: As long as you want
Kelly says: The best of its kind in Central Florida

Most of the Land of the Dragons is given over to a series of loosely connected climb-up, crawl-through, slide-down play areas that can keep little ones occupied for hours. I have given them the rather cumbersome name of "interactive play areas," but each has its own identity and special attractions, as we shall see.

Dominating the north end of the area is the **Dragon's Nest**, an elaborate two-story structure colorfully painted and shaded by a large tarp covering and towering live oak trees. On the lower level, it features a net climb, an "air bounce" (a large inflated floor on which kids can jump to their heart's content), and a "ball crawl" (a pit filled with colored plastics balls into which kids can literally dive). The upper level is reached either via the net climb or, for less agile adults, a stairway. There you will find a two-level, kids-sized, climb-through, maze-like environment forming a delightful obstacle course. No one higher than 56 inches is allowed in this one, so Mom and Dad are excused.

From this upper level extend two rope bridges. Both go to the **Tree House**, one directly and the other via an intermediate tower, from which kids can zip down a corkscrew slide to ground level. The Tree House itself is a kid's fantasy of a humongous old tree girdled by a spiral wooden staircase leading to a "secret" room at the top. Along the way, climbers can detour into jungle gym-like environments that snake off through the Land of the Dragons. Kids will love it; nervous parents may find it hard to keep track of their little ones.

At the foot of the Tree House lies **Mizzly Marsh**, a watery play area where kids can really get soaked. The marsh leads through and around the old tree and comes complete with a friendly dragon whose snake-like body appears and disappears beneath the water.

Set apart and surrounded by a fence is the **Dragon Diggery**, a large and ingeniously designed sandbox with adorable playhouses, one in the shape of a giant mushroom.

The overall effect of these interlocking entertainments is pure delight. Not only is virtually every activity conceived by the preschool mind represented here, but the design and attention to detail are wonderfully imaginative. Even the trash cans are part of the theme. They're called Gobblety Goop, and let you shove your candy wrappers and soda cups down a dragon's throat.

Tip: If your kids are old enough to be turned loose in the Land of the Dragons, you can draw some comfort in the knowledge that there is only one way out, at the southern end. There is no entrance at the north end, near *Lory Landing.*

Kiddie Rides

Rating: ★ ★ ★
Type: Mechanical rides for toddlers
Time: A few minutes each
Kelly says: Variations on a single theme

Sprinkled around Land of the Dragons are small kiddie rides. You know the kind of thing: tiny vehicles that go round and round in a tiny circle with tiny little people sitting in them. The ones here are better designed and executed than most, with cutesy names like *Eggery Deggery, Chug-A-Tug,* and *Dapper Flappers. If* your kids are the right age (under three) they should have a ball here.

Captain Kangaroo

Rating: ★ ★ ★ +
Type: Live outdoor show
Time: About 15 minutes
Kelly says: Politically correct tale for tots

This a delightful little singalong and audience participation show for the kids. Adults should check their sophistication at the door. If you're expecting Captain Kangaroo himself, you will be disappointed. It seems that the good Captain and Mr. Green Jeans have been called away — for an animal rescue no less. So it falls to a lowly stage sweeper to improvise the show with the help of a number of costumed characters and puppets.

. The show teaches kids those famous magic words "please" and "thank you" and urges them to be kind to each other. You know, the sort of thing the schools aren't allowed to teach because it might be construed as favoring religion.

There is an adult mindset, with which I am afflicted, that finds this sort of "P.C." pabulum a bit on the cloying side. Fortunately, the kids don't have these silly hang-ups and seem to enjoy the show immensely.

Lory Landing

Rating:	★ ★ ★ +
Type:	Walk-through animal exhibit
Time:	As long as you like
Kelly says:	Close encounters with inquisitive charmers

Lorys and lorikeets are the main attraction in this aviary within an aviary. About halfway between parakeets and parrots in size, lorys are as curious as they are colorful. As you walk through their jungle-themed aviary, they are likely to land on your head, shoulder, or arm to check out your shiny jewelry or cadge a handout. Busch Gardens encourages this by selling "lory nectar" ($2) just in case you forgot to bring your own.

This is great fun for kids (grown-ups, too!) and well worth a visit. In the antechamber to the lorys' digs are large cages displaying their larger cousins — cockatoos, macaws, and the like.

Shopping and Eating in the Land of the Dragons

The vest pocket kiosk **Dragon's Den** sells inexpensive toys and t-shirts ($15) as well as the sort of sandals that might come in handy in nearby *Mizzly Marsh*. There are also dragon towels ($17) to dry off with afterwards.

Fine dining is not on the menu in the Land of the Dragons and heaven forbid that there should be anything healthy on hand. But the cleverly named **Snack Dragon** kiosk features ice cream and strawberry bars for about $2, plus hot dogs and chips for about $4.

Stanleyville

Stanleyville is a compact, heavily shaded area with plenty of places to sit and survey the passing scene. The theme is African exploration and a lot of the window dressing includes piles of crates, cargo netting, and other expedition gear. In the middle is a shaded amphitheater flanked by two enjoyable water rides and at the southern end are some very entertaining **orangutans**.

Trans-Veldt Railroad

Rating:	★ ★ ★
Type:	Steam railroad journey
Time:	30 to 35 minutes for a complete circuit
Kelly says:	Shuttle with a view

Board a reconstruction of the type of steam railroad that served as mass transit in turn-of-the-century Africa, rest your weary feet, and get some great views of the animals of the *Serengeti Plain*. This is one of two vehicular viewing venues for the Serengeti (the *Skyride*, described in the Crown Colony section below, is the other). It makes a leisurely circuit of the park in a generally counterclockwise direction with stops in Nairobi (the closest stop to the main entrance) and the Congo (near Timbuktu). Since you can board or exit at any of the three stops, the *Trans-Veldt* is a great way to cut down on your walking time, and it provides glimpses of animals you probably wouldn't see otherwise.

As you travel from Nairobi through Egypt to the Congo, you will pass right through the superstructure of *Montu* and enter the Serengeti where you will see giraffes and a variety of veldt antelopes. Too bad you can't stop for a longer look. After the Congo stop, the train loops around the Congo and back to Stanleyville. The portion of the journey from the Congo to Nairobi is the least scenic, although it does provide some intriguing "backstage" glimpses of the park (including close-up looks at three roller coasters) as well as a preview glimpse of *Rhino Rally* (described in the Nairobi section below).

Tip: The left-hand side of the train generally offers the most interesting views.

Stanley Falls Log Flume

Rating:	★ ★ ★ +
Type:	Water ride
Time:	About 2 minutes
Kelly says:	The last drop is a doozy

This is a fairly ordinary log flume ride, especially when compared to more recent variations on the theme. On the other hand, it is one of the longest in the nation, they say. The car in which you ride is a log-shaped contraption with two seating areas scooped out of it. Each car holds four people, adults or children. However, when the lines aren't too long you can ride two to a car.

Your log rumbles along at a moderate pace in a water-filled flume, takes a few turns, and then climbs slowly to a modest height. The first small drop is merely preparation for the finale, a slow ride up yet another steep grade and an exhilarating drop to the bottom in full view of the passing crowds. Like all water rides, this one has a warning about getting wet, but the cars, with their scooped out fronts, seem designed to direct the wave generated by the final splashdown away from the passengers. It's unlikely that you'll get seriously soaked on this one.

As you exit, pause for a moment to commune with the black and white ruffed lemurs with their beautiful coats and long, bushy tails.

Tanganyika Tidal Wave

Rating: ★ ★ ★ ★
Type: Water ride
Time: About 2 minutes
Kelly says: A first-class soaking

If the nearby *Stanley Falls Log Flume* lulled you into a false sense of security about staying dry, this one will dispel any such notions. Like the log flume ride, this is all about the final drop. In fact, until then, this ride is far tamer. It snakes lazily through a narrow waterway past stilt houses, whose porches are piled high with Central African trade goods, before taking a slow climb to the top.

Then, all bets are off as the 25-passenger car on which you're riding plunges wildly down a sharp incline into a shallow pool of water, sending a drenching wave over not just the passengers but the spectators who have eagerly gathered on a bridge overhead. No two ways about it. This one really soaks you. Even with a poncho you'll still be pretty darned damp. Since you're probably soaked to the skin anyway, why not top the ride off by standing on the bridge and waiting for the next car to come by? For those who don't want to take the ride or get soaked on the bridge, there is a glassed in viewing section that offers the thrill of a wall of water rushing at you, without the soaking effects.

See *Good Things to Know About...Getting Wet*, earlier in this chapter, for some tips on negotiating Busch Gardens' water rides.

Stanleyville Theater Variety Shows

Rating: ★ ★ ★ +
Type: Rotating variety shows
Time: About 25 minutes
Kelly says: Varies from good to great

The Stanleyville Theater is a well-shaded amphitheater with open sides. A round, bare stage thrusts forward from a proscenium arch and curtain. The configuration lends itself to straightforward variety show entertainment that doesn't require much in the way of sets or complicated effects, and that's just what is presented here. Shows change much more quickly than they do at other Busch Gardens venues, so it's difficult to predict exactly what you will see when you visit.

The shows tend to feature circus, acrobatic, or dance and music acts involving a dozen or so performers. The Akishins, a Russian troupe of comic circus performers, have been frequent visitors to this stage. Chinese acrobats have also held forth as has a dance troupe from West Africa. During the fall and spring, Busch presents a series of weekend big band concerts on this stage. Whoever books these shows for Busch has a keen eye for talent and the shows I have seen have never been less than engaging. Frequently, as with the Akishins, they have been well worth fitting in to your touring schedule.

Eating in Stanleyville

Stanleyville Smokehouse

What:	Fast food barbecue
Where:	Next to the wart hogs
Price Range:	$$ - $$$

This is Busch Gardens' barbecue joint and as an aficionado of this cuisine I can report it ain't half bad. A rib dinner is about $9 with chicken about $7. A combination of the two is $8. Those with less of an appetite can get a small chicken dinner for about $6.50. Cole slaw and corn on the cob are available as side dishes. Desserts are $3 and there is beer and the usual array of soft drinks. Service is at walk-up windows and all seating is outdoors.

Shopping in Stanleyville

Tropical Wave

Strategically located next to the *Tanganyika Tidal Wave*, this kiosk offers (in addition to $5 ponchos) t-shirts celebrating not just the *Tidal Wave* but also Adventure Island, Busch Gardens' next-door water park (which is covered in the next chapter).

Stanleyville Bazaar

This long shed-like building offers an unusually wide range of miscellaneous merchandise, mostly clothing, along with sunglasses, watches, costume jewelry, stuffed animals, small toys, candy, and postcards.

Kenya Clayworks

It has nothing to do with Kenya, but it's an intriguing idea. Here you can choose from any of several dozen white pottery objects — everything from animal figurines, to platters, to cups and teapots, to menorahs. Then you take them to a table where you can paint them anyway you wish. The shop will glaze them, fire them, and mail them to you anywhere in the United States. The all-inclusive price for the whole experience, including the shipping, is remarkably low ($15 to $30). Unfortunately, they don't ship overseas.

If you'd rather not paint your own pottery, the entrance to the shop is lined with finished products, mostly pots, bowls, mugs, vases, and plates. Styles range from the traditional to the jazzily postmodern. Again, prices are surprisingly moderate ($10 to $70). If you'd like to spend more, there are wooden occasional tables from Thailand, with elephant trunks serving as legs ($170 to $400).

Livingstone's Photo Studio
At the *Trans-Veldt Railroad* station you will find an "antique" photo studio. Here you and your family can dress up as Wild West heroes or Victorian gentry and have your sepia-toned photo snapped. Prices range from $20 to $40 depending on the size of both the group and the photo.

The Congo
The Congo is another compact, cleverly designed area with twisting tree-shaded walks and a number of spectator bridges over rides and animal habitats. Most of the space is given over to some of Busch Gardens' premiere thrill rides, although the Congo is also home to the park's ravishing and much-ballyhooed white Bengal tigers. The predominant architectural motif is round buildings with conical wooden stick roofs.

In addition to the major attractions profiled below, the Congo contains a bumper car ride (**Ubanga-Banga Bumper Cars**), a trio of kiddie rides (**Pygmy Village**), and remote control trucks and boats. There is also a stop for the *Trans-Veldt Railroad* (described in the Stanleyville section, above).

Kumba
Rating: ★ ★ ★ ★ ★
Type: Steel roller coaster
Time: Just under 3 minutes
Kelly says: The next best (i.e. scariest) thing to *Montu*

Before *Montu* opened (see Egypt, below), *Kumba* was Busch Gardens' blockbuster ride. It's still pretty amazing and is the largest of its kind in the southeastern United States.

Kumba means "roar" in a Congolese dialect, the P.R. people say, and it's well named. Riders are braced with shoulder restraints into 32-seat vehicles (eight rows, four abreast) that roar along almost 4,000 feet of blue steel track that winds up, around, over, and through the surrounding scenery. There are loops, camelbacks, and corkscrews to terrify or thrill you, as the case may be. One of the more disorienting maneuvers takes you on a "cobra roll" around a spectator bridge, which is a great place for the faint of heart to get an idea of what they're missing. Remember to wave to Aunt Martha as you whiz by.

Claw Island

Rating:	★ ★ ★ ★
Type:	Animal habitat
Time:	Continuous viewing
Kelly says:	A treat for tiger fanciers

Claw Island is the Hollywood-ish name for an intriguing habitat housing some of Busch Gardens' most beautiful residents. Here, in a deep pit, on a small, green, palm-dotted island, you'll find five magnificent Bengal tigers. One bears the tawny coat we are all familiar with, three have dark stripes on white coats, and the fifth is completely white. These rare white tigers were prized by Indian royalty, and no wonder. They are truly awe-inspiring.

Claw Island's pit is surrounded by gazebo viewing areas and a wooden spectator bridge, all of which have heavy rope netting to make doubly sure that no one climbs or falls in. By walking around the perimeter you should be able to get good views of the tigers.

Most of the time, they are just lounging around (these are cats, after all). If you're lucky enough to chance by at feeding time things can get a bit livelier. Unfortunately, feedings are haphazard, to prevent the animals from becoming habituated. You can ask at the nearby gift shop when feeding time will be, but the information provided is not always accurate.

The Python

Rating:	★ ★ ★ ★
Type:	Small roller coaster
Time:	About a minute and a half
Kelly says:	Roller coasters 101A

Along with *The Scorpion* in Timbuktu (see below), this is one of Busch Gardens warm-up coasters for *Kumba* and *Montu*. It's hard to differentiate the two lesser coasters, but I rate this as slightly more advanced than *The Scorpion* if only because it has two up-and-over loops. It's also a good place to test your resolve before braving the bigger coasters. The business end of the ride, between the slow climb to the top and the slowdown before returning to the start, lasts just 30-some seconds. You can hold your breath the whole way.

Congo River Rapids

Rating:	★ ★ ★ ★ ★
Type:	Water ride
Time:	About 3 minutes
Kelly says:	The best of the water rides

It doesn't have the steep drops of the flume rides in Stanleyville, but for me *Congo River Rapids* provides the most enjoyable overall water ride experience in Busch Gardens. Here you climb aboard 12-seater circular rafts which are then set adrift to float freely along a rapids-filled stretch of river. The raft twists, turns, and spins as it bumps off the sides and various cunningly placed obstacles in the stream. In addition to the raging waters, which periodically slosh into the raft, the course is punctuated with waterfalls and waterspouts all of which have the potential to drench you to the skin. The most insidious threat of all comes from your fellow park visitors who are encouraged to spray you with water cannon (at 25 cents a shot) from the pedestrian walkway that skirts the ride.

Despite all the white water, the raft proceeds at a relatively stately pace and the "river" drops only several feet over its quarter-mile course. The real excitement is generated by the ever-present threat of a soaking. How wet you get is only somewhat a matter of chance. It seems that the wetness quotient has been increased since the ride first opened. Time was that some people emerged virtually unscathed, while others got soaked. Now it seems that almost everyone get thoroughly doused. On a hot Florida afternoon, that seems to be just the ticket, which makes this my favorite water ride and explains the five-star rating.

Eating in The Congo

ViVi Storehouse Restaurant

What:	Sandwiches
Where:	Near Claw Island
Price Range:	$$ - $$$

This cafeteria-style eatery (open seasonally) specializes in sandwiches. Deli sandwich platters and fajita sandwiches are both about $7. There are also salads and the usual array of desserts. Seating is outdoors at trestle tables under circular wooden-roofed pavilions.

Python Soft Serve

For those who missed (or lost) lunch while riding the nearby roller coaster of the same name, Python Soft Serve offers a quick sugar jolt in the form of soft ice cream waffle-cone sundaes for about $4.

Kumba Refreshments
Located hard by its namesake, this walk-up stand sells ice cream bars and popcorn for around $2, in addition to the usual array of soft drinks.

Shopping in The Congo

Congo River Rapids Outpost
Also called the Kinshasa Outpost, this large open-sided building, with its heavy wooden supporting posts and tin roof, mimics a trading warehouse deep in the jungle. They advertise "Dry Goods and River Gear," which means, among other things, you can pick up a poncho for about $5. You'll also find sports sandals, t-shirts (about $13), sun hats, and beach towels.

Tiger's Den
This open-sided kiosk celebrates the nearby Bengal tigers in a bewildering variety of media, from beach towels to posters to bookmarks. There are also some lovely t-shirts ($12 to $27) and plush tiger dolls ($12 to $100).

Timbuktu
Timbuktu is, of course, the legendary sub-Saharan trade crossroads that figures prominently in the popular imagination of adventure and exploration. It is, in fact, a dusty remnant of its past glory. Here at Busch Gardens, Timbuktu is an open, sun-drenched plaza dotted with palm trees and featuring architecture that mimics the mud towers of its namesake. There is precious little shade here unless you venture indoors.

The attractions in Timbuktu are a mismatched assortment, having little to do with either Timbuktu or even Africa. But then, Timbuktu is emblematic of far-flung trade, so perhaps it's not so farfetched that it contains an eclectic grab bag of themed attractions from around the world.

There are no zoo animals here, but there are dolphins and a sea lion in the large amphitheater at the north end. At the opposite end you'll find, of all things, a German restaurant! In between are a variety of typical **amusement park rides**, including Busch Gardens' only **carousel** and several other **kiddie rides**. Also at hand are a collection of **midway games**, cleverly disguised as a sub-Saharan marketplace, and a **video arcade** housed in a vaguely Saharan edifice with a vaguely Saharan name, *The Sultan's Arcade*. The major rides and attractions are described below.

The Scorpion
Rating: ★ ★ ★ +

Type:	A "baby" roller coaster
Time:	About a minute
Kelly says:	Roller coasters 101

This is the place to come to decide if you have what it takes to tackle the bigger coasters in the park. In my estimation, *The Scorpion* is the tamest of the lot, although it does have one up-and-over loop. So if you've never been "inverted," this is as good a place to start as any. Otherwise, it's no more terrifying than, say, Disney's Thunder Mountain.

Dolphins of the Deep (Dolphin Theater)

Rating:	★ ★ ★ ★
Type:	Live show
Time:	About 30 minutes
Kelly says:	A little bit of SeaWorld

The dolphin show that is a fixture at SeaWorld Orlando has found a second home here in Tampa. It's well worth taking in, even if you have seen SeaWorld and Discovery Cove, since the Busch version is somewhat different.

In this show, two dolphins named (what else?) Mich and Bud are put through their paces in a show that follows the edutainment formula — fascinating facts interspersed with even more fascinating "behaviors." This show even features a pint-sized version of Shamu's tail-splashing stunt. Adding a touch of humor is an interloping sea lion who hopes to land a spot in the show with an audition. It's all great fun and is topped off by a spectacular leap.

The show takes place in an open amphitheater with a roof for us and a sun shade for the dolphins. In the distance, you can see *Kumba*'s roaring loops. If you're hungry, you will find popcorn, ice cream, and soft drinks at the back of the auditorium.

The Phoenix

Rating:	★ ★ ★
Type:	Amusement park ride
Time:	5 minutes
Kelly says:	Only if you haven't done it before

This is a very familiar amusement park ride. A curved boat-like car seating 50 people swings back and forth, gaining height. At the apex of its swing, it pauses and the passengers hang briefly upside down, screaming merrily. Then on the next swing it goes completely up and over.

Chances are, there's a ride like this at an amusement park somewhere near your home, which leads to the question: Ride this one or spend the time doing things you can't do near home? I'd recommend the latter.

International Celebration (Das Festhaus)

Rating:	★ ★ ★
Type:	Musical variety show
Time:	About 20 minutes
Kelly says:	Best with a meal

Backed by a nine-piece band with an accent on brass, a sunny ensemble of young performers (Are there any other kind at these parks?) takes you on a musical tour of the world — or at least selected portions thereof. By my count, the show visits France, Mexico, Germany, Italy, and Ireland.

It's all great fun and there is some audience participation built in, which is a big hit with the younger members of the crowd who get a chance to dance with some of the performers. If your child is the outgoing type, grab a seat near the wide central aisle. After the show, the performers linger to mingle, making for a great **photo op**.

One of the best things about this show is that the busy tourist can combine it with a hearty lunch from the Festhaus cafeteria (described below).

Eating in Timbuktu

Das Festhaus

What:	German beer hall
Where:	South end of the plaza
Price Range:	$$ - $$$

It must be hard to make every shop and every restaurant fit into the right theme at a park this size. And at the Festhaus they don't even try. At least the theme at this cavernous restaurant harkens back to Anheuser-Busch's German origins. The dining area of this "German Festival Hall" seats 1,000 at trestle tables. To the front is a stage for the variety show and high overhead is a mammoth chandelier hanging from the tent-like ceiling. The walls are decorated with painted panels that conjure up a Bavarian town square and the air conditioning is like a fresh breeze from the Alps.

To your left as you enter, tucked away, is the cafeteria line. The menu, in a nod to American tastes, offers both German and Italian entrees. You can stick with the theme and have a German sampler platter ($6) of wursts and sauerkraut or opt for an Italian dinner ($7). The Das Alpine ($7) is a "mile-high" corned beef on rye. Beer is served here for about $3 to $4 depending on the size and the brand. Desserts are about $2.

After the Crown Colony Restaurant (see below), Das Festhaus offers Busch Gardens' most enjoyable dining experience, largely because of the chance to be royally entertained while eating.

Oasis Juice Bar

At the other end of the plaza, next to the midway games, this small kiosk serves fresh-squeezed juices, chicken strips, and corn dogs ($4 to $5).

Shopping in Timbuktu

West Africa Trading Company

Echoing Timbuktu's mercantile roots, this shop focuses on small decorative objects and gifts from far off sources. Preeminent among them are wooden crafts from around the world. Prices start at under $10 and go up to $1,200 or so, but you should be able to find a lovely gift here for under $30. An ever-changing variety of other types of international crafts is also on offer. For other tastes, the shop has a walk-in cigar humidor stocked with imported stogies from Honduras and the Dominican Republic as well as the handiwork of Tampa's own hand rollers.

Outside, in a setting that mimics a bazaar in a dusty sub-Saharan crossroads, you will find still more crafts products, including Ugandan baskets, Chinese pottery, and other decorative objects, along with straw hats and the ever-present Busch Gardens t-shirts. Prices on the crafts are modest to moderate.

Rhino Rally Photo

This kiosk features a remarkably realistic statue of a raging rhino in the act of dismembering a Land Rover. It serves as a backdrop for family photos that you can compose as your imagination dictates. Sample photos give you an idea of the wacky possibilities, although I must say that posing people on the rhino's back tends to detract from the realism. Photos cost from $10 to $13 depending on size.

Nairobi

This is Busch Gardens' most zoo-like themed area. To the east, the plains of Serengeti stretch as far as the eye can see. On the other side are a string of animal exhibits ranging from the merely interesting to the truly wondrous. In addition to those described below, there is a display of **Aldabra tortoises**, with occasional Meet The Keeper sessions. The showpiece of Nairobi, however, is the *Rhino Rally* attraction, which is part African animal encounter and part thrill ride.

Rhino Rally

Rating: ★ ★ ★ +
Type: Drive-through animal tour and water ride

Time:	7 minutes
Kelly says:	Nifty idea that's more clever than thrilling

Rhino Rally artfully blends safari-style animal encounters with a tame water ride. The ride is carved out of a 22-acre patch of the *Serengeti Plain* near the border between Nairobi and Timbuktu. But, unlike rides at other parks that use animated robotic figures, *Rhino Rally* calls on its cast of exotic African water buffalo, zebras, antelope, elephants, and rhinos to play themselves in a real-life action adventure.

The adventure begins as you board a 17-passenger converted Land Rover with your guide and driver to take part in the 34th annual running of *Rhino Rally*, an off-road race along the Zambezi River across the rugged and dangerous terrain of the African veldt. One adult in the group is chosen to ride next to the driver (a great seat, by the way) and serve as the navigator who, in off-road rally tradition, will be blamed if anything goes wrong. Along the way, your vehicle splashes through crocodile-infested waters and comes almost face to face with elephants, rhinos, and other wild critters. The course has been cleverly designed to allow the Land Rovers to nosedive into streams and water holes and cross narrow bridges over deep ravines. It's all great fun.

The trip provides close-up, although brief, encounters with elephants, Grant's zebras, cape buffalo and scimitar-horned oryx. The ancient Egyptians, we learn, domesticated these beasts and forced their long curving horns to grow together into a single horn, creating the myth of the unicorn. After driving past two rare white rhinos (which are actually gray), the vehicle fords a stream filled with real crocodiles cruising just a few feet away.

Then, as often happens in theme park thrill rides, things go awry and, of course, it's all the navigator's fault. A fateful wrong turn takes your vehicle into a tree-shaded gulch just as a cloudburst hits, obscuring the view out the front window. As your driver nervously tries to cross a rickety pontoon bridge, a freak flash flood comes roaring over a cliff on the left. Before you can say "Dr. Livingstone, I presume," the bridge breaks apart carrying you and your vehicle on an unscheduled ride down a meandering river. After drifting through a narrow canyon and under a drenching waterfall, the bridge fragment on which your vehicle is riding crashes against yet another washed out bridge and comes to a bumpy halt. Fortunately, your intrepid guide is able to drive out of this fix and up the side of the river bringing everyone safely to the finish line.

A great deal of the fun of this ride is supplied by the driver/guide. The best ones really get into the spirit of things, teaching you a few handy Swahili phrases and getting everyone involved in the action. So you'll probably want to ride more than once. The problem with that is the line quickly grows to daunting lengths. Figure on an hour's wait unless you arrive at opening time.

Tip: If you are alone or if there are just two of you, you may be able to get in a vehicle a bit sooner by following the sign for the single riders line. If you are waiting in the main line, you can accomplish much the same thing by holding one or two fingers aloft during the boarding process. Ride attendants sometimes look for singles or couples to fill in empty spots on the Land Rover that's about to depart.

The best seats in the house. The seats on the left hand side of the vehicle offer not only the best views of the wildlife but a front row seat to the spectacular flash flood. You will, however, get wet.

Myombe Reserve: The Great Ape Domain

Rating:	★ ★ ★ ★ ★
Type:	Ape habitat
Time:	Continuous viewing
Kelly says:	The zoo's crown jewel

Of all the animal habitats at Busch Gardens, this is the hands-down winner. The beautifully imagined setting here would be almost worth the visit without the chimps and gorillas. But it is these fascinating primates that we come to see, and the scenic designers and landscape architects have given them a home that provides plenty of variety for the animals while making it easy for us to spy on them. The achievement is remarkable and ranks right up there with the spectacular habitats at SeaWorld.

The habitat is divided in two, with the first area given over to a band of nine chimpanzees in a rocky, multi-leveled environment complete with spectacular waterfalls, calm pools, and a grassy forest clearing with plenty of climbing space. Best of all is a glassed-in viewing area that allows us to spy on the chimp's private behavior.

Passing through a tunnel, we arrive at the lowland gorilla habitat. There's a wonderful theatricality to this entrance as we pass through a simulated jungle fog to "discover" the gorillas grazing on our left. Talk about gorillas in the mist! In addition to a glassed viewing area, this habitat features a small amphitheater for extended observation and video cameras that allow us to observe individuals in the far reaches of the habitat.

There's plenty of explanatory information provided on blackboards (the conceit here is that we are visiting a jungle outpost of a scientific expedition), drawings in large, plastic-covered notebooks that we can leaf through, and voice-over narration in the hidden viewing area. If you only have time for one zoo exhibit between roller coaster rides, make it this one. The entrance to *Myombe Reserve* is opposite the Moroccan Palace Theater; the exit leads you into the rest of the Nairobi section.

Nairobi Station Animal Nursery

Rating:	★ ★ ★ ★
Type:	Newborn animal exhibit
Time:	Continuous viewing
Kelly says:	Lifestyles of the cutest and cuddliest

One of the main missions of today's enlightened zoological parks is the propagation of species, especially threatened and endangered ones. Busch Gardens takes this responsibility very seriously and, rather than leave things to chance, they scoop up newborns, bring them here, and give them the kind of tender loving care that will best ensure their survival. What you see here will, naturally, depend on who's been giving birth in the days and weeks prior to your visit. Question and answer sessions with the keepers of the nursery are held several times a day. Times are posted on a sign at the entrance.

Asian Elephants

Rating:	★ ★ ★ ★
Type:	Animal habitat
Time:	Continuous viewing
Kelly says:	Come at show time

A small herd of female Asian elephants is housed in a spacious, if rather barren, habitat at the northern end of Nairobi. The Meet The Keeper shows featuring these enormous creatures are highly entertaining and invariably feature one of the ponderous pachyderms getting a bath. The attendant will also make sure that photographers get a good shot of the elephant in an alluring pose. Happily, these shows are presented more frequently than the other animal presentations in the park.

Curiosity Caverns

Rating:	★ ★ +
Type:	Walk-through exhibit
Time:	Continuous viewing
Kelly says:	A real "Bat Cave"

Decorated to evoke a prehistoric cave, complete with wall paintings, this darkened walk-through tunnel displays, behind plate glass windows, a variety of critters that most people thing of as "creepy," although the nocturnal marmoset is positively cuddly. Aside from the snakes and reptiles, the main attractions here are the bats. Fruit bats cavort in a large enclosure decorated with bare trees artfully draped with bananas, apples, and other yummy treats. Nearby, in a smaller display, are the vampire bats (yes, they really exist!), the animal blood on which they thrive served up on dainty trays.

Eating in Nairobi

Kenya Kanteen

What:	Quick snacks
Where:	Between the elephants and the tortoises
Price Range:	$

Funnel cakes, soft serve ice cream, and soft drinks are the order of the day here, with nothing costing more than $4. You can sit at umbrella-shaded tables and observe the animals in the Serengeti across the way. Nearby are some attractive, slightly smaller than life size hippo sculptures that make a great place to take yet more pictures of your kids.

Shopping in Nairobi

J.R.'s Gorilla Hut

Just outside the *Myombe* exit, this outdoor kiosk sells, you guessed it, t-shirts, dolls, and other souvenirs that celebrate our primate relatives. Best of the lot are the t-shirts with white on black gorilla portraits ($18). You will also find a small selection of books on gorillas and chimps, aimed mostly at the younger set, as well as some cute plush dolls.

Crown Colony and the Serengeti Plain

This area takes its theme from the great British colonial enclaves of East Africa, where the well-heeled lived the good life and played cricket and polo while being waited on by the unshod. A real British Colonial would probably not recognize the place, but for the rest of us it'll do just fine. The overall impression is one of casual elegance and good taste.

Crown Colony serves as a comfortable home to several attractions (like *Akbar's Adventure Tours*, the Clydesdale stables, and the **Show Jumping Hall of Fame**) that stretch the African metaphor a bit. It is also the home of Busch Gardens' only full-service sit-down restaurant.

Edge of Africa

Rating:	★ ★ ★ ★ ★
Type:	Brilliant animal habitat
Time:	Continuous viewing
Kelly says:	Up close and personal with lions and hippos

With *Edge of Africa*, Busch Gardens has created an animal habitat to rival *Myombe*. Here, on a looping trail that evokes a number of African themes, are displayed a compact colony of adorable meerkats, a pride of lions, a pack of hyenas, a few hippos, and a troop of baboons. The genius of the design is in the glass walls that allow you, literally, to come nose to nose with some of these animals.

The lion display is built around the metaphor of a scientific encampment on the Serengeti that has been invaded by a pride. Two Land Rovers are built into the glass wall that separates you from the lions, allowing you to climb into the vehicles and re-create an actual safari experience. At feeding time, the handlers drop meat morsels into the lion enclosure from above the Land Rovers, encouraging the lions to climb into the backs and onto the hoods of the vehicles. The effect is breathtaking as you sit a hand's breadth away from a snarling lion.

The hippo exhibit evokes an African river village with the huts raised over the water on stilts. The viewing area is nicely shaded by the huts and the extensive glass wall allows a terrific underwater perspective on these beasts. While they may seem lumbering on land, under water they are surprisingly graceful as they lope past swarms of freshwater tropical fish. One visitor compared them to flying pigs.

The key to really enjoying *Edge of Africa* is to come at feeding time when the animals will be at their most active and most visible. At other times they will most likely be off relaxing in the shade somewhere. The attendants doing the feeding are all experienced animal handlers who are more than happy to share their extensive knowledge with you, so don't be shy about asking questions. Unfortunately, there is no regular feeding schedule. Feeding times are varied to mimic, to some small extent, life in the wild, where animals can never predict when their next meal is coming.

The solution is to ask the attendants at the attraction when feeding time will be. You may have to be persistent and you must also be willing to drop whatever you're doing elsewhere in the park to return at the appointed time. Take it from me, it's worth it.

Note: The main entrance to *Edge of Africa* is in Crown Colony but you can also reach the attraction from Egypt.

Serengeti Safari Tour

Rating: ★ ★ ★ ★ ★
Type: Guided tour
Time: 30 minutes
Kelly says: A safari for those who can't get to Africa

First the bad news: There is a hefty extra charge for this attraction of $30 for everyone five and older (annual passholders get a $2 discount). That will probably be a budget-buster for many families; but if the cost doesn't scare you off, this one will provide experiences you'll remember for a good long time. If it's any consolation, it's a heck of a lot cheaper than going to Africa.

The tour begins when about 20 people are loaded on to the standing-room-only back of a flatbed truck. A small awning provides some shade at the front, but since it is lowered for the animal feedings much of the time you will be in the searing sun; a hat, not to mention water, is not a bad idea. Your friendly tour guide, a Busch Garden's education staffer, lays down a few simple safety instructions and then it's off to the interior of the Plain for the real highlight of the tour — a chance to hand feed the ostriches, giraffes, maribou storks, and elands.

The adult giraffes tower over you, while the youngsters just get their heads over the edge of the truck. They are remarkably tame and will let you pet their stiff, tawny necks and soft muzzles. You may also get a demonstration of how they use their long black tongues to pluck the dainty leaves off thorny acacia bushes. For most people, this is the highlight of the tour. To have two or three of these gentle giants leaning into the back of the truck as you feed them and stroke their powerful necks is a very special experience indeed.

The best seats in the house. The back of the truck where you stand has a padded rail around the rim. I suggest positioning yourself at one of the back corners since giraffes will often trail after the slow-moving vehicle looking for another handout.

Tip: The trucks have a maximum capacity of 20 people and on a typical day there are just five tours. While the high price keeps the crowds down, tours do fill up quickly. You can reserve ahead for the first tour of each day only, which departs at 11:15 a.m. and is the only morning tour. The morning tour also offers the advantage of beating the heat of midday. Call (813) 984-4073 or (813) 984-4043 to make your reservation. When you arrive at the park, head to Crown Colony and look for the Expedition Africa gift shop, where you can pay for your tour with cash or credit card. If you don't reserve ahead, you must sign up in advance for one of the afternoon tours when you get to the park; it is wise to do so early.

Serengeti Plain

Rating:	★ ★ ★
Type:	Extensive animal habitat
Time:	Continuous viewing but access is limited
Kelly says:	Takes persistence to see it all

This is one of Busch Gardens' major zoological achievements. A 50-acre preserve that evokes the vast grasslands of Eastern Africa. (Serengeti is a Masai word meaning "plain without end.") Here, Busch displays a representative cross-section of African plains dwellers, from charming curiosities like giraffes and the endangered black rhinoceros, to the herd animals — lithe gazelles and lumbering wildebeest (or gnus). There are some African birds here, too, like the maribou stork, but most of the birds you will see are what Busch Gardens calls "fly-ins," Florida species that recognize a good deal when they see one. The rule of thumb is that if it's a bird and white, it's a Tampa Bay local.

It's a brilliant idea and, by and large, well executed, although it still looks far more like Florida scrub land than the real Serengeti. The concept and the design involve a number of tradeoffs. By mimicking nature, the designers have made the animals hard to see — just like in the wild. Although you can see into the Serengeti from Nairobi or the terrace of the Crown Colony House, the only way to get a good look is to go inside. Unless you are willing to pay the stiff extra fee for the *Serengeti Safari Tour*, that can be accomplished only by the *Skyride* (see below) and by the *Trans-Veldt Railroad* (see the Stanleyville section, above) which circles the perimeter. So your routes through the Serengeti are predetermined as are the lengths of your visits. This creates a number of minor problems. There's no guarantee that the animals will be in prime viewing position (or even visible) when you pass by, although it's unlikely that you will miss much. And, if an animal catches your fancy or is doing something particularly interesting, your vehicle simply keeps on going; you don't have the luxury of stopping. You also have no control over how close you can get to the animals (with the notable exception of the *Serengeti Safari Tour*).

That being said, the *Serengeti Plain* remains a major feather in Busch Gardens' zoological cap. The animals enjoy a much more spacious and natural environment than they would have in a more "traditional" zoo and we probably shouldn't complain too much about the compromises we must make for their comfort.

Those who want to make the investment of time and money can visit the Serengeti many times — on the *Skyride* over the plain, the train ride around it, the truck tour, and from vantage points in *Edge of Africa* and around the perimeter. The nature of the park experience, however, suggests that most people will glimpse the animals briefly on the short rides. And that's too bad.

The Skyride

Rating: ★ ★ ★
Type: Suspended gondola ride
Time: 5 minutes
Kelly says: Shortcut with a view

If you've been on the sky ride at Disney World, you know what this one's all about. This isn't intended as a tour of the *Serengeti Plain*, although it does pass over *Edge of Africa* and *Rhino Rally* and offers a glimpse of the plains animals in the distance. Rather, this is a one-way shortcut from Crown Colony to the Congo, or vice versa. Your vehicle is a small four-seat gondola suspended from an overhead cable. You can board at either end, but you cannot stay aboard for a roundtrip. The ride dips down for a dog-leg left turn at a checkpoint on the northern end of the *Serengeti*. This is not a disembarkation point but is used primarily to adjust the spacing between gondolas to assure a smooth arrival. It also gives you a swell view of the camels.

You can get some good views of the *Serengeti Plain* from this ride, although most people will take the opportunity to check out the action on *Montu* and *Kumba* or perhaps to spot the towers of Adventure Island, Busch Gardens' water park, down the road.

Akbar's Adventure Tours

Rating:	★ ★ ★ +
Type:	Simulator ride
Time:	10 minutes
Kelly says:	Not bad of this kind

Join the intrepid, if slightly desperate, Akbar as he tries to fend off the repo man and save his failing Egyptian tour operation with a "homemade simulator" operated by his baby brothers. That's the premise of this dotty exercise in simulated insanity. Amazingly enough it works pretty well.

After you snake through the line to the attraction's doors, groups of 60 are led into a pre-show area where Akbar (played with manic abandon by comedian Martin Short) explains his ingenious idea, only to be interrupted by a sleazy collection agent bent on repossessing everything Akbar owns. Akbar begs, pleads, and finally kidnaps this nemesis to show how his brilliant idea can make them both rich.

That's your cue to enter a simulator that seems to be the twin of the ones used at SeaWorld's Wild Arctic ride; only the interior decoration is different. We get to sample three of Akbar's tours, a ride through an Egyptian market on camel-back, a visit to the Sphinx that succeeds in destroying the ancient wonder, and a visit to a mummy's tomb that goes seriously awry and occasions a truly scary response from the owner.

If this is your only shot at a simulator ride, it's well worth the trip. Otherwise, SeaWorld's *Wild Arctic* does much the same thing better.

The best seats in the house. As you line up along the illuminated circles on the floor to enter the simulator, the screen (or front window of Akbar's homemade simulator) will be on your left as you go in. Your best view will be towards the back in the center. Attempt to arrange yourself accordingly.

Clydesdale Hamlet

Rating:	★ ★ +
Type:	Horse stables
Time:	Continuous viewing
Kelly says:	For horse lovers and Bud fans

This is a smaller version of the Clydesdale Hamlet at SeaWorld. The horses are magnificent; there may be a foal on view during your visit. Even if you aren't a horse lover, the stroll through the stables makes a convenient shortcut to *Akbar's Adventure Tours*. The Clydesdales also pose for **photo ops** several times a day. Check the Meet The Keepers schedule on the back of the large map you picked up at the main entrance when you arrived.

Eating in Crown Colony

Crown Colony House

What:	Full-service restaurant
Where:	Opposite the *Skyride* entrance, overlooking the *Serengeti*
Price Range:	$$ - $$$$

The only full-service restaurant at Busch Gardens is the 240-seat Crown Colony House, a droll evocation of a posh East African club during the heyday of British colonialism. It was founded, so they would have us believe, by an eccentric group of explorers, including Sir Edison Fitzwilly who unearthed the only known sphinx skeleton in addition to the Crystal of Zed. The walls are decorated with old cricket bats, polo mallets, and tennis racquets, as well as antelope horns and buffalo heads. The best dining area is the front room with its sweeping semicircular expanse of windows giving out onto the *Serengeti Plain.*

If the decor is British Colonial a la East Africa, the menu is standard American. Standouts include the Chicken Fettuccini and the Captain's Choice, a platter of broiled or fried shrimp, scallops, and grouper served with grilled vegetables. In the salad department, check out the large and beautifully presented Grilled Chicken Salad and, for vegetarians, the vegetable or fruit salad platters. Entrees range from $11 to $14; salads are $8 to $10 and sandwiches about $8. The big bargain offered here is the family-style dinner (fried chicken or fish) for $10, or $5 for those 12 and under. A limited selection of wine by the bottle is available ($14 to $24).

Tip: In addition to the luxury of being waited on, the main draw here is the great view of the *Serengeti Plain.* No reservations are accepted so you can't call ahead and reserve a table by the great semicircular sweep of window overlooking the *Plain,* but you can request one and wait until it becomes available. If you're not on a tight schedule I highly recommend doing so. The view alone makes this one of the nicest places to eat in Central Florida. And don't forget to bring your binoculars!

Provisions

What:	Fast food eatery
Where:	Downstairs in Crown Colony House
Price Range:	$$ - $$$

On the ground floor of the Crown Colony House you will find Provisions, a fast-food eatery serving up sandwich platters and pizza for about $5 to $7. Across the large room is a polished bar serving Anheuser-Busch beers for about $3 to $4. There is indoor seating in a dark, cool, clubby atmosphere (which can get noisy when full). Perhaps a better choice is to carry your tray past the bar to the curved windows overlooking the *Serengeti*; the view is almost as good as upstairs. If the weather cooperates, you can also eat outdoors where the view is even better.

Shopping in Crown Colony

Trader Jim's

This stone building with its wooden stick roof is located at the juncture where Morocco meets Nairobi and Crown Colony begins. The merchandise leans heavily to plush animals, animal themed t-shirts (about $13 to $20), and Busch Gardens baseball caps in a wide variety of styles (about $13 to $15).

Expedition Africa

After you make your way past the obligatory t-shirts with *Edge of Africa* themes and logos ($12 to $20), you will find some very nice upscale clothing for both men and women. In the back of the shop are tops for women ($20 to $25) and men ($25 to $35), a line of plush animals for the kids, and a smattering of African crafts. This shop is also the place to come to reserve and pay for a trip on the *Serengeti Safari Tour*.

Wilde and Wonderful Gallery

Near Provisions, this small shop sells some very nice wildlife photos and paintings. Most of the art on display is the work of Walter and Cheryl Kuck, although other artists are represented. Some pieces were done at Busch Gardens, others in East Africa. The prices are quite moderate for the obvious quality of the work. A very nice series of animal photos framed with an African postage stamp featuring the same animal are about $45. Unframed pieces range from $45 to $95.

Egypt

This is Busch Gardens' newest "land" and one of its smallest, at least in terms of strolling space and amenities. Its primary purpose is to give the mega-coaster *Montu* a home. The King Tut attraction seems a bit of an after-thought, and the only eatery here is a kiosk dispensing snacks. The shopping is a bit more elaborate but not much.

The design evokes upper Egypt as it might have looked about the time Howard Carter was unearthing King Tut's treasure. The scale is appropriately grandiose but the statuary and wall carvings fall well short of the originals. Still, it's pleasant enough. There's a clever "archaeological dig, " called **Sifting Sands**, that is, in fact, a shaded sand box in which little ones can uncover the past. A small selection of **midway games** is also offered.

For most people, however, Egypt will be glimpsed briefly en route to the massive temple gates at the end, beyond which lurks the terrifying *Montu*.

Montu

Rating:	★ ★ ★ ★ ★
Type:	Inverted roller coaster
Time:	About 3 minutes
Kelly says:	Busch Gardens' best roller coaster

This one is truly terrifying. It is also, for those who care about such things, the tallest and longest inverted steel roller coaster in the southeastern United States.

Montu (named for a hawk-headed Egyptian god of war) takes the for-mula of *Kumba* and, quite literally turns it on its head. Instead of sitting in a car with the track under your feet, you sit (or should I say "hang") in a car with the track overhead. Once you leave the station, your feet hang free as you pass over a pit filled with live crocodiles and climb to a dizzying 150 feet above the ground before being dropped 13 stories, shot through a 360 de-gree "camelback loop" that produces an eternity of weightlessness (actually a mere three seconds), and zipped, zoomed, and zapped along nearly 4,000 feet of track that twists over, above, and even into the ground. Fortunately, when you dip below ground level you do so in archaeological "excavation trenches," in keeping with the Egyptian theme. There's not much to see in these trenches, but then you don't spend much time in them and you'll probably have your eyes jammed shut anyway.

Each car holds 32 passengers. At maximum capacity, 1,700 guests can be pumped through this attraction each hour. Nonetheless, lines can be formi-dable. If this is your kind of ride, plan on arriving early during busy seasons.

The best (and scariest seats) are in the front row. Otherwise, the outside seats are the ones to hope for. Given the overhead design of this ride, the interior seats offer a very obstructed view, which may not be a problem if you tend to ride with your eyes shut most of the time. Getting the front seats is pretty much the luck of the draw, although every once in a while you may be able to step in when the faint of heart opt out of the front row.

Even if you can't or don't ride roller coasters, *Montu* is worth a visit for a close-up view of the crazy people who are riding. Position yourself at the black iron fence that you see as you pass through the massive temple gates that lead to the ride. Here you'll get an exhilarating close-up look of 32 pairs of feet as they come zipping out of the first trench.

If you do ride, don't forget to look for your terrified or giddy face on the instant photos they sell. It's $10 for a photo, $14 for two key chains, and $16 for your mug on a mug.

King Tut's Tomb

Rating: ★ ★ +
Type: Walk-through attraction
Time: About 10 minutes
Kelly says: A "spirited" guide to an ancient tomb

Here's your chance to walk in the footsteps of Howard Carter, the legendary archaeologist who discovered King Tut's tomb in the 1920s. As you wait in the darkened entrance to the tomb, old newspaper headlines and period newsreels re-create the excitement and wonder of the discovery. Then, the projector jams, the film melts and, as you enter the tomb proper, the spirit of Tut himself takes over as tour guide.

What you see is a re-creation of the tomb as it looked at the time of discovery, the many treasures and priceless artifacts piled in jumbled disarray. As lights illuminate specific artifacts, Tut tells us about his gilded throne, his golden chariot, and his teenage bride. Moving to the burial chamber, we see his solid gold sarcophagus and the golden goddesses who guarded the cabinet containing alabaster urns filled with his internal organs.

For newcomers to Egyptology, this attraction will serve as an intriguing introduction. The marvelously air-conditioned tomb also makes for a pleasant break from the burning Florida sun. Those who are more familiar with Tut, and especially those who saw the resplendent Tut exhibition that toured the world in the eighties, may want to skip this one.

Eating in Egypt

Pyramid Joe's is a snack kiosk with a limited menu of refreshments. Strawberry bars and Shamu bars are about $2. If you need anything more substantial, the Crown Colony House restaurant is just a short stroll away.

Shopping in Egypt

The Golden Scarab

Located at the exit to King Tut's Tomb, this shop specializes in Egyptian-themed curios and statuettes of so-so quality that struck me as over-priced. Far more attractive are the costume jewelry and the hand-blown Egyptian glass objects in ancient designs. There is also a small selection of books about ancient Egypt aimed at youngsters. Another nifty souvenir is a mug that features your name in hieroglyphics as well as Roman letters.

Montu Gift Shop

You walk through this gift shop on your way out of *Montu*, so you may be tempted to stop for something tangible to commemorate your survival. One of the "I Survived *Montu*" t-shirts ($15 to $16) should do the trick nicely. Somewhat surprisingly, this shop also features some nice sundresses for women and classy tops for guys ($25 to $35).

Guided Tours

Busch Gardens Tampa offers a number of special tours in addition to the *Serengeti Safari Tour* (see Crown Colony, above). These offer special perks, behind-the-scenes access, and up-close encounters with some of its animal charges. There is a hefty extra charge for these special experiences, but if you have the budget I think you'll find it money well spent. The fees given below (which do not include tax) are in addition to regular park admission and no annual passholder or other discounts are offered. Prices were accurate at press time but are subject to change, so it's best to call prior to your visit to double check prices and availability. You can call toll-free at (888) 800-5447 and ask to be connected to the tour department. The direct lines are (813) 984-4043 or (813) 984-4073. Children under five are not permitted on these tours; bilingual guides can be arranged with prior notice.

Animal Adventure Tour

This two-hour tour focuses on the animals of the park, with an emphasis on the newest additions to the Busch Gardens family. Consequently, the menu may change depending on who's given birth most recently. At each stop, you get a personal briefing from the keepers. The tour starts at the Expedition Africa gift shop near Crown Colony House and visits the Clydesdale stables and *Edge of Africa*. Then you climb aboard a truck for your own

Serengeti Safari Tour (see above). From there, you visit the rhinos and the elephants. A stop at the *Nairobi Nursery* might also be included. At most stops you will get to hand feed the animals and the tour guide will provide you with free ice-cold water during the tour.

There is just one *Animal Adventure Tour* each day, at 1:30 p.m. The tour, which is accessible to handicapped guests, costs $75 for all ages and is limited to seven people, so prior reservations are recommended. Otherwise, you can stop by the Expedition Africa shop to see if any slots are available. This tour is a sure-fire hit for animal lovers. If you are planning on taking the $30 *Serengeti Safari Tour* anyway, you may want to consider upgrading to this very special experience.

Guided Adventure Tour

This four- to five-hour guided tour combines the animal encounters of the *Serengeti Safari Tour* with visits to *Edge of Africa* and the park's major rides and shows. Guests on this tour get front of the line access to *Kumba*, *Gwazi*, and *Montu* and the best seats in the house for the dolphin and ice skating shows. You also receive a 20% discount on all park merchandise and free stroller and wheelchair rental.

The tour costs $59 for adults and $45 for kids and is limited to 15 people. Make a reservation before arriving or look for the "Guided Tour Adventure Center" in the entrance plaza to the park. Tours depart once a day at 10:20 a.m.

Ultimate Adventure Tour

This $199 all-day extravaganza is Busch Gardens' VIP tour and it can last as long as you wish, although at this price you'll probably want to arrive early and stay until the park closes. The Ultimate Adventure Tour includes the *Animal Adventure Tour* along with the front of the line access, priority seating, and discounts of the *Guided Adventure Tour*, plus a free continental breakfast and a free Fuji camera. This one must be booked at least 24 hours in advance, but large groups should book at least a week in advance.

Adventure Camps

If you really want to be nice to your kids, you won't just take them to Busch Gardens, you'll leave them there. Busch Gardens operates a number of sleepover camps for kids from grade six through high school. There's even a program that takes college kids. With nifty names like Zooventures and Terratrekkers, these camps last from three to nine days and cost from $550 to over $1,000. Housing is dorm style on Busch Gardens property.

And if you think it's unfair that kids have all the fun, ask about the three-day Family Fun weekend adventures, which let adults tag along. For more information and to request a catalog of camp programs at all of the Busch parks (the SeaWorlds in Orlando, San Antonio, and San Diego also offer programs) call (800) 372-1797.

CHAPTER TEN:

Water Parks

*O*rlando is the home of the water park as we know it today. George D. Millay, a former SeaWorld official, started it all in 1977 with the opening of Wet 'n Wild. Since then, the concept has been copied, most noticeably by Disney, whose nearby complex has three water-themed parks — Typhoon Lagoon, Blizzard Beach, and River Country — all of them beautifully designed in the Disney tradition. Despite its deep pockets and design talent, Disney hasn't buried the competition. Wet 'n Wild is still going strong and nearby Water Mania has its fans. To the west, the folks at Busch have built Adventure Island, right next to Busch Gardens Tampa. All of these water parks offer plenty of thrills at a competitive price.

An often overlooked selling point of these non-Disney water parks is that they all have numerous hotels and motels just a short drive away. Wet 'n Wild has many hotels within walking distance. This makes them especially easy to visit. If you are staying near one of these parks, there is little need, in my opinion, to trek all the way to Disney for a water park experience.

Like any self-respecting theme park, a water park has rides. But the rides here don't rely on mechanical wonders or ingenious special effects. Indeed they are the essence of simplicity: You walk up and then, with a little help from gravity and a stream of water, you come down. The fun comes from the many variations the designers work on this simple theme.

Slides

These are the most basic rides. After climbing a high tower, you slide down a flume on a cushion of running water, either on your back, on a rubber mat, in a one- or two-person inner tube, or in a raft that can carry anywhere from two to five people. Virtually every slide will have a series of swooping turns and sudden drops. Some are open to the sky, others are completely enclosed tubes. All slides dump you in a pool at the bottom of the run.

Speed Slides

Speed slides appeal to the daredevil. They are simple, narrow, flat-bottomed slides; some are pitched at an angle that approaches the vertical, others descend in a series of stair steps. Most culminate in a long, flat stretch that allows you to decelerate; a few end in splash pools. They offer a short, intense experience.

Wave Pools

These large, fan-shaped swimming pools have a beach-like entrance at the wide end and slope to a depth of about eight feet at the other. A clever hydraulic system sets waves running from the wall to the beach, mimicking the action of the ocean. Most wave pools have several modes, producing a steady flow of varying wave heights or a sort of random choppiness. Sometimes rented inner tubes are available for use in the wave pool.

Good Things To Know About . . .

Dress Codes

Simply put: wear a swimsuit. Most parks prohibit shorts, cut-off jeans, or anything with zippers, buckles, or metal rivets, as these things can scratch and damage the slides. Those with fair skin can wear t-shirts if they wish. Some rides may require that you remove your shirt, which you can usually clutch to your chest as you zoom down. Most people go barefoot, as the parks are designed with your feet's comfort in mind. If you prefer to wear waterproof sandals or other footwear designed for water sports, they are permitted.

Leaving the Park

All the parks reviewed here let you leave the park and return the same day. Just make sure to have your hand stamped before leaving.

Lockers

All water parks provide rental lockers and changing areas. Most people wear their swimsuits under their street clothes and disrobe by their locker. At day's end, they take their street clothes to a changing area, towel down, and get dressed, popping their wet suits into a plastic bag. The plastic laundry bag from your hotel room is ideal for this purpose.

Safety

Water park rides are safe, just as long as you follow the common sense rules posted at the rides and obey the instructions of the ride attendants. You are more likely to run into problems with the sun (see below) or with physical exertion if you are out of shape. You will climb more stairs at a visit to a water park than most people climb in a month. If you're not in peak condition, take it slow; pause from time to time and take in the sights.

The Sun

The Central Florida sun can be brutal. If you don't have a good base tan, a day at a water park can result in a painful sunburn, even on a cloudy day. Don't let it happen to you. Use sun block and use it liberally. Most overlooked place to protect: your feet. The sun also saps your body of moisture. Be sure to drink plenty of liquids throughout the day.

Towels

At Wet 'n Wild and Water Mania you can rent towels for a modest fee. Adventure Island, at my last visit, was not renting towels but said they were considering doing so, "because we get so many requests." It's easy (not to mention cheaper) to bring your own, even if it's one borrowed from your hotel.

Eating at the Water Parks

Water parks are like a day at the beach. Consequently, dining (if that's the right word) is a pretty basic experience. Most park eateries offer walk-up window service, paper plates, plastic utensils, and outdoor seating, some of it shaded. The bill of fare seldom ventures out of the hot dog, hamburger, pizza, barbecue, and ice cream categories. The prices are modest. You really have to work hard to spend more than $10 per person for a meal. In short, food at the water parks has been designed with kids and teenagers in mind, so I have not covered the restaurants in the reviews that follow. Suffice it to say you won't go hungry.

However, in my opinion, the best way to eat at the water parks is to bypass the fast-food eateries altogether and bring your own. All of the parks offer picnic areas, some with barbecue pits, some of them quite enchanting. If you are the picnicking type, I don't have to tell you what to do. Others should be aware that Florida supermarkets are cornucopias of picnic supplies. The folks at the deli counter will be more than happy to fix you up with a sumptuous repast. Many supermarket meat departments offer marinated or stuffed meat entrees ready for the grill. You can even pick up an inexpensive cooler while you're there along with ice to keep things cool. All the parks prohibit alcoholic beverages and glass containers.

Most people simply find a suitable picnic bench when they arrive and stake it out with a beach towel and their cooler, returning at lunch time. If you feel uncomfortable doing this, you can leave your cooler in the car and retrieve it at lunch time. (Don't forget to get your hand stamped!) Another option would be to use one of the rental lockers.

Shopping at the Water Parks

The casual attitude of these parks toward eating is echoed in the shopping. Don't worry, you'll be able to get that nifty t-shirt or the key chain with the park's logo if you must. But the shops are fairly basic even at their most spacious. The best thing about them is the canny selection of merchandise. If you get to the park and find yourself saying, "Oh no, I forgot my . . ." chances are you'll be able to find it in the shop.

In addition to the usual gamut of souvenirs and t-shirts are swim suits (some of them quite snazzy), sandals, sun block and tanning lotions, film, combs, brushes and other toiletries, towels, sunglasses, trashy novels — in short everything you need for a day at the beach. Forgetful picnickers will also be pleased to know that they can find soft drinks, snack foods, and candy bars at most of the shops.

Which Park Is Best?

We all have our favorites. My personal favorite of the parks covered in this chapter is Wet 'n Wild. However, if you have never been to a water park, I can virtually guarantee you will have a wonderful time at any of these parks. Then, too, comparing these parks is always something of an apples and oranges exercise. Each park has its unique attractions. Wet 'n Wild has the tow rides in its large lake. Water Mania has its simulated surfing ride. Adventure Island has the *Everglides*.

If you have a choice of parks, use the descriptions below to help decide which will most appeal to your tastes. Otherwise, pick the most convenient for your touring plan or the one that's offering the tastiest discount at the time of your visit.

Wet 'n Wild

6200 International Drive
Orlando, FL 32819
(800) 992-WILD; (407) 351-1800
www.wetnwild.com

The original Orlando water park is still the best. Add to that its location in the heart of Orlando's tourist country and its partnership in the Orlando

FlexTicket program (see *Chapter 1*) and you have a real winner.

The park layout is compact and efficient with little wasted space. The style is sleekly modern and the maintenance is first rate — even though Wet 'n Wild is the oldest water park in the area, it looks as if it opened just last week.

Getting There

Wet 'n Wild is located in the heart of Orlando's prime tourist area on International Drive at the corner of Universal Boulevard. It is less than a half mile from I-4 Exit 30A.

Opening and Closing Times

Thanks to heated water on its slides and in its pools, Wet 'n Wild is the only non-Disney water park that is open year-round, although it can get plenty chilly in the winter months. The hours of operation vary from 10:00 a.m. to 5:00 p.m. from late October to around the end of March to 9:00 a.m. to 10:00 p.m. at the height of the summer. Call the information lines above for specific park hours during your visit.

The Price of Admission

The following prices include tax:

Adults:	$32.81
Children (3 to 9):	$26.45
Children under 3 **free**.	
Seniors (55+):	$16.41
Annual Pass (all ages):	$95.35
Summer Season Pass (May 1-Labor Day; all ages):	$58.25

Parking is $5 for cars, $6 for RVs and vans.

Wet 'n Wild participates in the Orlando FlexTicket program described in *Chapter 1: Introduction & Orientation*. Prices (including tax) are as follows:

4-Park, 14-Day Pass — Universal, IOA, SeaWorld, Wet 'n Wild

Adults:	$180.15
Children (3 to 9):	$143.05

5-Park, 14-Day Pass — adds Busch Gardens Tampa

Adults:	$215.46
Children (3 to 9):	$175.12

In addition, the park offers discounts for entry in the afternoon year round. Call for details.

Rentals

The following are available for rent or loan at the round kiosk located to your right as you enter the park:

Lockers are $5, plus a $2 deposit.

Inner tubes are $4, plus a $2 deposit.

Towels are $2, plus a $2 deposit.

Life vests are **free**.

A Combo of 2 towels and a locker is $9, plus a $4 deposit.

Rides and Attractions at Wet 'n Wild

Wet 'n Wild is a compact and tightly packed park that somehow avoids feeling cramped. For the purposes of describing its attractions I have divided the park into three slices. I will start on the left-hand side of the park (as you enter the front gate), then proceed to the center section, and finally describe the slides and such on the right-hand side.

Kid's Playground

This delightful, multi-level water play area is a sort of Wet 'n Wild in miniature for the toddler set. At the top, there are some twisting water slides that can be negotiated with or without tiny inner tubes. On the other side is a mini-version of the *Surf Lagoon* wave pool surrounded by a Lilliputian *Lazy River*. In between are shallow pools with fountains, showers, water cannons, and a variety of other interactive play areas, all watched over by vigilant lifeguards. Rising above the pools is a blimp into which kids can climb; once aboard they can use a battery of water cannons to spray those below. Surrounding the *Kid's Playground* is a seating area filled with shaded tables and chairs where Mom and Dad can take their ease while junior wears himself out nearby.

Mach 5

The massive tower that houses *Mach 5* and two other rides looks like a giant pasta factory after a nasty explosion; flumes twist every which way. At the entrance, you grab a blue toboggan-like mat; the front end curves up and over two hand holds. Then there is a very long climb to the top where you will find three flumes labeled A, B, and C. They all seem to offer pretty much the same experience, but you'll probably want to try all three anyway. I sure did. You ride belly down on your mat and take a few gently corkscrewing turns. But then there is a quick drop followed by a sharp turn followed by another drop and so on until you zip into and across the splashdown pool. Keeping your feet raised will decrease the coefficient of drag and give you a slightly zippier ride.

Raging Rapids

This inner tube ride shares the tower with *Mach 5* but starts about halfway up. Once again, you pick up your inner tube, bright pink this time, at the bottom and carry it up. This is a comparatively gentle ride with a series of short slides into shallow pools, in each of which there is an attendant to send you over the next drop-off. The excitement comes when you find yourself going down backwards, unable to see what's ahead. One slide takes you under a delightfully drenching waterfall, and there is a sharp drop to the final splashdown. If you hit the bottom pool just right (or just wrong) you may find yourself unceremoniously dumped from your tube. It's a great way to end a fun ride.

The Flyer

This newer ride also shares the *Mach 5* tower and, while it starts at about the same height as *Raging Rapids*, it's a much faster, scarier ride. This time there's nothing to drag to the top with you; your vehicle awaits at the launching area. It's a bright green two-, three-, or four-person raft (no single riders), with built-in hand grips. Hang on tight because the turns are sharp and the raft gets thrown high up the curved side walls as you zoom quickly to the bottom. This is a justifiably popular ride with a lot of repeat riders.

The Surge

The Surge has a tower all to itself. One reason is the size of the rafts, large five-person circular affairs. You sit in the bottom of the raft, facing toward the center, and grab hand holds on the floor. Then the attendant gives the raft a good spin as he sends you on your way down the first fall. The flumes are larger versions of those at *Mach 5* and the descent seems somewhat slower. The turns, however, are deceptive. Depending on where you're sitting as the raft enters a turn, you can find yourself sliding high on the curved walls, and when you hit one of the frequents drops backwards you'll feel your tummy do a little flip.

Fountain Pool

Near the exit to *The Surge* is a small, shallow play area with waterfalls and fountains for the younger set, a good place for the littler members of your party to wait for you while you ride *The Surge*.

The Black Hole

The last slide ride on this side of the park, *The Black Hole* works an interesting variation on the theme. Here you ride a two-person, Siamese inner tube down completely enclosed black tubes. It's not totally dark, however; a thin line of light at the top gives some illumination and lets you know which way the tube will twist next. Although the darkness adds a special thrill, *The*

Black Hole is not especially scary or fast, especially compared to, say, *Mach 5*. If you choose the tube to your right as you enter the launch area, you'll get a few extra bumps. A single person can ride alone, occupying the front hole in the inner tube.

Knee Ski

Rounding things off on the left side of the park is something completely different — a modified water-skiing experience. You kneel on a small surfboard specially designed for this sort of thing; molded rubber impressions make it easy to stay on and a mandatory life-jacket protects you if you fall off. And instead of a speedboat, your tow line hangs from a sort of cable-car arrangement that tows you in a long circle around a lake. The entire course is surrounded by a wooden dock and, should you fall, you are never more than a few strokes from the edge. Ladders like those in swimming pools are provided at regular intervals, making this a very safe ride.

Dunkings are rare, however. Given the special design of the board, the low center of gravity, and the moderate speed of the tow line, most people complete the circuit easily. So don't let a lack of experience with water skiing keep you from enjoying this ride.

Surf Lagoon

Moving to the center section of the park we find, appropriately enough, the centerpiece of Wet 'n Wild. This is an artificial ocean. Well, actually, it's a fan shaped swimming pool with a hydraulic system that sends out pulsing waves in which you can jump and frolic. You can also bounce around on top of them in an inner tube. At the "ocean" end of the pool, a waterfall splashes off the back wall and onto swimmers bobbing in the waves below. At the "beach" end of the pool, you'll find plenty of lounge chairs for soaking up the sun.

Volleyball Courts

Squeezed between the back of the wave pool and the arcade are two side-by-side volleyball courts. The surface is soft beach sand. Balls can be obtained free of charge at the Courtesy Counter at the front of the park. If there are people waiting, you are asked to limit games to 15 minutes or 11 points, whichever comes first. The courts are occasionally reserved for the use of private groups visiting the park.

Arcade

A video arcade. 'Nuff said.

Wild One

Head past the volleyball courts on to the dock and hang a right. Down at the end is *Wild One*, the only ride at Wet 'n Wild that requires an additional charge over and above the admission to the park, $4 including tax. The ride is worth the extra expense. You are towed in a large inner tube behind a jet ski as it races around the Wet 'n Wild lake. The fun here is in the turns as the two inner tubes being towed accelerate sharply in wide arcs to keep up with the jet ski's tight turns. The ride lasts about two minutes.

Bubble Up

As you move to the right side of the park, you encounter *Bubble Up*. This attraction is just for kids. Too bad, because it looks fun. In the center of a pool stands a large blue and white rubber mountain; at the top is a circular fountain producing a steady downpour. The object is to grab the knotted rope hanging down from the summit and pull yourself to the top up the slippery sides. Once there you can slide back down into the pool.

Bubba Tub

This is a deceptively simple ride that packs a wallop. Five-person circular rafts zip down a broad, straight slide that features three sharp drops on the speedy trip to the bottom. The ever-helpful attendant gives the raft a spin at takeoff so it's hard to predict whether you'll go down backwards or not. It's a short ride, almost guaranteed to raise a scream or two, and a lot of fun.

Lazy River

Circling *Bubble Up* and the *Bubba Tub* is a swift-moving stream, about 10 feet wide and three feet deep. There are a number of entrances and you can enter or exit at any of them. Grab one of the floating tubes or, to assure you'll have one, bring your rented tube and float along with the current; it takes about five minutes to make one complete circuit. It is also possible to swim or float down *Lazy River* unaided, and many people choose this option.

The Storm

Riders of *The Storm* zip down a towering chute into an open air bowl, where they spin wildly around at speeds of up to 45 miles per hour as spectators cheer them on. Then they drop through a hole in the middle of the bowl into a waiting splash pool.

Der Stuka

Behind the *Bubba Tub*, you will find a high tower housing three speed slides — *Der Stuka*, *Bomb Bay*, and *Blue Niagara* — billed as the tallest and fastest in the world. Like all speed slides, *Der Stuka* is simplicity itself. You lie down on your back, cross your ankles, fold your arms over your chest, and an attendant nudges you over the edge of a precipitously angled free fall. You'll reach speeds approaching 50 mph before a long trough of shallow water brings you to a halt.

Bomb Bay

Bomb Bay is right next to *Der Stuka*. Its slide is precisely the same height, length, and angle of its neighbor. So what's the difference? Here you step into a bomb-shaped capsule which is then precisely positioned over the slide. The floor drops away and you are off to a literally flying start down the slide. Thanks to the gravity assisted head start, speeds on this slide are even faster than on *Der Stuka*, or at least they seem that way.

Blue Niagara

After *Der Stuka* and *Bomb Bay*, *Blue Niagara*, which shares the same tower with the two speed slides, seems tame by comparison. But looks are deceiving. *Blue Niagara*, which takes off from a point slightly below the top of the tower, consists of a pair of blue-green translucent tubes that corkscrew around each other at a seemingly modest angle.

You enter feet first, riding on your back. If you're wearing a t-shirt, you'll be asked to remove it. The reason quickly becomes clear. The speed you pick up as you hurtle down the ride could wrap a t-shirt around your face very quickly. As it is, you may get a nose-full of water as you splash down at the end of this exhilarating twist-a-rama.

Hydra Fighter

This clever little bit of fun is billed as the "first interactive water ride." Essentially, it is a series of tandem swings in which the riders sit back to back with a high power water cannon between their legs. With a bit of teamwork, riders can use their water cannons to swing themselves higher and higher. Or they can just squirt anyone in range while they bounce around aimlessly. Before hopping on yourself, take some time to observe the proper technique.

There are two towers with three arms, at the end of which dangle the two-seat gondolas; so the three-minute ride can accommodate 12 people at a time.

Water Mania

6073 West Irlo Bronson Highway
Kissimmee, FL 34747
(800) 527-3092; (407) 396-2626
www.watermania-florida.com

Water Mania is Kissimmee's answer to Orlando's Wet 'n Wild. It's slightly larger than its Orlando neighbor (36 acres), but it has only six slides (as opposed to nine) and doesn't have the lake and tow rides that Wet 'n Wild boasts. It is, however, the only water park in Florida with a "continuous wave form" allowing surfers a chance to hone their skills on the boogie board.

Water Mania positions itself in the Orlando water park sweepstakes as a park for families; they see Wet 'n Wild as more for teenagers. The park is right next to bustling route 192 but, unless you are right at the front fence, you'll hardly notice. The picnic area at the other end of the park, in fact, is an oasis of cooling shade and you will find it hard to believe you're in the heart of Kissimmee's tourist belt. The rest of the park is very nicely landscaped, too, with more green areas than you're likely to spot at Wet 'n Wild.

Getting There

Water Mania is easy to find, just a half mile east of I-4 Exit 25A on US 192, on the left between Mile Markers 8 and 9. Parking is at the back.

Opening and Closing Times

Water Mania is open seasonally, from March through October only. Hours are daily, 10:00 a.m. to 5:00 p.m.

The Price of Admission

Compared to nearby Wet 'n Wild, Water Mania's prices are a real bargain. Of course, the hours are shorter but most people will find that seven hours in a water park is plenty.

The following prices include tax:

Adults:	$21.35
Children (3 to 9):	$18.14
Children under 3 **free**.	
Seniors (55+)	$13.86
Annual Pass (all ages):	$53.45

Parking is $5 per vehicle, with in and out privileges.

Rentals

The following are available for rent or loan at the Rental Warehouse, located to your left as you enter the park:

Small lockers are $4, plus a $3 deposit, for a total of $7.28 when tax is added. Small lockers are cramped but doable for two people unless you are schlepping a great deal of stuff.

Large lockers are $6, plus a $3 deposit, for a total of $9.42.

Single tubes $4, plus a deposit of $1, for a total of $5.28.

Double tubes $6, plus a deposit of $1, for a total of $7.42.

Basketballs and volleyballs are free, but require a deposit of $5 and some form of ID.

Life vests are **free**, but require an ID.

Towels $3, plus a $1 deposit, for a total of $4.21.

Rides and Attractions at Water Mania

As you enter the park and turn right, you will see (on your right) a large wall-mounted map of the park that you can use to get your bearings. All of the rides are to the right as you enter the park. I describe them in the approximate order in which you will encounter them as you walk around the park in a counterclockwise direction.

Twin Tornadoes

This is the first of four slides sharing the same tower. Grab a blue mat and climb about halfway to the top. There you can choose from two flumes, A and B, for a 320-foot twisting ride to the bottom. The B flume gets off to a quicker start with an early drop but thereafter it's hard to distinguish the two. Both send you through a series of tight, fast turns to the final splashdown. *Twin Tornadoes* strikes me as being faster and more dizzying than Wet 'n Wild's *Mach 5*; otherwise, the two rides are very similar.

The Abyss

Right next to the *Twin Tornadoes* flumes is the jump-off point for *The Abyss*. This ride requires a two-person inner tube (no single riders). You find your tube at the bottom and tote it up the stairs.

The Abyss is a bit longer (380 feet) than *Twin Tornadoes* and the turns are even tighter. On top of that, the entire journey is enclosed in deep blue darkness. This is a really exhilarating ride, much more fun than *The Black Hole*, which is Wet 'n Wild's equivalent.

The Screamer

Leave the tubes and mats at the bottom and climb all the way to the top of the tower to reach Water Mania's speed slides. *The Screamer* offers a sheer drop of 72 feet into a lengthy deceleration area. Lie on your back, cross your arms and ankles, and scream your way to the bottom.

The Double Berzerker

Right next to *The Screamer*, but kicking off from a few feet lower down, are two identical slides that descend in three stages rather than one. To my mind, they offer an added twist to the speed slide experience. There is a millisecond of weightlessness (is it imagined?) as you go over each drop. Some people "cheat" on this one by riding sitting up and holding the sides, which slows their descent.

Wipe Out

Surf's up!

This is Water Mania's premiere ride and worth the trip if you're a surfer or would like to become one. A "continuous wave form" machine sends a swift cascade of water into and over a shallow trough, which you enter on a body board (a sort of truncated surf board) via a small angled slide from the side. Once into the trough, those who know what they're doing assume a kneeling position on the board and "ride" the artificial wave, weaving, swooping, even spinning completely around, all the while maintaining their position relative to the sides of the fast flowing stream of water. The real hot-doggers can ride forever but the attendant whistles them to give others a chance after they have shown off long enough.

Most people, of course, don't know what they're doing, making for a short but exhilarating ride. They loose their balance, the board, or both as they attempt to mimic the more advanced riders. When this happens you are either pitched out the far side or swept over the rear of the artificial wave into a long spillway that dumps you unceremoniously into *Cruisin' Creek*. The water here is quite turbulent and fast-moving, so prepare yourself for a dunking. If you don't have a firm grip on the board, it will be ripped from your grasp.

This is a must-do ride, even if you've never surfed. If you have the patience to wait in line and stick at it a bit, you can start to get the hang of it. The only downside to this ride is that the waiting line is right next to the wave, giving everybody a perfect view of your form, such as it is. It's a good test of your ability to maintain your self-esteem in the face of adversity.

Rip Tide

This short but sweet ride takes advantage of the spillway from *Wipe Out* to *Cruisin' Creek* (see below). You can ride on your tush or (more fun) on an inner tube down a short slide, through the spillway, and back into the rough and tumble entrance to the creek. If you decide after watching *Wipe Out* for a while that you'll wind up in the spillway, you might decide to come straight here.

Cruisin' Creek

This is a circular stream like *Lazy River* over at Wet 'n Wild. It circles past *Wipe Out* and under the speed slides over an 850-foot course. If you want to float through on a tube, you can grab one of the complimentary ones floating by. Be aware, however, that the complimentary tubes go fast. You may find it more convenient to rent one for the day. The complete circuit takes about five minutes.

The Rain Forest

This kiddie pool varies in depth from nine inches to two feet. There are baby-sized slides and a pirate ship in the middle, as well as floats and water cannons to keep the kids busy. There's also plenty of lounging space (much of it shaded) to keep Mom and Dad happy.

The Anaconda

This 420-foot slide starts 50 feet up and brings you to splashdown through a series of gently swooping curves. The flume is 14 feet wide to accommodate a variety of vehicles. You have your choice of a single inner tube, a double tube, or a four-person circular raft, all of which you must collect at the bottom and carry to the top. As you descend, watch out for a cascade of water halfway down that can drench those lucky enough to pass beneath it.

The Banana Peel

This is a sort of speed slide with training wheels. Two people in a Siamese inner tube swoop down a 176-foot slide in a single sharp drop to a bumpy landing. Screams galore and a good way to "test the waters" before tackling *The Screamer*.

Tot's Town

Smack in the middle of the major attractions for the big kids, you'll find this colorful interactive play area for wee ones that evokes a miniature city. In a refreshing break from the water theme, this one is set in a wooded picnic area. Parents will welcome the opportunity to take a break while their toddlers "go to town" here.

Squirt Pond

The second kiddie play area is a slightly less elaborate version of *The Rain Forest*. Next door is a white sand play area with a large climb-up, clamber-through, slide-down locomotive for little ones.

Rain Train

Although aimed at younger kids, this life-sized locomotive seems to attract kids of all ages. Water sprays from the train's stacks and wheels, while kid-sized slides offer lots of wet fun. The *Rain Train* sits in a pond that is billed as "zero-depth," in other words enough to get your feet wet and splash around in but not deep enough to make parents worry about the safety of their littler charges.

Whitecaps Wave Pool

By now, you have come full circle to the park's front entrance, in front of which is this 720,000-gallon wave pool surrounded by scores and scores of chairs and lounges for the sunbathing set. The wave machine runs in 10-minute cycles, kicking up rocking waves just crying out for you and your inner tube. Peppy rock music plays constantly as you splash about. There is a stage behind the pool and on special occasions entertainment is laid on.

Big Chipper

Behind the shaded rest area to the left of the pool is a vest-pocket 18-hole miniature golf course. Just pick up a putter and ball at the Rental Warehouse. The course is pretty flat and the holes are quite short — nothing here to rival the mega-mini-golf courses just a short drive away — but it makes a good break from the water park routine.

Volleyball

Water Mania boasts half a dozen sandy volleyball courts, scattered about the grounds. All are well maintained, but the ones towards the rear of the park seem to me to be preferable if only because they are not smack in the middle of all the crowds. Balls may be obtained, free of charge, at the Rental Warehouse with a $5 deposit.

The Woods

This is not an ride but your best bet for fine dining al fresco. It's not a fancy restaurant with a clever name; it is just what the name suggests — a heavily wooded, gloriously shady, three-acre picnicker's retreat at the rear of the park. The management guarantees that, in summer, it will be at least 10 degrees cooler here than on the pool deck. Most people bring their own food. However, Water Mania has a catering staff for groups of all sizes; call (407) 396-2626 and ask for the sales department to make arrangements. *The Woods* offers spacious picnic tables and plenty of barbecue pits. Volleyball and basketball courts are just a short stroll away. Even if you're not eating here, it's worth a peek.

Adventure Island

10001 McKinley Drive
Tampa, FL 33674
(813) 987-5660
www.adventureisland.com

Busch's entry into the Central Florida water park market is a winner, and if your only shot at a water park is during a visit to Tampa, it's the obvious choice. While I give a slight edge to Wet 'n Wild, Adventure Island, with its artful design and pleasing layout, runs a close second.

Getting There

Adventure Island is right across the street from Busch Gardens Tampa, two miles west of I-75 and two miles east of I-275. Drive past the Busch Gardens parking lots (heading north) and keep a sharp lookout for the entrance on your right. The main gate is easy to miss if you're not careful.

Opening and Closing Times

The park is open daily from mid March to early September and then weekends only to late October. It is closed the rest of the year. Park hours are generally 10:00 a.m. to 5:00 p.m. with closing time extending to as late as 8:00 p.m. during the warmer months. Call for the exact schedule, or request a brochure that has a calendar chart with operating hours.

The Price of Admission

The following prices include tax:

Adults:	$29.91
Children (3 to 9):	$27.77

Children under 3 are **free**.

Annual Pass

Adults:	$80.20
Children & Seniors:	$69.50

An *Annual Passport*, good for Adventure Island and adjacent Busch Gardens, is $123 for adults, $112.30 for kids. A *Value Pass* for a one-day visit to each of the parks is $64.15 for grown-ups, $53.45 for kids. You can also get annual passes that include SeaWorld. See *Chapter 9: Busch Gardens* for price information.

In addition, Adventure Island offers discounts for entry in the afternoon.

Call for details.

Parking is $5 per vehicle, motorcycles park **free**. If you hold any Busch Gardens annual pass, parking is **free**.

Rentals

Small lockers are $3, plus a $3 deposit.

Large lockers are $5, plus a $3 deposit.

Beach umbrellas are $2, plus a $3 deposit.

Volleyballs are **free** with a $10 deposit.

The admission price includes **free** use of inner tubes in designated areas of the park and life vests for all guests.

Rides and Attractions at Adventure Island

Adventure Island is laid out in a sort of figure eight. I have described its attractions in the approximate order you would encounter them on a counterclockwise circumnavigation of the park.

Beach Areas

As you move from the entrance plaza and walk down the steps into the park proper, you see a delightful sandy expanse in front of you. It's ideal for sunning and relaxing (although not for picnicking) with its many lounge chairs. Many people prefer to spread a beach towel on the pristine white sands. The entire area is ringed by an ankle-deep stream so as you exit you can rinse the sand off your feet. Similar areas are dotted around the park.

Runaway Rapids

This series of five water slides is so ingeniously snaked through a simulated rocky canyon that you are hard-pressed to spot the flumes as you wend your way to the top. To the left are two child-sized slides on which parents and tots can descend together. To the right and higher up are the three adult flumes. Here, as at other slides in the park, red and green traffic lights regulate the flow of visitors down the slides.

You ride these slides on your back or sitting up; there are no mats or tubes used. As a result, they can get off to a slow start but they pick up speed as you hit the dips and turns about a third of the way down. Of the three adult slides, the one on the left seems the zippiest, while the one in the middle is the tamest. None of them are super scary, however, and most people should thoroughly enjoy the brief ride to the shallow pool below.

Paradise Lagoon

This is a swimming pool with pizzazz. At one end, two short tubes (one slightly curved) let you slide down about 15 feet before dropping you from a height of about 3 feet into 10-foot deep water. A short distance away, you can leap from an 8-foot high rocky cliff, just like at the old swimmin' hole. Although the pool seems deep enough (10 feet), head-first dives are not allowed. At the pool's narrowest point, you can test your balance and coordination by trying to cross a series of inflated stepping stones while holding on to an overhead rope net.

Endless Surf

Adventure Island's 17,000 square-foot wave pool generates five-foot-high waves for body surfing as well as random choppiness for what is billed as a "storm-splashing environment." This is the smallest of the wave pools at the three parks reviewed here, with a correspondingly small lounging area at the beach end. Waves are set off in 10-minute cycles, with a digital clock at the deep end counting down the minutes 'til the next wave of waves.

Fabian's Funport

Adventure Island's kiddie pool follows the formula to a "T." The ankle-to calf-deep pool is abuzz with spritzing and spraying water fountains, some of which let kids determine when they get doused. A raised play area features mini water slides and water cannons with just enough range to spray unwary adults at the pool's edge. A unique touch here is an adjacent mini version of the wave pool, scaled down to toddler size. A raised seating area lets grown-ups relax while keeping an eagle eye on their busy charges.

Rambling Bayou

Adventure Island's version of the continuous looping river is delightful, with a few unique touches — a dousing waterfall that is marvelously refreshing on a steamy day, followed by a gentle misting rain provided by overhead sprinklers.

Spike Zone

This is by far the nicest volleyball venue at any of the water parks reviewed in this book. In fact, these 11 "groomed" courts have hosted professional tournaments. Most of the play, however, is by amateurs. Even if you're not into competing, the layout makes it easy to watch.

Water Moccasin

Three translucent green tubes descend from this moderately high tower. The center one drops sharply to the splashdown pool, while the two other tubes curve right and left respectively for a corkscrew descent. This is a body slide (you ride lying down on your back) that offers the thrill of a speed slide in the middle tube and a rapidly accelerating descent through the others.

Key West Rapids

The tallest ride at Adventure Island attracts long lines due in part to slow loading times. Fortunately the wait is made easier to take by the spectacular view of next-door Busch Gardens. In the distance, past the loops and sworls of Montu, you can see the downtown Tampa skyline.

Here you pick up a single or two-rider tube at the bottom and climb up for a looping and swooping descent on a broad open-air flume. The ride is punctuated twice by rapids-like terraces where attendants (I call them the Rapids Rangers), regulate the flow of riders. Thanks to the two pauses, this ride never attains the speed of similar rides at the other parks, but it offers an enjoyable descent nonetheless.

Splash Attack

This is a more elaborate version of *Fabian's Funport* and draws an older crowd — kids from 8 to about 15. The multi-level play area (much like that found in Land of the Dragons at nearby Busch Gardens) is alive with spritzes, sprays, spouts, and hidden geysers that erupt to catch the unwary. A variety of ingenious hand-operated devices lets kids determine to some extent who gets doused and when. A huge bucket at the summit tips over every now and then soaking everyone below.

Caribbean Corkscrew

This ride is almost identical to *Blue Niagara* at Wet 'n Wild, although to my untutored eye the angle of descent seems slightly narrower. You probably won't care as you spiral down and around one of these two tubes, which are twisted around each other like braided hair, picking up speed until you are deposited in the long deceleration pool. Holding your nose is highly recommended for this one.

Tampa Typhoon

These twin speed slides are the park's highest at 76 feet. The ride down is fast and seems more like falling than sliding. Riding on your back is recommended but some thrill seekers come down sitting up.

Gulf Scream

Right next to the *Tampa Typhoon*, these two slides offer a toned down speed slide experience and, by comparison, the ride down is leisurely. If you're uncertain about tackling the *Typhoon*, test your mettle here.

Aruba Tuba

Aruba Tuba shares a tower with the *Calypso Coaster*. As with *Key West Rapids*, you pick up your single or double tube at the entrance and climb to the top. This ride, as the name implies, descends through a tube which is mostly enclosed with a few brief openings to the sky. Periodically, you are plunged into total darkness adding to the excitement generated by the speed, sudden turns, and sharp dips of the ride. All in all, one of Adventure Island's zippiest experiences. You emerge into a pool with a convenient exit into *Ramblin' Bayou*, just in case you feel a need for a marked change of pace.

Calypso Coaster

Unlike its sister ride, *Aruba Tuba*, *Calypso Coaster* is an open flume. It is also wider, allowing for more side-to-side motion at the expense of speed. But there's no drop-off in excitement as you are swooped high on the sides of the flume in the sharp turns you encounter on the way down. Of the two, I give *Aruba Tuba* slightly higher marks in the thrills department, but it's a very close call.

Everglides

This ride is unique among the parks reviewed in this book. It is a slide — a speed slide in fact — but instead of descending on your back or in a tube you sit upright on a heavy yellow, molded plastic gizmo that's a cross between a boogie board and a sled. As you sit in the ready position, held back from the steep precipice by a metal gate, you might start to have second thoughts. But then the gate drops, the platform tilts, and you are sent zipping down the slide. The best part of the ride is when you hit the water. Instead of slowing down quickly, you go skimming across the surface for about 20 yards before slowing to a stop. If you're doing it right, you'll hardly get wet. The major error to be made on this ride is placing your center of gravity too far back. If you do, you're liable to be flipped over backwards for a very unceremonious dunking.

Wahoo Run

Adventure Island's newest ride is a twisty, turny mega slide designed for large rafts holding up to five riders. As you zip down 600 feet of corkscrewing blue tunnels at up to 15 feet per second, you pass under four waterfall curtains that guarantee a thorough drenching before you are deposited in a splash pool at the bottom. This is a great family ride.

CHAPTER ELEVEN:

Dinner
Attractions

The concept of the "dinner attraction" is not unique to Orlando, but surely there can be few places on earth where there are so many and such elaborate examples of the genre. At a typical dinner attraction (there are exceptions, as you'll see) the dinner is not a separate component; instead, the meal and the theme of the show are closely intertwined and usually something will be going on as you eat. Beer and wine (along with soft drinks) are poured freely from pitchers throughout the evening. The shows have been created specifically for the attraction; everything from the decorations on the wall to the plates you eat off reflect the theme. By and large, the shows are permanent, whereas a dinner theater changes shows regularly.

Dinner attractions are unabashedly "touristy." You'll have plenty of opportunity to buy souvenir mugs, a photo souvenir (often in the form of a key ring), and other tourist paraphernalia. There is plenty of audience participation; in fact, sometimes it's the best part of the show. Many (but by no means all) dinner attractions have an element of competition built in, with various sections of the audience being assigned to cheer on various contestants. And finally there is the matter of scale. With the exception of the murder mystery shows, Orlando's dinner attractions are huge productions put on in large arenas and halls, some of which seat over 1,000 people. You will find exceptions to these rules in individual attractions but, by and large, they describe the dinner attraction experience.

In this chapter, I have reviewed all the non-Disney dinner attractions (and one true dinner theater) in the Orlando area. For pageantry and large-scale spectacle there are *Arabian Nights*, *Medieval Times*, and *Pirates Dinner Adventure*. For musical entertainment there are *Aloha! Polynesian Review*,

Capone's, and the *Mark Two Dinner Theater*. For magic fans there are *Masters of Magic* and WonderWorks' *Night of Wonder*. In a class by itself is the small-scale *Treasure Chest Quest* game show. Finally, for comedy/mystery fans there are *Capone's* (again), *MurderWatch Mystery Theater*, and *Sleuths*. I have tried to give you an good idea of the nature of each experience, bearing in mind that not everyone shares the same taste. You should also be aware of the combination ticket offered by Splendid China (see *Chapter 6*) for dinner and their evening theatrical extravaganza, *Mysterious Kingdom of the Orient*. This is yet another excellent choice for dinnertime entertainment.

In my opinion a trip to Orlando is not complete without a visit to one of these attractions. If you have the time (and the stamina), catch two or more shows representing different genres. I don't think you'll regret it.

Tip: Discounts to most dinner attractions are readily available. Look for dollars-off coupons on web sites or in coupons booklets or reduced price tickets at ticket brokers (see *Chapter 1: Introduction & Orientation*).

Aloha! Polynesian Luau

In the SeaWorld park
(407) 351-3600

Prices:	Adults $35.95, juniors (8 to 12) $25.95, children (3 to 7) $15.95. Plus tax and tip.
Times:	Daily at 6:30 p.m.
Directions:	In the SeaWorld park, in an annex to the Bimini Bay restaurant.

In a low ceilinged room adjacent to the Bimini Bay restaurant in SeaWorld, you are transported to the lush South Seas. Family-style tables radiate out from the semicircular stage, and tropical flowers and large green leaves hang down from the rafters.

The show, which begins as the crowd settles in, is hosted by a suave crooner in the manner of Don Ho. It takes us through a leisurely history of Hawaii, as the islands move from the worship of volcano gods to the coming of the missionaries, to the bustling, pulsating Hawaii of today. Along the way, it offers a tour of the pageantry and dancing of other Pacific islands, Samoa and Tahiti prominent among them.

Backed by a small band, most of the show is given over to the dancers, four bare-chested men and four lissome young women who constantly reappear in new and ever more colorful costumes to evoke a variety of styles and moods. The dancing, though a bit suggestive at times, seems to offend no one. In fact, the loudest hoots and cheers come from the women in the audience when the male dancers leer, grind their hips, and grab their buttocks. How times change! Most of the evening is far more genteel than that, however. Indeed, this is a rather stately show compared to other dinner attractions, much like what you'd expect in a fairly upscale Hawaiian nightclub.

The singing by our host is mellifluous and soothing, ranging from Hawaiian language songs (including a "Hawaiian yodel"!) to the more familiar "Stranger in Paradise" from *Kismet*. The dancing is never less than enchanting and in the war chant numbers rather exciting. Volunteers are dragooned from the audience to dance the hula, which is always good for a laugh. The Samoan Fire Knife Dance finale is literally incendiary, as a dancer wearing nothing but a brief loincloth twirls a flaming baton and rests the burning ends on his tongue and the soles of his feet.

The food may not be quite as good as the show, but there is plenty of it, all served family style. First comes a selection of fresh fruit and salad. Among the three entrees, the mahi-mahi in piña colada sauce is a standout. The sweet and sour chicken and smoked pork loin are okay, as are the mixed steamed vegetables. Dessert varies with the season and is accompanied by coffee. The admission price includes the meal and complimentary soft drinks, coffee, or unlimited iced tea. For the drinkers in the crowd, a cash bar is available.

All in all, this show is a real crowd-pleaser, but I can't keep from wondering just how authentic it all is. Am I seeing the real thing or the Hawaiian equivalent of Pat Boone singing a Little Richard song?

Arabian Nights

6225 West Irlo Bronson Highway (Route 192), Kissimmee 34746
(800) 553-6116; (407) 239-9223; from Canada: (800) 533-3615
www.arabian-nights.com

Prices:	Adults $42, children (3 to 11) $26, seniors (55+) get a $5 discount. Show an AARP card and get $6 off an adult ticket, $3 off a child's. Prices do not include tax or tip.
Times:	Daily. Show times vary, so check. Matinees sometimes available.
Directions:	I-4 to Exit 25, then east on Route 192 for less than a quarter of a mile. The entrance road is on your left, with the theater itself set well back from the highway.

Orlando residents have voted *Arabian Nights* their favorite dinner attraction year after year, and it's easy to see why. Beautiful horses, impeccably trained and put through their intricate paces by a young and vivacious team of riders, are hard to beat. The show may appeal most to horse lovers and riders, but the old clichés "something for everyone" and "fun for the whole family" are not out of place here.

Arabian Nights is huge; it has to be to accommodate the 20,000 square foot arena the horses need to strut their stuff. Each side of the arena is flanked by seven steeply banked rows of seats; all told, the house can hold 1,200 spectators and every seat provides a good view of the action.

The "seats" are actually a series of benches, each seating 12 people at a small counter on which you will be served your dinner. The fare is simple but satisfying — salad, a slab of prime rib with roasted potatoes and a medley of vegetables, plus dessert. Vegetarian lasagna is also available. Unlimited beer, wine, and soft drinks are included in the price. Carafes of fancier wine can be ordered separately (for $18 and up), as can mixed drinks.

The doors open about an hour and a half prior to showtime if you'd like to come for pre-show drinks and a bit of nonequestrian live entertainment, which usually takes the form of a singer. On most nights, seating begins at about 7:00 and the show gets underway shortly after 7:30. We are guests at a feast celebrating the marriage of the Sultan's daughter, Scheherazade, to Prince Khalid. But the real emcee is the sultan's genie, a wisecracking sprite who smacks more of the Borscht Belt than Baghdad. It's just enough of a "plot" on which to string a series of scenes that show off the beauty and skills of *Arabian Nights'* $4 million stable of horses. More than 50 appear in each show.

While there are plenty of stunts involved in this show, the main emphasis is on the horses themselves, with their trainers and riders playing important supporting roles. Much of the evening involves intricate dressage and group riding in which the training of the horses and the precision of the riders are essential. Horses dance, prance, and strut to the music. They even do a square dance. Snow-white Lipizzans, the imperial breed of Austria, leap in the air and do a tricky double kick. One of the evening's most stunning moments comes when a magnificent, riderless black stallion performs an intricate series of movements in response to the subtle signals of his trainer.

Action fans won't be disappointed here. A circus sequence offers a chance for daring bareback riders to show their stuff and contains a hilarious comedy bit. There are cowboys and Indians with stunts straight out of the movies. Riders race around the arena standing up on the backs of two horses. There is even a Roman chariot race, complete with a spectacular "accident." All of this is performed by a remarkably small cadre of talented performers who change costumes and wigs with amazing rapidity to reappear over and over in new guises. Still, it is the horses that command our admiration. At show's end, many of the equine performers romp about spiritedly in the arena; many people linger just to watch them play. If you still haven't had enough, private VIP stable tours can be arranged.

Capone's Dinner & Show

4740 West Highway 192, Kissimmee 34746

(800) 220-8428; (407) 397-2378

Prices:	Adults $39.95, children (4 to 12) $23.95. 50% discount for seniors (55+) and Florida residents. Plus tax and tip.
Times:	8:00 p.m. nightly during spring and summer, 7:30 during fall and winter.
Directions:	On the south side of 192, a short distance east of the junction with SR 535, between Mile Markers 12 and 13.

Somewhere along the tawdry, commercial strip of Route 192 in Kissimmee you'll find an innocent ice cream parlor. But as with so much in the Orlando area, there's more here than meets the eye. For you see, the ice cream parlor is just a front for a speakeasy, Prohibition style. Yes, we've gone back in time again to 1930s Chicago, where the action owes a lot to Damon Runyon via *Guys and Dolls* and the Chicago accents sound straight outta Brooklyn.

Capone's Dinner & Show is a cheerfully amateurish mishmash of Broadway show, nightclub cabaret, sketch comedy revue, and all-you-can-eat buffet — that's buffet, as in Warren or Jimmy. Dinner includes the usual soft drinks, plus beer, sangria, and rum runners. In addition, there's a cash bar for serious drinkers.

The fun begins when you arrive and pick up your tickets at the box office. You're instructed to knock three times at the secret door and give a password. Then you get in line outside, where black-vested waiters warm up the crowd with the wisecracking rudeness that is to become the evening's hallmark.

Once the show's ready to begin, each party is led to the secret door, knocks three times, and gives the password — and they don't let you in until you get it right. Once inside, you're in a spacious nightclub with a large stage. The waiters — with names like Babyface — take drink orders and keep up a cheerful patter laced with film noir gangster patois. Much of the seating is in long rows of tables, so you'll have a chance to chat with the folks on either side of you; it's a fun way to get an idea of the wide cross section of types and nationalities drawn to Orlando.

The show, which has a weak plot about star-crossed lovers and even weaker dancing, is like the buffet — not great but hearty and lots of it. As with most amateur productions, some performers are better than others and, with the exception of some minor characters, they give it the old college try. It's hard not to like this bunch, even if they don't always shoot straight.

Mark Two Dinner Theater

3376 Edgewater Drive, Orlando 32804
(800) 726-6275; (407) 843-6275
www.themarktwo.com

Prices:	$35.50 to $49 depending on performance and seating. Plus tax and tip. Children (under 15) $10 off. Seniors (55+) $1 off.
Times:	Performances Wednesday through Sunday; matinees Wednesday, Thursday, and Saturday. Matinees: Dining 11:30 a.m., Curtain 1:15 p.m. Evenings: Dining 6:00 p.m., Curtain 8:00 p.m. Sundays: Dining 4:30 p.m., Curtain 6:30 p.m.
Directions:	I-4 to Exit 44, then west on Par Street, which deadends into Edgewater. The theater is at the back of the mall in front of you.

Of all the dinner attractions in Orlando, this is the only one that is a "dinner theater" in the classic sense of the term — you have dinner and then watch a Broadway musical or play. It is also a fully professional theater, employing only members of Equity, the actors' union.

The Mark Two is somewhat off the beaten tourist track, tucked away in the College Park neighborhood of Orlando's northeast. It is open year round and presents about eight shows a year, each running about six weeks. Most of the shows are familiar Broadway musicals, although the occasional British sex farce or Broadway comedy creeps into the repertory.

The theater is at the back of a none-too-prosperous looking retail mall. While the space was obviously intended for other uses, it has been cleverly converted to a 320-seat theater with tables arrayed on tiers around three sides of the stage floor; ramps slope gently down to the stage, which doubles as the buffet line for the pre-show dinner. (Thanks to the use of ramps, every part of the theater is wheelchair accessible.) The entire space is gaily decorated in accents of valentine red, with large Broadway posters ringing the walls. The tiny lamps on each table add a touch of elegance and intimacy.

The all-you-can-eat buffet will appeal primarily to the meat and potato lovers in the crowd. Typically, there are a chicken and a fish entree on the steam table, but the line culminates in a carving board where prime rib and ham are sliced to order. The food, while hardly exceptional, is abundant and you are encouraged to return again (and again, if you must). There is an extra charge for desserts and specialty coffee, but the key lime pie is worth it.

Dinner is served for about an hour and a half, with the line closing a half hour before show time to allow for the removal of the food and setting of the stage. Dessert is served during the intermission. There is a bar in the lobby and drinks are also served at your table.

The show I saw was enjoyable and the performances sturdily professional if perhaps not quite up to Broadway standards. Still, the Mark Two compares favorably to other dinner theaters I have visited and, if you arrive with modest expectations, you are not likely to be disappointed. In any event, the live performance of first-class musicals offers a refreshing change of pace from Orlando's usual evening fare for tourists. And considering the huge meal, the price is a bargain.

Tip: Tables have two or four seats. If you are a couple, request a two-seat table. If none is available, you will be seated at a four-seat table and may be joined by another couple (unless you purchase every seat at the table).

Masters of Magic Show

8560 International Drive, Orlando 32819
(407) 352-3456
www.mastersofmagic.net

Prices:	Adults $29.95, children (4 to 12) $19.95. Prices do not include optional dinner at a nearby restaurant.
Times:	Wednesday through Sunday, 6:30 and 9:00 p.m. Box office open 2:00 to 9:00 p.m.
Directions:	East side of I-Drive between the Mercado and Pointe★Orlando shopping centers.

Las Vegas-style entertainment comes to Orlando in the shape of Typhoon Lou and his razzle-dazzle extravaganza of large-scale magic tricks. Indeed, you'd have to travel to Vegas to see more major illusions in a single show. There are other magic shows in the Orlando area, but none can touch this one for sheer size and showbiz spectacle.

Backed by a cadre of four beautiful gals and two hunky guys, Typhoon Lou performs one jaw-dropping stunt after another. He has himself hoisted aloft on a roaring Harley in a steel cage and when the cage collapses both he and the Harley disappear, but Lou instantly reappears in the audience. In another extended bit, he unfolds a small box, has one of his lovely assistants step in, and then refolds the box to its former size, and just for good measure runs it through with a few swords. Not only does the girl reemerge at the end of the trick, she does so in a new outfit. Later he performs a variation on the girl-sawed-in-half trick that is quite simply the best I have ever seen. Lou intersperses the major illusions with charming close-up magic featuring audience volunteers. In my favorite bit, he pours six different beverages from the same milk carton, which he hands into the audience for close-up inspection lest you think it contain separate compartments for the various liquids.

This is a major production. Running one and a half hours with intermission, it features great choreography and some of the best dancing to be seen in Orlando. The set elements and costumes are also first-rate. And Typhoon Lou himself is a genial and affable master of ceremonies who uses his Native American and Hawaiian roots to disarming effect.

The theater seats 210 in nightclub style at long tables, with every seat facing the stage. Soft drinks and snacks are available and a beer and wine license is in the works. In the lobby, you can buy magic tricks and books on the magician's art, as well as meet Lou and his crew after the show. The dinner part of the equation comes in the form of a discount offered by nearby Tony Roma's restaurant to those showing ticket stubs from the show. More restaurant choices may be available when you visit.

Medieval Times

4510 Highway 192, Kissimmee 34746
(800) 229-8300; (407) 396-1518; from Orlando: (407) 239-0214
www.medievaltimes.com

Prices:	Adults $44, children (3 to 11) $28. Plus tax and tip. 10% discount for seniors (55+).
Times:	Nightly. Show times vary from month to month. Call for current schedule.
Directions:	On the south side of 192, between Mile Markers 14 & 15.

Back in time to the year 1093 we go as we cross a drawbridge over a murky moat and enter a "climate-controlled castle," guided by wenches and squires with a decidedly contemporary look about them. *Medieval Times*, in Kissimmee, is a cheerfully gaudy evocation of a time most of us know so little about that we'll never know if they've got it right — although I strongly suspect that Ethelred the Unready wouldn't recognize the joint.

Actually, *Medieval Times* tells us more about American tourism than it does about eleventh century Europe. The emphasis here is more on showing visitors an old-fashioned good time than on chivalry and historical accuracy. The medieval theme is merely a convenient excuse on which to hang a display of horse-riding skills.

Medieval Times is a bit like a large ride at one of the nearby theme parks. As you enter, you are issued a color-coded cardboard crown and have your picture taken for the inevitable (and optional) souvenir photo of yourself in chivalric garb. The large, banner-bedecked anteroom in which you wait for the show to begin does a brisk trade in tourist items and souvenirs, including some lovely goblets and very authentic looking swords.

A burly bearded knight is your host. His booming voice, with its idio-syncratic mock-formal cadences, will become familiar over the course of the evening as he explains the seating process, exhorts you to be of good cheer, introduces you to the players, and chides you for not having enough fun.

The dinner show itself takes place in a long, cavernous room in which guests are arrayed on six tiers of seats flanking a 70-yard-long, sand-covered arena. Each row consists of a long bench and counter arrangement so that everyone can eat and have a good view of the show. Each side of the arena has three color-coded sections which correspond to the color of the crown you have been given. Where you sit determines which of the color-coded knights you cheer for during the festivities.

The meal and the show unfold simultaneously. The meal is simple — soup, a small, whole roasted chicken, a pork rib, a roasted potato — but the herbed chicken is roasted to perfection and the ribs melt off the bone. In addition, you get to eat with your fingers: It's 1093, remember. I can't explain the psychology, but it helps put you in a suitably barbaric mood to cheer on your knight. (Vegetarians will be accommodated on request.)

The show begins slowly and builds to a climax of clashing battle-axes and broadswords that throw off showers of sparks into the night. Demonstra-tions of equestrian skills and the royal sport of falconry give way to our six mounted knights, young men who race back and forth on their charging steeds, plucking rings from the air and throwing spears at targets. Successful knights are awarded flowers which, in the spirit of chivalry, they share with young women in the crowd who have caught their eye. These guys are good at what they do and you may find yourself wondering if there's a career in this and, if not, what their day job is.

The show is wrapped in twenty-first century showbiz, with swooping computer-guided lighting, pyrotechnics, and a sound system that just might blast you back into the eleventh century. The main event is the joust in which the knights compete against each other, charging full tilt down the lists, shattering their lances on their opponents' shields, and taking theatrical falls to the soft earth beneath. The battle continues on foot with mace and sword and at least as much verisimilitude as you get in professional wrestling.

All of this is narrated with much portent and hokum by your host. The victorious knight chooses a "princess" from the crowd, who is escorted to the throne at the end of the hall for investiture.

This ain't art but it's a lot of fun. And the folks putting on the show ob-viously know their business. On the night I visited *Medieval Times*, the sold-out house, tepid at first, grew more and more enthusiastic until, by the end of the show, they were pounding the tables and cheering lustily for their ar-mor-clad champions.

This is a major production with a huge cast and considering the over-head, the cost is moderate. *Medieval Times* supplements its box office by sell-ing souvenirs (remember that photo that was taken when you came in?) and they find a lot of takers.

MurderWatch Mystery Theater

1850 Hotel Plaza Boulevard, Lake Buena Vista 32830
(in Baskerville's Restaurant in the Grosvenor Resort Hotel)
(800) 624-4109; (407) 827-6534
www.murderwatch.com

Prices:	Adults $34.95, children (4 to 9) $10.95. Prices include tax but not gratuity.
Times:	Saturdays only at 6:00 p.m. and 9:00 p.m.
Directions:	I-4 to Exit 27, west on SR 535 (Apopka-Vineland Road), then left on Hotel Plaza Boulevard (opposite the Crossroads Shop-ping Center). The Grosvenor Resort is on the right just before Disney Village Market-place.

In the elegant confines of Baskerville's Restaurant, decorated with etch-ings of scenes from the works of Sir Arthur Conan Doyle, a sumptuous buf-fet is being served. A cabaret act has been laid on for the entertainment of the guests but, as is so typical of the underbelly of show biz, jealousies and in-trigue are waiting just off stage. Before long, murder most foul has reared its ugly head and the game is afoot.

This entertaining dinner party cum murder mystery features a female hostess-detective — "My name is Holmes, Shirley Holmes" — who clues us in on the rules of the game, keeps track of the body count, and catalogues the growing number of clues.

The action, which cleverly involves the professional and personal jeal-ousies of the lounge-singing act that is the evening's nominal entertainment, takes place throughout the large dining area. While it is always possible to see what is happening, it's not always possible to hear, given the distance of your seat from the action of the moment. Audience members are encouraged to get up, move around the room, eavesdrop, and ask pointed questions, but good manners seem to keep most people in their seats. Nonetheless, by the time the evening winds to its conclusion, you will know all the dramatis per-sonae and their relationships with each other and have your own suspicions about who dunnit.

As amateur detectives, the audience's task is to solve the crime by listen-ing to four widely divergent versions of "what really happened" and then voting with their feet by gathering in different corners of the room with the cast member they believe to be telling the truth.

In this show, the action is virtually continuous throughout the meal and wraps up shortly after everyone has had dessert — about two and a half hours. The cast is smoothly professional, good singers and expert kibitzers with the audience (some of whom wind up becoming suspects in the final line-up). Virtually every table in the restaurant is visited by one or more cast members during the course of the evening, giving you a chance to size up the suspects at close range. The humor, while sometimes on the racy side, is strictly PG and the kids seem to love it. In fact, there is a special kids' version of the show which is used when the number of children in the audience reaches critical mass. After the show, you can have your picture taken with cast members in a nearby room decorated to re-create Sherlock Holmes' study at 221B Baker Street.

One of the drawbacks of the show is that it only takes place on Saturdays. On the plus side is that it takes place in Baskerville's, a lovely restaurant at the upscale Grosvenor Resort Hotel, which probably explains why the food here is the best of any Orlando area dinner attraction. It's an all-you-can-eat affair, with at least three entree choices in addition to carved-to-order roast beef au jus and Yorkshire pudding. The dessert array is especially bountiful and of the highest quality. Unlimited beer and wine and full bar service are available for an additional fee.

Finding the show can be a bit tricky if you're not familiar with the hotel's layout. Depending on which elevator you get on, push either "5" or "M" (for Mezzanine); they both take you to the fifth floor where the restaurant is located. Perhaps the simplest way is to avail yourself of the valet parking at the hotel entrance ($6) and have the doorman direct you to the staircase in the lobby that leads upstairs to the restaurant. Dreamland Productions, which puts on *MurderWatch Mystery Theater*, may have other shows taking place at other venues in the area during your visit.

Night of Wonder

At WonderWorks
9067 International Drive, Orlando 32819
(407) 352-0411
www.wonderworksonline.com/nightofwonder.html

Prices:	Adults $31.75, children (4 to 12) $26.45, tax included. For show and food only, adults $15.95, children $13.95.
Times:	Nightly at 6:00 and 8:00 p.m.
Directions:	From I-4 Exit 29, drive east on Sand Lake

Road, turn right on International Drive;
the show takes place in WonderWorks, next
door to the Pointe★Orlando shopping center.

As I watched this enthralling show, I was reminded of what a terrific disappearing act top-notch magic has done over the last few decades. Thanks to the demise of the great television variety shows, there's a good possibility that your kids (or maybe even you!) have never seen a really good magician perform up close. You can remedy that sorry circumstance by heading for WonderWorks, the interactive attraction in the upside down house (see *Chapter 12: Another Roadside Attraction*).

Every night, in a small 130-seat nightclub-like room at the back of Mazzerella's Pizzeria, you can catch a one-hour show featuring some truly first-rate prestidigitation. The show will probably change from time to time (the one I saw was called *Shazam*) but the formula should remain the same. This is a Vegas-style show complete with live music, singing, and a healthy dose of showbiz razzle-dazzle, albeit on a much smaller scale than *Masters of Magic* just down the road. I watched in increasing amazement as magician Tony Brent and his lovely partner Jamie Bowie progressed from standard disappearing card and ball tricks to amazing stunts like one in which a $100 bill borrowed from an audience member is burned only to reappear embedded in the pulp of a lemon. Some tricks involve elaborate contraptions in which the stars are locked and sometimes chopped, sliced, and diced (or so it would seem).

There is great emphasis placed on audience involvement, with pride of place given to the youngsters, whose sense of awe and wonder is evident in their fresh faces. Adults get their chance to shine as well in routines that are as light-hearted and humorous as they are mystifying. The result is a thoroughly entertaining interlude.

What makes this a dinner attraction is the all-you-can eat pizza and all-you-can drink beer, wine, and soda. The pizzas, which are quite good and don't skimp on the cheese, are half plain and half pepperoni, and as one disappears another arrives to take its place. The doors open and food service begins at 7:00 p.m.; the show starts at about 7:30 p.m., and service continues throughout the show.

The price of the show includes admission to the WonderWorks attraction (see *Chapter 12*); the wrist band you receive when you arrive for the show is your open sesame to the rest of the building. You can also opt just to eat and see the show, in which case the show becomes one of Orlando's best entertainment bargains. Reservations are recommended, especially during busier periods, because seating is limited. The only nearby parking is in the lot of the next door Pointe★Orlando shopping mall. Unfortunately, Wonder-

Works does not validate parking tickets, so expect to pay about $2 for it.

Pirates Dinner Adventure

6400 Carrier Drive, Orlando 32819
(800) 866-2469; (407) 248-0590
www.orlandopirates.com

Prices:	Adults $46.47, children (3 to 11) $28.03. Prices include tax but not gratuity.
Times:	Nightly at 7:30 p.m., doors open at 6:30 p.m.
Directions:	From I-4 Exit 29, drive east on Sand Lake Road, one block past International Drive to Canada Drive and turn left. Entrance to parking is on Canada.

If there were Academy Awards for Orlando dinner shows, *Pirates Dinner Adventure* would have to get the best set award. This cheerful melange of old-time Technicolor pirate movie, Broadway musical, and big top circus unfolds in a fog-shrouded domed arena dominated by a towering and ghostly pirate vessel a-sail on the watery deep (into which not a few of the performers take some spectacular falls).

The fun starts in a large antechamber where a Festival, celebrating the arrival of Princess Anita, welcomes arriving guests with Gypsy fortune tellers, face painting for kids, hors d'oeuvres, and a cash bar. There's even a tiny arcade for die-hard video game freaks. The show proper gets under way with the explosive entrance of a band of oddly friendly pirates who kidnap the princess and a comely gypsy wench. For good measure, they shanghai the entire audience, shepherding us to their outlaw realm.

We know these pirates can't be all bad when they announce that they will serve us a sumptuous meal, just to prepare us for the torture, maiming, and certain death that will follow shortly. The meal, served by the pirate crew, is a hearty one. Yellow rice with sliced beef and spicy chicken barbecued to a turn on pirate swords.

Then we settle back for a celebration of swashbuckling derring do on the high seas. In a plot that defies rational explication, we find ourselves caught up in a story that involves crew rivalries, the love of a young pirate lad for a princess, long dead pirates, trampolines, basketball, and — would you believe? — a circus aerial act. There is also a delightfully droll and smarmy pirate captain, complete with black beard and a wig of cascading ringlets; his wife is a brassy blonde with a voice like cannon fire. They make a highly entertaining couple.

Punctuated by song, the fast and furious action moves left and right, up and down, comes from behind us, and soars high over our heads. The "Golden Gypsy" dances high above, the pirates compete in wacky games of skill, and kids from the audience are taken aboard to be sworn in as swashbuckling buccaneers. All too soon it seems, the King's army arrives to save the day. There will probably be times during all this when you don't know what the heck is going on, but you'll probably be enjoying yourself too much to care.

All of this cheerfully chaotic mayhem is carried forward by a game and talented young cast. The male pirate chorus is especially fine. Don't be surprised if you find yourself singing along to the refrain of "Drink, Drink, Drink." And speaking of drinking, beer, wine, and soda flow freely during the meal and afterwards.

For those who care to linger after the show, there is a "Pirates' Buccaneer Bash" where crew members lead the crowd (kids mostly) in silly song and dance routines.

Sleuths Mystery Show & Dinner

7508 Universal Boulevard (Republic Square), Orlando 32819
(800) 393-1985; (407) 363-1985
www.sleuths.com

Prices:	Adults $40.95, children (3 to 11) $23.95. Prices do not include tax or gratuity.
Times:	Varies. Call for current schedule.
Directions:	Exit 30 off I-4, south on Kirkman Road and right on Carrier Drive. The theaters are in the Republic Square mall at the corner of Carrier and Universal.

Nestled incongruously in a suburban-style strip mall just past Wet 'n Wild is one of Orlando's most enjoyable attractions. Sleuths presents a rotating menu of a dozen hilarious whodunits served up with relish before, during, and after dinner.

You may find yourself invited to Lord Mansfield's Fox Hunt Banquet or discover yourself one of the alumni attending a reunion at genteel Luray Academy. Whatever the premise, the hilarity is virtually guaranteed, thanks to an ensemble of accomplished (and wonderfully hammy) local actors with a gift for improvisation and the quick comeback. Most of the fun and the biggest laughs come from the unscripted interactions with the "guests" who are made to feel very much part of the action.

As you arrive for dinner, you will meet some of the cast members ushering guests to their tables and passing hors d'oeuvres. After the salad course, the murder mystery proper unfolds on a minuscule set at the front of the house. Don't be surprised if you're called from your seat to participate in some bit of lunacy. At one show I saw, four people found themselves galloping through the house on make-believe horses while the rest of the audience bayed like hounds. But, if you're shy, don't fret; cast members seem to have an uncanny knack for not disturbing those who'd rather not be chosen for "stardom."

The humor is broad, with a healthy dose of double entendre. The cast members throw themselves into their parts but occasionally drop out of character in gales of suppressed laughter. And the audience never hesitates to pitch in, gleefully pointing out telltale clues that those on stage have missed. Before long, someone turns up dead and everyone in the cast seems to have a motive.

Now it's your turn to play detective. Each table of eight is asked to name a spokesperson. During dinner, each table mulls over the clues and tries to come up with one telling question that will uncover some yet-unknown fact that will point to the murderer. Each audience member is asked to write down their solution to the crime — who dunnit, with what, and why.

Another bit of good news is that the food, while simple, is quite tasty. The choices are limited — Cornish hen, prime rib (for an extra charge), and vegetarian or meatball lasagna. I'd recommend the Cornish hen. Beer, wine, and soft drinks are poured freely.

After dinner, the cast reappears and submits itself to the interrogation of the audience. This is no dry exercise in forensic logic. Thanks to the expert kibitzing of the cast, the laughter continues virtually nonstop. Ultimately, the wrongdoer is identified and audience members who guessed right win a prize.

Sleuths has become so popular that it now supports three separate theaters in its strip mall home. One of them regularly features a **Merry Mystery Dinner Adventure** especially for kids aged 3 to 12. The first show in this series (there will be more, they say) is called *Faire of the Shire* and offers cameo roles for the kiddies in a mystery that includes magic but no mayhem. Prices are cheaper for this show ($28 for adults, $16 for children 3 to 12) and the kids' meal is a marvelous creation called Worms Underground — a toadstool formed by a pizza atop a ramekin of buttered noodles sits on green pea grass studded with chicken nugget rocks. I'm told it's what the actors in the show always order.

One indicator of the success of the Sleuths experience is that, by show's end, the audience feels part of the family. The cast members graciously thank you for your attendance and point out the valuable service you perform in helping a local business survive and thrive without being owned by Disney or ABC. Hear! Hear!

Treasure Chest Quest

Amerihost Resort Maingate
7491 West US Highway 192, Kissimmee
(407) 396–6000, ext. 5059

Prices:	Adults $22, children (9 and under) $17. For games only, adults $10, children $5.
Times:	Tuesday and Friday 8:00 p.m.; buffet from 6:30 p.m.
Directions:	Between Mile Markers 5 and 6, next to Knights Inn

Always wished you could be on *Family Feud*? Think you're smart enough for *Who Wants to Be a Millionaire?* Well dream no more. Thanks to the enterprising people at Dreamland Productions, who also produce the slicker *MurderWatch Mystery Theater* (see above), you have an excellent chance of getting on one of the game shows crammed into this two-hour entertainment.

This is not strictly speaking a dinner attraction since the buffet is optional and takes place a few steps away from the vest pocket theater in which the game show itself unfolds. Skipping the buffet makes this an extremely attractive entertainment buy for the Orlando area.

There are four game shows presented under the watchful eye and quick wit of Martin Winkendale and his beautiful assistant Mallory, keeper of the chest of the title. The shows are *Name That Toon, The Matching Game, Family Food*, and *The Not-So-Newlywed Game*, titles cleverly designed to signal their sources of inspiration while keeping lawyers at bay.

Contestants are drawn from the audience and my impression is that if you have a burning desire to participate letting the staff know in advance will enhance your odds of being selected. The games are familiar, the banter lighthearted and often quite funny, and a great time is generally had by all. There are prizes, too, which are fairly modest until the grand finale when the stakes rise considerably.

The single contestant in the final segment of the show, the "Treasure Chest Quest" of the title, is drawn by lot and plays for $1,000 in cold hard cash in a game clearly patterned after *Who Wants To Be A Millionaire?* For added visual effect they actually produce the cash, a stack of what appear to be well-worn bank notes of small denominations. Get all ten questions correct and the money is yours.

This show has an appealing homegrown, handmade quality that I found quite endearing, and the performers and staff are clearly having a ball putting it on. As long as you don't come expecting big-budget, TV-quality production values, you should have a very good time indeed. And you just might go home $1,000 richer.

CHAPTER TWELVE:

Another Roadside Attraction

E arlier, I mentioned the great American tradition of the roadside attraction — those weird, often wacky, always wonderful come-ons
that beckoned from the highway's edge, all designed to amuse or
entertain or mystify, all designed to part the tourist from his money and keep
him happy while they did it. Fortunately for us, the tradition is alive and well
and flourishing in the fertile tourist environment of Central Florida. Gathered together in this chapter is a cornucopia of museums, monuments, mys-
teries, and amusements that, in my opinion, partake of this noble legacy of
American showmanship and hucksterism. Enjoy!

Astronaut Hall of Fame

6225 Vectorspace Boulevard, Titusville 32780
(321) 269-6100
www.astronauthalloffame.com

Admission:	Adults $13.95, children (6 to 12) $9.95, 5 and under **free.** The Astronaut Hall of Fame is nonprofit, so no tax is added to these prices.
Hours:	Daily 9:00 a.m. to 5:00 p.m. (hours are ex- tended in summer); last ticket sold 4:00 p.m.
Location:	On SR 405, just off US 1, on the way to Kennedy Space Center

Just before you reach Kennedy Space Center you pass the home of U.S.
Space Camp, a camping program for kids. Attached to the camp, and open to
the general public, is a beautifully designed museum/simulator attraction
called the U.S. Astronaut Hall of Fame. It's no substitute for a visit to the Space

Center but, if you have an extra day, it makes for an enjoyable supplement.

The museum portion of the experience pays homage to the seven Mercury and 13 Gemini astronauts who worked in the days when space travel was new enough that we could all keep track of who was who. More recently, 22 Apollo and Skylab astronauts were added to the Hall of Fame. Also on display are actual Mercury, Gemini, and Apollo capsules. There is even a Mercury model into which you can squeeze yourself— or try to. If you ever wondered why the early astronauts referred to the Mercury program as "man in a can," this experience will explain it all.

Probably of more interest to most visitors, especially the younger ones, will be the variety of simulated experiences this attraction has to offer. They range from the mildly interesting to the rather spectacular. At the lower end of the spectrum is *Shuttle to Tomorrow*, a film shown in the cargo bay of the model Space Shuttle. The film offers a brief overview of current and future space activities. Also in this category is *To Explore*, a ponderous 10-minute salute to the astronauts in the Hall of Fame.

Things get more interesting with the **Shuttle Landing Simulator**, a sort of video game in which you use a joy stick to guide the Shuttle to a safe landing. The best experiences are the true simulators. The **G Force Trainer** puts you in a centrifuge that simulates 4-Gs of acceleration. A video screen in front of you shows what a jet pilot might see while zooming through the wild blue yonder. Amazingly, there is no sensation of spinning, just eight minutes of the rather uncomfortable pull of rapid acceleration. The **Mission To Mars** simulation takes you on a bumpy ride across the surface of the Red Planet. The 16-seat **3D-360** takes you for a flight on what's billed as "the most realistic flight simulator ever created." They're probably right because this one takes you on actual barrel rolls, two in a row at one point, as the entire simulator rotates rapidly through 360 degrees. This 7-minute ride is not for the squeamish but it's a lot of fun. The less intrepid will probably have just as much fun watching their friends and family on the video monitors of the interior and seeing the simulator buck, roll, and spin. The video serves a double purpose; if you decide you can't take any more, you can wave your arms and the attendants will stop the ride to let you off.

The **U.S. Space Camp** is a five-day residential program for children 9 to 13. Tuition is $699 to $799, depending on dates. I am told that many parents drop their kids off while they take a Florida vacation on their own. There is also a program that lets parents and kids do everything together. You can get a look at the Space Camp Training Center as you return from the film aboard the shuttle mock-up.

Allow about two to three hours to fully experience this attraction. If you just want to hit the highlights, it will take far less time. A snack bar, the Cosmic Cafe, serves inexpensive breakfasts from 9:00 a.m. to 11:00 a.m. Lunch is served from 11:00 to 4:00 p.m. There is, of course, the obligatory **Right Stuff Shop** where you can pick up the Honorary Astronaut certificate included in the admission.

Citrus Tower

North US 27, Clermont 34711
(352) 394-4061

Admission: (Elevator to top of tower) Adults $3.50, children (3 to 15) $1

Hours: Monday to Thursday, 9:00 a.m. to 6:00 p.m.; Friday and Saturday, 9:00 a.m to 9:00 p.m.; Sunday, 11:00 a.m. to 5:00 p.m.

Location: Half a mile north of SR 50

The Florida Citrus Tower is a monument to a vanished industry. While I was visiting, another tourist told of coming here as a child in the fifties. "All you could see was miles and miles of orange trees," he remembered. "There's not much to see now." A series of devastating freezes over the past two decades has forced Florida's citrus industry farther south. Today, the fields around the Tower are more likely to hold Christmas tree farms or a new subdivision. Most of the fields are empty.

From the observation platform at the tower's top you can see 35 miles in all directions. You can even make out downtown Orlando and the taller buildings at Disney World in the hazy distance. Later, you'll be able to argue that you were as high as it is possible to get in the state of Florida. (The Bok Tower in Lake Wales, see *Chapter 15*, also claims this distinction.)

Nearby: House of Presidents, Lakeridge Winery.

Fantasy of Flight

P.O. Box 1200, Polk City 33868
(863) 984-3500
www.fantasyofflight.com

Admission: Adults $24.95, seniors (55+) $22.95, children (5 to 12) $13.95. Annual pass $63.55

Hours: Daily 9:00 a.m. to 5:00 p.m. Closed Christmas and Thanksgiving. Restaurant open 8:00 a.m. to 4:00 p.m.

Location: Exit 21 off I-4, about 50 miles west of Orlando

Vintage aircraft collector Kermit Weeks has turned his avocation into an irresistible roadside attraction that is definitely worth a visit if you are traveling between Orlando and Tampa. Just off I-4, Fantasy of Flight, with its Compass Rose restaurant, makes a great place to take a breakfast or lunch break. You can tour the exhibits and have a meal in less than two hours. Come for lunch and the afternoon if you want to take the free tours.

There are three major sections to Fantasy of Flight. The first is a **walk-through history of manned flight**, with an accent on its wartime uses. Using dioramas, sound, film, and life-sized figures, it's the equivalent of a Disney World "dark ride" without the vehicles. You start your journey in the hold of an old war transport. Suddenly, the jump master is ushering you out the open door of the plane. The engines roar, the cold wind whistles through your hair, you step out into the pitch blackness of the nighttime sky; all you can see is stars. Soon you find yourself at the dawn of flight, as a nineteenth century hot-air balloon is preparing to take off. Then you are in the trenches of World War I, a tri-plane about to crash into your position. Next you are at a remote World War II airstrip. As a new replacement in the 95th Bomber Group, you receive a briefing and then step aboard a restored B-17 Flying Fortress. As you walk through the aircraft you hear the voices of the crew during a mission over Europe, antiaircraft fire bursting all around you. Stepping across the bomb bay catwalk, you see the doors open beneath you as 500-pound bombs rain down on the fields and cities below. All of this is beautifully realized. The sets are terrific, the lighting dramatic, the soundtrack ingenious, the planes authentic in every detail. I found the B-17 mission to be truly moving.

The second section is a large, spotless, sun-filled **hangar** displaying Weeks' collection. There are reproductions of the Wright brothers' 1903 flyer and Lindbergh's "Spirit of St. Louis." There are a few oddities, like the 1959 Roadair, an attempt to build a flying automobile. But most of the planes are the real thing. The oil leaks, captured in sand filled pans, tell you that many of these planes still fly. You'll see the actual 1929 Ford Tri-Motor used in the film *Indiana Jones and the Temple of Doom.* There are World War II immortals as well, the B-24J Liberator, a heavy bomber, and the Grumman FM2 Wildcat, the U.S. Navy fighter that shone in the early days of the war. There's even a Nazi short-take off and landing plane, the Storch, that once saved Mussolini's neck by plucking him from a remote mountain resort.

There are three tours given in the afternoon; arrive by 1:00 and you can see them all. The **Backlot Tour** provides a good overall look at the hangar, while the **Restoration Tour** focuses on some current projects. Each day they choose an **Aircraft of the Day**; after giving you a thorough briefing on the plane's history, they take it aloft and put it through its paces.

By this time, you may wish you were able to get behind the controls of one of these great machines. Fortunately the price of admission includes unlimited flight time aboard the eight simulators in **Fightertown**, Fantasy of Flight's third main section. Past a wrecked Zero and a restored Corsair, lies a land of virtual reality fantasy where you can strap yourself into a Wildcat and go gunning for Zeroes over tropical islands in "Battle over the Pacific." Each sortie lasts seven minutes.

The experience is surprisingly realistic. A flight instructor monitors your progress and provides helpful hints — like don't fly upside down. You can fly against the computer or against another pilot in a different simulator. It's also possible for teams to fly against each other. After your own flight, you'll probably want to go to the control tower to see how things look from the flight instructor's point of view.

When you leave the hangar area, you find yourself back where you began. If you'd like to walk through the dioramas again (and you might), help yourself. Otherwise you can visit the gift shop (leather bomber jackets just $300!) or stop into the **Compass Rose restaurant**, a beautifully designed re-creation of the kind of Art Deco restaurant you might have found at a fancy airport in the 1930s. The Compass Rose opens at 8:00 a.m. and makes a good choice for breakfast. The regular menu features burgers, sandwiches, and salads (all named after aircraft) in the $5 to $8 range. Daily specials are about $7 and the desserts are scrumptious.

If a visit puts you in the mood to take to the air, check into the hot air balloon and plane rides available here (see *Chapter 17: Moving Experiences*).

Flying Tigers Warbird Restoration Museum

231 North Hoagland Boulevard, Kissimmee 34741
(407) 933-1942
www.warbirdmuseum.com

Admission:	Adults $9, seniors (60+) $8, children (6 to 12) $6, all plus tax. Children 5 and under **free**
Hours:	Daily 9:00 a.m. to 6:00 p.m. (to 5:00 p.m. on Sundays)
Location:	About half a mile south of Highway 192

That's not a pile of junk behind that hangar. That's history.

The dusty hangar at the end of a runway at the Kissimmee Airport is home to the very serious (and expensive!) business of restoring battered and crumpled warplanes to flying trim once again. Fortunately, owner Tom Reilly and his wife Suzzie couldn't bear to keep this labor of love all to themselves, so they opened their treasure trove of restored planes, historical oddities and, well, junk to the general public.

You can wander through the hangar on your own, but unless you're a real military aviation expert, it will probably make little sense to you. Far better to wait for one of the regular tours that take you around, through, and under the hodgepodge of planes and into the workshop where once proud fighting machines are being resurrected by dedicated craftsmen.

Tours last about 45 minutes but the length varies depending on the number of people and the number of questions they ask. Feel free to give your curiosity free rein. The guide will be more than happy to explain the intricacies of what goes on here. The style of these tours is wonderfully lacking in theme park polish and long on easy-going macho anecdotes about mid-air crashes and 400-degree-per-second spin ratios. These guys know what they're talking about and obviously love what they do.

And of course there are the planes. Everything from a wood and canvas 1909 "pusher" (so called because the engine sits behind the pilot and pushes the plane through the air) to an A4 Skyhawk (made famous by the movie *Top Gun*) to a MiG 21 (once part of the Latvian air force and confiscated from an arms dealer). The shop is in the process of renovating not one but two B-17s as well as two Corsairs. Don't worry, they'll still be there when you visit. It takes about five years to restore one of these babies. There are occasional visitors, too, like the nifty little French-built Israeli fighter trainer that lost its canopy on takeoff and was in for repairs when I visited.

There are also occasional poignant reminders of what war is all about. On one visit I saw the fuselage of a World War II P-40 that had crashed into a Florida swamp on a training mission. It was discovered 40 years later, the pilot still strapped into his seat. Some 2,000 aviators lost their lives in Florida while training for World War II; in fact, Kissimmee Airport was a U.S. Army Air Corps base, maintained by a crew of German and Italian POWs.

A lot of old-timers visit here and I'm told that it's not unusual for tears to be shed. It's not surprising. After spending an hour or so poking your head into the cramped spaces of these old war machines, you'll have a deeper appreciation of the special breed of men who took them aloft to fight for our freedom. If you're really lucky, you may arrive in time to see a B-25 bomber rumble down the runway and make a flyover escorted by a Mustang fighter, just as in its heyday. If you attend the monthly, week-long vintage aircraft restoration course ($995), you'll be treated to a spin in a B-25 on your graduation.

There is a small, rather helter-skelter, collection of military aviation memorabilia on display in the Museum's office. A few items are for sale, as are aviation books and souvenirs.

Nearby: Green Meadows Farm, Stallion 51, Warbird Adventures.

Guinness World Records Experience

8437 International Drive, Orlando 32819
(407) 248-8891

Admission: $14.99 adults, children (5 to 12) $9.99
Hours: Daily, 10:00 a.m. to 10:00 p.m.
Location: In front of the Mercado shopping and din-
ing complex

Housed in a snazzy modernistic building, this harmless time-passer uses film, stage sets, and interactive displays in an attempt to breath life into the *Guinness Book of World Records*, the small-print compendium of facts and figures that has been settling barroom bets since 1954.

A short film introduces the concept and your two loony scientist hosts. They shrink you down to enter the "Guinness database" where you take a Guinness Records trivia test and roam at will through a black-lit room representing the bowels of a computer. When you tire of this (it won't take long) you are un-shrunk in yet another chamber to enter a space shuttle mock-up to view videos of various space-related records. From there it's on to Guinness Town, a large stage set showing off such earth-shattering "personal" records as the world's largest female breasts. Then, you get to sit through a five-minute motion simulator film that is ostensibly an attempt to show the most world records in the shortest period of time. It is, in fact, a fairly incoherent attempt to separate you from your lunch, in which it just might succeed. The best seats are in the third row in the middle and there is a row of stationary seats up front.

Finally, you wobble into a gift shop where you can pick up a paperback copy of the latest edition of *Guinness World Records* for $7, which may just be the best thing in the whole experience.

Nearby: Titanic, Trainland.

House of Presidents
123 U.S. 27 North, Clermont 34712
(352) 394-2836

Admission: Adults $9.95, children (4 to 13) $4.95
Hours: Daily 9:00 a.m. to 5:00 p.m.
Location: About half a mile north of SR 50, near
Grand Citrus Tower

Next to the Grand Citrus Tower (see above) sits a small porticoed house that is home to an even smaller porticoed house. This is House of Presidents, a meticulous scale model of the White House that has been the life's work of Orlando resident John Zweifel and his wife Jan. Anyone who's into modeling or anyone who's helped a child build a doll house will want to visit this astonishing work.

Inside you'll find life-sized wax-museum-style statues of all the U.S. presidents, from Washington right down to "Dubya." They will remind you of just how few presidents you can recognize by sight. They also form a fascinating chronicle of the evolution of upscale American male clothing over the past 225 years or so. A recent addition is *Tribute to the Presidents*, 43 display cases containing menus, photos, personal items, and other mementos that were meaningful to each president.

In the first of the two display rooms in this small museum is a 16-foot square diorama depicting the building of the White House as it might have looked in 1797, three years before its completion. At a scale of three-quarters of an inch to one foot, we can watch the dozens of stonemasons, carpenters, and laborers ply their trade while George Washington himself surveys their progress. Washington, by the way, was the only president not to live in the White House, even though he supported the project.

The pièce de résistance, however, awaits in the much larger second room. Here you will find the 60- by 22-foot model of the White House executed in a scale of one inch to the foot. It took Zweifel, his wife, and hundreds of volunteers over 500,000 man-hours to bring the model to its present state and apparently they're not done yet, since the work is billed as an ongoing project. The result is impressive. They have re-created not just the main building but the East and West wings as well, all in astonishing detail.

As you enter the room, you see the front of the building. Peek through the windows and you can glimpse details of the rooms inside. But walk the length of the model and around to the back and the entire White House will be revealed to you. In doll house fashion, there is no rear wall and here the full extent of the Zweifels' accomplishment becomes apparent.

The scope of the re-creation and the attention to detail are astounding. You can spot pens on tables, cigar burns on tabletops, even the occasional gravy stain. The clocks tick, the phones ring, the television sets are on (picking up Orlando stations oddly enough). Along the wall behind you are dioramas of the Oval Office as decorated by a series of recent presidents.

The gift shop offers a surprising number of books about the White House and the presidents who have lived in it along with an assortment of more traditional souvenirs. A few items (not for sale) are worthy of *Ripley's Believe It or Not!* You can see, through magnifying lenses, the flags of all nations painted on a grain of wheat or a portrait of the Kennedys, John and Jackie, executed on the head of a pin. What possesses people to do this sort of thing?

Some of the exhibits go on tour from time to time and so may not be there when you visit (*Tribute to the Presidents*, for example, traveled to the 2000 Republican Convention). On the other hand, the House of Presidents sometimes hosts exhibits on loan from presidential libraries and other museums.

Nearby: Citrus Tower, Lakeridge Winery.

Lakeridge Winery Tour

19239 U.S. 27 North, Clermont 34711-9025
(800) 768-WINE; (352) 394-8627

Admission: **Free**

Hours: Monday to Saturday 10:00 a.m. to 5:00 p.m.;
Sunday 11:00 a.m. to 5:00 p.m.

Location: About 5 miles north of SR 50 and 3 miles
south of Florida Turnpike exit 285

Believe it or not, American wine making began in Florida, thanks to some French Huguenot settlers who started fermenting the local wild Muscadine grapes near present-day Jacksonville in about 1562. Viticulture was a thriving Florida industry until the 1930s, when a plant disease wiped out most of the grapes. Now, thanks to Lakeridge, the only winery in Central Florida, wine making is starting to make a comeback in the Sunshine State. Lakeridge currently produces some 50 thousand gallons a year with plans for expansion. Perhaps one day it will fill up all the acres abandoned by the citrus industry. (See Citrus Tower, above.)

The attractive Spanish-style building that sits atop a small hill on a bend in the highway has been cleverly designed to serve as both a working winery and a welcome center for passing tourists. Despite its out-of-the-way location and low-key promotion, Lakeridge attracts a steady stream of visitors. I wonder if it's the lure of free wine?

Tours run constantly, as long as there are people arriving, and take about 45 minutes. After a short video about the history of wine making in Florida and Lakeridge's operations, you are taken on a short tour. It leads you, via an elevated walkway, over the compact wine making area at the back of the building, onto a terrace that overlooks the vineyards and the rolling, lake-dotted countryside of the Central Florida Ridge, and then back over the U-shaped wine making room.

After the tour, there is a 15-minute wine tasting that lets you sample six or seven of Lakeridge's 13 wines, including Crescendo, their *methode Champenoise* sparkling wine. You will also get to taste their mulled wine and, if you like, purchase a bag of spices to make your own. And speaking of purchases, all of Lakeridge's wines are available for purchase. In addition to a varying menu of specials, full cases are sold at a 20% discount. Buy three cases and get 25% off. Lakeridge also sells its own line of salad dressings, sauces, mustards, jams, and jellies.

The winery throws special events on a regular basis throughout the year, ranging from "Jazz at the Winery" to vintage auto shows. There is an admission of $1 to $5 for most of these events, although some are **free**.

Nearby: Citrus Tower, House of Presidents.

Medieval Life Village

4510 West Irlo Bronson Highway, Kissimmee 34746
(800) 229-8300; (407) 396-1518

Admission:	Adults $8, children (3 to 12) $6, plus tax
	Free with tickets to *Medieval Times*
Hours:	Daily, 4:00 p.m. until showtime at *Medieval Times*
Location:	At the *Medieval Times* dinner attraction

What's a medieval castle without a village to supply all its needs? Fortunately, the owner of *Medieval Times*, the popular Kissimmee dinner attraction, is a Spanish count. So it wasn't too much of a stretch for him to clear out the attics and barns of his estates, buy up an old village on Majorca, and ship the whole lot to Central Florida.

The result is an intriguing re-creation of a twelfth century village, complete with a cadre of artisans and craftspeople plying their trades in much the way their medieval predecessors did. The buildings are modern construction, but the doors, the wooden windows, the furniture, and many of the other objects to be found in the village are all originals, some of them 800 years old.

The tiny village is set around a small courtyard and cobblestone street. Much of it is given over to a series of workshops and ateliers, including a basket shop, a carpenter's workshop, a metalsmith, and a blacksmith creating chain mail armor one link at a time. There is also a cloth weaver working at an 800-year-old loom. Many of the items produced here can be purchased in the gift shop.

One of the more intriguing displays is "The Dungeon," a collection of implements of torture. There is an additional $2 fee for this section. A sign outside cautions that the display may not be suitable for small children and it is advice well worth heeding. The implements themselves (all apparently genuine) are ghastly enough but, for those with poor imaginations, mannequins have been added to illustrate the hideous uses to which these bizarre inventions were put. It may not be the best thing to see before sitting down to a meal and a night's entertainment.

Admission to the village is included in the price of your ticket to the dinner attraction (see *Chapter 11*), which is one of the best in the Orlando area. Whether the village is worth the admission if you are not seeing the show will depend on your interest in things medieval. There is a fair amount to see here, but much of it is unidentified and unexplicated. The artisans who "inhabit" the village, however, are friendly and knowledgeable and are a great source of information about the strange objects you'll encounter.

Nearby: Airboat Rentals U-Drive, Jungleland.

Old Town

5770 West Irlo Bronson Highway, Kissimmee 34746

(407) 396-4888

Admission: **Free**. Rides are extra.

Hours: Daily 10:00 a.m. to 11:00 p.m.

Location: About 1 mile east of I-4

Take away the window dressing and Old Town is just a mall filled with gift, novelty, and souvenir shops. But the window dressing is fun and obviously popular with the crowds that make Old Town a lively place to visit and shop during those sultry Florida evenings.

Behind a small, brightly lit amusement park facing route 192, a vaguely Western Main Street stretches through a few blocks of 70-plus shops, cafes, and entertainments to a tiny carousel and mini roller coaster on the edge of the Kissimmee night. It's pedestrians only, with frequent benches for weary strollers and a constant swirl of visitors from around the world.

The 18 rides are of the carnival midway variety and are paid for with tickets purchased from a booth at the front ($1 per ticket). Rides cost anywhere from two to five tickets, so a $25 ride-all-day pass will pay for itself fairly quickly. A tiny go-kart track collects a separate fee of $6 for a 13-lap, 4-minute ride. Old Town also boasts a haunted house, the **Haunted Grimm House**. Admission is $7 ($5 for kids 10 and under) for a 5- to 10-minute stroll through 20 rooms of shocks and surprises courtesy of special effects and a handful of live actors. If you don't plan on visiting the more elaborate *Skull Kingdom* (see below), and absolutely must visit a haunted house, the Grimm establishment is a satisfactory substitute.

Lazer Blast, the resident laser tag game, works an interesting variation on the theme — the floors are inflated and the walls padded, allowing the shoeless players to dive and roll like action movie heroes as they fire off their laser weapons at all and sundry. For the fearless (or foolhardy, depending on your point of view), the **Human Slingshot** beckons. For $25, you can be shot into the sky in a seat powered by a giant rubber band.

Old Town lays on a number of **free** events to draw crowds and keep them entertained between bouts of shopping. An outdoor stage down one of the side streets offers musical entertainment on an irregular schedule. More predictable is the 8:30 p.m. **Friday and Saturday Night Cruise** of vintage automobiles. Over 350 cars show up on the average Saturday, and Old Town claims it's the largest such event in the world. It's great fun for anyone who grew up in the age of those great finned monsters. Live rock 'n' roll adds the perfect musical accompaniment to the nostalgia.

Nearby: SkyCoaster, Water Mania.

Ripley's Believe It Or Not

8201 International Drive, Orlando 32819

(407) 363-4418

www.ripleysorlando.com

Admission:	Adults $14.95, children (4 to 12) $9.95, plus tax
Hours:	Daily 9:00 a.m. to 1:00 a.m.; last ticket sold at midnight
Location:	Next to the Mercado on I-Drive

Is that an ornate Italian villa sliding into a Florida sinkhole on International Drive or is it just Ripley's Believe It Or Not? It's Ripley's, of course, and the zanily tilted building is only one of the illusions on display here (and one of the best).

Robert Ripley was a newspaper cartoonist whose series on oddities and wonders, man-made and natural, made him a very wealthy man and an American institution. The Orlando Ripley's is one of several monuments to Ripley's weird and wonderful collections, gathered in the course of visits to some 198 countries at a time when such globe-trotting travel was still a challenge. On display here are objets collected by Ripley himself, along with others gathered after his death, and a series of show-and-tell displays illustrating a variety of optical and spatial illusions.

Where else are you going to see a real two-headed calf? Or the Mona Lisa recreated in small squares of toasted bread? Or a three-quarter scale Rolls Royce crafted from over a million matchsticks? Most displays here are fascinating, although a few are not for the squeamish and some may strike you as tasteless. Best of all are the show-and-tell displays, like an elaborately tilted and skewed room in which the balls on a pool table seem to roll uphill. There is also a giddily disorienting catwalk through a rock-walled tunnel. From the outside, it is obvious that the walls are moving, but step inside, onto the catwalk, and suddenly the walls seem to be rock solid and it is the catwalk that seems to be rotating.

Nearby: Guinness World Records, Titanic, Trainland.

Skull Kingdom

5933 American Way, Orlando 32801

(407) 354-1564

www.skullkingdom.com

Admission:	Adults and children 8 and up $12.50; not recommended for younger children
Hours:	Monday to Friday 6:00 p.m. to 11:00 p.m.; Saturday and Sunday noon to 11:00 p.m.

Location: Across from Wet 'n Wild.

The art of stylish entertaining may be dying elsewhere but it's alive and decomposing at *Skull Kingdom* where gracious ghouls invite you in for a tour of their decrepit digs on I-Drive. If you've ever been to one of those haunted houses that spring up as fundraisers around Halloween, then you have a pretty good idea of what awaits you, although the experience here is probably a good bit more elaborate. For those new to the genre, the experience goes something like this: Once a group of likely victims, er guests, congregates, the doors open and the group is sent on a leisurely 20-minute stroll through two floors of mazes and cavernous rooms past all manner of yucky surprises. Most of the creatures you encounter are mechanical dummies but some are scarily real, and the living (or at least undead) entertainers carry off their tasks with great aplomb. If it's any consolation to the squeamish, the unwritten rule of the game is that the performers never actually touch you.

Skull Kingdom also has a spiffy new building, a brooding castle with an enormous skull shaped entrance, and it uses a bit more technology than similar attractions elsewhere — film, mechanical monsters, voiceover recordings, and the like.

Nearby: Wet 'n Wild, Universal Orlando.

Spook Hill

Admission: **Free**
Hours: 24 hours
Location: South on 27 to 17A (before Lake Wales), turn left (east) and follow signs

I don't get it. A sign at this "attraction" (which is just a line drawn on a road in the small town of Lake Wales) talks about a legendary Indian chief, an epic battle with an alligator, and the belief of early pioneers that the place was somehow haunted. Then you are instructed to stop your car on the white line painted in the street, place it in neutral, and then marvel as the car mysteriously rolls backwards uphill!

The only problem with this scenario is that it seems to me screamingly obvious that your car is rolling downhill. Maybe I'm perceptually challenged. Or maybe the locals are hiding in the bushes laughing at tourists making fools of themselves on Spook Hill. But what the heck, it's a local legend, it's free, and it's on the way to Bok Tower Gardens if you're heading that way. Maybe you can explain it to me.

Titanic, The Exhibition

8445 International Drive, Orlando 32819
(877) 410-1912; (407) 248-1166

www.titanicshipofdreams.com
Admission: Adults $16.95, children (6 to 12) $11.95
Hours: Daily 10:00 a.m. to 8:00 p.m.
Location: In the Mercado shopping and dining complex

Fans of the movie *Titanic* (and they are legion) will welcome the opportunity to visit this extremely well-done evocation of the most famous cruise ship in history. The exhibition takes the form of "guided tours," which depart every half hour or so and are led by actors representing historical characters, from the designers of the Titanic to crew members and passengers aboard the ship's ill-fated maiden voyage.

Among the highlights of the tour are re-creations of staterooms and other areas of the ship. And if the grand staircase looks smaller than the one in the film, that's because this one is accurate; the filmmakers took some liberties and made the staircase higher and broader. Then there are the artifacts, including actual chinaware, deck chairs, and life jackets from the ship. If you're in the right mood, these can be rather chilling. And some visitors may get a few goose bumps from seeing a costume worn by Leonardo himself in the movie.

But the real goose bumps come from the boarding passes you are handed at the start of your voyage into history. Each one bears the name of an actual Titanic passenger. At the end of the "voyage" you can consult a memorial wall and learn whether or not you survived. The historical character-guides handle their roles extremely well, giving equal time to historical trivia (like the fact that the ship's linoleum floors were the height of luxury at the time) and the somber human drama of the ship's tragic end.

Tickets are purchased at a sort of steamship office near the International Drive entrance to the Mercado. (Dollars off coupons are readily available.) Tickets in hand, you proceed to the Mercado's inner courtyard where you wait for the next "departure."

Trolley and Train Museum
8990 International Drive, Orlando 32819
(407) 363-9002
Admission: For museum only: Adults $6.95, children, $4.95, seniors (55+) $5.95, tax included
Hours: Monday to Saturday, 10:00 a.m. to 9:00 p.m.; Sunday 10:00 a.m. to 8:00 p.m.
Location: Just south of Pointe★Orlando shopping mall

If you think your old HO-gauge model train set was pretty nifty, you may want to do a reality check at the Trolley and Train Museum. This combination train store/museum boasts one of the largest G-gauge layouts in the world — and G-gauge is four times bigger than HO.

The layout occupies 4,800 square feet of space in its own room and required more than 3,000 feet of track and some 4,700 man-hours to complete. The result is impressive, rising high overhead and twisting and turning through mountain passes, quaint small towns, industrial zones, and idyllic farm valleys. There's even a spur line to Santa-Land. The elaborate landscape is microscopically imagined with a wealth of telling details. The rivers have fish in them and the mountaintops are home to Bigfoot and the Abominable Snowman.

The Trolley and Train Museum is a labor of love, as you will quickly discover if you fall into conversation with one of the managers on duty. They take great pride in their creation and obvious joy in sharing its wonders with visitors. Model train devotees will find them a virtually inexhaustible font of modeling tips and train lore.

By the way, if you're so taken with the layout that you just can't live without your very own, Trainland will reproduce it on your premises for a mere $125,000. Trains will run you about $8,000 extra.

Nearby: Ripley's Believe It or Not, SeaWorld, Titanic, WonderWorks.

WonderWorks

9067 International Drive, Orlando 32819
(407) 351-8800
www.wonderworksonline.com

Admission:	Adults $15.95, children (4 to 12) and seniors (55+) $11.95, plus tax
Hours:	Daily 10:00 a.m. to 11:00 p.m.
Location:	On International Drive, next to Pointe★Orlando

If you liked the subsiding building that houses Ripley's Believe It Or Not, wait 'til you see WonderWorks. The fantasy here is that a mysterious neoclassical building has crashed out of the sky, upside down, right in the middle of Orlando's glitziest tourist strip. Inside, the normal laws of physics are likewise turned upside down. The exterior of WonderWorks may be its best feature; it has become Orlando's most-photographed building.

In fact, WonderWorks is packed with the kind of games and gimmicks (over 100) used by science museums to teach basic principles of physics, and it turns them into a highly enjoyable interactive amusement arcade. Here, on three noisy levels, you can experience an earthquake or a hurricane and get some idea of what it would be like to be fried in the electric chair. Then test your reflexes, your pitching arm, the strength of your grip, and your visual acuity. Or maybe you'd just prefer to play around with soap bubbles as big as you are. There's plenty more to keep you amused and entertained for as long as you'd like to hang out.

The "world's largest" laser tag arena occupies the third level. Next door is Pointe★Orlando, an elaborate shopping, dining, and movie venue that is an attraction in its own right.

Nearby: Guinness World Records, Ripley's Believe It Or Not, Titanic, Trainland.

World of Orchids

2501 Old Lake Wilson Road, Kissimmee 34747
(407) 396-1887

> *Admission:* **Free**
> *Hours:* Tuesday to Sunday 9:30 a.m. to 4:30 p.m.
> *Location:* From I-4, take US 192 West and turn left on Old Lake Wilson, about one mile

If the last orchid you saw was on a corsage at the high school prom, a visit here may remind you why this delicate bloom is the symbol of choice for proms and other events. World of Orchids is actually a working greenhouse that will ship its orchids and other plants nationwide. To educate and enchant the public, they have constructed a vast greenhouse covering some three-quarters of an acre. In the carefully controlled warm, humid air some 1,000 orchids are displayed in a natural jungle setting, complete with waterfalls, babbling streams, and squawking parrots. The total varies seasonally and can double at certain times of the year.

World of Orchids also has a "nature walk," a 1,000-foot-long boardwalk that meanders off into a nearby wetlands.

Nearby: Splendid China, Water Mania.

CHAPTER THIRTEEN:

Do It!

A vacation in Orlando doesn't mean always being a spectator. There are plenty of activities that will put you right in the middle of the action. In this chapter, I will discuss some of them. Of course, there are many sports-oriented activities as well. They are discussed in *Chapter 18: Sports Scores*.

Airboat Rentals U Drive

4266 West Irlo Bronson Highway, Kissimmee 34746
(407) 847-3672
www.airboatrentals.com

Cost:	$5 to $27 an hour
Hours:	Daily 9:00 a.m. to 5:00 p.m.; last boat leaves at 5:00 p.m.
Location:	East of *Medieval Times*, near Mile Marker 15

Just east of the *Medieval Times* dinner attraction, US Highway 192 crosses Shingle Creek. You'd never notice if it weren't for this unassuming rental operation. Here in the middle of Kissimmee's major commercial strip is a little fragment of old Florida wetlands that you can explore in that most traditional of vehicles, the airboat.

The four-person airboats, which rent for $27 an hour, are so easy to drive that even a child can pilot them (as long as an adult is present). The driver sits in a slightly elevated seat right in front of the shielded, rear-facing propeller. A lever, operated with the left hand, steers the boat right and left; the throttle is on the right.

You can explore upstream (under the highway bridge) for about a mile and a half before the water gets too shallow for even the low-draft airboat. Or you can head downstream for about two miles toward Lake Kissimmee. Since the airboats do about 8 to 10 miles per hour, this makes a comfortable hour's outing.

There are other boats available. A six-seat rowboat powered by a tiny electric outboard is $22 an hour or $50 for the day; rent a fishin' pole for another $5. Canoes are $5 an hour or $20 a day. Alligators are spotted here occasionally; river otters are seen more frequently: A family of six or seven frequents the area near the dock.

Nearby: Jungleland, Medieval Times.

Fun Spot

5551 Del Verde Way, Orlando 32819
(407) 363-3867
www.fun-spot.com

Cost:	$3 to $30 as explained below; kids ride **free** with paying adult
Hours:	Weekdays noon to 11:00 p.m.; Saturday and Sunday 10:00 a.m. to midnight
Location:	Just off International Drive near the intersection of Kirkman Road and International

Fun Spot easily wins the Orlando go-kart sweepstakes with its intriguing, twisting, up and down, multilevel tracks. There are four of them here, with the 1,375-foot, three-level *QuadHelix* the most popular.

There are also bumper cars, bumper boats, and a 101-foot high ferris wheel that offers a panoramic view of the upper end of International Drive and Universal Orlando across the Interstate. A 10,000 square foot video arcade (tokens at 25 cents each or $6 for as long as you want) and a snack bar round out the offerings at this compact amusement park.

Rides are paid for with tickets that cost $3 each, although most people will opt for a package deal. The *QuadHelix* requires two tickets for a four-minute, four-lap, one-mile ride. The other go-kart tracks cost two tickets each. All the other rides are one ticket each. If you'd like to pig out at Fun Spot you can buy an armband that gives you unlimited access to all rides and the arcade for $30. For $15, you get the same deal for a three-hour period.

Nearby: Skull Kingdom, Universal Orlando, Vans Skatepark, Wet 'n Wild.

Kartworld

4708 West Irlo Bronson Highway, Kissimmee 34746
(407) 396-4800

Cost:	$3.50 per lap, 4 laps for $12, 8 for $20

Hours: Daily usually 11:00 a.m. to 11:00 p.m.
Location: 1 mile east of SR 565 at Mile Marker 13

Nothing fancy here, just go karts conveniently located on Kissimmee's main tourist strip. Go karts come in three sizes here — a large and a small single-seater and a two-seater — and the price is the same for all sizes of kart. The almost one-mile track snakes around three loops with a bridge and overpass arrangement allowing the karts to end up where they started. The bumper boat pool and a small kiddie-sized track are nearby. Tickets for the go-kart track can also be used on the bumper boats ($3.50 for 4 minutes), which are like large truck inner tubes with a motorized center.

Nearby: Jungleland, Medieval Times.

Lake Eola Swan Boats

Lake Eola Park, Orlando
(407) 839-8899

Cost: $7 per half hour, including tax
Hours: Weekdays 11:00 a.m. to 6:00 p.m., week-
               ends to 9:00 p.m.
Location: Downtown, near the intersection of
               Rosalind Avenue and Robinson Street

Right in the heart of Orlando's super-serious business district is this charming bit of whimsy. Lake Eola is Orlando's signature park, with its spectacular floating fountain. Along its shore, at a tiny kiosk called the Lake Eola Cafe, you can rent paddle boats decked out as graceful white swans and take them for a spin on this picture postcard lake. A sunset cruise on a swan makes a lovely way to get your evening off to a flying . . . er, floating start.

Nearby: Orange County Regional History Center.

Magical Midway

7001 International Drive, Orlando 32819
(407) 370-5353

Cost: $2.50 per ticket, $20 for unlimited rides
Hours: Sunday to Thursday noon to 10:00 p.m.;
               Friday noon to midnight; Saturday 10:00 a.m.
               to midnight
Location: On I-Drive, two blocks south of Wet 'n
               Wild

Magical Midway is a smaller version of Fun Spot, described above, but due to the absence of kiddie rides it draws an older teen clientele. The main attractions are the two elevated wooden go kart tracks, but there are also midway-style rides including a scaled down version of Universal's *Dr. Doom* shot tower. Individual tickets cost $2.50, with most rides requiring two tickets. At that rate, the $20 ride-all-day option quickly begins to make sense.

Nearby: Skull Kingdom, Universal Orlando, Wet 'n Wild.

Naskart Family Raceway

5071 West Irlo Bronson Highway, Kissimmee 34746
(407) 397-7699

Cost:	$5.35 for a 5-minute ride, including tax
Hours:	Daily 10:00 a.m. to 11:00 p.m.
Location:	Between Mile Marker 10 and 11 on the north side of US 192

There are no video arcades or other distractions at Naskart. Go karts are the central and only attraction at this small venue on the busy 192 tourist strip. There are two fairly short tracks. The "Naskar" track features fully enclosed stock-car-like karts (the roof closes over your head) and an oval track, while the "Indy" track offers one- and two-seater karts and a winding course. Buy five rides and get the sixth ride **free**.

Nearby: Old Town, Water Mania.

Paintball World

3445 Vineland Road, Orlando 32811
(407) 648-8404
www.paintball-world.com

Cost:	$25, plus tax, plus paintballs
Hours:	Day games, Saturday and Sunday noon to 5:00 p.m.; night games, Friday and Saturday 6:00 p.m. to 11:00 p.m.; private games by appointment
Location:	Near I-4 and Conroy Road; coming from I-4, turn right on Vineland

Hunkered down under a moonlit sky behind a sandbag bunker with a remorseless "enemy" bearing down on you or running like mad through the scrub forest from barricade to barricade, with bursts of gunfire going off all around, you begin to understand why the owners of this paintball field call it "the ultimate adrenaline rush."

Paintball World lets you play John Wayne (or Rambo, or Chuck Norris) in refereed "battles" that last about 15 minutes and pit two teams of five to eight players against each other. The challenge — and the fun— comes in the form of the tiny paintballs that give the game its name. Fired from small CO_2 powered guns, they zip along at 190 miles an hour, splatting against whatever they come in contact with, leaving a telltale mark. They hit with quite a sting and raise a lovely red welt so when you get hit, you'll know it.

The games are highly structured with an emphasis on good sportsman-ship and safety. Anyone breaking the rules will be removed from the game. According to the management, paintball causes fewer participant injuries than bowling and golf. And, lest you think paintball is a game just for young boys and grown men who act that way, a surprising number of women play here — and make formidable opponents.

All games are played outdoors on a 30-acre championship course com-prising four separate game areas. The sections I have played are very imagina-tively designed, well executed, and meticulously maintained. Game sessions last about four or five hours and you can play as long as you wish during any session. Night games are especially exhilarating and highly recommended. If you have, or can assemble, a group of ten or more players, you can schedule a private game session, day or night, on any day of the week and get yourself some discounts.

Schedules are somewhat loose and most of the local groups schedule their games for other days of the week to avoid the weekend crush. There's always a possibility that you'll be able to join a private group, so it's worth dropping by or calling in to check. Kids as young as ten may play with signed parental approval.

The basic entry cost is $25, plus tax, which includes admission, a paint-ball gun, 100 paintballs, and the mandatory face mask. If you bring your own equipment, you pay only a $10.85 admission fee. Additional paintballs (which you will need) cost extra but are reasonably priced. Make sure to dress down for your game and make sure to wear the required footgear, ei-ther boots or athletic shoes. The optional jumpsuits ($5 rental), many of them camouflaged, are highly recommended. They provide concealment and some protection from the sting of a direct hit.

Nearby: Holy Land Experience, Universal Orlando.

If paintball catches your fancy or if you're a diehard player, you may also want to check out **Orlando Paintball**, a 300,000 square foot, air-condi-tioned, indoor playing area housed in a former shipping warehouse well off the tourist track on the northeast side of Orlando. Indoor paintball is a dif-ferent experience and is best in the cooler months or when it's raining. The floor here is well cushioned with sawdust, and the low-tech layout of ply-wood and rubber tire barricades is imaginative and challenging with many dangerous cul de sacs to trap the unwary. This is sort of the urban guerilla version of paintball and vaguely reminiscent of those post-apocalypse shoot-em-up movies. A game called "Siege Camelot Castle," played in and around a two-story crusader's castle complete with turrets and towers, is especially challenging.

Prices are $20.95 per person Sunday through Thursday and $25.95 Friday and Saturday. Orlando Paintball is located at 7215 Rose Avenue, Orlando 32810. The phone is (407) 294-0694. Call for directions or check their web site at www.orlandopaintball.com.

Skate Reflections

1111 Dyer Boulevard, Kissimmee 34741
(407) 846-8469; (407) 239-8674 (from Orlando)
www.skatereflections.com

Cost:	$4 to $5; skate rentals $1
Hours:	Vary by day
Location:	Just south of Highway 192

This roller skating rink specializes in good clean fun with strict rules against smoking and gum chewing and a dress code that bans such things as "muscle shirts" and "obscene wording" on clothes. The large rink is impeccably maintained with subdued disco lighting and a small snack bar area with seating. Wednesday and Thursday nights are reserved for private parties.

Nearby: Green Meadows Farm and the many attractions along US 192.

SkyCoaster

2850 Florida Plaza Boulevard, Kissimmee 34746
(407) 397-2509

Cost:	$37 for one person, $64 for two, $81 for three
Hours:	Daily noon to midnight
Location:	On US 192 near Old Town, between Mile Markers 9 and 10

Those odd looking white towers, floodlit at night, that stick up over the Kissimmee tourist strip will lead you to SkyCoaster where for under $40 a head you can swing high and low over an artificial lake. The experience begins when you are strapped into a full body harness, on your stomach, in a prone position. Up to two friends can ride with you, with discounts for the additional riders.

Next you are hoisted 300 feet in the air to the rear tower and . . . well, dropped. But this is not bungee jumping. There is no gut-wrenching jolt at the bottom. Instead you glide suspended on stainless steel airline wire along a path mathematicians call an "arcuate curve" between the other two towers. The result is a remarkably smooth and — once you recover from the initial shock — relaxing ride. After about three swings of ever decreasing arc, you are lowered to a platform and released. For $16 you can have your adventure immortalized on video.

Nearby: Million Dollar Mulligan, Old Town, Water Mania.

SkyVenture

6805 Visitors Circle, Orlando 32819

(407) 903-1150

www.skyventure.com

Cost:	Adults $38.50, children (2 to 12) $33.50
Hours:	Monday to Friday 2:00 p.m. to midnight; Saturday and Sunday noon to midnight
Location:	Off I-Drive, opposite Wet 'n Wild

The folks that brought you SkyCoaster bring you this freefall skydiving adventure. SkyVenture is housed in an odd looking tower that packs quite a punch. Inside is a powerful fan that creates a 120 mile per hour rush of air in a vertical wind tunnel.

Following a course of instruction in the fine art of skydiving, you are suited up and walked high into the tower where, along with your instructor, you step out into mid air and learn to fly. The upwards rush of air keeps you aloft as your instructor takes your hand and shows you how to negotiate the updraft. Around you, a 360 degree virtual reality display heightens the sensation of free falling thousands of feet above the ground below. The entire experience takes about an hour, although the free fall portion lasts only about two minutes, which they say is about as much as first-timers can take. A video of your adventure costs $16.

Nearby: Fun Spot, Skull Kingdom, Universal Orlando, Wet 'n Wild.

Stallion 51

3951 Merlin Drive, Kissimmee 34741

(407) 846-4400

www.stallion51.com

Cost:	$1,950 (half hour) to $2,750 (one hour)
Hours:	Monday to Saturday, by appointment
Location:	At the Kissimmee Airport off North Hoagland Boulevard

In my *Universal Orlando* guidebook, I boldly stated that *Back to the Future* at Universal Studios Florida is the best thrill ride in Orlando. Allow me to rephrase that: *Back to the Future* is the best thrill ride in Orlando that costs less than $1,950. If you have the bucks, you might just want to enlist for an adventure that could quite literally be the thrill of a lifetime.

At the Kissimmee Airport, you can strap yourself into a beautifully maintained and painted P-51 Mustang and spend an hour soaring and swooping central Florida. These World War II vintage warbirds are powered by V-12 Rolls Royce engines and are capable of speeds up to 500 mph, although you'll be held to a more sensible 280 or 300 mph. You're not alone, of course. These Mustangs have dual-control cockpits and you ride in back, but you will have actual control of the plane at least 90% of the time — if you want to, that is.

To make doubly sure you get your money's worth, your flight is meticulously documented on video using cameras mounted on the stabilizer and the glareshield. You also get a pre/postflight briefing, a cockpit briefing, a photo, and a certificate as part of the package. If you decide you're cut out to be an aerial ace, ongoing training is a mere $3,050 an hour.

Nearby: Flying Tigers Warbird Restoration Museum, Green Meadows Farm, Warbird Adventures.

Vans Skatepark

5220 International Drive, Orlando 32819
(407) 351-3881

Cost:	$7 to $10 per session ($5 to $7 for members); membership $50 per year
Hours:	Daily 10:00 a.m. to 11:00 p.m.
Location:	Off I-Drive, near Belz Outlet Mall

Part of a nationwide chain, Vans Skatepark in Orlando is the second largest indoor skateboard facility in the world. This is the place to come to practice your skateboarding and extreme skating skills on a bewildering array of ramps, jumps, and chutes, ranging from beginner to professional level. An elevated walkway affords easy viewing and makes a visit to Vans a fun excursion even for those who would never think of attempting the wild stunts going on below.

Sessions last two hours, with the more expensive ones between 2:30 p.m. and 9:00 p.m. weekdays and all day on Saturday and Sunday. Bring a report card and for every "A" kids get $1 off a single session. Safety gear is mandatory and if you don't have your own you can rent helmet, elbow and knee pads for $5 a session. Beginners can take advantage of the daily two-hour Skate Clinics at 4:45 p.m.

Nearby: Fun Spot, Universal Orlando, Wet 'n Wild.

Warbird Adventures

233 North Hoagland Avenue, Kissimmee 34741
(407) 870-7366
www.warbirdadventures.com

Cost:	$150 (15 minutes) to $450 (one hour)
Hours:	Daily, by appointment
Location:	At the Kissimmee Airport, south of US 192

If you blanched at the cost of flying one of those Mustangs at Stallion 51 (see above), you'll be glad to know that just a short distance away, in more modest surroundings, you can fly their baby brothers at a fraction of the cost. The North American T-6/SNJ/Harvards flown here were the premier fighter-trainers of World War II, renowned for their excellence for teaching pilots and preparing them for bigger planes (like the Mustang).

The experience is similar to that offered at Stallion 51, except that here you get to pilot from the front seat. The planes are also not quite as zippy, although that will hardly matter to most folks. The Pratt and Whitney 1340 radial engines are capable of speeds up to 240 mph, although typical cruising speed during these flights is 160 mph. The three planes in the fleet are painted with the historically accurate markings of the Navy, Marines, and the Army Air Corps; you have your pick.

Warbird Adventures uses an a la carte approach to pricing. It costs $150, $250, and $450 for 15-, 30-, and 60-minute flights, with additional charges for options like aerobatics ($30), video tapes of your flight ($40), and so forth. Flights are timed from takeoff to landing.

Nearby: Flying Tigers Warbird Restoration Museum, Green Meadows Farm, Stallion 51.

World Bowling Center

7540 Canada Avenue, Orlando 32819
(407) 352-2695
www.worldbowlingcenter.com

Cost:	Adults $3.75, children $2.25, seniors (60+) $2.50 per game
Hours:	Daily noon to 11:00 p.m.
Location:	Near *Pirates Dinner Adventure*

Here is a moderately-priced, basic 32-lane bowling alley right in the heart of the I-Drive district. What makes World Bowling Center a bit out of the ordinary is the wacky decor, which features murals of astronauts bowling, among other whimsical touches. Prices are always the same, regardless of the time of day. However, on Sundays the adult price drops to $2.50 per game. Shoe rental is $2.

Nearby: Pirates Dinner Adventure, Magical Midway, Ripley's Believe It Or Not, Titanic, Wet 'n Wild.

CHAPTER FOURTEEN:

A Who's Who of Zoos

Animals have always held a fascination for us humans, especially the younger members of our species. So it's hardly surprising that in a tourist-saturated area like Orlando, you'd find a number of attractions built around this ancient allure. The attractions I describe in this chapter run the gamut from a true zoological park, to roadside attractions, to Gatorland clones, to conservation and preservation efforts; what they have in common, of course, is animals even though the context may differ from place to place. Other animal-themed attractions such as SeaWorld, Busch Gardens, and Gatorland are described in earlier chapters.

Amazing Exotics

SR 452, Umatilla 32784
(352) 821-1234
www.amazingexotics.com

Admission:	$34 to $119
Hours:	Daily by appointment
Location:	North of Eustis on SR 452

What Discovery Cove (*Chapter 3*) is to dolphins, Amazing Exotics is to servals, lynxes, lemurs, and tigers. If you ever thought what fun it would be to have a tiger sink its teeth into you, this is the place to come.

Amazing Exotics, located on a sprawling ranch on the northern fringes of the Orlando area, began as a rescue facility for macaque monkeys that escaped during the filming of the *Tarzan* movies in nearby Silver Springs. Today it is a nonprofit educational facility dedicated to caring for a variety of exotic animals (many of them show biz retirees) and training animal handlers for zoos and other animal preserves. One way the facility pays its way is by offering instructional tours and close-up animal encounters with wild beasts to folks like you and me.

The priciest option here, and the one I chose, is the **Safari Tour**. Your adventure begins in a suitably hair-raising fashion. You are handed a multi-page legal disclaimer in which you attest to your understanding that you might be maimed or even killed during your visit and that this is just fine by you. And just to make sure, they require that you initial each and every bloodcurdling paragraph. Of course dealing with any wild animal carries risks, but I suspect the real vicious animals in this scenario are the ones in three-piece suits with "esquire" at the end of their names.

After you've cheerfully signed away your right to sue, a charming young animal handler, most likely a recent graduate of Amazing Exotics' training program, takes small groups of people on a tour of the compound's extensive collection of animals. It's a bit like a visit to the zoo except that all of the animals here have a personal story — one is a rescued throwaway, another a former Las Vegas star — and a personal relationship with your tour guide. The narration has the usual tidbits of natural history lore but the emphasis is on the nuts and bolts and challenges of caring for these animals. It's an insider's viewpoint and it offers the visitor an unusual perspective on the ironies of working with caged wild animals. The guide's enthusiasm is contagious and I'm sure that most of the guests contemplate a career change at some point during the tour.

But the main attraction, and the reason people shell out serious money to take the Safari Tour, is the chance to get up close and personal with animals that few people are lucky enough to approach closely, let alone touch. There are three separate animal encounters, with small cats, primates, and large cats. Which exact animals you might interact with when you visit is hard to predict. It will depend to some extent which animals are how old at the time of your visit and which animals seem to be in the right mood to tolerate a bunch of fawning tourists. (One of the major elements in the training program is the fine art of how to "read" an animal's facial expression and body language.)

During the small cat encounter, I was able to pose with and pet a regal serval (a large-eared spotted cat from northern Africa that was a favorite of ancient Egyptian royalty) and a lynx. They are both beautiful animals and being able to pet them was a special thrill but, what can I say? They're cats and they studiously ignored the tourists who were so captivated by them. The lynx took far more interest in a passing beetle than in any of us. Far more enjoyable was the primate encounter which took place indoors with a brown lemur, two small siamang apes, and two capuchin monkeys, one of them a minuscule specimen that had been born prematurely and would never reach full size. We adults sat crossed-legged on the floor while the primates literally bounced off the walls and off us, landing on our heads and shoulders, licking our hair and swinging from our arms. It was as much fun as, well, a barrel full of monkeys.

The finale is the big cat encounter. During our tour I had heard of a five-month-old tiger cub named Apollo and asked if we could visit with him as our big cat encounter. All the other tour guests seconded the motion and, after some discussion, it was decided that Apollo and his handler could oblige us. While the small cats ignored us, Apollo seemed to see us as a chance to practice bringing down large prey and he made regular attempts on our legs. He sure looked adorable and cuddly but he was a wiry little guy with incredibly sharp teeth. Petting a tiger cub had long been a dream for me, so the scrape on my calf was a small price to pay. (In fact, I went out of my way to brag about it in the days that followed, much to my wife's embarrassment.)

Amazing Exotics is the antithesis of a theme park, which is a major part of its immense charm. Staff members wear faded blue jeans with gaping holes at the knees or wander about stripped to the waist, showing off rippling muscles and lavish tattoos. The facility is launching a major expansion and perhaps things will be less casual by the time you visit, but I certainly hope not.

The three-hour Safari Tour described above costs $119 from November through February and $94 the rest of the year. The two-hour **Encounter Tour** includes an encounter with one small cat and the primates and costs $54 year round. The one and a half hour **Discovery Tour** costs $34 year round and only includes the behind the scenes tour with no animal encounters. Since Amazing Exotics is a bona fide nonprofit organization, no tax is added to these prices and the admission price is treated as a contribution, making it tax deductible (at least for US citizens).

Reservations are mandatory. When you call, you will be booked for a specific time and you are expected to arrive promptly. Since slots for the Safari and Encounter Tours are strictly limited, it is advisable to book as far in advance as possible.

To reach Amazing Exotics from Orlando drive north on US 441, to SR 19 north, to CR 452. When you see the sign that welcomes you to Marion County, look for the entrance on your right. Depending on where in Orlando you start your journey, the trip should take about an hour and a quarter to an hour and a half.

Nearby: Not a thing. This really is the country.

Audubon Center for Birds of Prey
1101 Audubon Way, Maitland 32751
(407) 644-0190
www.adoptabird.org

Admission:	Adults $5; children (4 to 12) $4; children under 4 **free**
Hours:	Tuesday to Sunday 10:00 a.m. to 4:00 p.m.
Location:	East of I-4, between Exits 46 and 47

One of the most enchanting animal encounters to be found in the Orlando area is also one of the cheapest. The Center for Birds of Prey is an endeavor of the Florida Audubon Society. Each year it takes in about 650 wounded and orphaned raptors from all over Florida, tends to their wounds, and nurses them back to health with the ultimate goal of releasing them back into the wild. About 40% make it.

You won't be able to see the rehabilitation process; these birds are shielded from public view lest they become habituated to humans, thus lessening their odds for survival back in the wild. You will be able to see the "flight barn" and the "rehabilitation mews," odd looking structures with slatted wooden walls, in which injured birds are nursed back to health.

You can also see, in a series of attractive aviaries, birds whose injuries are so severe that they cannot be released. Here they lead the good life (at least they eat well and regularly) and perform a useful role in educating Florida school children and others about the wonders of wildlife and the need to protect it. There are about 32 different species of raptors housed here. They range from tiny screech owls to vultures. There are also a fair number of ospreys, red-tailed hawks, kites, and others. A pair of bald eagles, Prairie and T.J., are particularly fascinating. A short video tells the story of their offbeat love affair and touching attempts to have young.

A visit here can be an educational as well as an uplifting experience. While here, I learned for the first time of the 1916 Migratory Bird Treaty Act, which makes it illegal to own or transport even a single feather from these birds. The Center collects every feather from molting birds, as well as feathers from specimens that don't survive. They are turned over to the government which in turn distributes them to Native American tribes for whom the feathers of eagles and other species have ritual significance.

A boardwalk leads down to a charming gazebo set in the wetlands along the shore of Lake Sybelia. From here you will be able to use binoculars to glimpse the birds exercising in the flight barn. A small museum tells the history of the Florida Audubon Society. Guided tours are available by reservation for groups of 10 or more and it's a good idea to call ahead to find out when volunteers will be on hand to answer questions. If a group comes through while you are visiting, feel free to join it. Finding Birds of Prey is a little tricky but it's worth it. Call ahead for detailed directions.

Nearby: Maitland Art Center, Maitland Historical Museum.

Back to Nature Wildlife Refuge

18515 East Colonial Drive, Orlando 32820
(407) 568-5138
www.btn-wildlife.org

Admission:	**Free**. Donations requested
Hours:	Daily 9:00 a.m. to 4:00 p.m.
Location:	East of central Orlando

Located incongruously next to an auto repair shop, with which it shares an office, this nonprofit organization is dedicated to the four R's — Rescue, Raise, Rehabilitate, and Release. In the average year, it plays host to some 1,500 critters, but unlike Birds of Prey (see above), Back To Nature Wildlife Refuge takes on all comers, except common household pets like dogs and cats. The ultimate goal is to release their charges back into the wild, a goal that often proves illusive. What you will see when you visit are the animals that, for a variety of reasons, will be living out their lives in captivity. Many of the cages are marked with the nicknames and histories of their occupants.

The tales told about these animals are a litany of abuse, abandonment, stupidity, and the random cruelty of nature and (more often) mankind. There's a fox presumably abandoned by its owner, but not before he lopped off its tail for a souvenir. There are "throw away" pets sold by unscrupulous dealers and abandoned when their owners discovered that porcupines, raccoons, and wild African cats don't make the charming pets they'd imagined. Then there are the birds and beasts damaged by pesticides or wounded by bullets. There are also many animals orphaned in the wild or born with disabilities that would have quickly killed them had they not been rescued first. Among the more impressive residents here are cougars, bobcats, bald eagles, and a hybrid wolf. A small nursery looks after the littlest guests, including baby raccoons and fledgling birds.

Back To Nature is a labor of love of David and Carmen Shaw and a dedicated group of volunteers. Donations are requested subtly via donation boxes scattered throughout the property. Many of the animal enclosures bear the names of donors who made them possible. It is unlikely that you will leave without becoming a donor yourself.

Nearby: C.A.R.E. Foundation, Fort Christmas Historical Park, Jungle Adventures.

C.A.R.E Foundation

P.O. Box 1012, Christmas 32709
(407) 482-4092

www.thecarefoundation.org

Admission:	**Free**; donations requested
Hours:	Sunday 11:00 a.m. to 2:00 p.m.
Location:	Three miles north of SR 50 on Fort Christmas Road

C.A.R.E. stands for Creating Animal Respect Education. Like nearby Back To Nature, it is a scrappy little nonprofit organization dedicated to rescuing abandoned animals, with an accent on "exotics." You will find it down a dirt road past an orange grove in a ramshackle collection of barns and volunteer-built animal pens. It's worth seeking out.

Among the more impressive animals here are an immense Siberian tiger, a leopard, a jaguar, two pumas, and several gorgeous Florida panthers. There are also homelier charges like Daphney, a duck with a broken beak, and Truffles, a Vietnamese potbellied pig, who have become the best of friends.

Visitors are treated to a guided tour by a friendly and knowledgeable volunteer. You'll learn the stories behind the animals and may even get to pet one or two. Entertainment is provided by the exercise sessions the animals are given in the large, communal exercise pen. On a recent visit I watched in delight as two volunteers romped and wrestled with a young Florida black bear. The facility is open to the public only on Sunday and just for a few hours. The best advice is to arrive promptly at 11:00 a.m. so as not to miss any of these sessions.

C.A.R.E. helps support itself by taking its animals to Orlando area shopping centers and such for educational displays. Check the web site for a calendar of upcoming public events.

Nearby: Back To Nature, Fort Christmas Historical Park, Jungle Adventures, Orlando Wetlands Park.

Central Florida Zoological Park

3755 NW Highway 17-92, Sanford 32747
(407) 323-4450; fax (407) 323-2341
www.centralfloridazoo.org

Admission:	Adults $7, children (3 to 12) $3, seniors (60+) $4 ($2 on Tuesdays), half price for all Thursdays 9 a.m. to 10:00 a.m.; **free** parking
Hours:	Daily 9:00 a.m. to 5:00 p.m. Closed Thanksgiving and Christmas
Location:	From I-4 Exit 52 drive south on US 17-92 and follow signs, less than a mile.

The Central Florida Zoo can't hold a candle to its bigger cousins in the Bronx and San Diego, but it does wonders with what it has. The collection is small, with an understandable strength in local species, many of which will be found in the excellent herpetarium (snake house). Among the more "exotic" species are two elephants, a hippo, a clouded leopard, and cheetahs in a lovely habitat viewed through one-way glass. Newer arrivals here include a rare and endangered Amur leopard and some delightfully colorful Hyacinth macaws.

What makes this zoo special is its design and layout. A series of lovely boardwalks carries you between exhibits that are graciously arrayed under a sheltering canopy of oaks. Especially nice is the **Florida Nature Walk** that snakes through a wooded and swampy area of the zoo grounds. Signs along the way do an excellent job of explicating Central Florida fauna and explaining the way in which minor differences in altitude produce major differences in plant life. There are many similar "nature walks" in the Orlando area; this one does the best job of making a stroll both an aesthetic and educational experience.

On weekends and holidays there are animal demonstrations involving the elephants, along with primate and feline feeding programs. Volunteer "docents" also roam the park with one of some 40 species used for educational purposes. You may get a chance to touch a boa or pet a possum. The zoo has a barebones snack bar, serving inexpensive hot dog and burger fare, with a lovely outdoor seating area nearby. Across from the entrance there are sheltered picnic tables and barbecue pits.

Green Meadows Farm

1368 South Poinciana Boulevard, Kissimmee 34741
(407) 846-0770
www.greenmeadowsfarm.com

Admission:	$15, including tax, for all those 3 years old and up; Florida residents $13; annual pass $35
Hours:	Daily 9:30 a.m. to 4:00 p.m.
Location:	Six miles south of Highway 192

This is where kids meet kids — and piglets, and ducklings, and chicks. If you have little ones between the ages of three and seven, this cleverly conceived and well-run petting farm is sure to be a favorite memory of their Orlando visit. Better yet, let their grandparents take them! Green Meadows is an ideal place for this sort of trans-generational bonding experience. Meanwhile, you and your spouse can take the in-room jacuzzi out for a spin.

The ethos of Green Meadows Farm is pretty well summed up by the quote from Luther Burbank that greets you on your arrival: "Every child should have mudpies, frogs, grasshoppers, waterbugs, tadpoles, mud turtles, elderberries, wild strawberries, acorns, chestnuts, trees to climb, animals to pet, hay fields, pine cones, rocks to roll, lizards, huckleberries, and hornets. Any child who has been deprived of these has been deprived of the best part of their education."

Green Meadows Farm is spread out over 40 acres under the dappled shade of moss-draped Southern oaks. The farm is experienced via a guided tour that lasts about two hours. If the park is busy, you may be asked to wait until the next tour begins but on slower days you'll be escorted to the tour in progress. ("When you get back to the chickens, you'll know the tour's over.") If you like, you can simply stay with the tour and repeat it over and over.

The tour includes a short ride on a miniature railway and a bumpy tractor-powered hayride, but the real stars of the show are the animals. This is not a working farm but more of a "farm zoo" with widely spaced pens holding a fairly representative cross section of American farm animals. There are also a few more exotic species, like llama, buffalo, and ostriches, that are showing up on your trendier farms. Visitors can enter most of the pens for a close-up encounter. This is the city kid's chance to hold a chicken, pet a baby pig, feed a goat, milk a cow, chase a goose, and meet a turkey that has yet to be served at Thanksgiving. Squawking guinea hens and stately peacocks (including a stunning all-white specimen) roam freely about the grounds. And, of course, there is a pony ride. The little ones love every minute. For doting parents and grandparents, it's a photographic field day.

The tour guides are the antithesis of theme park attendants. There are no spiffy uniforms or carefully rehearsed spiels here. These folks look and talk like they're down on the farm, dirty jeans and all. It's truly refreshing. But don't expect to escape the edutainment. You'll be treated to spot quizzes ("Who can tell me what a baby goose is called?") and little known facts ("The pig is a very clean animal.") as the guide shepherds you from pen to pen. Thanks to this tour I now know that the gestation period of a Vietnamese potbellied pig is three months, three weeks, and three days.

Of course everyone's favorites are the farm babies, and you can increase your odds of seeing them by visiting during the spring or around harvest time. During October there is pumpkin picking, another winner with the wee set.

There's little in the way of food here. At the General Store (or the Chuck Wagon during busier months) you can get sandwiches for about $3 and ice cream bars for about half that. Soft drinks are available from vending machines. You can also bring a cooler and have a picnic. Judging from the number of tables provided, quite a few people do just that.

Remember to wear sensible shoes — this is a farm, after all, and after a rain, it can get muddy. The tour is long and covers a fair amount of ground.

You can rent a "little red wagon" for $3 in which to lug the kids.

Nearby: Old Town, Water Mania.

Jungle Adventures

26205 East Colonial Drive, Christmas 32709

(407) 568-2885

www.jungleadventures.com

Admission:	Adults $16, children (3 to 11) $8.50, seniors (60+) $12.50, all plus tax
Hours:	Daily 9:30 a.m. to 5:30 p.m.
Location:	On SR 50, about 17 miles east of Orlando

It's hard to miss Old Swampy. He's a 200-foot foam and cement alligator stretched smilingly alongside SR 50 on the way to the Space Coast. Step into (or more precisely, around) his jaws and you enter Jungle Adventures, a small attraction that has many things in common with Gatorland (see *Chapter 5*) but a few unique surprises of its own.

At its most basic, Jungle Adventures is a small zoo with a familiar cast of characters — two black bears (Boris and Natasha), some spider monkeys, some crocs, macaws and cockatoos, and a small collection of injured birds of prey, including two bald and two golden eagles. The zoo's most distinguished specimens are its big cats, two hybrid panther-cougars (siblings Sparkles and Junior) and two young tigers (Tiananmen, a Bengal, and Tanya, a Siberian). But mostly there are alligators. Like Gatorland, Jungle Adventures is part of a larger alligator farming operation. There are some 200 gators living in the 20-acre park but just a stone's throw away are 10,000 more being grown out for their skin and meat.

What sets Jungle Adventures apart, and makes a visit worth consideration, are its fascinating setting and its shows. The setting is in the midst of a swamp, with the main zoo across a bridge and completely surrounded by water fed from a sulfurous spring. At first it seems that there's something terribly wrong with the water; it's completely covered by what looks like a chartreuse slime. Actually, it's duckweed, a tiny four-leafed water plant that grows in the billions. It adds a marvelously primordial touch to the alligators that swim through it, coating their horny hides with gooey green.

Two short **jungle nature trails** take you around the back of the animal cages and let you take a close look at the natural Florida setting from the safety of a boardwalk.

The shows at Jungle Adventures are refreshingly low key, one might almost say amateurish, although in the very best sense of the term. There are three shows and a boat ride that are timed so that you can move seamlessly from one to the next. A complete cycle takes about two and a half hours and there are four cycles each day.

The 15-minute **pontoon boat ride** circles the island zoo as gators swish thorough the duckweed, leaving a telltale trail in the green coating on the water's surface. Along the way, your guide tells tales of Jungle Adventures' past and present, and its future plans. An eclectic **animal show** features a small alligator which everyone gets a chance to hold while their picture is taken. Next comes a passel of snakes, draped languorously on the presenter's shoulders, followed by the opportunity to watch the guide feed the pan-ther-cougars and four wolves.

In the **Indian Village** tour that follows, you will hear about the Calusa, Seminole, and Cherokee tribes and have the opportunity to buy Native American flutes, necklaces, and dream-catchers.

Finally, there is an **alligator feeding show** reminiscent of the *Jumparoo* at Gatorland. Sometimes, the gators are fed from a dock-like platform over the water, but from time to time the handler chooses to work the shore, drawing the enormous reptiles from the green waters to leap and snap just a few feet away from the audience. Even for those who have toured Gatorland, this will be an exciting spectacle.

The staff is young and wonderfully free of the heavily rehearsed spiels that some parks insist on using. Also, Jungle Adventures doesn't draw the larger crowds that the Orlando attractions have to deal with, so there's more occasion for an easy give and take between the staff and the visitors. It can be a lot of fun.

Nearby: Fort Christmas Historical Park, Midway Airboat Tours.

Jungleland Zoo

4580 West Irlo Bronson Highway, Kissimmee 34746
(407) 396-1012
www.junglelandzoo.com

Admission: Adults $14.95, children (3 to 11) $9.95, se-niors (55+) $12.95, all plus tax; AAA, AARP, and military discounts

Hours: Daily 9:00 a.m to 6:00 p.m.

Location: 6 miles east of I-4; 2 miles east of SR 535

The 120-foot plaster alligator outside might make you think this is a Gatorland clone but, while Jungleland has a first-rate gator show, it is pri-marily a small zoo specializing in "exotic" animals, including a number of big cats who have their own show.

Plan your visit around the schedule for the shows which begin at about 10:00 a.m. and end around 3:00 in the afternoon. The latest you can arrive and see all the shows is 2:00, but the schedules can vary, so call ahead. The

Bushmasters Gator Show takes place three times every day. This 25-minute display is first-rate "edutainment" and well worth the price of admission. Jungleland compresses all its gator lore and trivia into this single show, whereas Gatorland spreads it out over your entire visit. Otherwise the shows are very similar, although I'd have to give the edge to Jungleland.

The show takes place in a 300-seat outdoor amphitheater with shaded seating areas. If you drop by early, you may be able to see the gator wrangler lasooing a likely looking co-star from the nearby gator pond. Once inside the arena, the wrangler puts the uncooperative gator through its paces, showing off its teeth and gaping maw. He also holds the gator's jaws shut with his chin, the piece de resistance of every gator wrestling show.

This show offers a different version of the origin of gator wrestling from the one I heard at Gatorland, attributing the practice to the Seminole Indians who hunted gators in this fashion for their skin and meat. Hunters usually worked in pairs, with one getting on the gator's back and clamping its jaws shut while his partner tied the jaws shut for the trip back to market. The trick of pulling back the gator's head and holding its jaws with the chin was developed, according to this version, by lone hunters who didn't want to share the sale price with a partner. By holding the jaws with their chin, they were able to free their hands to tie the gator's jaws shut single-handed. All in all, the Jungleland version has the ring of truth to it.

Every bit as good as the gator show (better, if you're a big cat fan) is the **Cat Show**, which takes place in a wooden arena toward the back of the zoo. Here a trainer shows off several tigers and a gorgeous puma, putting them through paces that are similar to a circus act, except that here the show biz razzle dazzle is replaced by fascinating facts about these magnificent creatures and a somber warning about their odds of surviving in the wild. The same trainer doubles as a magician in **Magic of the Rainforest**, which takes place in a small, dark theater near the food stand in the middle of the park. It's fairly standard magic show fare, with a variety of birds, monkeys, and other forest critters appearing and disappearing in a succession of clever tricks, as the host cites ominous statistics about the world's disappearing rainforests. In addition to the shows, there are three **primate feedings** each day.

Between the shows, stroll along the half-mile looping path through Jungleland's **zoo** which houses some 300 specimens. You can get closer to the animals here than at most zoos, and Jungleland is far less concerned about your feeding the animals than many. In fact, there are 50-cent food dispensers dotted along the route just for that purpose. There are some lovely members of the big cat family here, ranging from African leopards and lions, to brother and sister Bengal tigers, to an older Siberian tiger. The North

American cats — cougars, lynx, and bobcats — are also represented. There are some unusual felines, too, like the African caracal with its distinctive ears and the dog-sized serval, once the house cat of Egyptian royalty.

Primates are another well-represented family. My favorite is the orangutan, Radcliffe, the zoo's only large primate. Radcliffe will respond to simple hand signals — waving your hand over your head, placing it on your forehead as if you have a headache, sneezing with your hand over your nose. He also seems to respond to the verbal command, "Smile." Like any good actor, he performs more willingly if you bribe him with food.

Most people seem to spend about two and a half hours at Jungleland which is just long enough to see all the shows and visit the other animals. Don't forget to take a family snapshot by the big gator outside before you leave. A helpful sign tells you the best place to stand.

Nearby: Kartworld, Medieval Times.

Reptile World Serpentarium

5705 East Irlo Bronson Highway, St. Cloud 34771
(407) 892-6905

Admission:	Adults $5.50, students (6 to 17) $4.50, children (3 to 5) $3.50; prices include tax
Hours:	Tuesday to Sunday 9:00 a.m. to 5:30 p.m.
Location:	East of St. Cloud, about 9 miles east of Florida Turnpike Exit 244.

This unassuming cinder block and stucco building houses an impressive collection (over 50) of snakes from around the world, ranging from the familiar and innocuous to the exotic and deadly. Here you'll find the Australian taipan, considered by some to be the world's deadliest snake, as well as a splendid 18-foot king cobra. All told, there are six species of cobra and 11 kinds of rattlesnakes. There are also snakes you may never see elsewhere, like the brilliant pea green East African green mamba and its less startling but nonetheless beautiful West African cousin. The snakes are housed in modest glass-fronted pens along a darkened corridor. Snakes are the main course, but there are also a 14-foot gator sulking in a shallow, murky pool, a passel of iguanas, and a pond full of turtles.

If all Reptile World had to offer was its snake displays, it might be recommended only to the certified snake fancier. But this is a working venom farm (if that's the right term). Though there may be only 50 snakes on public display, behind the scenes are hundreds of venomous snakes just waiting to be milked for their valuable venom. Reptile World ships this precious commodity worldwide for use in medical and herpetological research. The regular milking of these dangerous snakes is done in public and makes Reptile

World more than just another snake house.

Venom shows are scheduled at noon and 3:00 p.m. daily. Sometimes the shows start a bit late, but any wait will quickly be forgotten once the show starts. After bringing out a large snake for guests to hold, owner George Van Horn retreats behind a glass wall to take care of business. About half a dozen snakes are plucked from their boxes and coaxed into sinking their fangs through a clear membrane stretched over a collection glass. The glasses range in size from small test tubes used for coral snakes to hefty pilsner glasses used for large rattlers and cobras. The view can't be beat; you are just three feet away from these fanged wonders and will be thankful for the glass window between you and the snakes.

The entire show is fascinating but the large snakes are the most impressive. The Eastern diamondback rattlesnake, the largest of its kind, bares huge fangs and spits copious venom into the collection glass. The black and white spitting cobra requires special care. As its name suggests, it spits its venom into its victim's eyes and the recommended treatment is to wash the eyes with urine. The monocled cobra, so called because of the eye-like marking on the back of its head, emerges from its box with hood flaring and head darting rapidly about. This is serious, not to mention dangerous business. Van Horn once received a near-fatal bite from a king cobra while 30 school children looked on enthralled, convinced it was part of the show.

Reptile World is on the extreme outer fringe of the Orlando tourist circuit. For anyone who has ever been fascinated by snakes, it's well worth the detour. By all means time your visit to the venom shows.

CHAPTER FIFTEEN:

Gardens & Edens

For those who feel the Orlando theme park experience is "so plastic!," help is at hand. Within the Orlando metropolitan area, or just a short ride away, are private gardens, public parks, and wilderness tracts where cool waters, fresh breezes, and quiet forests await to soothe the simulation- and stimulation-weary tourist.

The most famous man-made garden in the area, Cypress Gardens, is described in *Chapter 4*. Here I describe the Harry P. Leu Gardens, right in the heart of Orlando, and the spectacular Bok Tower Gardens in Lake Wales, a short drive from Orlando and not too far from Cypress Gardens. Of course, these attractions involve the cunning hand of man and are, in a way, just as artificial as any theme park — although some would argue they are a good deal more beautiful.

Then there are the state, county, and city parks, many of which have been only slightly modified by humans. It comes as a surprise to many visitors that the "real Florida" (to use a phrase pushed by the state's public relations campaigns) lies all around them. Just a short drive from your motel, you can hike miles and miles of pristine trails and never see another human, or swim in a crystal clear spring bubbling up from deep in the earth, or canoe down a river that still looks much as it did when the first Europeans arrived in this part of Florida.

This is nature, let us not forget, so in addition to sunscreen, a good bug repellent will come in handy for hikers. Be aware too that deer ticks carrying Lyme disease are found here. Common-sense precautions should be used with wildlife — don't pick anything up and don't feed the alligators (it's against the law!). The words to live by when visiting these beautiful areas are:

"Take nothing but pictures, kill nothing but time, leave nothing but foot-prints."

The parks listed here are just the beginning. If this type of unspoiled recreation is to your taste, you may want to venture farther afield — to Blue Springs State Park to the north, where manatees come to warm up in the winter, or to Homosassa Springs State Park to the west, or to Lake Kissimmee State Park to the south. An excellent (and free) guide to Florida's state parks is available from the Department of Environmental Protection, Division of Recreation and Parks, MS#535, 3900 Commonwealth Boulevard, Tallahassee, FL 32399-3000. Or ask for *Florida State Parks . . . the Real Florida* at the ranger station of any state park. For more on Orlando's city parks, go to the city's web site, www.cityoforlando.net, and click on "parks."

Big Tree Park
General Hutchinson Parkway, Longwood 32750
No phone

Admission:	**Free**
Hours:	Daily 8:00 a.m. to sunset
Location:	Take I-4 Exit 49, drive east on SR 434; turn left on Route 17-92 and left on General Hutchinson

Pay a brief visit to this small Seminole County park to gawk at the oldest cypress tree in the U.S. "The Senator" (nicknamed to honor the senator who donated the land) stands 126 feet high and measures 47 feet around. It's estimated that the behemoth is some 3,500 years old.

Bok Tower Gardens
1151 Tower Boulevard, Lake Wales 33853
(863) 676-1408
www.boktowergardens.org

Admission:	Adults $6, children (5 to 12) $2; **Free** for all on Saturday mornings from 8 a.m. to 9 a.m.
Hours:	Daily 8:00 a.m. to 6:00 p.m. (last admission at 5:00 p.m.)
Location:	Off Burns Avenue in Lake Wales. Take US 27 South to Mountain Lake Cutoff and follow the signs

Once upon a time, before the age of Leona Helmsley and Donald Trump, the wealthy knew how to spend their money. One such individual was Edward W. Bok, a Dutch immigrant born in 1863 who came to the United States at the age of six and made his fortune as a writer and magazine publisher. In the twenties, after his retirement, he set out to create an Eden on an unprepossessing patch of land whose only claim to fame was that it was reputedly the highest point on the Florida peninsula. He enlisted Frederick Law Olmstead, Jr. (son of the creator of New York's Central Park and a major landscape architect in his own right) to do the landscaping and hired noted architect Milton B. Medary to build a setting for a very special musical instrument. In 1929, he presented the result as a gift to the American people. The "result" is the Bok Tower and its magnificent carillon that stands majestically in the midst of an artfully designed wooded park, specifically conceived as a refuge from the bustle of "the world."

Bok Tower Gardens, now a National Historic Landmark, is a very special and a very quiet experience. Unlike nearby Cypress Gardens, where the landscaping is over-the-top and in-your-face, the effect here is far more subtle, almost ethereal. The bark-chip covered paths through the woods are meant for leisurely strolls and quiet moments alone with one's thoughts. The vistas, powerful as they are, are contemplative and softly romantic.

Olmstead's design is devilishly clever in the way he leads you to the tower. He only lets you see it when he wants you to. Your first glimpse is across a reflecting pool, framed by palm fronds and Spanish moss. Then it vanishes as you walk through a palm-fringed glade to approach more closely. Suddenly, the tower rises above you, standing on an island barely larger than its base, surrounded by a moat crossed by marble bridges and guarded by massive wrought iron gates. It's as if you have come upon a magical remnant of an ancient city in a storybook land, part cathedral, part castle keep.

The storybook aspect is heightened by the pink and gray Georgia marble that forms the tower's base and accents its flanks, the odd and complex sundial mounted on the side of the south wall, the highly polished brass door on the north, the mysterious red door behind the ornately carved balustrade above the sundial, by the very fact that you cannot cross the moat for a closer look. It must be a wondrous experience on a foggy morning.

The tower was never intended to welcome guests; the only way to get a look inside is to see the orientation film screened at the **Visitors Center** on a regular schedule. The tower exists solely to house the 60 precisely tuned bronze bells operated by a massive keyboard played with the fists. The carillon occupies the upper third of the structure. The unique sound produced by this massive instrument rolls out across the surrounding woods through 35-foot high grilles in the form of Art Deco mosaics of drooping trees and animals in colorful shades of turquoise and purple.

Every afternoon at 3:00 there is a 45-minute carillon recital. Many of the pieces played were composed specifically for carillon, others have been adapted to the unique requirements of the massive instrument. A schedule of

"Daily Carillon Music" lists the day's program, everything from old folk tunes to opera. It's a wonderful experience on a warm, sunny day and, unless you're a carillon connoisseur, probably unlike any other concert you've ever heard. When the performance is live (rather than recorded), a video monitor mounted in what appears to be a small green shelter lets you watch the carillonneur play.

Tip: Most people sit on the grass or on benches under the shady oak trees near the tower's base during the recitals. You will have a better musical experience if you move somewhat farther away. Stroll down the slope away from the tower until the tower's mosaic grilles reappear over the tops of the oak trees. Then find a spot with an unobstructed view of the top of the tower. This way, the music will roll over the tree tops and cascade down the slope towards you.

Don't leave without exploring the rest of the grounds. Past the reflecting pool that marked your approach to the tower lies an "exedra," a semicircular marble bench that looks out from the top of Iron Mountain to the west. At the northern edge of the grounds is a more recent, and ingenious, addition, the **Window By The Pond Nature Observatory**. It's a small wooden building on the lip of a pond. You sit behind a large picture window, unseen by the wildlife outside. A sign notes that this is nature's show and that the performance schedule is erratic. On the back wall are drawings of the local animals you might glimpse from your hiding place.

From here you can take a one-mile hike through the **Pine Ridge Preserve**, one of the few remaining fragments of the sort of longleaf pine forest that once covered millions of acres of the southeastern United States. Preserving this patch of woods is not as easy as it may sound. A carefully orchestrated series of controlled burns is used to mimic ageless natural processes. Otherwise, evergreen oaks would invade the habitat and eventually kill the pines with their shady branches. An informative brochure that explicates the habitat can be found at the trailhead.

The **Visitors Center** houses a modest but finely executed exhibit that provides background on Bok, the tower, and the carillon it houses. The cafeteria-style **Carillon Cafe** serves simple sandwich platters and hot dogs. A meal will cost about $6 or $7. There is also a tasteful gift shop where you can get cassettes and CDs of Bok Tower carillon recitals. It carries a good selection of books about gardening, wildlife, conservation, and Florida's natural wonders. Framed photos and posters of the gardens make nice souvenirs.

In 1970, the Bok Tower Gardens Foundation acquired the nearby **Pinewood Estate**, formerly known as "El Retiro," a palatial summer home built for a steel mogul. Although it dates to only 1929, it has the look of a much older Mediterranean villa and has been meticulously restored inside. Both the house and the grounds were designed by architects associated with the Olmstead firm. You can tour the house from October to mid-May. Tours depart daily at 11 a.m. and 1:30 p.m., by appointment only, and are limited to 12 guests. The price is $5 for adults, $4 for children 5 to 12. From Thanksgiving to Christmas, the house is decorated for the holidays and is open without reservations. For more information and reservations, call (863) 676-1408.

Bok Tower Gardens is accessible to the physically challenged. It offers complimentary wheelchairs and strollers and mobility vehicles for a fee.

Nearby: Spook Hill, Cypress Gardens.

Forever Florida and Crescent J Ranch

4755 North Kenansville Road
St. Cloud, FL 34773
(888) 957-9794
(407) 957-9794
www.foreverflorida.com

Admission:	**Free** admission and parking; there is a charge for most activities
Hours:	Daily 8:00 a.m. to 9:00 p.m.
Location:	Take US 192 east from Kissimmee for about 24 miles to Holopaw; turn south on US 441 for about 7 miles to the entrance on your left. (The address given above is the corporate office.)

Did you know that wild hogs kill more people than any other wild animal? Did you know that red carpet lichen grows only where the air is especially pure? Did you know that the berries of poison ivy plants are the sole source of vitamin C for the animals of Florida's forests? These are just a few of the fascinating facts you'll learn as you explore a patch of the "real Florida" that is as much a family affair as it is a tourist attraction.

Forever Florida was founded by Dr. Bill Broussard as a living monument to his son Allen, a devoted ecologist who died well before his time. The attraction combines Dr. Broussard's ranch (he's a tenth generation rancher as well as an ophthalmologist) with a swampy wilderness tract next door that had been sold in parcels as part of a classic Florida land scam back in the sixties. It was in these woods, that young Allen fell in love with Nature and found his vocation. Also part of Forever Florida is the former country retreat of another doctor, whose house will be converted into a bed and breakfast and whose private grass airstrip welcomes fly-ins so long as they call ahead.

You begin your visit to Forever Florida at the **Visitor Center**, which contains a gift shop and restaurant. Near the Visitor Center are a free **petting**

zoo and pony rides ($8 by reservation). But the real attraction here is access to the nearby wilderness, much of which has remained untouched by the hand of man, despite the fact that this part of Florida was a thriving logging center in the nineteenth century.

You can reach the wilds in a number of ways: by foot, on a trail bike, on horseback, by horse-drawn covered wagon, or on a wacky-looking green "Cracker Coach" designed by Dr. Broussard and unique to Forever Florida. Most people choose the last alternative.

Your tour vehicle is a 32-seat open-sided coach raised well above the ground on large tractor tires. The bucket seats are comfortable and the tour guides extremely knowledgeable experts, many with degrees in biology or ecology.

There are several tours a day, but I highly recommend the sunset tour, which leaves at about 6:00 p.m. in the warmer months. Not only do you avoid the heat of the day, but you are more likely to see the local wildlife which is smart enough to avoid the blazing midday sun. On the tour I took, we sighted white-tailed deer, armadillos, gators, wild turkey, and gopher tortoises. We even sighted some of those elusive wild hogs, albeit in hog traps. One lucky tour group sighted the Florida panther that roams this preserve. There are fewer than 30 left in the wild, so don't count on seeing one on your visit. Photographers should make sure to bring along their best telephoto lenses.

The highlight of the tour is the narration by your guide. These folks love this scruffy patch of Florida wilderness and it shows. They mix an in-depth knowledge of the local ecology with a passion for its preservation. You will leave this tour knowing why you should never buy cypress mulch for your garden and why wild hogs (descended from those abandoned by the Spaniards when they discovered there was no gold in Florida) should be removed from the Florida ecosystem. In fact, you will see ample evidence of the damage the preserve's estimated 800 hogs inflict on the local ecology. Those trapped hogs, by the way, are fattened up on yummy farm feed and then relocated elsewhere or given away to local groups for barbecues.

The **motorized tours** cost $28 ($18 for children 5 to 12; kids under five are free) and last about two and a half hours. This is also the only tour given at sunset. The horse- or mule-drawn **covered wagon tours** last about one hour and cost the same but must be reserved in advance. The **guided horseback tours** are offered daily, by reservation only, and cost $35 for one hour, $48 for two, and $52 for three. There is no reduced price for children on these tours. Trail bike rentals are $8 an hour ($5 for children 12 and under). The hiking fee is a flat $5.

The restaurant offers a straightforward and familiar menu of country-style cooking, although you are not likely to find the Fried Gator Tail Plate on too many other local menus. Sandwiches range from about $2 to $4, while the more elaborate steak, chicken, and catfish platters range from $5 to $15. Homey desserts are about $3. The restaurant opens at 11:00 a.m. during the week and at 7:00 a.m. on weekends, when a country breakfast with grits and a biscuit is offered for $4. The gift shop sells clothing, some interesting crafts, and books on Florida ecology and cooking.

Forever Florida offers an evolving menu of special events and programs. One recent offering was a two-night sleepover for kids that included a nighttime outing to find nocturnal critters. To celebrate Earth Day, the preserve hosted "Cracker Survivor Island" inspired by the TV show. Typically, when a special event is on, there will be a modest parking charge. Call ahead or check the web site to see what's going to be on during your visit.

Katie's Wekiva River Landing

190 Katie's Cove, Sanford 32771
(407) 628-1482 (from Orlando); (407) 322-4470 (from Sanford)
www.ktland.com

Cost:	Canoe runs: Adults $16.50 to $25, depending on canoe route and number in party; children (3 to 11) half price. Canoe rentals: $14.50 minimum (for 2 hours) up to $25 maximum per day. A 7% sales tax is added to all fees.
Hours:	Daily 8:00 a.m. to sunset
Location:	Take I-4 Exit 51, go west on SR 46 for 5 miles, then right onto Wekiva Park Drive for 1 mile

What easier way to appreciate the pristine wilderness of the "real Florida" than to glide gently past it in a canoe? Katie's is a small RV and camper resort along the banks of the Wekiva River that offers canoe excursions along some of Central Florida's most beautiful waterways. There are six expeditions to choose from.

The Little Wekiva River Run is their most popular and it's easy to see why. The scenery is drop-dead gorgeous and there are plenty of turtles and birds to be seen. You might also glimpse an alligator. The shoreline varies from well-manicured backyards to impenetrable jungles. They estimate five to six hours for this nine-mile trip, although inexperienced paddlers may take longer. The Rock Springs Run is a 19-mile, all day marathon and paddlers have the option of making it an overnight trip (for an additional $10.50), with primitive camping in Wekiva State Park. For these trips, you are driven to drop-off points upstream and end your trip back at Katie's.

Two other trips head downstream from Katie's and require that you arrive at pick- up points by specified times. They are the St. John's River Run (6 miles, 2 to 3 hours) and the Blue Springs Run (12 miles, 5 to 6 hours). The latter involves some six miles on the St. John's River with its motorized traffic and is recommended for experienced canoers only. Both these trips require a minimum of four adults. If you'd like to spend the night, Katie's can accommodate you in one of six air-conditioned log cabins. Rates are $60 double per night with a two-night minimum or $375 for the week. RVs pay $20 per day for two people plus $2 per day for each additional person age two or older. Campers get a 20% discount on canoe rentals.

Nearby: Rock Springs Run State Reserve, Wekiva Falls Resort, Wekiwa Springs State Park.

Kelly Park, Rock Springs

Kelly Park Drive, Apopka
(407) 889-4179
http://parks.onetgov.net/15kelly.htm

Admission:	Adults and children $1, children under 5 are **free.**
Hours:	Daily 9:00 a.m. to 7:00 p.m. in summer; 8:00 a.m. to 6:00 p.m. in winter
Location:	Take Rock Springs Road north from Apopka, then right onto Kelly Park Road and follow signs

This 248-acre Orange County park is built around one of the Apopka area's crystal clear springs. As its name suggests, Rock Springs bubbles up from a cleft in a rock outcropping and, instead of spreading out into a pool, becomes a swiftly running stream that quickly slows to a meander. The activity of choice here, and the major reason for the park's obvious popularity, is riding down the stream in an inner tube or on a float.

Kids, and not a few grown-ups, jump into the headwaters by the dozens and bob and splash their way downstream for about a mile. The trip takes about 25 minutes at a leisurely float. There are exits from the river along the way and an excellently maintained network of boardwalks (with flooring designed to protect the barefooted) let you carry your tube back to the beginning for another go. You can also go down without a tube but, for most adults at least, the stream is too shallow for swimming during most of its course. At the middle of the tubing course, the stream blossoms into a series of lagoons and pools that form the centerpiece of the park. This is the place to come for a cooling, if somewhat crowded, swim. Or join the sunbathers thronging the shores and islands. This is a great park for kids and, if you don't have any, you may feel a bit overwhelmed by other people's.

Tubes are not available in the park, so unless you bring your own, stop at one of the tube rental shops near the park entrance. The cost is modest, about $3 for a day's rental.

Most of the rest of the park is given over to nicely shaded picnic tables, most with a barbecue nearby. The park also offers camping sites ($10 a night for Orange County residents, $15 for all others); electricity is another $3. Your admission receipt lets you leave the park and return the same day. No pets are allowed in the park, and there's no fishing here.

Leu Gardens

1920 North Forest Avenue, Orlando, 32803
(407) 246-2620; fax (407) 246-2849
www.leugardens.org

Admission:	Adults $4, children (grades K–12) $1.
Hours:	Daily 9:00 a.m. to 5:00 p.m. Closed Christmas day.
Location:	Take I-4 Exit 43 (Princeton Street), go east to Mills (US 17-92) and turn right. Turn left on Virginia Drive and follow signs

Strolling through Harry P. Leu's magnificent formal gardens on the shores of Lake Rowena, it's hard to believe that you're in the heart of the city, just a short drive from the bustling "Centroplex" as Orlando rather inelegantly refers to its central business district. There's nothing inelegant about this luxurious estate, however. Deeded to the city by a local industrial supplies magnate and amateur botanist, the 50 acres of manicured grounds and artfully designed gardens offer a delicious respite from the cares of the world.

Camellias were Harry Leu's first love and the place is full of them — over 2,000, making this the largest documented collection of camellias in North America. But there are many other trees, flowers, and ornamental plants to catch the fancy of amateur gardeners, who will appreciate the meticulous signage which provides the full scientific name for the thousands of species represented. They can flag down a passing staff member, who will be more than happy to answer their questions. The rest of us will simply enjoy strolling through this artfully constructed monument to the gardener's art, stopping now and then to smell the roses.

The estate is given over to a number of gardens which blend seamlessly one into another. Camellias bloom under tall Southern oaks dripping with Spanish moss in the North and South woods, while the palm garden allows botanists to test the hardiness of various species during the nippy Central

Florida winters. In the center is a formal rose garden that is at its best from April through October. The Tropical Spring Garden features tropical vines and plants that are native to or can be grown in Florida. By the lake, the aquatic wetland garden is home to swamp hibiscus, lizard's tail, loblolly, and dwarf wax myrtle, all under the shade of stately cypress trees. And don't miss the small hothouse tucked away in a corner of the estate. There you will find orchids, ferns, aroids, and other cold-sensitive plants.

Another not-to-be-missed highlight is the 50-foot floral clock. The mechanism was purchased in Scotland and now sits on an intricately planted sloping hill at the foot of a formal garden. Later, a stroll down to the lake takes you past the Ravine Garden, lush with tropical plants. At the water's edge a spacious wooden terrace offers a peaceful spot to sit and admire the wading birds. Benches and a gazebo encourage you to sit and stay awhile. Your patience may be rewarded with a glimpse of Lake Rowena's resident eight-foot alligator.

Every half hour from 10:00 a.m. to 3:30 p.m., volunteers conduct tours through the **Leu house**. Don't miss it. You'll be treated to a wonderfully gossipy recounting of the building's evolution, through several changes of ownership, from humble farm house to rich man's estate, spiced with tales of a sheriff gunned down in the line of duty and a home-wrecking New York actress. (That's her as Cleopatra in the photo in the living room.) Nearby is a cemetery in which the unfortunate lawman lies buried with many of his kin.

The antebellum-style **Garden House**, where you pay your modest admission to the gardens, houses a 900-volume horticultural library (open to visitors) and spacious meeting rooms. The terrace at the back of the building offers a stunning view of the lake. There are frequent arts and crafts exhibits in the Garden House, as well as a regular schedule of musical events. Wheelchairs are available free of charge.

A small gift shop offers a tasteful array of floral themed merchandise, including birdhouses, garden tools and accessories, and other small items. Leu Gardens t-shirts range from $10 up. There is a small selection of educational toys aimed at awakening a youngster's interest in gardening and nature. There are also hundreds of gardening books on sale here.

Pets are not allowed in either the gardens or the houses.

Nearby: Mennello Museum of Folk Art, Orlando Museum of Art, Orlando Science Center.

Orlando Wetlands Park

Wheeler Road, Christmas
(407) 568–1706

Admission: **Free**

Hours:	Daily, January 21 to September 30 only, Sunrise to sunset
Location:	East on SR 50, then left on County Road 420 (Ft. Christmas Road); go 2.3 miles and turn right onto Wheeler Road

Tucked away on the far eastern fringes of Orlando is an ingenious combination of the practical and the aesthetic. To the untrained eye, the "Iron Bridge Easterly Wetlands" that comprise this park look like a preserved sliver of the "real" Florida. It is, in fact, part of the City of Orlando's wastewater treatment system. Every day, 16 million gallons of highly treated reclaimed wastewater from parts of Orange and Seminole counties are pumped into this 1,200-acre, man-made wetlands where aquatic plants continue the process of removing nutrients as the water slowly makes its way to the St. John's River. If visions of open sewers spring to mind, banish them. The result is enchanting, combining open fields, gently rolling woods, a small lake, and a thick forest.

In the parking area, go to the wooden announcement board. There you can sign in (don't forget to sign out!) and pick up a park map and a *Field Checklist of Birds*. The best way to get acquainted with the park is to walk (or jog) the four-mile "walk/jog loop." If you'd like, you can veer off onto a more primitive hiking trail through the woods; it eventually rejoins the main trail. The map thoughtfully points out the best bird-watching spots along the park's 18 miles of raised roads. More than 150 species frequent the park. The *Checklist* lists them and the seasons in which they visit and notes whether they are common, uncommon, or rare.

Biking is permitted on the berm roads and there is a sheltered picnic area in a broad grassy area near the parking lot. The Florida Trail skirts the property, allowing serious hikers to extend their explorations. The Orlando Wetlands Park is a bit out of the way (it is about a 40-minute drive east of the city), but a visit will reward bird watchers and those looking for a more exciting jogging trail than the motel parking lot.

Nearby: Back to Nature Wildlife Refuge, C.A.R.E., Fort Christmas Historical Park, Jungle Adventures, Tosohatchee Reserve.

Osceola District Schools Environmental Study Center

4300 Poinciana Boulevard, Kissimmee 34758
(407) 870-0551

Admission:	**Free**
Hours:	Saturday 10:00 a.m. to 5:00 p.m.; Sunday noon to 5:00 p.m.
Location:	13 miles south of Highway 192

During the week, this 19-acre patch of Reedy Creek Swamp serves as an educational resource for the school children of Osceola County. On weekends, it's open to the public and well worth a visit from the wildlife-loving tourist. In the winter and spring, you might even be able to spot a nesting bald eagle.

Begin at the Visitors Center, which houses one of the best introductions and reference guides to Central Florida wildlife you are likely to find. If you've spotted some critter that you couldn't identify, you'll probably find it here. Most impressive are the taxidermy of birds like the bald eagle and osprey. There are also stuffed panthers and black bears. Most of these specimens were killed accidentally, typically by an automobile. Now they help teach school kids. These three-dimensional examples are supplemented by quite lovely color photographs of the native species taken right here at the Study Center. On another wall are photos of the local flora. Add to this charts of bird silhouettes and animal tracks and you have a remarkably complete resource for enjoying the Florida wilderness. Pick up a free copy of *The Reedy Creek Swamp Nature Guide* and the trail guides to guide the rest of your visit.

There are three short trails to explore. An 1,800-foot raised walkway takes you into Reedy Creek Swamp and its 400-year-old cypress trees. At the end, an observation platform lets you eavesdrop on the osprey nests. The short Pine Woods Trail features a reconstruction of the portable logging railroads that once ferried felled trees out of the swamp. The rails were made by Krupp, the famous German industrial giant. Another trail leads to a modest Indian mound formed by snail shells discarded by the aboriginal inhabitants. A small picnic area is available.

Nearby: Green Meadows Farm.

Rock Springs Run State Reserve

SR 433, Apopka
(407) 884-2008; (407) 884-2009 - recorded information
www.dep.state.fl.us/parks/district3/rocksprings/index.asp

Admission:	$4 per vehicle (up to 8 people); $1 for walk-ins and bikers
Hours:	Daily 8:00 a.m. to sunset
Location:	From I-4 (Exit 51), take SR 46 West about 7 miles; turn left onto route 433

This sprawling park is bounded by Rock Springs Run and the Wekiva River, which might suggest that water activities abound. Not so. There is no water access and a sign at the gate directs you to nearby resorts and parks if that's what you have in mind.

What the Reserve has to offer, in abundance, is solitude and well-maintained hiking trails that meander through 8,750 acres of the kind of terrain that's referred to as "Florida's Desert." Depending on how far you trek, you'll see sand pine scrub, pine flatwoods, bayheads, hammocks, and a few swamps. Depending on how lucky you are, you may glimpse a black bear. If you do, report the sighting by calling (407) 884-2008.

There is one "primitive" camping site in the Reserve for those hardy enough to backpack to the far side of the park. Or you can ride your horse there. The camping fee is $3 per adult, $2 per child 6 to 18, and $5 per horse. Children under six camp free. If riding is your cup of tea, the Rock Springs Run Riding Stables has horses for hire for $22 per hour; children must be at least six to ride alone. Call (352) 735-6266.

Nearby: Katie's Wekiva River Landing, Wekiva Falls Resort, Wekiwa Springs State Park.

Sylvan Lake Park

845 Lake Markham Road, Sanford 32771
(407) 322-6567
www.co.seminole.fl.us/parks/sylvan.asp

Admission:	**Free**
Hours:	Daily 8:00 a.m. to 10:00 p.m. Closed Thanksgiving and Christmas
Location:	From I-4 Exit 51, drive west on SR 46 3.2 miles, turn left onto Lake Markham Road. Park is less than a mile on left

This Seminole County park offers cut-rate tennis and racquetball, along with four soccer fields. Tennis courts are $2 an hour before 5:00 p.m. and $4 per hour thereafter; racquetball courts are $4 an hour at all times; soccer fields go for $10 an hour before 5 p.m. and $20 per hour thereafter. Use of the facilities is open to all, even to tourists, but you must call for reservations

Otherwise, the park offers picnicking, a jogging trail, and an intricate network of boardwalks that take you through the woods and across the swampy fringes of Sylvan Lake, where you can sit in a spacious gazebo and bird watch or just while away the time. A small dock offers fishing or a place to launch your own canoe or other non-motorized boat.

Tibet-Butler Preserve

8777 State Road 535, Orlando 32836
(407) 876-6696

Admission:	**Free**
Hours:	Wednesday to Sunday 8:00 a.m. to 6:00 p.m.

Location: About five miles north of I-4 Exit 27

Just a stone's throw from Walt Disney World and SeaWorld, amid the gated communities of Orlando's burgeoning southwest district, lies this 440-acre patch of Florida wilderness. The spiffy new Vera Carter Environmental Center building, with its state-of-the-art interpretive displays, is the kickoff point for four miles of beautifully maintained trails and boardwalks that meander through bay swamps, marshes, cypress swamps, pine flatlands, and Florida scrub. The park borders the Tibet-Butler chain of lakes from which it takes its name, but you can't get down to the water. You can get close, though, on a lovely pavilion at the end of Osprey Overlook Trail. This is a great spot for bird watching and an excellent place to escape the bustle of tourist Orlando. The Preserve is home to bobcats and foxes, although it is unlikely you'll spot any of these elusive creatures. Special programs and guided nature hikes are offered from time to time. Call for details.

Nearby: SeaWorld, Discovery Cove.

Tosohatchee State Reserve

3365 Taylor Creek Road, Christmas, 32709
(407) 568-5893

Admission: $2 per vehicle (up to 6 people)
Hours: Daily 8:00 a.m. to sunset
Location: 3 miles south of SR 50 in Christmas
www.dep.state.fl.us/parks/district3/tosohatchee/index.asp

If you really want to get away from it all, this mammoth (28,000-acre) state park is an excellent choice. I visited one Wednesday afternoon and was the only person there. The park borders 19 miles of the St. John's River and includes wetlands, pine flatwoods, and hammocks. The name is a contraction of Tootoosahatchee, an Indian word for "chicken creek," and the eponymous stream flows through the northern portion of the park.

Hiking, biking, and horseback riding are the activities of choice here. If you want the purest experience of this enchanting and sometimes spooky ecosystem stick to the primitive Florida Trail, marked with white (or sometimes blue) blazes. The trails marked with rectangular or diamond-shaped orange blazes allow bikes and horses (bring your own horse; there are none for hire here). Walking softly and quietly will increase your chance of spotting wildlife. There are white-tailed deer, bobcat, gray fox, and several varieties of raptors to be seen here. The Florida panther is said to put in a rare appearance. More likely, you will flush large vultures or hawks as you proceed through the semi-gloom of the forest past tea-dark streams and pools, their still surfaces like obsidian mirrors.

If a casual visit is not enough, why not spend a few days? The camping here is "primitive," that is no recreational vehicles or pop-up tent trailers are allowed. Most of the campsites have nearby parking areas but for the truly adventuresome, there are two backpacking campsites, one of them seven miles from the nearest road. Campers must make reservations by phone at least two weeks (but no more than 60 days) in advance. There is a fee of $3 per adult per night ($2 for those under 18). The regular admission fee is waived for campers.

When you arrive, sign in and pay your vehicle fee (envelopes are provided). You must also sign out to let the park caretaker know that you are not lying wounded in some far flung corner of the wilderness. Also, be aware that hunting is allowed in this park. The deer season runs from late September to about Thanksgiving. The wild hog (yes, wild hog) season is in January and wild turkey have their turn in March and April. All of these hunting seasons have gaps, that is, periods of three days to two weeks when hunting is not allowed. Being in the woods when trigger happy hunters start thinking that deer wear orange vests is never a great idea; call to check the schedule, which is also posted at the sign-in area. If you want to hunt, you have to get a special permit from the state even if you are a local resident.

Nearby: Back to Nature Wildlife Refuge, C.A.R.E., Fort Christmas Historical Park, Jungle Adventures, Orlando Wetlands Park.

Turkey Lake Park

3401 Hiawassee Road, Orlando 32835
(407) 299-5594

Admission:	Adults $2, children (3 to 12) $1
Hours:	Daily 7:30 a.m. to 5:00 p.m. November to April, 7:30 a.m. to 7 p.m. May to October
Location:	From I-4 Exit 30 take Kirkman north, turn left onto Conroy then right onto Hiawassee to park entrance, about 4 miles total

Just a stone's throw from the hurly-burly of Universal Orlando, the city of Orlando has created a 300-acre oasis along the shores of Turkey Lake. This beautifully landscaped and maintained park offers picnicking, hiking along seven miles of nature trails, biking along a three-mile bike path, and a number of other diversions. The picnic areas are close to the lake with beautiful shaded tables and "picnic pavilions" (additional charge). There are nearby kiddie play areas and sandy "beaches" but no lake swimming. Instead there is a large pool overlooking the lovely lake. A fishing pier lets you test your angling skills against largemouth bass and other species. If you prefer to fish from a boat, you can rent one for $5.00 Thursday through Sunday, 7 a.m. to 11 a.m. only. Call (407) 299-1248 to make a reservation.

Across the park, an "all children's" playground offers an enormous wooden and car-tire wonderland that will offer little ones hours of exploration and fun. Shaded gazebos nearby keep Mom and Dad out of the sun. No eating here, however, as food draws rats and other not-so-welcome wildlife. Next door is a "Cracker" farm featuring an authentic 100-year-old barn, to give kids an idea of what pioneer Florida looked and felt like.

There's camping here, too. Cabins that sleep up to 10 are available for $27.50 per night. "Family" camp sites for trailers and RVs are $14.38 per night including tax, electricity, and water. If you need a sewer hookup as well, the price is $16.60. The area is beautifully shaded, with picnic tables and barbecue pits. A "primitive" camping area nearby is less shady, but at $6.61 per tent, the price may be right. Camping requires reservations.

Nearby: Universal Orlando.

University of Central Florida Arboretum

UCF Campus
4000 Central Florida Boulevard, Orlando 32816-2368
(407) 823-2978
http://pegasus.cc.ucf.edu/~arbor/

Admission:	**Free**
Hours:	Daily 9:00 a.m. to 6:00 p.m.
Location:	On the UCF campus in east Orlando; ask at the campus information booth for directions and parking information

The University of Central Florida has a quite extensive "collection" of trees and other flora, and it is displayed in this tranquil oasis in the midst of its ultramodern campus on the eastern fringes of Orlando. The emphasis is on Florida species but the collection ranges far and wide. A maze of nature trails takes the visitor through a number of plant "communities" including oak hammock, cabbage palm, and pond pine. Informative signage identifies individual species and, when appropriate, gives tips to gardeners. Best of all, secluded tables and benches, some with thatched shelters offer quiet spots for contemplation or study.

Nearby: Back to Nature Wildlife Refuge.

Wekiva Falls Resort

30700 Wekiva River Road, Sorrento 32776
(407) 830-9828; (352) 383-8055

Admission:	Adults $5, children (2 to 11) $3, seniors (65+) $4. Prices include tax
Hours:	Daily 8:00 a.m. to 6:00 p.m.

Location:	From I-4 Exit 51, drive west on SR 46 for 5.5 miles, turn left on Wekiva River Road; entrance is 1.4 miles on left

This homey camping resort welcomes day guests for picnicking, canoeing, and swimming. For most visitors the centerpiece of the resort will be Mastodon Springs, where slightly sulfurous but crystal clear water bubbles up from a 68-foot-deep aquifer vent forming a long, narrow pool that's ideal for splashing and wading. The pool is flanked by steep grassy slopes ringed on top by shaded concrete picnic tables. (Bring your own grill if you want to cook.) Another ring of tables is at the bottom of the slope at the edge of the sandy beach that surrounds the spring. A structure in the middle of the water lets kids climb up and slide down six tubular slides into the cool water. The pool spills out into a shallow stream for wading or tubing; about 100 yards downstream a wooden bridge blocks passage. This is very much a kids' place; most adults hang out on the shore or tend to the barbecuing. Pets are not allowed in the resort.

On the other side of the bridge the stream opens into an small lagoon from which canoes depart. Canoes rent for a modest $5 for the day or $3 for two hours. Or you can explore without paddling on the 45-passenger Wekiva Queen II, which offers daily one-hour "jungle cruises" on the Wekiva River. The Queen departs on the hour from 9 a.m. to 5 p.m. The fare is $15 for adults and $10 for children 2 to 11.

If you'd like to stay here, camping fees start at $18 a day for two people with weekly and monthly rates available.

Nearby: Rock Springs Run State Reserve, Katie's Wekiva River Landing.

Wekiwa Springs State Park

1800 Wekiwa Circle, Apopka 32712
(407) 884-2008; (407) 884-2009 – recorded information
www.dep.state.fl.us/parks/district3/wekiwasprings/index.asp

Admission:	$4 per vehicle (maximum of 8 people)
Hours:	Daily 8:00 a.m. to sunset
Location:	From I-4 (Exit 49) take route 434 West to Wekiva Springs Road, then about 3 miles to the park entrance

This gem of a park boasts what must be the most beautiful spot to take a swim in all of Central Florida. The spring that gives the park its name bubbles up at the base of an amphitheater of greensward, forming a crystal clear circular pool of pure delight. The water is a steady 72 degrees year-round, making for a bracing dip in the heat of summer and a heated pool for snowbirds in the winter. The pool is fairly shallow, seldom more than five feet deep. Bring a snorkel and mask for a peek down into the spring itself.

The spring is one source of the Wekiva River, which flows from here northeast to the St. John's River. You can rent a canoe to explore this lovely stretch of river. Rates (including tax) are $14 for two hours and $2 for each additional hour, up to a maximum of $25 for the day. If you'd like to rent a canoe to do some overnight camping, the rate is $50 per night, but half of that will be returned to you when you return the canoe. No portage or pickup is available: you have to paddle back (upstream) on your own or make your own transportation arrangements. Trail bikes can be rented for $5 for one hour, $9 for two, $12 for three, $15 for four, or $18 for the day. Call (407) 880-4110 for canoe and trail bike rentals.

The river is gorgeous from a canoe but some daring souls snorkel it. The park police tell me this is a foolhardy venture given the population of large alligators who have lost their fear of man, thanks to being fed by ignorant tourists. Shortly before one of my visits to the park, an 11-foot gator was pulled from the waters of nearby Wekiva Marina. Because of its aggressive behavior and total lack of fear of humans, the trapper was forced to kill it.

If you get hungry after your swim, there's a barebones snack bar at the top of the hill. But a better choice might be the picnic area at the other end of the park, where you'll find a couple of dozen picnic tables artfully sited around the shores of Sand Lake. There are alligators here, so be careful.

In between there are some beautifully maintained trails. If you begin from the spring-fed swimming pool, a boardwalk takes you from the swampy jungle of the river's edge to the sandy pine forest of the drier uplands. This is one of the nicest spots I found in Central Florida for a visitor to get a quick appreciation of just how different Florida's ecosystems are. There's plenty of wildlife, too. I've spotted white-tailed deer fawns leaping through the woods and armadillos grubbing in the underbrush.

Family campsites are available by reservation if you'd like to stay longer. The fees for up to four people are $16.65 per night without electricity and $18.77 with, plus $2.12 per night for each additional person or pet and $3.18 per night for each additional vehicle. The park requires written proof that pets have had a rabies vaccination. Call Reserve America, (407) 326-3521, for campsite reservations. More primitive camping is also available. Call the park at (407) 884-2008 for more information.

Note: In 2001, a pine-beetle infestation devastated acres of parkland. In response, the park closed most hiking trails and campsites to log out the infected trees. Many were still closed as this book went to press. So call ahead before making plans to hike or camp here.

Nearby: Katie's Wekiva River Landing, Rock Springs Run State Reserve, Wekiva Falls Resort.

CHAPTER SIXTEEN:

Artful Dodges

Those who assume that Orlando, with its high concentration of theme parks and "mindless" entertainments, is a cultural wasteland have got it dead wrong. In fact, the Orlando area boasts some world-class museums, a lively and growing theater scene, and a number of modest local history museums.

HISTORICAL & SCIENCE MUSEUMS

Fort Christmas Historical Park & Museum

1300 Fort Christmas Road, Christmas 32709
(407) 568-4149
http://parks.onetgov.net/10Christmas.htm

Admission: **Free**

Hours: Museum is open Tuesday to Saturday 10:00 a.m. to 5:00 p.m.; Sunday 1:00 p.m. to 5:00 p.m. Park is open daily 8:00 a.m. to 8:00 p.m. (to 6:00 p.m. during winter months)

Location: Two miles north of SR 50, a major artery between Orlando and the Kennedy Space Center

This is not the actual Fort Christmas but a re-creation. The original was built a short distance away in 1837 during the Second Seminole Indian War (1835-1842) and has long since rotted away. The re-created fort, with its log cabin-like blockhouses and pointed palisades, is remarkably evocative of a frontier that most Americans associate with the West, not the South.

Display cases in the blockhouses provide a fragmentary history of the Seminole Wars, the culture they destroyed, and the early days of white settlement. In the nearby Visitors Center, which is built in the style of a "Cracker" (old-time Florida cowboy) farm house, you can get a pamphlet that explicates the museum's exhibits and provides a short history of the Seminole Wars. Scattered about the property is a small but growing collection of original Cracker architecture. Yesterday, disreputable shacks. Today, cherished history. Regular tours of these seven old houses are conducted daily at 11:00 a.m., 1:00 p.m., and 2:00 p.m.

Fort Christmas is also a county park complete with picnic tables (many with barbecues), a shaded playground, a baseball diamond, and tennis, volleyball, and basketball courts.

Nearby: Back to Nature Wildlife Refuge, C.A.R.E., Jungle Adventures, Orlando Wetlands Park, Tosohatchee Reserve.

The Holocaust Memorial Resource & Education Center

851 North Maitland Avenue, Maitland 32751
(407) 628-0555
www.holocaustedu.org

Admission:	**Free**
Hours:	Monday to Thursday 9:00 a.m. to 4:00 p.m.; Friday 9:00 a.m. to 1:00 p.m.; Sunday 1:00 p.m. to 4:00 p.m.
Location:	At the intersection of Maitland Boulevard and Maitland Avenue, about a mile east of I-4 Exit 47

Someone once observed that for there to be peaks there must be valleys. The reference was to art, but the metaphor holds true for history too. This modest and moving museum commemorates one of the darkest valleys of human experience — the martyrdom of the six million Jews who, along with homosexuals, Gypsies, and other "undesirables," were ruthlessly exterminated by the Nazis in the 1930s and 1940s.

A small chapel-like room houses "The Holocaust in History," a permanent collection of multimedia displays documenting the horrors of institutionalized hate. A separate room houses rotating exhibits on aspects of the Holocaust; these change every three to four months. A rapidly expanding 6,000-volume library is devoted exclusively to Holocaust history.

A visit here can be a profoundly disturbing experience, which is not to say it is something to shy away from. Stepping out once again into the Florida sunshine, we are reminded that we have been blessed to live on one of history's peaks — a lesser peak, it might be argued, but a peak nonetheless. A visit here will put the pleasures of your Orlando vacation in a richer perspective.

Nearby: Maitland Art Center, Maitland Historical Museum, Waterhouse Residence, Birds of Prey Center.

Maitland Historical Museum

221 West Packwood Avenue, Maitland 32751
(407) 644-2451
www.ourfrontporch.com/osi/mhs

Admission:	Suggested donation $2 ($5 for a family)
Hours:	Thursday to Sunday noon to 4:00 p.m.
Location:	From I-4 Exit 47 go east on Maitland Boulevard, then turn right onto Maitland Avenue and right onto Packwood.

This modest museum, housed in a former residence next to the Maitland Art Center (see below), houses memorabilia of the tiny town of Maitland, which began its life as Fort Maitland in 1838, serving as a way station between larger forts in Sanford and Orlando. There are photographs of old houses and early residents along with the contents of Maitland's attics — old radios, cameras, glassware, and household implements. A small room houses old desks and class photos from the turn of the century, when children would row through Lakes Faith, Hope, and Charity to reach the Maitland School.

The real attraction here, however, is the **Telephone Museum** housed in a building out back. Telephone service in this part of Florida began in 1909, when the Galloway family grocery store installed 10 phone lines so their good customers could order by phone. The service mushroomed into what came to be known as the Winter Park Telephone Company, which remained independent and family-owned until 1976 when it was sold to the company that became Sprint. There are several old magneto switchboards here, dating back to 1900, and a large collection of phones, from the old-fashioned, wall-mounted, hand-cranked varieties to a sleek one-piece 1970 Swedish Ericofon. Also on display are samples of copper wiring and other telephony paraphernalia, including wooden conduits once used to snake wire beneath city streets. Some more recent switching equipment is housed here and volunteers hope to get it working again for demonstration purposes.

There are very few explanatory labels, so ask for a guided tour. On my visit, I was escorted by a charming lady who once worked for the Galloways themselves.

Nearby: Maitland Art Center, Waterhouse Residence, Birds of Prey Center.

Orange County Regional History Center

65 East Central Boulevard, Orlando 32801

(407) 836-8500

www.thehistorycenter.org

Admission:	Adults $7, seniors (60+) $6.50, children (3 to 12) $3.50
Hours:	Monday to Saturday 10:00 a.m. to 5:00 p.m.; Sunday noon to 5:00 p.m.
Location:	In downtown Orlando; from the north take I-4 Exit 42, from the south Exit 40

Unlike most county historical museums, which are dusty hodgepodges of miscellaneous objects displayed in a donated and threadbare house of "historical" interest, Orange County's museum is housed in a magnificent 1927 courthouse, its collection attractively and professionally displayed. This is one of the best looking local history museums I have visited and well worth a look if you venture downtown.

The impressive ground floor entrance features a marble inlay map of the world with Orlando at the center; above is a wonderfully zany multimedia sculptural dome dotted with references to Central Florida's natural, cultural, and social history. Your best bet is to head for the fourth floor, enjoy the short orientation film, and then work your way down through a chronologically arranged series of exhibit rooms.

After an introduction to Florida's natural environment and its first Paleo-Indian inhabitants, the focus shifts to the settler period in which both the Europeans and the Seminoles, the latter forced from their homelands in Georgia and the Carolinas, were newcomers. A fascinating display on tourism takes us back to the 1920s and the first RVs, converted Model Ts that brought penny-pinching "tin can tourists." The then governor of Florida said of these pioneers, "They came with one pair of underwear and one twenty dollar bill and changed neither." How times change!

Other highlights are a perfectly preserved courtroom, a reminder of the building's previous life, and a display on the pre-World War II training of military pilots, when Central Florida was so little-known that it was the perfect place for a top-secret government base.

The History Center is one of the high points of Orlando's revitalized downtown. In front is a small but lovely park. The Public Library, with free Internet access, is on one side and Wall Street Plaza, a charming pedestrian street with cafes and restaurants, on the other.

Nearby: Lake Eola Swan Boats, Leu Gardens, Mennello Museum, Orlando Museum of Art, Orlando Science Center.

Orlando Science Center

777 East Princeton Street, Orlando 32803

(407) 514-2000

www.osc.org

Admission:	Adults $9.50, seniors (55+) $8.50, children (3 to 11) $6.75
Hours:	Monday to Thursday 9:00 a.m. to 5:00 p.m.; Friday and Saturday 9:00 a.m. to 9:00 p.m.; Sunday noon to 5:00 p.m.; closed most Mondays in the fall and winter
Location:	From I-4 Exit 43, go east and follow Loch Haven Park signs about one quarter mile

The Orlando area is gaining a reputation as another high-tech business corridor with specialties in laser and simulation technologies. The Orlando Science Center's smashing new home is a fitting monument to the technological explosion going on around it and should serve as a launching pad for future generations of scientists. The accent is on kids and science education but, thanks to its ingenious hands-on approach, the Center offers plenty to keep even the dullest adult occupied.

The Center's 42,000 square feet are crammed with eye-catching exhibits that illustrate the many faces of science and how it interacts with our everyday life. Power Station teaches about energy, LightPower about lasers and optics, The Cosmic Tourist about earth and the solar system, and Body Zone about health and fitness. There's even a section, ShowBiz Science, that explains the technology underlying some of the man-made wonders you've been gaping at during your Orlando visit.

The 310-seat CineDome features IMAX movies and planetarium shows on a screen eight stories high, with a state-of-the-art sound system. There is an additional admission charge for these shows ($6.00 adults, $5.50 seniors, $4.50 children). The Combo Experience ($12.50 adults, $11.50 seniors, $9.25 children) gives you one "CineDome experience" in addition to basic admission. The Double Combo Experience ($14.50 adults, $13.50 seniors, $11.25 children) offers a choice of two CineDome shows. My advice would be to go for the Combo Experience ticket; if you want to see more IMAX films, the admission is just $2.00 additional per film. This is the largest such theater in the world and seeing an IMAX movie on the vast curved screen is an experience not easily duplicated elsewhere.

There's a spacious cafeteria so you can plan a visit around lunchtime and then spend the rest of the day exploring the wonderful world of science, with side trips to the nearby art museums.

Nearby: Mennello Museum, Orlando Museum of Art, Leu Gardens.

Spence-Lanier Pioneer Center

750 North Bass Road, Kissimmee 34746
(407) 396-8644

Admission:	Suggested donation, adults $2, children $1
Hours:	Thursday to Saturday 10:00 a.m. to 4:00 p.m., Sunday 1:00 p.m. to 4:00 p.m.
Location:	Half a mile south of Irlo Bronson Highway (US Route 192)

Sometimes referred to as the Pioneer Museum, this open-air venue is a labor of love of the Osceola County Historical Society. The highlights are two old wooden buildings, rescued from oblivion and moved to this site as reminders of Central Florida's not too distant but nonetheless vanished past.

The Lanier House, which has been dated to about 1887, is a Cracker-style residence made from broad cypress boards which have aged to a lovely cafe au lait shade of beige. The broad, shaded porches and airy central breeze-way, or "possum trot," were designed to let air circulate through the four rooms. The spare interior rooms, including a kitchen with a wood stove, touchingly evoke the rhythms of life in a simpler time. Next door is the smaller, two-room 1890 Tyson Home, now used to re-create a turn of the century general store. Books of local history and locally produced crafts are sold here.

A nearby modern prefab building holds a growing and random collection of antiques and memorabilia donated by the local community. Many of these touchstones to the past seem to have been passed from generation to generation before finding their way here. This is the living, collective memory of Osceola County and reflects not just Florida history but the many ways in which foreign and national events impinged on small towns like Kissimmee.

Across the street from the four-acre site of the museum is the **Mary Kendall Steffee Nature Preserve**. This 7.8-acre patch of wilderness lies in the very heart of tourist Kissimmee and yet remains remarkably isolated. A short walk on marked trails brings you to a raised boardwalk that juts out into Shingle Creek Swamp. A shaded seating area beckons the footsore. Aside from the intermittent drone of small planes landing at the nearby Kissimmee Airport, this is an oasis of tranquillity where you can glimpse the occasional eagle or other large raptor. The numbers on the trail markers correspond to a trail guide which the museum will lend you. Or you can purchase a copy for $2.

Nearby: Flying Tigers Warbird Restoration Museum, Kissimmee Rodeo, Medieval Times, and the many other attractions along Route 192.

Waterhouse Residence & Carpentry Museum

820 Lake Lilly Drive, Maitland 32751

(407) 644-2451

www.ourfrontporch.com/osi/mhs

Admission:	Suggested donation $2 ($5 for a family)
Hours:	Thursday to Sunday noon to 4:00 p.m.
Location:	From I-4 take Exit 47 East onto Maitland Boulevard, then turn right onto Maitland Avenue and right onto Lake Lilly Drive

William H. Waterhouse, a home builder and cabinetmaker by trade, came to Central Florida in the early 1880s and put his obvious skills to use building a handsome family residence overlooking tiny Lake Lilly. Today, it serves as a monument to gracious living in a simpler, less stressful time.

Lovingly restored and maintained by volunteers, the house contains many items of furniture fashioned by Mr. Waterhouse in the carpentry shop behind the home. The home itself is furnished throughout and looks as if the Waterhouse family had just stepped out for a moment. Do-it-yourselfers will marvel at the fine detail work and the lavish use of heart of pine, a favorite of builders of the period because it was impervious to termites. It is rare today because few loggers are patient enough to let pines go unharvested long enough for this prime lumber to develop.

Tours are conducted by knowledgeable volunteers who will provide you with many insights into this charming home and the people who lived here. If you arrive when a tour is in progress, you may find the door locked. Just take a seat in the comfortable chairs on the porch; a volunteer will be with you shortly. Tours last about 30 to 40 minutes.

The museum offers two children's programs that transport kids back to the late 1800s. *Carpentry Crew* ($12) showcases woodworking and building techniques while *Hats and Teas* ($10) focuses on social etiquette. These programs are designed for kids in grades three and up. Call for more information and to make reservations, which are required.

Nearby: Maitland Art Center, Maitland Historical Museum, Birds of Prey Center.

Winter Park Historical Association Museum

200 West New England Avenue, Winter Park 32790

(407) 647-8180

Admission:	**Free** (Donations requested)
Hours:	Thursday and Friday 11:00 a.m. to 3:00 p.m.; Saturday 9:00 a.m. to 1:00 p.m.; Sunday 1:00 p.m. to 4:00 p.m.

Location: In downtown Winter Park next to the park

This fledgling historical museum is housed in one room around the corner from the building in which Winter Park's Saturday Farmer's Market is held. The display is simple, relying heavily on photographs of now-vanished buildings and assorted household items and artifacts that speak less of Winter Park than of American consumerism.

The best part of this museum is the central display area, a sort of room within a room. It houses changing exhibits artfully put together by a local architect and interior decorator using donated and loaned furniture and artifacts. Past exhibits have included a Victorian parlor decked out for a Christmas celebration and an upper middle-class kitchen circa 1932. The exhibit changes every six months or so.

While perhaps not worth a special trip, you may want to consider a visit if you are touring the many other attractions in Winter Park.

Nearby: Morse Museum, Cornell Museum, Albin Polasek Galleries, Winter Park Scenic Boat Tour.

ART MUSEUMS & GALLERIES

Albin Polasek Galleries

633 Osceola Avenue, Winter Park 32789

(407) 647-6294

www.polasek.org

Admission: Suggested donation $3

Hours: Tuesday to Saturday 10:00 a.m. to 4:00 p.m.; Sunday 1:00 p.m. to 4:00 p.m.; closed during July and August

Location: From I-4 Exit 45, follow SR 426 East about 3 miles

The studio-home and gardens of the late Czech-American sculptor, Albin Polasek, have been turned into a loving memorial by his widow. The quietly luxurious home was designed by Polasek himself and constructed in 1950 overlooking Lake Osceola. Today it is on the Register of Historic Places and houses some 200 of his works. The paintings are originals while most of the sculptures are reproductions.

Polasek was a devout Roman Catholic and a self-taught woodcarver who, as a young immigrant, found work carving religious statues in the Midwest. Later, he received formal art training and eventually became a highly respected academic artist. The work on display here ranges from the mawkish to the quite impressive. He was a better sculptor than painter and some of his bronzes, like The Sower and Man Carving His Own Destiny, possess real power. The former is a classically inspired bronze, the latter depicts a muscular figure in the process of carving itself out of stone.

One of his most affecting pieces is The Victorious Christ, a larger than life sculpture of the crucified Christ gazing heavenward. The original hangs in a cathedral in Omaha, Nebraska. There are two reproductions here. One dominates his two-story studio but the real stunner is the bronze version in the back garden. Mounted on a large wooden cross and sited under a theatrically towering oak tree, facing the lake, it is a powerful work.

Nearby: Cornell Fine Arts Museum, Morse Museum of American Art, Winter Park Scenic Boat Tours.

Cornell Fine Arts Museum

1000 Holt Avenue, Winter Park 32789
(407) 646-2526
www.rollins.edu/cfam

Admission:	**Free** (Donations accepted)
Hours:	Tuesday to Friday 10:00 a.m. to 5:00 p.m.;
	Saturday and Sunday 1:00 p.m. to 5:00 p.m.
Location:	On the campus of Rollins College, at the foot of Holt Avenue

Travel guru Arthur Frommer lists the Cornell Fine Arts Museum as one of the top 10 free attractions in the world, but don't come here just to save money. The collection's emphasis is on European and American painting of the last three centuries. It boasts a permanent collection of some 6,000 objects, ranging from Old Masters to twentieth century abstractionists, making it the largest public museum collection in Florida.

The Cornell is also the oldest museum in the state, having recently celebrated its centennial. The current museum building, a handsome Spanish style villa, was dedicated in 1978.

Typically, the lion's share of the gallery space is given over to a special exhibition, while a smaller gallery features some choice examples from the permanent collection. Many exhibits are locally curated and draw either from the permanent collection or from private and public collections in Florida, offering the art lover the opportunity to view works that would otherwise be impossible to see. For other exhibits, the Cornell joins forces with smaller museums across the country to mount distinguished traveling shows. Exhibits, which run from six to eight weeks, range from retrospectives of a single artist, to highlights of distinguished private collections, to surveys of important movements, to themed shows illuminating genres and techniques.

In addition to its exhibits, the Cornell offers a generous selection of other free programs including lectures by prominent artists, chamber music recitals, and showings of art-related films. Call for details.

Nearby: Albin Polasek Galleries, Morse Museum, Winter Park Scenic Boat Tours.

Frank Lloyd Wright Buildings at Florida Southern College

111 Lake Hollingsworth Drive, Lakeland 33801

(863) 680-4110

www.flsouthern.edu/fllwctr

Admission:	**Free**
Hours:	Visitor Center is open Tuesday to Friday 11:00 a.m. to 4:00 p.m., Saturday 10:00 a.m. to 2:00 p.m., Sunday 2:00 p.m. to 4:00 p.m.; grounds are accessible 24 hours a day
Location:	On the shores of Lake Hollingsworth

Devotees of Frank Lloyd Wright (and they are legion) will want to make a pilgrimage to Lakeland, about 54 miles west of Orlando, to marvel at the largest group of Wright buildings in the world. Wright designed 18 buildings for Florida Southern, a liberal arts college affiliated with the Methodist Church. Twelve were built.

To get there from Orlando, drive west on I-4 and take Exit 18. Follow US 98 South. From Tampa take Exit 14 and follow US 92 East. The two routes join in downtown Lakeland. When they part ways again, follow route 98 and, shortly, turn right onto Ingraham Avenue. Follow Ingraham until it deadends at Lake Hollingsworth Drive (you'll see the campus of Florida Southern College on your right).

Turn right onto Lake Hollingsworth, then right again onto Johnson Avenue. Look for the parking lot on your right opposite the William F. Chatlos Journalism Building. In front of you will be a red and white sign; on it is clear plastic box containing brochures that outline a self-guided walking tour that circles the grounds.

The buildings were designed for a tight budget (much of the early construction was done by students in the forties) but the results are impressive. Many buildings are unlocked and open to the casual visitor. Inside, look for the tiny squares of colored glass embedded in the exterior walls — a delightfully whimsical touch. Take a moment to sit in the quiet splendor of the Annie Pfeiffer Chapel; the smaller but equally arresting Danforth Chapel is nearby. One of the most interesting buildings to be seen here is the only planetarium Wright ever designed.

The buildings are starting to show their age, but Wright's designs are so idiosyncratic, his decorative elements so unique, that this extensive example of his "organic architecture" seems to exist outside the time/style continuum we carry around in our heads. Instead, it is easy to imagine you are in a city built a long time ago in a galaxy far, far away.

The buildings are linked by one and a half miles of covered esplanades which Wright, in his charmingly perverse way, scaled to his own rather short height. "It makes it kind of difficult to recruit a basketball team," a college executive confided. But for those who fit underneath, the effect is rather cozy and Florida Southern students must say a silent prayer of thanks to Wright as they scurry between classes during an afternoon downpour.

Maitland Art Center

231 West Packwood Avenue, Maitland 32751
(407) 539-2181
www.maitartctr.org

Admission:	**Free**
Hours:	Monday to Friday 9:00 a.m. to 4:30 p.m.; Saturday and Sunday noon to 4:30 p.m.
Location:	From I-4 take Exit 47. Go east on Maitland Boulevard, then turn right onto Maitland Avenue and right onto Packwood

The Maitland Art Center is both a gallery and a working art school. It was founded in the late 1930s by the artist and architect André Smith as a "laboratory" for the study of modern art. Smith built a charmingly eccentric complex of tiny cottage/studios for visiting artists. He decorated the modest buildings with cast concrete ornaments and detailing heavily influenced by the art of the ancient Aztecs and Maya.

Today the gallery plays host to a regular succession of exhibits by local and national artists as well as exhibits of private collections. After visiting the gallery, take some time to stroll the grounds. The place must have been idyllic in its heyday, before Maitland became quite so built up. Across the street from the gallery and studios is a roofless outdoor concrete chapel with a lattice-work cross. Shaded by oaks dripping in Spanish moss and surrounded by lush vegetation, the chapel offers a peaceful corner for contemplation. Right next to it is an open courtyard whose exuberant decoration owes a debt to the boisterous paganism of pre-Columbian Mexico; it makes for quite a contrast.

The Maitland Art Center hosts occasional half-day and day-long work-shops on topics such as papermaking as a sculptural art and casting silver jewelry, with tuition ranging from $35 to $100. Artists may want to call ahead for a schedule. There are also regular lectures and gallery talks.

Nearby: Maitland Historical Museum, Waterhouse Residence, Birds of Prey Center.

Mary, Queen of the Universe Shrine

8300 Vineland Avenue, Orlando 32821
(407) 239-6600
www.maryqueenoftheuniverse.org

Admission:	**Free**
Hours:	Daily 7:30 a.m. to 5:00 p.m.; museum 10:30 a.m. to 4:00 p.m. (closed Wednesday)
Location:	Near I-4 Exit 27

This Roman Catholic shrine had humble beginnings as a tourist ministry; today it is a large modern cathedral named by the Pope as a "house of pilgrimage." There is some striking architecture and religious art to be seen here, especially a lovely, abstract, blue stained-glass wall in a chapel dedicated to Our Lady of Guadalupe. A small museum off the gift shop hosts rotating exhibits of religious art from around the world, such as a recent exhibit of Russian crosses and icons.

Nearby: SeaWorld, Discovery Cove, Arabian Nights.

Mennello Museum of American Folk Art

900 East Princeton Street, Orlando 32803
(407) 246-4278
www.menellomuseum.com

Admission:	Adults $4, students and seniors (55+) $1, children under 12 **free**.
Hours:	Tuesday to Saturday 11:00 a.m. to 5:00 p.m. (Thursday to 8:00 p.m.); Sunday noon to 5:00 p.m.
Location:	In Loch Haven Park, near I-4 Exit 43

Art collectors Marilyn and Michael Mennello fell in love with the work of "naïve" artist Earl Cunningham and purchased virtually his entire life's output. The City of Orlando, meanwhile, had been collecting Florida and southern folk art as part of its Public Art Collection. Now these two visionary endeavors have been brought together in a small gem of a museum located in a renovated private residence overlooking picturesque Lake Formosa in Loch Haven Park.

Cunningham was a Maine sea captain who gradually worked his way south, all the while painting imaginative and idealized coastal landscapes with a Caribbean sense of color. His works form the backbone of the Mennello Museum's collection. They are displayed using a clever halogen lighting system, designed by the museum's director, that heightens the colors in the paintings to almost neon intensity.

Other rooms in the museum showcase items from the Orlando city collection and traveling exhibits of other folk artists. The museum's small shop offers some unique folk craft items at very reasonable prices.

Nearby: Orlando Museum of Art, Orlando Science Center, Leu Gardens.

Morse Museum of American Art

445 Park Avenue North, Winter Park 32789
(407) 645-5311
www.morsemuseum.org

Admission:	Adults $3, children and students $1; **free** Friday 4:00 p.m. to 8:00 p.m. September to late May
Hours:	Tuesday to Saturday 9:30 a.m. to 4:00 p.m.; Sunday 1:00 p.m. to 4:00 p.m.
Location:	On Park Avenue, just past the fancy shopping district

Could the Charles Hosmer Morse Museum of American Art be the best museum in Central Florida? Well, for my money, it's hard to beat the world's largest collection of Tiffany glass. That's Louis Comfort Tiffany, the magician of stained glass who flourished at the turn of the twentieth century. The works on display here are absolutely ravishing and, if you have any interest in the decorative arts, your visit to Orlando will be poorer for not having found the time to visit this unparalleled collection.

When most people think of Tiffany glass they think of those wonderfully organic looking table and hanging lamps with the floral designs. Those are here, of course, as are some stunning examples of his large-scale decorative glass windows and door panels. But there's much else, some of which may come as a surprise.

As brilliant a marketer as he was an artist, Tiffany saw the World's Fair of 1893 as an opportunity to spread his fame worldwide. So he put his best foot forward by creating an enormous chapel interior for the exhibit. Everything in it, from a massive electrified chandelier, to a baptismal font, to intricate mosaic pillars to stunningly beautiful stained-glass windows was of Tiffany design. The chapel has been lovingly restored by the Morse.

The faces on Tiffany's glass pieces were painted with powdered glass that was fused to clear glass, but much of the other detail and molding is created by the rich colors and tonal fluctuations in the glass itself. Tiffany is less well known as a painter, but several of his paintings, including some very deft watercolors from his worldwide travels, are to be seen here. There are also miniature glass pieces, vases in delicate, psychedelic-colored favrile glass, inkwells, jewelry, and other decorative objects.

In a rear gallery are some lovely examples of American painting of the last century, including a deft portrait by John Singer Sargent and one by Samuel F. B. Morse, a distant cousin of the man for whom the museum is named and better known as the inventor of the telegraph and the code that bears his name.

The Morse's collection focuses on the decorative arts and is extensive, comprising some 4,000 pieces. In addition to the permanent displays, the museum dips into its collection to mount special exhibits illuminating various aspects of American decorative arts, including "vignettes," small rooms in which interior designers show off the museum's collection of furniture and decorative objects as they might have looked in the well-to-do homes for which these lovely objects were created.

Nearby: Albin Polasek Galleries, Cornell Fine Arts Museum, Winter Park Scenic Boat Tours.

Orlando City Hall Galleries

Orange Avenue and South Street, Orlando 32801
(407) 246-2221

Admission:	**Free**
Hours:	Monday to Friday 8:00 a.m. to 9:00 p.m.; Saturday and Sunday 12:00 noon to 5:00 p.m.
Location:	Just off I-4 Exit 36

The City of Orlando has a long-standing policy of supporting the arts and an extensive public collection of art, much of which is on display at City Hall. The ground floor gallery, just off the impressive entry rotunda, is used for special exhibits that rotate every three months or so. The third-floor gallery just outside the mayor's office displays selected works from the permanent collection; continue down the stairs to the second floor and see more art on display. In fact, if you wander through the building, you will see that most of the hallways are alive with art. Much of the collection focuses on Florida artists, with an accent on folk art, but some major artists with national reputations are also to be found here.

If you like what you see here, more of the city's folk art collection is on display at the Mennello Museum of American Folk Art, described above.

Nearby: Lake Eola Swan Boats, Orange County Regional History Center.

Orlando Museum of Art

2416 North Mills Avenue, Orlando 32803

(407) 896-4231; fax (407) 896-9920

www.omart.org

Admission:	Adults $6, children (4 to 11) $2, students and seniors (55+) $4; more for special exhibits
Hours:	Tuesday to Saturday 9:00 a.m. to 5:00 p.m.; Sunday 12:00 noon to 5:00 p.m.
Location:	In Loch Haven Park, near I-4 Exit 43

The Orlando Museum of Art (OMA) was founded in 1924 to present local, regional, and national artists and develop art education programs for the community. Today, its handsome modern building with its arresting circular hub houses a permanent collection of nineteenth and twentieth century American paintings. There is also a distinguished collection of pre-Columbian art housed in its own gallery.

On any given day, the galleries may host a special exhibit, a selection of works on loan, and a selection of works from the permanent collection. The museum also offers regular video, film, and lecture series, most of which require an additional admission charge. Wheelchairs and lockers are provided free of charge.

A small but very classy gift shop offers a tasteful range of small art objects, reproductions, calendars, glossy art books, and artisanal works you are unlikely to find elsewhere. You can even get an Orlando Museum of Art t-shirt.

On the first Thursday of each month, from 6:00 to 9:00 p.m., the museum throws a party with a cash bar, live music from local bands, and themed art by local artists. The $5 admission also allows entry to the galleries.

Nearby: Mennello Folk Art Museum, Orlando Science Center, Leu Gardens.

Osceola Center for the Arts

2411 East Irlo Bronson, Kissimmee 34744

(407) 846-6257

www.ocfta.com

Admission:	**Free** to art gallery
Hours:	Monday to Friday 10:00 a.m. to 6:00 p.m.; Saturday 10:00 a.m. to 4:00 p.m. and whenever there is a theater performance
Location:	A mile east of Florida Turnpike Exit 244

This community-based arts organization mounts exhibits of Florida artists. Based on what I've seen, the standards for exhibition are quite high. Exhibits change monthly. The Center also hosts special events, such as a recent exhibition of work by established and emerging local artists.

In addition to presenting art work, the Center hosts a regular schedule of theatrical and musical presentations. Among these are tours by the Orlando Ballet and the productions of a local community theater group.

Oval on Orange

29 South orange Avenue, orlando 32801
(407) 648-1819
www.ovalorlando.org

Admission:	**Free**
Hours:	Thursday 11:00 a.m. to 2:00 p.m.; Friday 11:00 a.m. to 10:00 p.m.; Saturday 3:00 p.m. to 10:00 p.m.; or by appointment
Location:	Downtown on the corner of Pine Street

This space in the heart of downtown houses a cooperative artists' gallery and working studio space, so during your visit you can not only browse the contemporary art on exhibit but watch the artists at work. Exhibits change monthly on the third Thursday, with an opening reception held between 5:00 and 10:00 p.m.

Wells'Built Museum of African American History

511 West South Street, Orlando 32801
(407) 245-7535

Admission:	**Free**
Hours:	Office hours Monday to Friday 9:00 a.m. to 5:00 p.m.; call for museum hours
Location:	Just west of I-4 near Church Street

Dr. William M. Wells was a prominent African-American physician in Orlando during the first half of the 20th century. He created the South Street Casino to host touring black bands and, since Orlando was rigorously segregated, he opened the Wells'Built Hotel next door to house the musicians. Ella Fitzgerald, Count Basie, Ray Charles, Cab Calloway, Ivory Joe Hunter, and many other musical greats played the Casino and stayed at the hotel over the years. White Orlando didn't know what it was missing.

The Casino is gone now, but the hotel remains. It has been converted into a modest museum housing memorabilia of Orlando's African-American community along with some African art on loan from local collectors.

Dr. Well's home has been moved to the site of the Casino and will be restored and opened to the public.

Zora Neale Hurston National Museum of Fine Arts

227 East Kennedy Boulevard, Eatonville 32751

(407) 647-3307

www.zoranealehurston.cc

Admission:	**Free**
Hours:	Monday to Friday 9:00 a.m. to 4:00 p.m.
Location:	From I-4 Exit 46 take Lee Road east and turn left almost immediately on Wymore; at the next light turn right on Kennedy for about a quarter mile

The tiny enclave of Eatonville is the hometown of the writer Zora Neale Hurston, one of the shining lights of the Harlem Renaissance of the 1920s. Her namesake museum is a small gallery hosting rotating exhibits of African-American artists from Florida and around the nation. The shows change about every six months. The museum also hosts an annual festival in Hurston's honor celebrating various aspects of African-American culture.

THEATER

Orlando and the surrounding communities have an extremely active theater scene. In addition to the companies listed here, you should be aware of the Mark II Dinner Theater, reviewed in *Chapter 11: Dinner Attractions*. There are also a goodly number of community theaters, as well as touring Broadway shows. You will find complete listings of the day's theatrical offerings in the Living section of the daily *Orlando Sentinel*. The "Calendar" section of the Friday *Sentinel* contains listings for the entire week. Listings also appear in the free weekly paper, *Orlando Weekly*, and on the web site Creative Orlando at http://www.creativeorlando.com.

Theater buffs will want to take advantage of **OTIX**, a half-price ticket service similar to those offered in New York, London, and other major theater centers. Located in the Official Orlando Visitors Center at 8723 International Drive, the service sells unsold day-of-performance tickets at half price, plus a service charge that ranges from $1.50 to $5 depending on the face value of the ticket. This is a specially good deal in the case of higher priced events, and the convenient location of OTIX in the heart of tourist Orlando makes it a convenient way to make entertainment decisions for the evening.

Annie Russell Theatre

1000 Holt Avenue, Winter Park 32789

(407) 646-2145

www.rollins.edu/theatre

The drama department of Rollins College holds forth in this lovely, 377-seat Spanish Mediterranean style theater, offering an eclectic season of modern classics, a contemporary musical, and an old farce or Shakespearean play. The season runs from August to April and ticket prices are a bargain — $15 to $17 a seat. The repertory is ambitious and the productions I have seen belie the fact that all the performers are undergraduates.

The Annie, as it's known locally, also presents touring dance companies of international renown. Pilobolus and the Paul Taylor Dance Company are among the troupes it has hosted.

Bob Carr Performing Arts Centre

401 West Livingstone Street, Orlando 32801
(407) 849-2001, (407) 426-1700
www.orlandocentroplex.com

Located downtown within sight of I-4, the Bob Carr is Orlando's venue for touring Broadway shows and other high-ticket, high-attendance performing arts events. The ultra modern 2,500-seat theater hosts the **Orlando Broadway Series**, presenting a season of six or seven shows for runs ranging from one week to a month. These are either touring companies of current or recent Broadway hits, or revivals showcasing a star you've probably heard of. It's mostly "feel-good" musicals like *Annie Get Your Gun* with Marilu Henner, but the occasional straight play, like *Master Class* starring Faye Dunaway, is also presented. Tickets for this series range from $40 to $60.

The **Orlando Philharmonic Orchestra** performs here six to eight times a year, presenting everything from straight classical evenings to Beatles tributes. Tickets range from $12 to $50. The Bob Carr also hosts tours of symphony orchestras with national or international reputations at ticket prices more in line with those of the Broadway series.

The Bob Carr is the venue of choice for local groups like the **Orlando Opera** and **Orlando Ballet**, described below, as well as one-night stands by comedians like George Carlin, magicians like David Copperfield, and the usual mix of pop and rock concerts.

Church Street Theatre

128 West Church Street, Orlando 32801
(407) 254-4930
www.orlandoyouththeatre.com

Located in the heart of Orlando's historic downtown district, the 100-seat Church Street Theatre is home to **Orlando Black Essential Theatre** and **Orlando Youth Theatre**, two separate companies with somewhat different missions.

The Orlando Youth Theatre produces age-appropriate plays for a young audience and all performers are under 18. They mount 15 shows a year for an eight-performance run. Tickets are $8 for all ages. The Orlando Black Essential Theatre is an African-American company that produces a five-show season, with each show running for four weekends. One play a year is a new play, often by a local playwright. Tickets are $12 for adults and $10 for childen and seniors (65+).

Impacte! Productions
237 University Park Drive, Winter Park
(407) 672-4868

This company of twentysomethings is built around the writing talents of Tod Kimbro, whose comic plays — with titles like *Zombie Doorman* and *Suckers* — have been consistent hits at the Orlando International Fringe Festival (see below). Now Kimbro has his own theater which opened with a continuing stage sitcom, *Caffeine*, billed as a "postmodern black-comic farce." More of the same is promised for the future. Performances are Fridays and Saturdays and tickets cost $10, $8 for students.

Mad Cow Theatre Company
105 East Pine Street, Orlando 32801
(407) 297-8788
www.madcowtheatre.com

This is Orlando's version of New York's Off-Off Broadway or London's Fringe. A dedicated group of non-Equity actors puts on contemporary plays and modern classics in a 77-seat venue in an historic building downtown. Although they are not in the actors' union, the performers are paid and, judging from what I've seen them do, the standards are quite high.

The selection of plays is eclectic, everything from Ibsen's *Ghosts* to Irving Berlin. Other recent productions include *The Laramie Project* and *As Thousands Cheer*. Don't expect Broadway-style production values or Broadway comfort. The budget for these shows ranges from the minuscule to the modest. But for those with an adventuresome taste in theater-going, Mad Cow will be well worth checking out. Tickets are $15 to $18 for adults, $15 for students and seniors; $12 for all on Monday nights.

Orlando Ballet
1111 North Orange Avenue, Orlando 32804
(407) 426-1739
www.orlandoballet.org

From September to May, this homegrown ballet company mounts

three-performance runs of three ballets, ranging from "timeless classics to in-novative contemporary works." They draw on a permanent company of 23 professional dancers and 2 apprentices, occasionally presenting guest artists and visiting choreographers. In addition, each year during the Christmas season, they present the ever-popular *Nutcracker*, in association with the Or-lando Philharmonic; it runs for 12 performances.

All major performances are given at the Bob Carr Performing Arts Center downtown (I-4 Exit 41). Single tickets range from $15 to $48. Call the number above to purchase tickets.

Orlando International Fringe Festival

398 West Amelia Street, Orlando 32801

(407) 648-0077

www.orlandofringe.com

If you're in Orlando during May and your tastes run towards experi-mental theater, you won't want to miss this theatrical feast. For 10 days, from noon to midnight, the streets of downtown are given over to an interna-tional smorgasbord of traditional theater, cabaret, performance art, and street acts. A typical Festival will see over 500 performances by more than 50 groups representing 10 or more countries. Most of the shows are indoors, but there is one outdoor performance venue.

To attend, you must first purchase a $5 button, which serves as a sort of cover charge for the Festival's shows. You may pay an additional $1 to $8 for each show you see, although some shows are free. A printed program lets you know what's coming up next, and since the Festival is geographically com-pact, it's easy to dash from site to site. Veteran Festival-goers suggest quizzing others making the round of shows for suggestions on what's worth seeing and what should be avoided like the plague. Call the number above for the exact dates and location of this year's bash.

Orlando Opera

1111 North Orange Avenue, Orlando 32804

(800) 336-7372; (407) 426-1700

www.orlandoopera.org

Dedicated to bringing the piercing sounds of Italians in pain to Central Florida, the Orlando Opera offers a season of three mainstage productions and two minor productions. The major productions feature the heavyweights (you should excuse the term) of the opera world; Pavarotti, Domingo, and Sills have all performed here. Recent major productions include *Tales of Hoffmann*, *The Barber of Seville*, and *La Bohème*. The minor productions feature resident artists. Recitals and concert performances with major artists have been discontinued but may make a comeback depending on the funding situation.

The season runs from September to May. Prices for tickets to individual performances range from $15 to $55; half-priced tickets are available to students with a valid ID.

Orlando Theatre Project

Seminole Community College

100 Weldon Boulevard, Sanford 32773

(407) 328-2040; (407) 328-4722, ext. 3323

www.otp.cc

After a decade of presenting plays in makeshift and temporary theaters throughout the area, the Orlando Theatre Project has settled into residence at Sanford's Seminole Community College, to the north of Orlando. This small Equity company (all of its actors are based in the Orlando area) presents primarily American plays by playwrights such as Arthur Miller and A. R. Gurney. It also produces original scripts by local playwrights.

The three-play season runs from November to May, with each production running for three weeks. Performances are Thursday through Saturday at 8:00 p.m. and Sunday at 2:00 p.m. Tickets are $18; students and seniors (65+) receive a $2 discount. Orlando Theatre Project also presents a free play reading once a year.

Orlando-UCF Shakespeare Festival

812 East Rollins Street, Orlando 32803

(407) 477-1700

www.shakespearefest.org

The Bard of Avon is alive and well in Orlando, thanks to this up and coming professional theater company whose home (renovated at a cost of some $3.1 million) in Loch Haven Park boasts three performance spaces. The 330-seat Margeson Theater features a thrust stage and plenty of theatrical bells and whistles, while the 120-seat Goldman Theater is for more intimate productions. There is also a 100-seat "black box" house for experimental shows, workshops, and readings.

The Festival is arguably the best theater group in Orlando, and the shows I have seen, including a top-notch production of *Taming of the Shrew*, have been excellent. Each season, the Festival (as they like to be called) presents five plays, which may or may not have a Shakespearean connection. In the spring, the company presents a Shakespeare play under the stars in the open-air 936-seat Walt Disney Amphitheater at Lake Eola. One play a year is an adaptation of a classic novel written by a local playwright.

Throughout the season, the Festival offers Play Lab, a series of professional readings of contemporary plays in development. These events usually take place on the second Monday of the month and are free. Otherwise, ticket prices range from $18 to $32. Mainstage plays run about six weeks with evening performances on Wednesday through Sunday and a matinee on Sunday.

Osceola Players

2411 East Irlo Bronson Highway, Kissimmee 34744

(407) 846-6257

www.ocfta.com

In addition to its fine-arts endeavors, the Osceola Center for the Arts is the home of the Osceola Players, a community theater troupe that presents a season of anywhere from six to ten contemporary comedies and musicals with the occasional Shakespeare play thrown in for good measure. The season runs from September to May or June and tickets range from $13 for adults and $12 for seniors (60+) to $8 for students and children. The Center also presents touring performances by the Orlando Ballet, two local dance studios, and the Orlando Opera.

SAK Theatre Comedy Lab

398 West Amelia Street, Orlando 32801

(407) 648-0001

www.sak.com

In the heart of downtown you'll find the Orlando home of improvisational comedy. "Improv," as its practitioners invariably call it, involves a group of agile and quick-witted actors creating a coherent and hilarious sketch based on frequently bizarre suggestions from the audience. More often than not, SAK succeeds. One indicator of SAK's success is that Wayne Brady of the TV show *Who's Line Is It Anyway?* is a SAK alumnus.

Typically, what you will see is *Duel of Fools*, which is described as "two teams of improv comedy stars . . . in an all-out battle for laughs with Olympic judges, official referees, the pink shoe of salvation, help from the audience, and free candy!!!" From time to time, they present "plays" based on improv principles, such as *Blank:The Musical* and *Suspect*, a murder mystery in which the audience gets to decide whodunit. Popcorn and soft drinks are served. Unlike many comedy clubs, SAK adheres to a strict PG policy; there's no bad language and no booze is served, making it an entertainment possibility for your hipper kids.

The SAK is open year round, Tuesday to Saturday. There is one performance on Tuesdays at 9:00 p.m. and, seasonally, on Wednesdays at 8:00 p.m.

and two on Thursdays and Fridays at 8:00 and 10:00 p.m. The Tuesday and Wednesday performances are by SAK's student company. On Saturdays they add a midnight show. Tickets are $13 for adults, but Florida residents with photo ID, and all students, seniors, and military personnel with ID, get in for $10.

Studio Theater

398 West Amelia Street, Orlando 32801

(407) 872-2382

www.orlandotheatre.com

This intimate venue in downtown Orlando is maintained by the non-profit Central Florida Theatre Alliance as a rental space for companies that don't have a permanent home. Among the groups that have performed here are the Orlando Black Essentials Theatre, People's Theatre, the Florida Children's Rep Theatre, and the Oops Guys, a duo presenting what is described as "schticky gay comedy."

Ticket prices are set by the group currently using the space and range from $1.50 to $15. The web site contains not only information about what's going on at the Studio Theater but a searchable database of the entire Orlando theater scene.

Theatre Downtown

2113 North Orange Avenue, Orlando 32803

(407) 841-0083

www.theatredowntown.net

Here is another Off-Off Broadway-style theater offering classics ranging from *A Doll's House* to *Twelve Angry Men* to the occasional much earlier work, like Sheridan's *The Critic*, at moderate prices. The theater, a converted industrial building, has two performing spaces — a 125-seat main stage with the audience on three sides of the stage and the more informal "drama-rama," a space which doubles as the lobby for main stage productions. The rock musical I saw there was vastly entertaining thanks to a spirited cast that made up in energy whatever they may have lacked in the talent department. Shows run for about a month with performances on Thursday, Friday, and Saturday evenings; there is one Sunday matinee each month. Tickets are $12 to $15 ($10 to $12 for students and seniors).

FILM

Orlando has the usual quota of mall-based multiplex movie theaters offering the latest Hollywood entertainment. The typical admission price is about $6.75 to $7.50 for adults. Some theaters have lower prices ($3.50 or $4) for all showings prior to 5:00 p.m. or for one late afternoon screening each day, and the **Park 11**, (407) 644-6000, in Winter Park, shows slightly older films for $1 to $2.50. The "Calendar" section in Friday's *Orlando Sentinel* lists the show times of every movie showing in the greater Orlando area (which extends to the Atlantic coast) along with helpful capsule reviews.

One local movie house deserves special mention:

The **Enzian Theater** (1300 South Orlando Avenue in nearby Maitland, (407) 629-0054, www.enzian.org), is the local art house. It shows subtitled European imports and the more adventuresome independent American films. From time to time, it runs special series built around a specific theme. Best of all, the films are screened in a 225-seat movie theater-restaurant. You can have a full meal, washed down with beer or wine, while soaking up culture. Appetizers run about $2 to $10, sandwiches are $5 to $6, and pizzas run from $7.50 to $13, with toppings extra. Beer is sold by the pitcher for about $9 to $13. Tickets are $4.50 for matinees (before 6:00 p.m.) and $7 for evening performances.

In June of each year, the Enzian hosts the **Florida Film Festival**, screening as many as 150 films in four venues. Many filmmakers journey to Orlando for the event and give seminars. Single tickets are $7 and $100 buys a pass that lets you see every film in the Festival. Two shorter festivals are held in February (the three-day South Asian Film Festival) and October (the two-day Central Florida Jewish Film Festival).

MUSIC

The Orlando music scene is far too fleeting and fluid to cover in a guidebook, but if you like your music live rest assured that you will have plenty of opportunity to indulge yourself during your Orlando vacation. In addition to the Philharmonic, mentioned earlier, Orlando's downtown arenas play host to the usual array of aging rock stars and pop headliners, while the local bar and club scene serves up a wide variety of musical offerings from folk, to ethnic, to rhythm and blues, to country-western. Orlando has also garnered a reputation as an incubator of teen pop groups. If your taste lies in this direction you may be able to catch some rising stars.

The best way to plug into the music scene is the "Calendar" section in Friday's *Orlando Sentinel* which lists all musical performances for the week, arranged helpfully by genre, along with a list of web sites for local bands. A "Calendar" page in the daily *Sentinel* lists that day's offerings. The free *Orlando Weekly* also has extensive coverage of the local music scene.

CHAPTER SEVENTEEN:

Moving
Experiences

N ot only are there a lot of things to see in the Orlando area, there
are a lot of ways to see them. If walking or driving around begins
to seem a bit boring, why not try some of these alternate modes of
taking in the sights? There are some sights you will be able to see in no other
way. Then again, some of these experiences are ends in themselves, with the
passing scenery merely a backdrop.

Gathered together in this chapter, then, are the many and varied ways to
get up in the air or out on the water during your Orlando vacation.

Balloon Rides

Up, up, and away in a beautiful balloon. It's a great way to start the day
and, if floating along on a big bubble of hot air appeals to you, that's when
you'll have to go — at dawn. The weather's capricious in Orlando and at
dawn the winds are at their calmest. A number of companies offer ballooning experiences in the Orlando area, and they all operate in much the same
fashion, providing much the same experience.

Typically, you make your "weather-permitting" reservation by phone;
your flight is confirmed (or called off) the night before. Then it's up with the
birds to meet at a central location in the predawn twilight for a ride to the
launch site, which will be determined by the prevailing weather conditions.

Most balloon operators let their passengers experience the fun (or is it
the hard work?) of unloading and inflating the balloon. When the balloon is
fully inflated, you soar aloft on a 45-minute to one-hour flight to points un-
known. Of course, the pilot has a pretty good idea of where he'd like to put

down, but the winds have a way of altering plans. After landing, once the balloon is packed away, a champagne toast is offered. With photographs and certificates, the passengers are inducted into the confraternity of ballooning. Some excursions include breakfast. The whole experience takes anywhere from three to four hours.

The balloons — or more properly the baskets that hang beneath the balloons — hold anywhere from two to 20 people, with six- to eight-passenger baskets being the most common. Usually, then, you will be riding with other people. If a couple wants a balloon to themselves (a frequent request), the price goes up. A few balloon operators try to float over Disney World whenever the winds cooperate, but it's hard to guarantee. The Disney folks are (understandably) less than happy about balloons landing on their property, so pilots must plan with care. Typically, your flight will be over the less-populated fringes of the metro area.

Hot-air ballooning is not cheap (most operators accept credit cards). Figure on about $165 to $200 per person, plus tax, for the brief flight and the attendant hoopla. Still, for those looking for a very special way to celebrate a birthday or an anniversary, the ballooning experience is not quite like any other. As one brochure puts it, "the ballooning adventure will last three to four hours, the memories will last a lifetime!"

AirSports Aviation
11475 Rocket Boulevard, Orlando 32824
(407) 438-7773
www.airsportsinternational.com
    Cost is $165 per person, $95 for children under 12, with groups of six or more receiving a 10% discount. Private flights for couples are $400. Prices include a champagne toast and a continental breakfast on landing, as well as a number of souvenirs of your flight.

Blue Water Balloons
P.O. Box 560572, Orlando 32856
(407) 894-5040
www.bluewaterballoons.com
    Sunrise champagne flights in the Disney area run $165 per person, with a $75 charge for children under 90 pounds. Special "couples only" flights are $400. Free hotel pickup in the Orlando area is included in the price and owner Don Edwards limits capacity to four passengers per balloon.

Fantasy of Flight
P.O. Box 1200, Polk City 33868

(863) 984-3500

www.fantasyofflight.com

This roadside attraction reviewed in *Chapter 12* now offers balloon rides. You must book at least 48 hours in advance. Cost is $160 per person. Fantasy of Flight is about 50 miles west of Orlando off Exit 21 from I-4.

Orange Blossom Balloons

P.O. Box 22908, Lake Buena Vista 32830

(407) 239-7677

www.orangeblossomballoons.com

Cost is $165 per person, $95 for children 10 to 15, with younger children riding free with a paying adult. Private flights for couples are $425. Meets at Days Inn Maingate West on US 192, where an all-you-can-eat breakfast buffet is served after the flight. Orange Blossom offers wedding packages for $825.

Painted Horizons Hot Air Balloon Tours

7741 Hyacinth Drive, Orlando 32835

(407) 578-3031

www.paintedhorizons.com

Cost is $175 per person, $275 per couple on private flights, which are available only on weekends. I'm told the couples-only flights book up fast.

Rise & Float Balloon Tours

P.O. Box 620755, Orlando 32862-0755

(407) 352-8191

"For Lovers Only" flights are $395, which includes an airborne champagne party with fresh pastries, cheese, crackers, and other treats. Regular flights are $165 per person, children (4 to 12) $95. An "introductory" flight for $85 involves groups of four or more people; half the group flies for half an hour, while the other half follows in the chase van; the two halves then switch places for another half hour flight.

SkyScapes Balloon Tours

5755 Cove Drive, Orlando 32812

(407) 856-4606

www.skyscapesballoontours.com

SkyScapes specializes in "couples only" private flights for $350 per couple. The flights culminate in a champagne brunch and party. The whole experience lasts about four hours.

Boat Rides

As you can easily see when you fly into Orlando, Central Florida is dotted with lakes, from the tiny to the fairly large. It also boasts its fair share of spring fed streams and rivers, as well as acre upon acre of swamps. It should come as no surprise, then, that the Orlando area offers the visitor plenty of opportunities to get on the water.

The signature Central Florida boat ride, of course, is aboard an airboat. These cleverly designed craft were created to meet the challenges of Florida's swamps and shallow estuaries. The pontoons allow the craft to float in just inches of water, the raised pilot's seat allows the driver to spot submerged obstacles (like alligators) before it's too late, and the powerful (if rather noisy) airplane propellers that power them let the boats skim across the water at a remarkable clip. The airboat is a raffish, backwoods sort of vehicle and it is used to give tourists a taste of what the old Florida of trappers and hunters was like. The "prey" is much the same — gators and such — but these days the only thing that gets shot is photographs.

There are other ways to cruise Central Florida's waters. One of the most popular is the pontoon boat, a flat rectangle set on two buoyant floats and designed for leisurely lake cruising. For many of Florida's lakeshore residents, they serve as floating patios; for the tourist trade, they make excellent sightseeing vessels. Central Florida even lays claim to a sort of cruise ship that takes passengers out on the broad St. John's River for an elegant dinner. All these options are listed below, along with the major airboat excursion companies.

A-Awesome Airboat Rides

P.O. Box 333, Christmas 32709
(407) 568-7601
www.airboatride.com

Cost:	Adults $30, children (3-12) $15, under 3 **free**
Hours:	Daily, 24 hours
Location:	Meets on SR 50 at the bridge over the St. John's River

"Captain Bruce" runs one of two operations offering private airboat tours of the St. John's River ecosystem near Christmas, to the east of Orlando. (The other is Old Fashioned Airboat, below.) The 90-minute tours are by reservation only. They offer a close-up look at alligators, bald eagles (September through May), and other denizens of this starkly beautiful landscape.

You can take a trip in the middle of the night if you wish, but you are better advised to consult with Captain Bruce on the best time to go to see what you want to see. There are two six-passenger airboats, but if you have a large group, Captain Bruce can round up enough boats to accommodate 30 people. There is a $70 minimum per boatload, which means that if only two people go they will be charged $35 a head instead of $30.

Adventures in Florida

1331 Palmetto Avenue, Suite 200, Winter Park 32789
(407) 331-0991
www.thefloridacompanies.com

Cost: $49 to $95 per person, per day trip; discounts
             available to groups
Hours: Weekdays
Location: Picks groups up at their hotel

Mike Kelley's innovative tour operation specializes in showing off the offbeat and natural Florida that all too many tourists never see. Many of his tours feature airboat, pontoon, and canoe trips, so I have listed them here.

The menu of tours ranges from half-day outings to event-filled 12-hour expeditions. The "Cowboys and Indians" tour, for example, features a morning of horseback riding followed by an afternoon of canoeing, while other tours feature airboat and pontoon boat expeditions in search of alligators and other wildlife.

The price includes transportation, a professional guide, and (on the longer tours) lunch. Some of the tours take you to places and use the services of companies listed elsewhere in this book. Call ahead and request a brochure, which describes the tours in detail; or ask at the Guest Services desk in your hotel.

Aquatic Wonders Tours

101 Lakeshore Drive, Kissimmee 34741
(407) 846-2814
www.florida-nature.com

Cost: Adults $21, children (12 and under) $14,
             plus tax, for 2-hour tours
Hours: 9:00 a.m. to dusk
Location: Departs from Big Toho Marina on the Kissim-
             mee waterfront

"Captain Ray" runs this friendly tour operation offering a terrific variety of waterborne experiences on Kissimmee's Lake Toho (Tohopekaliga). You cruise aboard the 30-foot wheelchair accessible pontoon boat "Eagle Ray," and since all tours are limited to just six people, there's plenty of elbow room. Most tours last two hours and are offered both during the day and at night.

The "Eagle Watch Tour" goes in search of bald eagles and ospreys. The "Sunset Sounds" and "Starlight Wonders" tours can be taken separately or combined for a full evening of entertainment. Other tours concentrate on Native American and local settler history, fishing for kids, and nighttime gator safaris. The half-day "Aquatic Wonders" tour ($35 for all ages) concentrates on the lake's ecology and features experiments and demonstrations in the boat's "on-board wet lab." Snacks and beverages are available on board and you are encouraged to bring along your own picnic cooler. Captain Ray will even put together a custom tour just for you and your family. Another option: for $15 per person, he will provide drop-off and pick-up service to a 125-acre island where you can picnic and hike on your own. Call ahead and ask him to send you his informative brochure, which describes all the tours in detail and lets you make an informed decision.

Boggy Creek Airboat Rides

1. 3702 Big Bass Road, Kissimmee 34744
(407) 344-9550
2. 2001 Southport Road, Kissimmee 34746
(407) 933-4337
www.bcairboats.com

Cost:	Adults $17.95, children (3-12) $12.95, under 2 **free**
Hours:	Daily 9:00 a.m. to 5:30 p.m.
Location:	1. About 8 miles from East Irlo Bronson Highway on the north shore of East Lake Tohopekaliga. 2. On the north shore of West Lake Tohopekaliga, about 20 miles from US 192 on Poinciana Boulevard (which becomes Southport Road).

Boggy Creek Airboats operates half hour tours from both locations. The East Lake Toho location uses both 6- and 18-passenger boats, while the one on West Lake Toho has only 18-passenger vehicles. The tours explore the northern shores of their respective lakes. The eastern location also covers the nooks and crannies of Boggy Creek, one of the few habitats of the endangered snail kite. On the wildlife menu for both are alligators, turtles, and a multitude of water fowl. On warm summer nights, both run hour-long alligator tours by reservation only. The tab is $25 per participant.

You'll find the Big Bass Road location at East Lake Fish Camp, a lovely camping and fishing resort. Several fishing guides operate from this base. You might want to consider spending a day (and perhaps a night) here.

Midway Airboat Tours

28501 East Highway 50, Christmas 32709
(407) 568-6790
www.midwayairboatrides.com

Cost:	Adults $15, children (11 and under) $7
Hours:	Monday to Saturday 9:00 a.m. to 4:15 p.m.; Sunday 9:00 a.m. to 5:00 p.m.
Location:	At the St. John's River, just past Christmas

The cheerfully ramshackle set of buildings perched on the edge of a swampy backwater in the middle of nowhere give Midway Airboat Tours the look of a movie set for some post-apocalyptic Mad Max adventure. But the featureless desolation of the immediate surroundings is deceptive because a short distance away, over the swamp grass, are the wide expanses of the St. John's River.

Midway runs economical 30- to 40-minute tours through the edges, nooks, and crannies of this fascinating ecosystem aboard 20-passenger airboats. Each trip covers about six or seven miles with gator sightings the primary goal. During the spring, this is also prime bald eagle habitat. Night tours are $25 for adults and $15 for children, with a minimum of five adults per boat; 24-hour advance reservations are required. The night tours use spotlights to point out unwary gators.

Old Fashioned Airboat Rides

24004 Sisler Avenue, Christmas 32709
(407) 568-4307
www.airboatrides.com

Cost:	Adults $37, children (2-12) $16, including tax; under 2 **free**
Hours:	By appointment
Location:	SR 50 at the public boat ramp about 45 minutes to an hour from Orlando

Captain John "Airboat John" Long runs this boutique operation from his home, specializing in private airboat tours on three six-passenger boats. Make your arrangements by phone and make sure you bring along lunch or a snack.

John's 90-minute nature trips are leisurely by the standards of most airboat tours. They explore a 40-mile roundtrip swath of river and swamp. There's plenty of gators and bald eagles to be seen along this remote stretch. On one side is the Tosohatchee Preserve, on the other large swaths of private ranch land. You can stop at a small island cabin or an ancient Indian mound for lunch and a great **photo op** of the boat on the water.

In the warmer months, John runs night trips in search of alligators. Gators have a reputation for being stupid but they avoid the blistering summer sun, making them smarter than the average tourist in some people's estimation.

Expect to ride with other folks, unless your party is three or more people. "Those boats burn a lot of gas," John explains. "Private tours" of one or two people are offered at $100. John doesn't recommend the trips for very young children (under 2), but if you insist and you get your child earplugs and the child sits on your lap, children under two ride free. Payment is strictly in cash; no credit cards.

Rivership Romance
433 North Palmetto Avenue, Sanford 32771
(800) 423-7401; (407) 321-5091
www.rivershipromance.com

Cost:	$35 to $50, tax included, plus drinks and tip
Hours:	Cruises at 11:00 a.m. daily and 7:30 p.m. Friday and Saturday; year-round
Location:	From I-4 Exit 51, 4 miles east on SR 46

The Rivership Romance is a refurbished, 100-foot, 1940s Great Lakes steamer that plies the waters of Lake Monroe and the St. John's River for leisurely luncheon and dinner cruises. It's not quite the "Love Boat," but for a nice change of pace from landlocked dining, it will do quite nicely.

There are three-hour luncheon cruises on Wednesday, Saturday, and Sunday; four-hour luncheon cruises on Monday, Tuesday, Thursday, and Friday; and three-and-a-half-hour dinner cruises on Friday and Saturday. Live entertainment is featured on all cruises and there is dancing to a sophisticated combo on the evening cruises. Reservations are required and all major credit cards are accepted.

The dinner menu is short but sumptuous and, in true cruise line tradition, the portions are generous. After starting off with plump chilled shrimp, you can choose from glazed chicken breast, seafood medley, eggplant parmesan, stuffed pork chops, or a Caesar salad with chicken, shrimp, or gator. The roast prime rib, however, seems to be the favorite.

The scenery's nothing to sneeze at either. The St. John's is one of just two larger rivers in the world that flow north and during the four-hour luncheon cruise, you'll get to see some 25 miles of its history-steeped shores. There's not much to see at night, of course, except for the stars. And for the romantic couples who take these cruises that's the whole point.

Toon Tours

4255 Peninsula Point, Sanford 32771

(407) 314-2954; (386) 753-1800

Cost:	Adults $18, seniors $15, children $12, plus tax
Hours:	Tuesday through Sunday; call for times
Location:	From I-4 Exit 51, follow SR 46 through Sanford, then turn left on SR 415

The 'toon in Toon Tours refers to pontoons, not cartoons.

The company offers nature cruises along the densely wooded shores of the St. John's River. There are two two-hour cruises daily that head south on the winding river for a leisurely roundtrip journey. Thanks to the river's many islands, estuaries, and bayous, the boat never traverses the same stretch of waterway twice. Much of the territory covered is wilderness, although there are a few homes to be seen. Wildlife is plentiful and the boat's leisurely pace makes critter-spotting easy. All tours are narrated and snacks and refreshments are available on board.

With a little advance notice, early morning and sunset tours can also be arranged.

Winter Park Scenic Boat Tour

312 East Morse Boulevard, Winter Park 32789

(407) 644-4056

www.scenicboattours.com

Cost:	Adults $8, children (2 to 11) $4, with tax
Hours:	Daily 10:00 a.m. to 4:00 p.m. on the hour
Location:	At the foot of Morse Boulevard, a short stroll from Park Avenue's fancy shops

The little town of Winter Park has 17 lakes. Thanks to the operators of these modest, flat pontoon boats, you can visit three of them on a leisurely one-hour cruise. You slip between the lakes through narrow canals originally cut by logging crews in the 1800s and barely wide enough to accommodate the tour boat. It's not quite Venice but it makes for an unusual and relaxing outing.

There's plenty of bird life to be seen on this tour and your guide will dutifully point out the wading herons, muscovy ducks, and ospreys nesting high in the cypress trees. Less frequently sighted, but there nonetheless, are alligators, some of them quite large. There's also a bit of local history to take in, from the campus of Rollins College to the palatial 1898 Brewer estate, the only Winter Park home on the National Historic Register.

But, this tour is really about real estate envy. As you glide past one gorgeous multimillion dollar home after another, their impeccably landscaped backyards cascading down to boathouses that coyly echo the architecture of the big house, you will find yourself asking, "Why them and not me? Why, why, why?"

Helicopter Tours

Small operations offering guided aerial sightseeing by helicopter pop up (and disappear) with some regularity. If the ones listed here are closed by the time you arrive, you'll probably spot new ones as you drive around the tourist areas. They all seem to offer much the same menu of tours, ranging from short five- to seven-minute hops for about $20 to half-hour surveys for about $125. Some offer extended trips that take in Kennedy Space Center for $400. Typically, these operators require a minimum of two passengers, although some offer special one-person rates.

Tip: The farther they have to fly the more expensive the trip. So if you especially want to see Universal Orlando, pick a helipad on International Drive; if Disney World is on your must-see list, try a tour that leaves from Kissimmee. You might save some money.

Air Florida Helicopters

8990 International Drive, Orlando 32819
(407) 354-1400
www.airfloridahelicopters.com

Cost:	$20 to $395 per person, with discounts for children 3 to 9 on some of the longer flights
Hours:	Sunday to Thursday 9:30 a.m. to 6:00 p.m.; Friday and Saturday 9:00 a.m to 7 p.m.; first flight at 10:00 a.m.
Location:	At Trolley and Train Museum, next to Race Rock

Air Ventures, Inc.

4619 West Irlo Bronson Highway, Kissimmee 34746
(407) 390-0111

Cost:	Adults $20 to $125, children (2 to 11) riding with an adult $20 to $115, children under 2 **free**
Hours:	Monday to Saturday 10:00 a.m. on; Sunday 1:00 p.m. on
Location:	At Mile Marker 14

Magic Air Adventure

5069 West Irlo Bronson Highway, Kissimmee 34746

(407) 390-7502

Cost:	$20 to $375 per person, with discounts for children 3 to 12 on some of the longer flights. Minimum fares apply on all flights; they range from $60 to $990.
Hours:	Daily 9:00 a.m. to sunset
Location:	Between Mile Markers 10 and 11

Orlando Helitours

5519 West Irlo Bronson Highway, Kissimmee 34746

(407) 397-0226

Cost:	Adults $15 to $125, children (under 11) $15 to $75
Hours:	Daily 9:00 a.m. to sunset
Location:	East of I-4

Parasailing

Ever been high as a kite? Well here's your chance. Parasail operators will strap you onto a small seat (sort of like a swing) and launch you into the sky on a gaudily colored parachute by towing it from the back of their boats. You're always attached, but the U.S. Coast Guard-certified boat captains maintain just enough slack on the rope to give you the sensation of gliding high above central Florida. You'll soar for 10 to 12 minutes before being gently reeled back in for a dry landing on the boat. The price you pay depends on how high you want to get. No experience is necessary and the safety record is impeccable.

Boggy Creek Parasail Rides

3702 Big Bass Road, Kissimmee 34744

(407) 348-2700

www.boggycreekparasail.com

Cost:	$45, $55, or $65 for 400-, 600-, and 800-foot starting heights
Hours:	Daily 9:00 a.m. to 5:30 p.m.
Location:	6 miles south of Orlando International Airport

Plane & Glider Rides

Air Florida Charter

Orlando Executive Airport, Orlando 32803

(407) 888-4114

www.airfloridacharter.com

Cost:	Adults $60, children (under 10) $40; $120 minimum
Hours:	By appointment
Location:	At the Orlando Executive Airport, near Fashion Square Mall on East Colonial Drive

This on-demand air charter service will fly you to the Bahamas or Key West if Orlando's attractions begin to pale. They also offer a 45-minute aerial sightseeing tour of Orlando aboard three- or four-seater fixed wing aircraft such as a Cessna 172. The narrated tour covers the major theme parks (Disney, Universal, SeaWorld) and includes a souvenir photo.

Fantasy of Flight

P.O. Box 1200, Polk City 33868

(863) 984-3500

www.fantasyofflight.com

Cost:	$49 per person
Hours:	Daily 10 a.m. to 5 p.m. weather permitting
Location:	Exit 21 off I-4, about 50 miles west of Orlando

Get a look at Central Florida from a vintage 1929 New Standard airplane. No reservations are necessary for the 20-minute flights. (See *Chapter Twelve* for Fantasy of Flight's other attractions.)

Seminole-Lake Gliderport

P. O. Box 120458, Clermont 34712

(352) 394-5450

www.soarfl.com

Cost:	$80 to $140, including tax
Hours:	Tuesday to Sunday 9:00 a.m. to dusk
Location:	Just south of Clermont, at the intersection of SR 33 and SR 561

If you look up in the sky and see puffy cumulus clouds against a warm blue sky, it's perfect gliding weather. You might just want to pop over to the

Clermont area for an air-powered glider ride. The folks at Seminole-Lake Gliderport will put you in a high-performance glider with an FAA-certified instructor, tow you into the wild blue yonder — and let you go.

The price depends on the altitude at which the flight starts and, hence, its length. An $80 flight starts from 3,000 feet and lasts 20 to 25 minutes. At $110 and 4,000 feet they'll throw in some aerial maneuvers for the 35-minute flight. The $140 flight tows you to 5,000 feet, offering a spectacular view of Central Florida on the 45-minute glide to landing.

Flights begin about 10:00 a.m., with the last flight about 4:00 p.m. Visa and MasterCard are accepted. Instruction is also offered; rated pilots can pick up a gliding add-on to their license in about three or four days.

Train Rides

Orlando-Mt. Dora Railway

150 West Third Avenue, Mt. Dora 32757
(352) 735-4667
www.mtdoratrain.com

Cost:	Adults $8.50 or $15, children (12 and under) $5 or $7.50, seniors (55+) $7.50 or $14
Hours:	Daily 9:00 a.m. to 5:00 p.m.
Location:	350 Huey Street in Orlando and Mt. Dora train depot

Vintage train buffs may want to take the long, leisurely trip from downtown Orlando to picturesque Mt. Dora, on the northern fringes of the Orlando area, just for the fun of riding in restored 1950s streamlined coaches pulled by **The Cannonball**, a 1913 Baldwin steam engine that has been converted from wood fuel to oil-fired locomotion. Much is made of the fact that the venerable engine has "starred" in a number of movies and television series over the years. The train leaves downtown Orlando at 9:00 a.m. and gets back at 5:00 p.m., giving you two and a half hours to eat lunch and explore Mt. Dora.

First-class passengers ride aboard the Calumet Club Car, which was built for the Illinois Central's famed "City of New Orleans." They are treated to complimentary continental breakfast and hors d'oeuvres, soft drinks, and coffee. Regular passengers ride in less lavish coaches of the same era. First-class fare is $60 for all; regular fares are $40 for adults, $35 for seniors (55+) and $32 for children 3 to 9.

Once in Mt. Dora, you have the option of shopping and dining while waiting for the return trip or of taking an additional one-hour round trip excursion to Tavares, aboard rail cars that date back to the 1880s, one of which is an open-air affair that is delightful on a balmy day. Taking this trip leaves little time for lunch, however, so you may want to pack a picnic to eat on the excursion.

The railway offers four round trips daily between the two communities. The noontime excursion is pulled by The Cannonball, the other three, by a 1950s Alco diesel engine. The fare is $12 for adults, $11 for seniors, and $8 for children, regardless of which engine is pulling the train.

This is a gentle attraction that will appeal most to hard-core train buffs, but it makes for a enjoyable excuse to visit Mt. Dora, a charmingly quaint little town that is something of a tourist attraction in its own right. Self-guided walking tours are available from the Chamber of Commerce, a stone's throw from the train depot. Antique buffs will appreciate the many downtown shops.

CHAPTER EIGHTEEN:

Sports Scores

PART I: PARTICIPANT SPORTS

The mild climate of Central Florida is an open and ongoing invitation to the active life. Sportsmen and women will find a wide array of choices to fit every taste and every budget. Prices quoted do not include tax.

Golf Courses

For golfers, Central Florida is a sort of demi-paradise, with 123 courses within a 45-minute drive of downtown Orlando. With that many, choosing one can be a daunting task. You can simplify matters by using the services of Tee Times USA, (888) 465-3356, (904)439-0001, or www.teetimesusa.com. They will help you pick a course and make the reservations for you; they'll even fax driving directions to your home or hotel. It's a free service and you will pay the regular greens fees. You'll get the best choice of courses and times if you book several months in advance, but they can arrange next-day tee times as well.

I have listed here golf courses in Orange and Osceola counties on the theory that most of my readers will be staying in Orlando (Orange County) or Kissimmee (Osceola County). If you want to explore farther afield, call (800) 864-6101 before you leave for Florida and order a copy of *Golfer's Guide* for the Orlando and Central Florida area. There is a $3 charge which can be paid for over the phone with a credit card. Or call the Orlando Convention and Visitors Bureau, (407) 363-5831, to find out where you can pick up a free copy in the Orlando area. You will also find an extensive listing of golf courses of all types in the Yellow Pages in your hotel room. All these courses are in the (407) area code.

Municipal Courses

Dubsdread Golf Course, Orlando, 246-2551
Winter Park Municipal, Winter Park, 623-3339

Public Courses

Boggy Creek, Orlando, 857-0280
Crystalbrook Golf Club, Kissimmee, 847-8721
Eaglewood Golf Club, Orlando, 351-5121
Forest Lake Golf Course, Ocoee, 654-4653
Hunters Creek Golf Club, Orlando, 240-4653
Remington Golf Club, Kissimmee, 344-9374
Walk-N-Sticks Golf Club, Kissimmee, 348-9555
Winter Pines Golf Club, Winter Park, 671-1651

Resort Courses

Eagle Pines (WDW), Lake Buena Vista, 939-4653
Falcon's Fire Golf Course, Kissimmee, 397-2777
Grand Cypress Resort, Orlando, 239-4700
International Golf Club, Orlando, 239-6909
Marriott's World Center, Orlando, 239-4200
Orange Lake Country Club, Orlando, 239-1050
Poinciana Golf and Racquet Club, Kissimmee, 933-5300

Semi-Private Courses

Bay Hill Club, Orlando, 876-2429
Buenaventura Lakes West, Kissimmee, 348-4915
Cypress Creek Country Club, Orlando, 351-2187
Eastwood Golf Club, Orlando, 281-4653
Kissimmee Bay Country Club, Kissimmee, 348-4653
Kissimmee Golf Club, Kissimmee, 847-2816
Lake Orlando Golf and Country Club, Orlando, 298-4144
Meadow Woods Golf Club, Windermere, 850-5600
Metro-West Country Club, Orlando, 299-1099
The Oaks, Kissimmee, 933-4055
Ventura Country Club, Orlando, 277-2640
Wedgefield Golf and Country Club, Orlando, 568-2116
Zellwood Station Country Club, Zellwood, 886-3303

Fishing

The best time to go fishing, the conventional wisdom has it, is when you can. And you can go fishing in Central Florida. Boy, can you ever. If you just want to throw a line in the water and drift into a semi-trance, you can do that just about anywhere. If you'd like to do some real fishing, I strongly suggest you hire a guide. There are a number of reasons for this:

- A guide has the in-depth local knowledge you lack.
- A guide may be your only means of access to private lakes that have not been overfished.
- A guide will provide tackle and bait, saving you the hassle of schlepping it with you.
- Many of Orlando's fishing guides are attractions in themselves, practitioners of a lifestyle that has all but disappeared in our homogenized fast-food culture.

Throughout much of the American Southeast bass fishing is virtually a state religion, and most of the Orlando area fishing guides seem to specialize in this feisty game fish. There are, however, other fish to be caught hereabouts. Here is a list of Central Florida species, with notes on their seasons:

American shad: Optimum, February and March, so-so January, April, and May.

Bluegill: Optimum, April to June, so-so the rest of the year.

Channel catfish: So-so all year.

Crappie: Optimum, December to March, so-so April and May.

Largemouth bass: Optimum, January to March, so-so the rest of the year.

Shellcracker: Optimum, May to July, so-so the rest of the year.

Sunshine bass: Optimum, December to February, so-so March, April, October, and November.

Striped bass: Optimum, December to February, so-so March, April, October, and November.

What you go after, then, will be a function of the time of your visit and your guide's predilections. Where you go will depend to a fair extent on the guide you hire and his location; each has his favorite (or even exclusive) areas. Among the more popular fishing spots are the Clermont chain of lakes (west of Orlando), the Wekiva River and the St. John's River (north of Orlando), and West Lake Tohopekaliga (in Kissimmee). Serious fishermen will want to pick up a copy of Kris Thoemke's *Fishing Florida* (Falcon Press, $18.95), which provides lake by lake, stream by stream commentary.

Guides do not come cheap; $250 for a full day and $200 for a half day is fairly standard, although some services charge as much as $350 for a full day and $250 for a half. The price covers two people, plus tackle and, sometimes, bait. If all you have time (or money) for is a half-day, make it the morning. Of course, you will also need a Florida State fishing license. A 7-day license for a nonresident is $17.50, an annual one is $31.50. You can get one at any fishing camp, or your guide will help you obtain one.

A #1 Bass Guide Service
P.O. Box 421257, Kissimmee 34742
(800) 707-5463
www.a1bassguideservice.com

A-Action Bass Guide Services
P.O. Box 701625, St. Cloud 34770
(800) 936-7398; (407) 892-7184
www.centralfloridabassfishing.com

A Pro Bass Guide Service
398 Grove Court, Winter Garden 34787
(407) 877-9676

Bass Anglers Guide Service
6526 SR 535, Windermere 34786
(407) 656-1052
www.tyree.net/bassanglers

Bass Charmer Guide Service
2920 West Washington Street, Orlando 32805
(407) 298-2974

Bass Challenger Guide Service
195 Heather Lane Drive, Deltona 32738
(407) 273-8045
www.basschallenger.com

Bass Fishing Unlimited, Bob Lawson
(407) 957-8900

Big Toho Marina
101 Lake Shore Boulevard, Kissimmee 34741
(407) 846-2124
www.kissimmeefishing.com

Lake Charters Guide Service
1820 Henry Street, Kissimmee 34741
(407) 933-2021

Richardson's Fish Camp
1550 Scotty's Road, Kissimmee 34744
(407) 846-6540

Shiner King Bass Guide Service
5035 Ponce de Leon Road, Kissimmee 34742
(407) 348-2202

Horseback Riding

There are a few places to go horseback riding in the Orlando area. Most stables offer leisurely trail rides of about an hour or so. Lessons are also available at these stables.

Devonwood Stables

2518 Rouse Road, Orlando 32817

(407) 273-0822

Cost:	$35 for one and a half hours
Hours:	Tuesday to Sunday 10:00 a.m. to sunset
Location:	Half way between East Colonial Drive and University Boulevard in eastern Orlando

English-style riding.

Grand Cypress Equestrian Center

1 Equestrian Drive, Orlando 32836

(407) 239-1938

Cost:	$45 (Western) to $100 (English), plus tax
Hours:	Daily 8:30 a.m. to 6:00 p.m. (to 5:00 p.m. on weekends)
Location:	On SR 535, about 4 miles from I-4 Exit 27

Both Western and English-style riding.

Horse World

3705 South Poinciana Boulevard, Kissimmee 34758

(407) 847-4343

Cost:	$32 (beginners, 45 minutes) to $49 (advanced, 90 minutes), plus tax
Hours:	Daily 9:00 a.m. to 5:00 p.m.
Location:	About 12 miles south of Highway 192

Western-style riding on 750 acres.

Miniature Golf

Just as the amusement park was revolutionized by Walt, miniature golf, once a homey mom-and-pop sort of attraction, has become a multilevel "themed" extravaganza with entrepreneurs competing with each other to create the most unusual, most atmospheric, most elaborate course yet. And the Orlando area boasts some of the finest examples of the genre. For most visitors, there's nothing quite like this back home, and I think a visit to at least one miniature golf attraction should be included in every Orlando vacation.

Most of the courses are concentrated in the International Drive area of Orlando and along US 192 in Kissimmee. During the warmer months, it's best to avoid the torrid heat of the day and play at night. Don't worry, they all stay open late. Discount coupons to most (if not all) of these courses can be found in brochure racks and throwaway magazines.

Bonanza

7761 West Irlo Bronson Highway, Kissimmee 34746
(407) 396-7536

Behind that towering rock formation over the Magic Mining Company restaurant ("Steaks & Seafood") lies a cleverly laid out miniature golf course with a Gold Rush theme. There are two complete 18-hole courses, "The Prospector" (the easier of the two) and "The Gold Nugget." Putt your way over this three-story mountain past cascading waterfalls, old mining sluices, trestle bridges, mountain pools, and cool grottoes. The course is compact, well maintained, and a lot of fun. The entrance to Splendid China (see *Chapter 6*) is just across the way.

Prices: $6 adults, $5 children under 9. The second 18 holes are half price.

Congo River Golf

6312 International Drive, Orlando 32819
(407) 352-0042
4777 West Irlo Bronson Highway, Kissimmee 34746
(407) 396-6900
531 West SR 436, Altamonte Springs 32714
(407) 682-4077

Here you can putt your way up, through, around, and over Livingston Falls in a setting that evokes a storybook Africa and the memory of Stanley and Livingston. There are two complete 18-hole courses, with the "Stanley" course being the easier of the two. If you find yourself having difficulties making par, it's "Livingston," I presume. The holes on both courses are lined with small rocks and large boulders, making for erratic and unpredictable bounces. The International Drive location offers views onto Wet 'n Wild's lake (see *Chapter 10*), where you will see screaming riders in inner tubes being towed by jet skis.

Prices: $11.50 for 36 holes, $7.95 for 18, $3.95 for replays. The Altamonte Springs location only has 18 holes and the fee is $7.50.

Million Dollar Mulligan

2850 Florida Plaza Boulevard, Kissimmee 34746

(407) 396-8180

Before there was Astroturf, there was turf, and Million Dollar Mulligan, located right next to Old Town (see *Chapter 12*), is unique in offering a miniature golf experience on honest to goodness Bermuda grass. The nine-hole "pitch and putt" course is impeccably maintained with each hole looking just like a grown-up golf hole, complete with sand traps.

Prices: The course is $11.75 for adults, $7.50 for kids under 12 and seniors (50+).

Pirates Cove
8601 International Drive, Orlando 32819
(407) 352-7378
Crossroads Center, Lake Buena Vista 32836
(407) 827-1242
2845 Florida Plaza Boulevard, Kissimmee 34746
(407) 396-7484
www.piratescove.net

Adventure on the high seas is the theme here with two 18-hole courses named after Blackbeard and Capt. Kidd. "Blackbeard's Challenge" is the more challenging of the two. The design and execution of these courses is on a par with that seen at Congo River (see above). I give Pirates Cove a slight edge, however, with the Lake Buena Vista location my personal favorite. It boasts extra height and higher waterfalls, not to mention its location next to Pebbles restaurant (a personal favorite for its tasty cuisine). At all locations, the courses are punctuated with signs offering the real-life history of their namesake pirates. (Will this edutainment never stop!) Prices are somewhat higher than at other area courses, but dollars-off coupons are fairly easy to come by.

Prices: "Blackbeard's Challenge" ranges from $7.50 to $8 for adults and from $6.50 to $7 for kids 12 and under; "Captain's Course" ranges from $7 to $8.50 for adults and from $6 to $7.50 for kids. Prices vary by location with Kissimmee charging the least. At the Orlando and Lake Buena Vista locations, you can play both courses for $12.50 for adults and $11.50 for children. This option is not available in Kissimmee.

Pirates Island Adventure Golf
4330 West Irlo Bronson Highway, Kissimmee 34746
(407) 396-4660

Once again the theme is piracy and once again the two 18-hole courses are named for Blackbeard and Capt. Kidd. This is one of the handsomest courses in the Orlando area, with a spectacular central waterfall cascading down in stages to a series of lagoons complete with artificial mist. The course is beautifully maintained, with smooth brick borders on each hole. There's edutainment here, too, with signs providing capsule biographies of well-known (and not so well-known) pirates.

Prices: Blackbeard is $8.50 for adults, $7.50 for children; Capt. Kidd is $8 and $7. All-day unlimited play costs $11 for adults, $10 for kids.

River Adventure Golf

4535 West Irlo Bronson Highway, Kissimmee 34746

(407) 396-4666

The spinning waterwheel that serves as this course's billboard says it all. A river bubbles up at the top of an artificial hill and tumbles down through a number of rocky streams to a placid lagoon below. There's just one 18-hole course with plenty of greenery. Hedges and ivy-covered rock outcroppings abound. This is yet another impeccably maintained course, with signs that announce not just the hole number and par but the distance to the hole as well. There's a "19th hole" where you can putt for a free game.

Prices: $7.50 for everyone 4 and older. The second game is $4. Children under 4 play **free** with a paying adult.

Skydiving

Skydive Lake Wales

Lake Wales Airport

440 South Airport Road, Lake Wales 33853

(863) 678-1003

www.skydivelakewales.com

Ever feel like throwing yourself out of a plane? Then this is the place to come and test your resolve. Actually, it's remarkably easy, since someone else throws you out.

Allow me to explain: Would-be skydivers can experience the joys of freefall on a "tandem jump." That means you are strapped securely to a certified instructor, who knows the ropes and controls the jump. After a flight to 13,500 feet, the fun begins, with a full minute of freefall and about five minutes under a parachute to landing. No experience is necessary, but jumpers must be at least 18 years of age and weigh no more than 230 pounds.

The cost, including tax, is $150. If you want your dive immortalized on video, add another $79. If you can talk two or more of your friends into jumping with you, you'll all receive a discount — $10 per person. For groups of seven or more people, the discount goes to $20 a head. Licensed skydivers with their own gear can jump for just $16.50.

The first jump is scheduled for about 8:00 a.m. and the last usually goes at sunset. But since the entire experience takes about four to six hours, including a very thorough pre-jump briefing, plan on arriving early. The best idea is to reserve your jump a few days in advance. Skydive Lake Wales is open daily year round but hours vary seasonally.

Jet Ski Rentals

Jet skis, those noisy motorcycles of the seas, are becoming increasingly popular (much to the dismay of those who prefer their lakes quiet and peaceful). If you'd like to take one out for a spin, there are a number of places that will accommodate you. No experience is necessary and driving a jet ski is the soul of simplicity. Rentals start at about $35 for as many minutes and go as high as $80 an hour for really fast three-seater machines. The places listed here also offer water skiing.

Buena Vista Watersports
13245 Lake Bryan Drive, Orlando 32830
(407) 239-6939
www.bvwatersports.com

Kissimmee Water Sports
4914 West Irlo Bronson Highway, Kissimmee 34746
(407) 396-1888

Wakeboarding & Water Skiing

Orlando Watersports Complex
8615 Florida Rock Road, Orlando 32824
(407) 251-3100
www.orlandowatersports.com

Sort of a cross between (or among) water skiing, surfing, and skateboarding, wakeboarding is an increasingly popular sport, and this 50-acre facility has quickly become its Central Florida epicenter. Here you can take advantage of two "cableways," overhead tracks that take the place of the more traditional speedboats and tow you along an oval course past (or over) a series of ramps and obstacles at speeds of up to 36 miles per hour. You can choose from the double skis popular with beginners or a variety of special discs and trick skis, but the platform of choice seems to be the wakeboard.

Although beginners are welcome (or at least tolerated), this place has become a hot spot for pros and semi-pros looking to brush up on their skills. The level of ability on display can be pretty intimidating for novices. If you'd just like to come and watch, that's okay, too. There is a snack bar and a terrace-like dining area with a good view of the action.

Note: Professional events are held here from time to time.

Rates range from about $20 for an hour to $37 for an all-day pass. Weekly passes are $196 and annual passes go for $1,000. A pro shop offers the latest in equipment and accessories.

Although the complex can be seen quite easily from the toll road to the airport, it's a little tricky to find. Perhaps the easiest route for tourists is to head south from Sand Lake Road on Orange Blossom Trail (US 17/441). Just before the junction with Florida's Turnpike, turn left on Landstreet Road and drive about two miles through a heavily industrial area before turning left onto Florida Rock Road.

PART II: SPECTATOR SPORTS

The more sedentary among us will find enough spectator sports in and around Orlando to keep them busy for quite some time. With the possible exception of the Magic, tickets are easy to come by and reasonably priced.

Arena Football

Arena football is a scaled-down, indoor version of pro football. Two eight-man teams square off on a field about a half the size of the outdoor version. Adding interest to the game, six players on each team play both offense and defense. Otherwise, the rules are much the same as those for pro football. There are 16 professional arena football teams in the United States.

Orlando Predators

600 West Amelia Street, Orlando 32801

(407) 447-7337

www.orlandopredators.com

Season:	April to July
Where:	In the T. D. Waterhouse Centre in downtown Orlando
Ticket Prices:	$7.50 to $40 (group rates available), through TicketMaster or the Arena box office

Auto Racing

Amateurs race for the love of it at two racing venues that lie within hailing distance of each other on the far eastern fringes of the Orlando metropolitan area. Orange County Raceway has several different tracks, all of them dirt or clay, which means their schedule is subject to the vagaries of the Florida weather. This is where you want to be for BMX bicycles, motocross, stock cars, and four-wheel-drive Mud Boggs (modified trucks). Speed World has a straight paved track with bleachers, including a platform for wheelchairs; this track is strictly for dragsters.

There's usually something going on at one or both tracks on the weekends, with additional events on some weeknights, but it's a good idea to call for current information.

Orange County Raceway

19444 East Colonial Drive, Orlando 32833
(407) 568-6693

Season:	Year round, call for schedule
Ticket Prices:	$10 and up, varies by race

Speed World Dragway

19442 East Colonial Drive, Orlando 32833
(407) 568-5522
www.speedworlddragway.com

Season:	Year round, call for schedule
Ticket Prices:	$10 and up

Baseball, Major League

Thanks to the arrival in 1998 of the Tampa Bay Devil Rays, an expansion team in the American League, Central Florida boasts its own professional baseball team. Despite the name, the team plays in St. Petersburg, not Tampa.

Tampa Bay Devil Rays

1 Tropicana Drive, St. Petersburg 33705
(813) 825-3137
www.devilrays.com

Season:	April to September
Where:	1 Tropicana Drive, St. Petersburg
Ticket Prices:	$5 to $125 for general admission

Baseball, Major League Spring Training

Many major league baseball teams find Florida's spring weather ideal for their preseason warm-ups. The training regimen includes a number of exhibition games in March that allow the teams a chance to limber up and practice under realistic conditions. They also give fans a chance to look over their favorite team's form and check out new players before the official season begins.

I have listed here the teams that have spring training camps within striking distance of Orlando, bearing in mind that a true fan's definition of "striking distance" could mean 100 miles. The prices listed below are for the 2002 season. A good source for current ticket prices is the web site of *Spring Training Magazine* at www.springtrainingmagazine.com.

Atlanta Braves
Disney's Wide World of Sports Complex
Lake Buena Vista 32830
(407) 939-4263; (407) 839-3900
>*Location:*　　West of I-4 in the Disney complex
>*Ticket Prices:*　$11 to $18

Cincinnati Reds
Ed Smith Stadium
2700 12th Street, Sarasota 34237
(941) 954-4464
>*Location:*　　I-75 Exit 40, west to Tuttle Avenue, left to ballpark
>*Ticket Prices:*　$5 to $12

Cleveland Indians
Chain O' Lakes Park
Cypress Gardens Boulevard, Winter Haven 33880
(941) 291-5803; (843) 293-3900
>*Location:*　　Intersection of US 17 and Cypress Gardens Boulevard (about 5 miles from Cypress Gardens)
>*Ticket Prices:*　$5 to $21

Detroit Tigers
Joker Marchant Stadium
2301 Lakeland Hills Boulevard, Lakeland 33805

(941) 686-8075; (686) 688-8075
> *Location:* South of I-4 Exit 19 about 3 miles
> *Ticket Prices:* $8 to $12

Florida Marlins
Space Coast Stadium
5800 Stadium Parkway, Melbourne 32940
(321) 633-9200
> *Location:* I-95 Exit 74, then 3 miles south on Fiske Boulevard
> *Ticket Prices:* $6 to $15

Houston Astros
Osceola County Stadium
1000 Bill Beck Boulevard, Kissimmee 34744
(407) 933-2520
> *Location:* Off US 192, just east of Kissimmee
> *Ticket Prices:* $8 to $13

Kansas City Royals
Baseball City Stadium
300 Stadium Way, Davenport 33837
(863) 424-2500
> *Location:* South of I-4 Exit 23, about 1 mile
> *Ticket Prices:* $6 to $10

Los Angeles Dodgers
Dodgertown
4101 26th Street, Vero Beach 32960
(561) 569-6858
> *Location:* Take SR 60 East from I-95, turn left on 43rd Avenue, then right on 26th Street
> *Ticket Prices:* $7 to $12

New York Yankees
Legends Field
1 Steinbrenner Drive, Tampa 33614
(813) 879-2244
> *Location:* I-4 to I-275 Exit 23, Dale Mabry North
> *Ticket Prices:* $10 to $16

Philadelphia Phillies
Jack Russell Memorial Stadium
800 Phillies Drive, Clearwater 33755
(727) 442-8496

Location:	SR 60 West to Highland Avenue, then north to Palmetto Street, turn left
Ticket Prices:	$7 to $13

Pittsburgh Pirates
McKechnie Field
1611 9th Street West, Bradenton 34208
(941) 748-4610

Location:	I-75 Exit 42, then west on SR 64, left on 9th Street West
Ticket Prices:	$6 to $9

Toronto Blue Jays
Dunedin Stadium at Grant Field
311 Douglas Avenue, Dunedin 34698
(727) 733-0429

Location:	From US 19, west on Sunset Point Road, right on Douglas Avenue
Ticket Prices:	$9 to $15

Baseball, Minor League
The Orlando area's two farm teams give you a chance to see some rising (and a few falling) stars in action. Many devotees of minor league baseball say it takes them back to a simpler time, before players started commanding multimillion dollar salaries. The prices are comfortably old fashioned, too.

Daytona Cubs (Class A, Chicago Cubs)
105 East Orange Avenue, Daytona Beach 32114
(386) 872-2827
www.daytonacubs.com

Season:	April to September
Where:	Jackie Robinson Ballpark; from I-95 take International Speedway Boulevard exit (SR 92) east to Beach, then south to East Orange
Ticket Prices:	$4 to $7 at the stadium

Orlando Rays (Class AA, Tampa Bay Devil Rays)

P.O. Box 10000, Lake Buena Vista 32830

(407) 939-4263

www.insidecentralflorida.com/sports/orlandorays

Season:	April to September
Where:	Disney's Wide World of Sports complex, west of I-4 Exit 25B
Ticket Prices:	$5 to $8, through TicketMaster or at the stadium

Basketball

The Magic are definitely the hottest sports ticket in town. Don't be surprised if you find them sold out well in advance, especially if they are playing the Lakers or the Bulls. Still, tickets are sometimes available. You can always try your luck outside the Arena on the day of a game; someone just might have an "extra" ticket. Florida law prohibits the sale of a sports ticket for more than $1 over its face value, but scalpers have commanded from $225 to $1,000 for tickets to Magic playoff games.

Far more accessible are the ladies of the Orlando Miracle, part of the Women's National Basketball Association. They play during the Magic's off season, and you can get a lot closer to the action for a lot less money.

Both teams play in the same arena, the T. D. Waterhouse Centre in downtown Orlando.

Orlando Magic

1 Magic Place, Orlando 32801

(800) 338-0005; (407) 896-2442

www.orlandomagic.com

Season:	November to April
Where:	T. D. Waterhouse Centre
Ticket Prices:	$10 to $150, at the Arena box office or through TicketMaster

Orlando Miracle

1 Magic Place, Orlando 32801

(407) 839-3900; (407) 916-9622

www.orlandomiracle.com

Season:	May to August
Where:	T. D. Waterhouse Centre

Ticket Prices: $8 to $41, at the Arena box office or through TicketMaster

Dog Racing

Orlando has two greyhound tracks, a short distance apart. Seminole Greyhound Track operates from May through October, while the Sanford-Orlando Kennel Club is open year round. Both are just across the Seminole County line, north of Orlando. Admission is cheap, starting at $1 for grandstand seats, and both tracks allow you to bet on dog and horse races elsewhere that are beamed in by satellite. Of the two, the Seminole Greyhound Track has a slightly nicer setting, with a backdrop of trees and open skies.

Sanford-Orlando Kennel Club

301 Dog Track Road, Longwood 32750
(407) 831-1600
www.orlandogreyhoundracing.com

Seminole Greyhound Park

2000 Seminola Boulevard, Casselberry 32707
(407) 699-4510

Jai-Alai

Jai-Alai is played on a sort of elongated racquetball court but, instead of a racquet, the players use a long curved wicker basket, called a cesta, strapped to their right hand, to catch and return the pelota (or "ball") at blinding speeds. To facilitate betting, the game is played in round-robin fashion by eight single players or two-man doubles teams. The first to reach seven points wins, with second and third place determined by point totals. Playoffs settle ties.

Reflecting the Basque origins of the game, most of the players have Basque or Spanish surnames. The action is fast and often surprisingly graceful. Points are determined much as they are in racquetball or squash. As one player (or team) loses a point, the next player takes his place. Although the program gives stats on the players, betting seems more like picking the numbers for a lottery game.

If you tire of the action unfolding in front of you, you can repair downstairs and bet on jai-alai matches in Miami or horse racing at New Jersey's Meadowlands, all of them shown on large video screens.

Orlando Jai-Alai

Highway 17-92 & SR 436, Fern Park 32730
(407) 339-6221
www.orlandojaialai.com

Season: Year round
Ticket Prices: $1 to $5, at the door
Game Times: Thursday to Saturday at 7:30 p.m. Matinees Monday, Thursday, Friday, and Saturday at noon, Sunday at 1:00 p.m.

Rodeo

A rodeo might seem a little too "Wild West" for Orlando, until we remember that Osceola County was the heart of Florida cattle country before Mickey arrived. Once a week, Central Florida cowhands and other rodeo enthusiasts get to show off their riding and roping skills for the general public. There's plenty of bareback riding, bull riding, bronco busting, and calf roping, along with a "calf scramble," in which kids from the audience get to chase after a mini-herd of skittish dogies.

Your host on horseback dispenses insight into the rules of rodeo along with cornpone humor ("How do you make a good impression on a lawyer?" "How?" "Steel-belted radials."). A large concession stand dispenses hamburgers, hot dogs, hot chocolate, and soft drinks, while a souvenir stand offers cowboy regalia, including straw cowboy hats for around $10.

Kissimmee Rodeo

958 South Hoagland Boulevard, Kissimmee 34741
(407) 933-0020
www.ksarodeo.com

Season: Year round, except first week of October, first two weeks of December, and third week of February
Ticket Prices: Adults $15, children (under 12) and Florida residents $7, children 3 and under **free**
Times: 8:00 p.m. Fridays, except as noted above

CHAPTER NINETEEN:

Shop 'Til You Drop

S een all the attractions? Got some money left? No problem! Orlando makes it easy to go home flat broke and maybe with a few genuine bargains to help convince the folks back home that you're not simply an unregenerate spendthrift. Of course, for many people shopping is an attraction in itself, bargain or no. Whatever category fits you best, you're sure to find plenty of opportunities to shop 'til you drop.

In this chapter I have concentrated on discount shopping opportunities on the theory that, a) you can always pay full price back home and, b) your wallet can probably use the break during an Orlando vacation. Basic information about other shopping venues in the Orlando area can be found on the Internet at orlando.retailguide.com. And don't forget all those gift shops in the various attractions described in earlier in this book.

Outlet Shopping

Once upon a time, "factory outlets" were just that — small shops located in or near the factory where seconds, rejects, overruns, and discontinued lines could be sold, at a discount, directly to the public. Factory outlets existed outside the standard retail channels and were a classic win/win proposition: The public got a bargain and the factory recouped at least some of its costs.

Today, factory outlets have become very much a part of the retail scene, located far from the factory in glossy malls and often featuring merchandise specifically designed for and marketed to the bargain-hunting segment of the market. And the words "Factory Outlet" have become a marketing buzzword used to suggest deep, deep discounts, whether they are there or not. Some factory outlets are run directly by the companies whose merchandise they sell. Others are run by entrepreneurs who contract with big name companies and then set their own prices. Still others are run by merchants who buy cheap merchandise from a variety of off-cost producers or from brokers who specialize in overstocked and "distressed" goods. All of which is to say that, when it comes to factory outlet shopping, the warning "caveat emptor" (let the buyer beware) is in full force. On the other hand, I do not mean to suggest that the outlet malls in the Orlando area are filled with shady operators out to fleece the unwary tourist. Far from it. Most of these outlets offer excellent deals on first-rate goods and any factory seconds or irregulars are clearly marked. Still, a wise shopper will arrive with a clear idea of what he or she is looking for and what the "going rate" for those items is back home.

What follows is a survey of the major factory outlet shopping venues in the Orlando area. Conveniently enough, most of them are located along International Drive in Orlando. I have listed them in the order you would encounter them when traveling from north to south along this well-traveled tourist corridor and then south to Kissimmee. The list is not meant to be all-inclusive. You may find other bona-fide outlets. On the other hand, there are many shops that use the words "factory outlet" rather loosely.

Finally, a note on sales tax. Orange County (Orlando) levies a six percent tax on all retail sales. In nearby Osceola County (Kissimmee) the sales tax is seven percent.

Belz Factory Outlet Mall
www.belz.com/factory/locations/orlando/

Location:	At the north end of International Drive, near the intersection of Oak Ridge Road
Information:	(407) 354-0126
Hours:	Monday to Saturday 10:00 a.m. to 9:00 p.m.; Sunday 10:00 a.m. to 6:00 p.m.

Belz is the 900-pound gorilla of the outlet scene with two malls and four "annexes" housing some 170 merchants who offer, according to Belz's management, up to 75% off every day. Like any self-respecting mall, this one features food courts and snack kiosks to refuel the flagging shopper. There are also games and rides for the kiddies.

Quality Outlet Center

Location:	On International Drive, just east of Kirkman Road

Information: (407) 423-3885
Hours: Monday to Saturday 9:30 a.m. to 9:00 p.m.;
Sunday 11:00 a.m. to 6:00 p.m.

There is a smaller selection of merchants at this strip mall, but they offer some excellent buys on brands such as Adidas Mikasa, and Samsonite. Just across the street is the excellent **Passage To India restaurant.**

Orlando Premium Outlets
Location: 8200 Vineland Avenue, off International Drive
just south of SeaWorld
Information: (407) 238-7787
Hours: Monday to Saturday 10:00 a.m. to 10:00
p.m.; Sunday 11:00 a.m. to 7:00 p.m.

The newest entry in the outlet shopping sweepstakes boasts 110 stores representing such upscale vendors as Coach, Bottega Veneta, Versace, and Burberry, plus a central food court with its own Starbucks. It claims to offer "everyday savings of 25% to 65%."

Lake Buena Vista Factory Stores
www.lbvfactorystores.com
Location: On SR 535, 2 miles south of I-4 Exit 27
Information: (407) 672-5644
Hours: Monday to Saturday 9:30 a.m. to 9:30 p.m.;
Sunday 10:00 a.m. to 6:00 p.m.

This mall of more than 40 shops is located on the well traveled state road that links I-4 to US 192. There's a small food court if you get hungry and a playground for the kids.

Value Outlet Shops
www.floridaoutlets.com
Location: One mile east of the intersection of SR 535,
on US Highway 192 (Irlo Bronson High-
way)
Information: (407) 396-8900
Hours: Monday to Saturday 10:00 a.m. to 9:00
p.m.; Sunday 11:00 a.m. to 5:00 p.m.

Not to be left out, Kissimmee has its own outlet mall, featuring more than 25 merchants, including Nike, Samsonite, Dress Barn, and Van Heusen. A separate discount shoe outlet is next door and an electronics store catering to an international clientele is across the highway.

Flea Markets

The flea market is an Old World concept. Originally the term was applied to impromptu markets, the yard sales of their day, where enterprising individuals at the frayed edge of the merchant class displayed a grab bag of merchandise, some of dubious provenance — hence the alternate term: "thieves' market." Like the term "factory outlet," the term "flea market" has evolved over the years. Today, as practiced in Central Florida, a flea market is a sort of alternate shopping mall. The market owner provides, at a modest rental, simple booths in covered arcades. The merchants are, for the most part, full-time professionals with long-term leases on their booths who differ from their counterparts in the glitzy malls only in the matter of scale.

Whereas the old flea markets of Europe held out the lure of uncovering some priceless antique at an unbelievably low price, the modern Florida flea market more often offers inexpensive merchandise, purchased from a wholesaler and offered at a price that might not be any better than you could get at Kmart. Still, savvy shoppers can find bargains here if they know what they're looking for (and at). The best bets, in my opinion, are the secondhand dealers, the craftspeople, the fresh produce vendors, and the purveyors of the sort of wacky and offbeat stuff you don't usually see elsewhere.

Whatever the drawbacks of flea market shopping, there's no denying that the atmosphere of these bazaars is a lot of fun. There's plenty of greasy and fattening food to keep your energy up and the very challenge of navigating the seemingly endless rows of wares tends to keep you going. For those who have never experienced this particular slice of Americana, I recommend it highly. For those of you who simply love the flea market experience (and you know who you are), the following flea markets should keep you busy. If you must have more, just look in the Yellow Pages in your hotel room under "Flea Markets."

Flea World

Location: Highway 17-92 in Sanford; I-4 Exit 50
Information: (407) 330-1792
Hours: Friday, Saturday, and Sunday 9:00 a.m. to 6:00 p.m.

Flea World bills itself as "America's largest flea market" with 1,700 dealer booths, most of which are occupied on any given weekend. There's bingo here and an amusement park next door to keep the kids occupied.

Main Gate Flea Market

Location: 5407 Irlo Bronson Highway (Highway

192) in Kissimmee
Information: (407) 390-1015
Hours: Daily 10:00 a.m. to 10:00 p.m.

This market is housed in a series of long metal buildings on the heavily traveled tourist strip of route 192, just east of I-4. There are over 400 booths here and a smattering of food stands, some of which offer some intriguing ethnic specialties.

192 Flea Market

Location: 4301 West Vine Street (Highway 192) in Kissimmee
Information: (407) 396-4555
Hours: Daily 9:00 a.m. to 6:00 p.m.

This is Kissimmee's original flea market. Over 400 booths offer a variety of wares, including plenty of Disney souvenirs and Florida t-shirts for the budget souvenir hound.

Osceola Flea & Farmers Market

www.fleaamerica.com
Location: 2801 East Irlo Bronson Highway (Highway 192) between Kissimmee and St. Cloud
Information: (407) 846-2811
Hours: Friday, Saturday, and Sunday 8:00 a.m. to 5:00 p.m.

A little farther off the tourist track, this flea market offers more fresh produce than the others. It also has a "garage sale" section, which draws folks with some junk to unload (as opposed to regular merchants). There are about 900 booths selling everything from Disney souvenirs to home improvement items to car stereos.

Visitors Market

Location: 5811 Irlo Bronson Highway (Highway 192) in Kissimmee
Information: (407) 390-9910
Hours: Daily 9:30 a.m. to 10:00 p.m. (to 6:00 p.m. in slower periods)

A modest market housed in a former retail location on Kissimmee's gaudy tourist strip, this has space for 250 booths, only a portion of which are open for business.

Index to Rides & Attractions

The Other Orlando

Free Updates

For free updates to this book and its companion volume, *Universal Orlando: The Ultimate Guide To The Ultimate Theme Park Adventure,* visit:

http://www.TheOtherOrlando.com

Other Books from The Intrepid Traveler

The Intrepid Traveler publishes money-saving, horizon expanding travel how-to and guidebooks dedicated to helping its readers make world travel an integral part of their everyday life.

In addition, we offer hard-to-find specialty books from other publishers. For more information visit our web site, where you will find a complete catalog, frequent updates to this and other of our books, travel articles from around the world, internet travel resources, and more:

http://www.IntrepidTraveler.com

If you are interested in becoming a home-based travel agent, visit the Home-Based Travel Agent Resource Center at:

http://www.HomeTravelAgency.com